YALE CENTER FOR INTERNATIONAL AND AREA STUDIES

YALE
RUSSIAN AND EAST EUROPEAN
PUBLICATIONS

YALE
RUSSIAN AND EAST EUROPEAN
PUBLICATIONS

VYACHESLAV IVANOV:
POET, CRITIC AND PHILOSOPHER

VYACHESLAV IVANOV:
POET, CRITIC AND PHILOSOPHER

EDITED BY
ROBERT LOUIS JACKSON
AND
LOWRY NELSON, JR.

NEW HAVEN
YALE CENTER FOR INTERNATIONAL AND AREA STUDIES
1986

YALE RUSSIAN AND EAST EUROPEAN PUBLICATIONS, NO. 8

314909

Distributed by Slavica Publishers, Inc.
P.O. Box 14388, Columbus, Ohio 43214

Library of Congress Card Catalog Number: 85–51637
ISBN: 0–936586–08–7
Typography by Brevis Press
Printed in the United States of America by BookCrafters, Inc.

Vyacheslav Ivanov

To the memory of
Lydia Ivanova
1896–1985

Contents

CRITIC

CLASSICAL SCHOLAR AND PHILOSOPHER

REMINISCENCES AND CHRONOLOGY

Note

The major source for citations from Ivanov's works is Vyacheslav Ivanov, *Sobranie sochinenij,* ed D. V. Ivanov and O. Deschartes, 3 vols. (Brussels, 1971–79). References are given in the text in brackets as "*SS*" followed by volume and page numbers.

The transliteration system is a modification of that used by the Library of Congress. In proper names used in the text, ю and я are transliterated as *yu* and ya, and й is omitted. Elsewhere, й, ю, я are transliterated as *j, ju, ja*; ё is rendered as *yo* in proper names and as *e* elsewhere.

Acknowledgments

The editors wish to express their thanks to those who have aided them in various capacities: as translators, editors, typists and consultants. Suzanne Fusso, Denis Crnkovich, Leslie Jackson and William Bidwell were particularly helpful in our general labors. In a collaborative volume such as this the ideal of complete consistency is not always achievable in matters of stylistic and typographical nuance. We have occasionally honored individual preference and, in a few cases, different translations of the same Russian passage.

Vyacheslav Ivanov: An Introduction
Robert Louis Jackson

When the mists lift entirely from the period now known as the Silver Age of Russian literature and culture (a period extending roughly from 1895 to 1915) they will reveal a landscape slightly changed from the one historians have marked out on their maps: the most noticeable difference will be the vastly increased stature of the poet, philosopher and theoretician of the Russian Symbolist movement, Vyacheslav I. Ivanov (1866–1949).

Yet the importance of Ivanov certainly transcends the limits of the brief Symbolist movement. Here two things deserve to be noted: first, that Ivanov plays a central role in literary history only midway in a long and productive life; and second, that prolonged stretches of Ivanov's life—the "Silver Age" excepted—were spent not in Russia, but in Western Europe. These unusual circumstances have complicated to some extent the task of assessing Ivanov's place in Russian literature, since his art can only transiently be seen in direct relation to a concrete literary scene or movement. These same circumstances, however, underscore certain truths about Ivanov: more than for most writers, perhaps, his art constitutes a self-created world with its main points of reference—on the horizontal map—in both Russia and the West. As Fyodor Stepun has observed, Ivanov is "in the highest degree a Russian-European, entirely Russian and simultaneously entirely European."[1] At the same time, the concerns of Ivanov's poetry, "with its distinctive, intimate sense of the cultural memory of humanity, of the 'anamnesis' which struggles with oblivion" (as S. S. Averintsev has put it[2]), merge organically with his concerns as historian of the past, cultural thinker and religious philosopher. What is especially characteristic of the poet Ivanov, then, and what must enter into any assessment of his importance in Russian literature is the historical and metaphysical, or vertical, dimension that so sharply defines his life and work and that complicates any effort to "place" him in a literary movement. Vyacheslav I. Ivanov was born in Moscow, February 16, 1866, the son of a land surveyor who, in the spirit of the times, was taken up by the atheistic ideas of Ludwig Büchner, Jakob Moleschott and David Friedrich Strauss. Ivanov himself was to pass briefly through a phase of atheism and materialism in his early years. "Suddenly I realized that I was an extreme atheist and revolutionary," he recalled later in his *Autobiographical Letter* (*Avtobiograficheskoe pis'mo*, 1918).[3] But the same young atheist who at the age of seventeen attempted suicide out of despair was writing poems with the image of Christ as his "main hero"; and in the same period, Ivanov recalls, he had "a passion for Dostoevsky." Ivanov's philosophical atheism was but the obverse of a deep religious feeling.

Ivanov's father died when his son was five, and his mother, a "passionately religious" woman who came of a clerical family, became the decisive influence in the young Ivanov's evolution. She provided him with a religious education and with an intimate knowledge of Eastern Orthodox liturgy and of Church Slavonic. "I inherited elements of my mother's spiritual nature," Ivanov wrote in his *Autobiographical Letter* [*SS*, II, 7]. A woman with a strong bent for German culture of the time of Goethe and Beethoven, she also encouraged Ivanov's intellectual proclivities and his poetic interests.

Ivanov began the study of ancient Greek on his own at the age of twelve, and was to maintain a love for the language and all things Greek to the end of his life. After graduating from a classical gymnasium in Moscow with highest honors, Ivanov attended the historical-philological faculty of Moscow University where, early in his studies, he received a prize for his progress in the study of ancient languages.

Recognizing his promise as a scholar, Ivanov's teachers arranged for him to go to Berlin in 1886. There he studied mainly Roman history for five years under the renowned German historian Theodor

Mommsen, and simultaneously continued work in his favorite area of classical philology.

Ivanov recalls his immersion at the time in Goethe, Schopenhauer, and German classical music. Yet no sooner had he arrived abroad than "the need to know Russia and its idea awakened." It was then that he read Vladimir Solovyov and Aleksey Khomyakov. Though attracted enormously by German classical culture, Ivanov recalls that he was also repelled by the "depersonalizing force of modern German culture, its philistine character." "Perplexed, I noted how the State system [*gosudarstvennost'*] could serve as the source of exalted sentiment even for such a free and freedom-loving man as Mommsen" [*SS*, II, 18].

In 1891 Ivanov went to Paris for a year and then left for Rome where he prepared his doctoral dissertation, a work he wrote in Latin on the Roman system of tax-farming in Italy. He also studied archeology. Much taken by his scholarly work, Ivanov's teachers offered him in 1896 the post of *Privatdozent* in Roman history in a German university. His teachers, Ivanov later told M. S. Altman, had predicted a brilliant future for him in classical history: "But to everyone's surprise, I veered off in an entirely different direction; I immersed myself in poetry and my whole life has followed a different course."[4]

Ivanov's creative scholarly interests in all aspects of European history and culture were to remain with him all his life. Yet his erudition, though awesome in its scope and mastery of ideas and detail, differed from the style of the scholarship of those days. Commenting on Ivanov's way of lecturing, of conducting polemics, analyzing poetry or simply arguing in a circle of acquaintances, Fyodor Stepun called attention to Ivanov's "unique combination of profundity and brilliance, erudition and improvisation, weightiness and winged flight." The same quality marked his literary and philosophical essays.

For all their scholarship they were not scientific tracts solidly constructed according to the rules of logic and method, but rather artfully and lightly woven wreaths made out of the living colors of friendly talks not only with contemporaries but also with "eternal interlocutors." The abundant references and citations [of these essays] were not scientific ballast, not the needlework-footnoting of a professor, but images of a living and grateful love for those geniuses of humanity with whom he carried on a warm exchange, and without whom he could not have lived a single day.[5]

At the time Ivanov turned down the offer of a teaching post in Germany he had already begun to concern himself seriously with poetry. Vladimir Solovyov, shown some of Ivanov's poems, spoke of their "absolute originality." Most immediately, Ivanov had plunged into a study of the works of Nietzsche. "Increasingly and ever more powerfully, Nietzsche became the master of my thoughts," Ivanov later wrote of his relationship to Nietzsche at the time.[6] Ivanov gave himself up to a study of the religion of Dionysus. "This study was prompted by a driving inner need: it was only by this means that I could overcome Nietzsche where matters of religious consciousness were concerned" [SS, II, 21]. An admirer of Dostoevsky and Solovyov, Ivanov ultimately diverged in fundamental ways from Nietzsche. Yet Ivanov could still write of Nietzsche in A Correspondence from Two Corners (Perepiska iz dvukh uglov, 1921) as "one of the great artificers of the ideal; from an iconoclast, he turns into an icon painter."[7] And as though reflecting on his own development, Ivanov observed that "it is doubtful whether any personal initiation can take place in the contemporary cultural climate without the 'initiate's' . . . meeting him [Nietzsche] as 'guardian of the threshold'" [SS, III, 402].

Ivanov met Lydia Zinovieva-Annibal in Rome in 1893 and began a relationship with her that was to leave a deep imprint on him for the rest of his life. Together with her he travelled widely, living for long periods in England, France, Italy, Switzerland and Greece, returning only occasionally to Russia. They visited Palestine and Egypt. In aggregate, Ivanov was to spend approximately forty-four years of his life abroad, though during these years he made frequent trips to Russia.

Ivanov wrote his first poems at the age of nine. He published his first collection of poems, *Pilot Stars* (*Kormchie zvezdy*) in St. Petersburg in 1903 at the age of thirty-seven. The book immediately drew attention to the poet. In 1904, Ivanov published his second collection of verse, *Translucency* (*Prozrachnost'*), his tragedy *Tantalus* (*Tantal*) and various essays on esthetic and philosophical themes. In the same year he published a series of lectures entitled *The Hellenic Religion of the Suffering God* (*Ellinskaja religija stradajushchego boga*), a study of Dionysian psychology and Dionysian sacrifice. In the same period, Ivanov published his important essays, "Crisis of Individualism" (*Krizis individualizma,* 1905) and "Presentiments and Portents" (*Predchuvstvija i predvestija,* 1906). In the first he insists that "individualism, in its contemporary, involuntary and unconscious metamorphosis, is acquiring features of ecumenicity" [*sobornost'*].[8] In the second, he anticipates the arrival of "a new organic epoch and the theater of the future" that will foreground the "choral and ecumenical element."[9]

When Ivanov returned to Russia for a prolonged stay in 1905 he was already well known. His fifth floor apartment on the corner of Tavricheskaya Street and Nevsky Prospect was known, because of its bay-window turret, as the "Tower" (*bashnja*); it became a historic gathering place for intellectuals, writers and artists of various interests and tendencies. Together with the poets Alexander Blok and Andrey Bely, the poet and philosopher Ivanov in these years was the center of a symbolism with a mystical, religious and realist tendency that set it apart from such earlier symbolists as Valery Bryusov and Konstantin Balmont who followed more directly in the tradition of French Symbolism. As Johannes Holthusen observed in *Vjačeslav Ivanov als symbolistischer Dichter und als russischer Kulturphilosoph* (1982), "the issues of the debate in the literary discussion of those years in Russia were in fact Ivanovian themes which corresponded to his effort to determine his own cultural position."[10]

Ivanov's wife, Lydia Zinovieva-Annibal, died in 1907. In 1909, he published a collection of philosophical, esthetic and critical essays entitled *By the Stars* (*Po zvezdam*). In 1911, he published a long-delayed volume of verse, *Cor Ardens* (followed by another volume under that title later the same year), containing poetry that dated back to 1904, but for the most part consisting of poems and sonnets dedicated to his wife's memory. He remained in St. Petersburg until 1912, teaching the history of literature and poetry. He spent the winter of 1912–1913 in Rome, working on the origins of the cult of Dionysus; the same year saw the publication in Russia of another volume of verse, *Tender Mystery* (*Nezhnaja tajna*). Ivanov had married Vera, the daughter of the first marriage of Lydia Zinovieva-Annibal and, together with her, he moved to Moscow in 1913, where he remained until 1920.

In this period, Ivanov worked especially on his translations from Aeschylus (the *Eumenides, Choephoroe, Persae* and *Seven against Thebes*); he had already completed his translation of the *Agamemnon* in Rome in 1913. In addition, he wrote a tragedy, *Prometheus* (*Prometej*, 1919) and published a second and third volume of collected essays, *Furrows and Boundaries* (*Borozdy i mezhi*, 1916) and *Matters Native and Universal* (*Rodnoe i vselenskoe*, 1917), completed and published an autobiographical poem, *Infancy* (*Mladenchestvo*, 1918), with its theme of childhood as an eternal paradise. Finally, Ivanov wrote a number of miscellaneous articles and verse, including a major lyric-philosophical "melopoieia," *Man* (*Chelovek*)—a work he began in the war years and completed in 1919.

The years of the revolution and civil war in Russia brought no little hardship for Ivanov and were marked by a second blow in his personal life with the death in 1920 of his thirty-year-old wife. In the years 1918–1919 Ivanov worked in various institutes. He suffered no persecution from the Bolsheviks. Unlike Blok, who had hailed the October revolution, or Merezhkovsky who had condemned it, Ivanov took no open political stand, though he spoke out in defense of religion on a number of occasions and wrote a short cycle of poems, *Songs of a Time of Troubles* (*Pesni smutnogo vremeni*), in which he was critical of militant atheism and the Red terror. Andrey Bely may have come closest to defining Ivanov's relation to the upheaval of the revolutionary years when he wrote in *The Sirin of a Scholarly Barbarism* (*Sirin uchenogo varvarstva*, 1922) that "the antinomies of our time intersect in Vyacheslav Ivanov."[11] Although the People's Commissar of Education A. V. Lunacharsky declared of Ivanov that he was not "attuned to the times," Ivanov's concern with the times reached deeply below the surface of cultural politics. In the same year that Lunacharsky declared Ivanov to be out of step with the revolution, Ivanov and M. O. Gershenzon published *A Correspondence from Two Corners,* a work which the German cultural historian Ernst Robert Curtius referred to as "the most important statement about humanism since Nietzsche" (*das Wichtigste, was seit Nietzsche über den Humanismus gesagt worden ist*).[12] In a series of six letters (counterbalanced by six letters of Gershenzon) Ivanov insisted on the continuity of culture and the vital meaning of memory. He criticized Gershenzon's anarchistic rebellion against culture and gave voice to his own religious optimism. "The disintegration of religion," he later wrote in his *Lettre à Charles Du Bos* (1930), "must be considered an infallible symptom of the extinction of memory in a given society."[13]

The years 1919 and 1920 were a period of intense poetic creation for Ivanov. It was then that he composed his moving *Winter Sonnets* (*Zimnie sonety,* 1919) and a brief cycle of sonnets, *De Profundis Amavi* (1920); in both cycles Ivanov gave expression to the tragic mood of the period and to his own efforts to surmount suffering. At the time Ivanov exchanged letters with Gershenzon he was at work on a translation of Dante's *Purgatory.* Ivanov's work on translations extended over his lifetime. Apart from almost the whole of Aeschylus, he translated the first ode of Pindar (1899), a dithyramb of Bacchylides (1904), poems of Alcaeus and Sappho (1914), most of Novalis's lyrics, a number of Petrarch's sonnets, Byron's *The Island,* some of Baudelaire's poems, Dante's *Vita nuova,* some of Michaelangelo's sonnets, Armenian and Lithuanian poems, and other works.

In 1920, Ivanov moved with his son and daughter to Baku, where for four years he occupied the University Chair of Classical Philosophy. There he completed and published (in 1923) his important study, *Dionysus and Predionysianism* (*Dionis i pradionisijstvo*), a work which constituted his doctoral dissertation. In the autumn of 1924 he obtained permission to leave Russia with his family and went to Rome. Ivanov was to remain in Italy until the end of his life.

Shortly after his arrival in Italy, Ivanov wrote his remarkable

cycle of poems, *Roman Sonnets* (*Rimskie sonety,* 1924), the first of
which, *Regina viarum,* begins with an invocation to the city of Rome
and ends on an apocalyptic note of destruction and fiery renewal.
It was in Rome at this time that Ivanov moved further along
a religious path that had always been integral to his spiritual evolution. In his *Lettre à Charles Du Bos,* in which he looks back on
the decade of the 1920s and its significance for him, Ivanov wrote:

> Indeed, the atmosphere I met with in this [western] world was
> scarcely calculated to cure my pessimism; everything combined to
> belie dark omens with a forced optimism that contained elements
> of presumption and of apathy, with a tolerance more lax and more
> skeptical than ever, with a tendency to try everything and to
> reconcile everything, providing all dogmatism should be weakened
> and softened in advance; with a dilettantism that fancied obscure
> aberrations; it is a world beset by the ugliness of soulless ma-
> chinery, where stupidity is a supreme symbol, steeped in a spir-
> ituality of nothingness coupled with an oriental cult of monsters;
> everything combined to belie those dark omens with a worn-out
> and glazed indifference propped up by a fatalistic doctrine of hu-
> manitarian progress, spreading out into a beatific dream of a so-
> ciety of human beings at peace and rationally responsible one for
> another, like a collective homunculus. In this atmosphere where
> the spiritual torpor of the bourgeois world corresponded by some
> sort of diabolical counterpoint with the revolutionary fever [in
> Russia], that familiar call sounded again imperiously in my soul;
> it was the persistent call which, ever since my youthful contact
> with that great and saintly man who was Vladimir Solovyov, had
> led me slowly but inexorably toward joining the Roman Catholic
> church [*SS,* III, 424].

Ivanov joined the Roman Catholic church in 1926, and "for the first
time felt [himself] to be Orthodox in the full, true sense of the
word," he wrote, again in his letter to Du Bos [*SS,* III, 426]. In
that same year Ivanov was invited to teach the Russian language and
literature at the University of Pavia and modern languages in the
Almo Collegio Borromeo. During these years he wrote various ar-

ticles for the Swiss review *Corona* and other journals, as well as a book on Dostoevsky, which included materials published in earlier collections of his essays. In 1934 he was offered the Chair of Russian Literature at the University of Florence, but the Italian government refused to confirm the appointment since he was not a member of the Fascist party. In 1934 Ivanov became professor of Slavonic Languages in the Pontificum Institutum Orientalium Studiorum. In his Roman years Ivanov led a generally retiring life, remaining aloof both from the emigré Russian community and from Western politics. It was in these years, however, that Ivanov established contacts with such notable figures as Martin Buber, Gabriel Marcel, Jacques Maritain, and others.

Ivanov's poetic output in the two decades following his departure from Russia was small, though he published a number of individual poems in emigré journals, as well as his long poem *Man*. A most significant work of those decades was his *Tale of Prince Svetomir* (*Povest' o Svetomire Tsareviche,* 1928–1949), an unfinished work in archaic prose in which elements from early Russian history and culture interweave with motifs from Ivanov's life.

In 1944, under the impact of the somber war years, Ivanov returned in a major way to poetry. It was in the last years of the war that he wrote his great verse cycle *Roman Notebook 1944* (*Rimskij dnevnik 1944*). During the war years Ivanov also worked on an edition of the Acts and Epistles of the Apostles and the Book of Revelation. One of his last works was an introduction and commentary to the Psalms.

Ivanov died in Rome, July 16, 1949.

Literary rediscoveries make us conscious not only of the tyranny of fashion but of the fact that irrespective of arrivals and departures on the cultural scene history has its own timetable. The great English poet, artist and mystic, William Blake (1757–1827), long reproached for his "obscurity," had to wait a century before criticism and scholarship were able to approach the uplands of his art and poetry and make an appreciation worthy of his genius. Like Blake, Ivanov was long relegated to the position of a difficult poet ("obscurity," "oracular obscurity," "bookish poet," "verbal hieroglyphics," *gelehrte Poesie*, etc.); and like him, a victim of anthologies, he has had to wait for a full appreciation of his stature.

A period of renown in the early part of the twentieth century was followed, after World War I and the Bolshevik revolution, by fifty years of neglect in criticism and scholarship. The first Russian emigration after the revolution, of course, remembered Ivanov and made some signal tributes and evaluations. Noteworthy are Bely's essay, "The Sirin of Scholarly Barbarism," an article by Ilya Golenishchev-Kutuzov (1930) and a group of essays in the Italian journal *Il Convegno*, 1933–1934 (Deschartes, Ganchikov, Ottokar, Pellegrini, Zelinsky). But it was only in the 1950s and, increasingly, in the 1960s that interest in Ivanov began to revive. Renato Poggioli's essay on Ivanov's *A Correspondence from Two Corners* (1950) and S. Makovsky's two essays on Ivanov in *Novyj zhurnal* (1952) were followed by Olga A. Deschartes' publication of a wide selection of Ivanov's lyrics and sonnets (accompanied by commentary) in *Oxford Slavonic Papers* (1955, 1958). Johannes Holthusen's valuable *Studien zur Ästhetik und Poetik des russischen Symbolismus* (1957) gave special attention to Ivanov.

Ivanov's important collection of verse, *Evening Light* (*Svet vechernij*) was published in 1962 with an introductory essay by Sir Maurice Bowra. Special mention should be made here of Fyodor Stepun's two important critical essays in 1962 and 1964. Yet more than fifty years after the era of Russian Symbolism and twenty years after Ivanov's death one could still speak of only a handful of essays, articles and memoirs, and one could search in vain for a single monograph on Ivanov. The situation changed in the late 1960s and early 1970s with the publication of Carin Tschöpl's *Vjačeslav Ivanov. Dichtung und Dichtungstheorie* (1968), James West's *Russian Symbolism: A Study of Vyacheslav Ivanov and the Russian Symbolist Aesthetic* (1970) and Armin Hetzer's study of Ivanov's tragedy *Tantalus* (1972). Since that time there has been a slow but steady increase in scholarly interest in Ivanov, the last examples of which are Johannes Holthusen's *Vjačeslav Ivanov als symbolistischer Dichter und als russischer Kulturphilosoph* (1982) and Fausto Malcovati's *Vjačeslav Ivanov: estetica e filosofia* (1983).

"The proof of a poet," Walt Whitman once wrote, "shall be sternly defer'd til his country absorbs him as affectionately as he has absorb'd it."[14] Ivanov, along with many other Russian writers and artists of the pre-revolutionary period, suffered a near total eclipse in the Stalinist era. A revival of interest among Soviet Russian literati was signalled by the publication in the scholarly *Annals* of Tartu University of M. S. Altman's important memoirs of Ivanov in Baku (1968) along with an article by N. V. Kotrelyov. In 1975 a selection of Ivanov's verse was published in the series *Biblioteka poeta*. The poems were accompanied by an introductory essay and commentary by S. S. Averintsev.

Whatever the larger reasons for the scant attention given to Ivanov in East and West in the last fifty or sixty years, one factor has been the complete absence of any scholarly apparatus for even the most elementary critical, scholarly or historical work, namely, a standard edition (or *any* edition) gathering together Ivanov's complete poetry, his abundant theoretical writings, literary criticism and philosophical essays, along with basic biographical and bibliographical materials. The works of Ivanov had remained scattered for decades in original editions and forgotten journals throughout the libraries and archives of Russia, Western Europe, and the United States. It was only the dedicated and massive work of the late Olga A. Deschartes, Ivanov's close friend, editor and biographer, and Lydia and Dmitri Ivanov, daughter and son of Vyacheslav Ivanov, that made any renewed interest in Ivanov a realistic possibility, at least from the scholarly point of view. In the years after Ivanov's death they carefully ordered, maintained and expanded the western archives of Ivanov and, in the general dearth of Ivanov information and materials, were generous in granting scholars and critics access to their archives and their rich fund of information. Out of these archives have come, to date, three volumes (2,500 pages) of a projected six-volume edition of the complete poetry and prose of Ivanov. With the appearance of the first three volumes (1971, 1974, 1979), the renaissance of Ivanov studies has begun in earnest.

The international symposium on Vyacheslav I. Ivanov at Yale University in 1981—the first gathering of any kind devoted exclusively to Ivanov—must be considered a watershed in the development of Ivanov studies. The success of this symposium, its signal achievements, would have been impossible without the long history of poetic appreciation and scholarly interest among an admittedly small but tenacious group of critics and scholars in East and West.

What the symposium did was to bring many of these people together, to review the state of Ivanov studies and to found Convivium, an international scholarly association devoted to the study of the work of Ivanov and all questions related to the period in which he wrote and lived.[15] Last but not least, the symposium generated a varied and stimulating group of papers on the poetry, criticism, philosophy, translations and life of Vyacheslav Ivanov. It is this material that we offer to the reader in the hope that it will further bring into the foreground the achievements of Vyacheslav Ivanov.

Notes

1. Fedor Stepun, "Wjatscheslaw Iwanow," in *Mystische Weltanschauung. Fünf Gestalten des russischen Symbolismus* (Munich: Carl Hanser, 1964), p. 208.

2. See Averintsev's essay in this volume, pp. 25–48.

3. *Avtobiograficheskoe pis'mo, SS,* II, 13.

4. M. S. Al'tman, "Iz besed s poetom Vjacheslavom Ivanovichem Ivanovym," in *Trudy po russkoj i slavjanskoj filologii XI. Literaturovedenie* (Tartu, 1968).

5. Stepun, "Vjacheslav Ivanov," in *Vstrechi* (Munich: Tovarishchestvo zarubezhnykh pisatelej, 1962), p. 143.

6. *Avtobiograficheskoe pis'mo, SS,* II, 19.

7. *Perepiska iz dvukh uglov, SS,* III, 403.

8. "Krizis individualizma," *SS,* I, 839.

9. "Predchuvstvija i predvestija," *SS,* III, 86, 102.

10. Johannes Holthusen, *Vjacheslav Ivanov als symbolistischer Dichter und als russischer Kulturphilosoph* (Munich: Verlag der Bayerischen Akademie, 1982).

11. Andrej Belyj, *Sirin uchenogo varvarstva* (Berlin: Izdatel'stvo 'Skify', 1922), p. 3.

12. Ernst Robert Curtius, *Deutscher Geist in Gefahr* (Stuttgart: Deutsche-verlaganstalt, 1932), p. 116.

13. "Lettre à Charles Du Bos," *SS,* III, 428.

14. "As I sat alone by Blue Ontario's Shore" (1856), in *Leaves of Grass* (Philadelphia: David McKay, 1900), p. 302.

15. The second international symposium on Vyacheslav Ivanov, sponsored by Convivium, the University of Rome and the Cultural Department of the City Council of Rome, took place in Rome and Frascati, April 24–28, 1983.

The Symbolist Ambience and Vyacheslav Ivanov

Victor Erlich

One of the salient features of the copious and vivid memoir literature bearing on the brilliant chapter in Russian cultural history, often referred to as the "Silver Age," is the insistence on its distinctive ambience, its heady, intoxicating "air."[1]

It is a matter of record that the Russian Symbolist movement spurred the resurgence of poetic craft after years of mellifluous monotony and high-minded bleakness, and significantly enhanced the emotional suggestiveness and associative wealth of the Russian poetic idiom. It is equally true that in its most characteristic manifestations Russian Symbolism, as Vladislav Khodasevich put it, "was not content to be a school of poetry"[2] and aspired to become a mode of creating life, a vehicle for transforming or transfiguring reality, an approach to higher esoteric truth that alone could provide the way out of the deep-seated crisis which had gripped the Western world.

The notion of the visionary, redemptive or, in the language of the period, "theurgic" nature of art, and, most notably, of poetry, was especially pronounced in the writings of the so-called younger Symbolists—a strand in early twentieth-century Russian literature associated with the names of Alexander Blok, Andrey Bely, and Vyacheslav Ivanov. To be sure, to call Ivanov a younger Symbolist is, in a strict sense, a blatant misnomer. Born in 1866, he was closer in age to the initiators of the Symbolist movement in Russia, Konstantin Balmont, Valery Bryusov or Fyodor Sologub, than to either Blok or Bely. Yet where literary rather than personal chronology is at issue, the designation might yet be salvaged: Vyacheslav Ivanov's relatively late and uncommonly mature poetic debut *Pilot Stars*

(*Kormchie zvezdy,* 1903), preceded as it was by two decades of total immersion in classical scholarship and Greek mythology, nearly coincided with the emergence of Russian Symbolism's most charismatic lyrical poet and most stunning prose writer. Moreover, and more importantly, Ivanov, Bely and Blok were linked by a spiritual affinity, anchored in their common indebtedness to the ambiguous legacy of Vladimir Solovyov—a strangely affecting blend of heterodox religious universalism and darkly apocalyptic prophecy, a vision shuttling uneasily between the notion of the Second Coming and that of an imminent advent of Antichrist.[3]

The catastrophic, "end-of-history" strain in Solovyov resonates throughout the *oeuvre* and the life of Andrey Bely, the dazzling polymath, the uncannily articulate, mercurial and frequently embattled spokesman of Russian Symbolism. The apocalyptic bent of Bely's imagination has by now been amply documented.[4] The leitmotif of his remarkable novel *Petersburg (Peterburg,* 1916), a brilliantly nightmarish vision of the early twentieth-century Russian capital, tottering at the edge of an abyss, is the ominous ticking of a time bomb which is about to explode and finally does. In Bely's discursive writings a keen sense of the precariousness of pre-1914 Russian society—an incisive eyewitness, Fyodor Stepun, called Bely "an immensely versatile and sensitive seismograph"[5]—blended with his "personal apocalypse" and anguished rebelliousness rooted in a conflict-ridden and conflict-generated childhood to produce a permanent, overpowering sense of crisis. Bely's retrospective attempt in his fascinating and often unreliable autobiographical trilogy to present himself as a revolutionary and a near-Marxist, intermittently led astray by politically treacherous traveling companions, is less than persuasive. This baffling protean figure was congenitally immune to consistency. What is consistent, indeed obsessive in Bely, is a yearning for an "explosion," less a considered ideological position than a vaguely metaphysical postulate and a deep-seated political need. "Politics will dissolve in spiritual war," he wrote on the eve of Armageddon. "The old forms of the old society will be blown up. I am dynamite, I know my fate."[6] Some ten years later, in *Notes of a Crank,* he declared characteristically: "Thus my eternal explosions

became worldwide."[7] The bomb remains his favorite metaphor and
his recurrent self-definition: "I am a bomb trying to explode into
pieces."[8]

In moments of iconoclastic frenzy Bely was apt to scorn his far-
flung sophistication to proclaim the cultural tradition useless and
gone to seed: "Culture is a rotten head. Everything in it is dead.
There is nothing left. Come the explosion," he exulted, "everything
will be swept away."[9] When the explosion did come, he welcomed
it in grandiloquent verse thrilling to his own imminent destruction:
"And you, stormy element, rage, burning me to ashes" (*a ty, burevaja
stikhija, bezumstvuj, szhigaja menja*).[10]

Though Bely's essential sincerity was hardly ever at issue, some
of his contemporaries were prone to dismiss such outbursts as ec-
centric posturing or *outré* moral histrionics. Yet few of them would
question the utmost seriousness of equally dire warnings and equally
self-destructive gestures on the part of the poet whom Anna Akhmatova dubbed, in retrospect, "the tragic tenor of the era." Alexander Blok has been credited, not without justice, with keen
responsiveness to the "music," the elemental rhythms of his nation's
history, and with the moral courage to face the inevitable. (There is
no question that in Blok the faculty which Lionel Trilling has called
the "imagination of disaster" was developed to the highest degree.)
By the same token, when on the eve of the First World War, he
refused "to judge" the imminent cataclysm, even if it were to spell
the destruction of "us the intelligentsia,"[11] he demonstrated an ability to reach beyond the vested interests of his group toward a wider
ideal of social justice. Yet it has become increasingly clear that this
selfless stance contained an element of sheer self-destructiveness, of
a morbid fascination with doom, akin to what Blok himself once
called the "love of perdition." (Anyone who cares about Blok the
man and the poet is apt to find the reference in his diary of April 5,
1912, to "an immense joy [he] derived from the news about the
wreck of the Titanic"[12] more than a little unsettling.) When in
January 1918, bewitched, as he put it, by the noise produced by
the collapse of the old world, Blok surrendered his sensibility and

indeed his poetic persona to the raging revolutionary elements, this
act of lyrical self-effacement produced one of the most striking and
truly innovative modern Russian poems, easily the finest poetic response to the October Revolution. The price of this Dionysian fling
was, we will recall, an ever-deepening depression. Significantly, as
he emerged from it, on the eve of his untimely death, to reaffirm
in his memorable speech "On the Calling of the Poet" the importance of craftsmanship and the necessity of creative freedom, the
language he used—"the gay truths of common sense," "the gay
name of Pushkin"[13]—was unmistakably, indeed pointedly Apollonian.

If both Bely and Blok appeared spellbound by Solovyov's apocalyptic mood, it fell to Vyacheslav Ivanov to carry forth and elaborate
both in his richly orchestrated, well-wrought verse and his stately
prose the positive aspect of Solovyov's thought—his abiding sense
of the underlying unity of the Christian tradition, his cultural and
religious ecumenicity. In fact, when in 1926 at the threshold of one
of the most creative periods in his career, Ivanov espoused Catholicism, he experienced this conversion not as an abandonment of his
earlier allegiance but as an organic outgrowth of his spiritual evolution, a reaffirmation of his persistent belief in the universality of
the Christian Church as well as a step toward the much overdue
rapprochement between the East and the West. By temperament and
endowment, he was a bridge-builder, a reconciler, a synthesizer, a
gatherer of cultural energies. It is these qualities, combined with a
learning formidable if lightly worn and an amazing intellectual and
esthetic sensitivity that made Ivanov so pivotal a figure in the lit-
erary-artistic Petersburg of 1905–11, so resourceful and beguiling
a moderator of that ongoing symposium, the "Wednesday evenings
at the Ivanovs." An active participant in these high-powered gatherings, Nikolay Berdyaev spoke of Ivanov's "fifth-floor apartment,"
known as the "Tower," as a place where against the backdrop of
social turmoil and political strife "values of spiritual and creative
life, of poetry, art, philosophy, mysticism and religion were upheld
and elaborated."[14] Another eminent habitué, Andrey Bely, recalled

half admiringly, half grudgingly: "It often seemed that Ivanov spun a fine ideational spiderweb, bringing together incompatible people and captivating them all" [*SS*, I, 94].

Ivanov shared with many of his contemporaries what Frank Kermode has called the "sense of an ending," the conviction of living at the turning point in Russian and European history. But even his eschatology had an affirmative, chiliastic bent: it was less a premonition of a disaster than a hope for the dawn of a "new religious consciousness" that would reach beyond the narrow confines of alienating individualism toward a *sui generis* Christian personalism, a collective state of mind which he often called *sobornost'* (ecumenicity), a lay theological term which hovers in meaning between spiritual community and spiritual communion. He paid his due to the prerevolutionary era's yearning for radical social change by lending at some point his prestige to the much contested concept of mystical anarchism. [15] But this former student of Mommsen was too strongly wedded to the classical tradition, too steeped in Aeschylus, Dante, Virgil and Goethe to yield, be it for a moment, to the utopian temptation of staking the prospect of spiritual renewal on a single climactic or cataclysmic event, let alone to succumb to the optical illusion of a totally new beginning, a clean slate.

How relevant is the cultural tradition in time of violence and social upheaval? This query lies at the core of the memorable dialogue between Vyacheslav Ivanov and his distinguished fellow humanist, a prolific literary and cultural historian, Mikhail Gershenzon. Slated by circumstances, in 1920, to share a room in a Moscow convalescent home for artists and scholars, the two old friends found themselves in an intense disagreement over a fundamental issue. After a few lively oral exchanges they decided to commit their contending views to writing. What ensued is that remarkable document, *A Correspondence from Two Corners* (*Perepiska iz dvukh uglov*, 1921). [16]

Writing to his roommate, Gershenzon gave vent to a mounting weariness with his erudition, to an urge to shake off the "tedious burden of mankind's accumulated intellectual achievements" [17] so as to recapture the freshness and spontaneity of the earlier phases of the Western civilization. Ivanov retorted: "To you it appears that oblivion is a source of liberation while cultural memory spells enslavement and death. To my mind, memory is the dynamic principle, oblivion is weariness and cessation of movement, decline and reversion to the state of relative stagnation."[18] "Culture will become again the cult of God and of the earth. It will be a miracle wrought by Memory."[19]

The insistence on the liberating, life-preserving power of memory is quintessentially Ivanovian. In his first collection of verse he hailed "eternal memory" as a triumph over death: "Over death eternally triumphs / he in whom eternal memory dwells" (Nad smert'ju vechno torzhestvuet / v kom pamjat' vechnaja zhivet [SS, I, 560]). In a 1908 essay, "Sporady," he said: "According to an old Orphic belief, in order to become divine and immortal the soul must find again the keys of memory and quench its thirst in the lake of subterranean Mnemosyne."[20] The theme of the organic connection between poetry and memory reappears in a straightforward, almost vernacular vein in a lyric contained in Roman Notebook 1944 (Rimskij dnevnik 1944 under February 11):

The poet, too, has something to teach,
But what he teaches is not his wisdom:
with it he would all the sooner
Embarrass or bore everyone.

Whether life is sweet or bitter,
You had better find out yourself,
And each has his own sorrows:
What he teaches is to remember.

I poèt chemu-to uchit,
No ne mudrost'ju svoej:
Eju on vsego skorej
Vsekh smutit il' vsem naskuchit.

Zhizn' sladka l' na vkus, gor'ka li,
Sam ty dolzhen raspoznat',
I svoi u vsekh pechali:
Uchit on—vospominat'.   [SS, III, 592]

To return, finally, to the Ivanov-Gershenzon correspondence: it is singularly fitting or, if one will, symbolic that it should have been Vyacheslav Ivanov who at one of the most trying moments of modern Russian history, on the eve of major dislocations and tragic discontinuities, spoke gravely and eloquently on behalf of memory as repository of values, a warrant of cultural continuity and a mode of civilized survival.

Notes

1. Vladislav Khodasevich, *Literaturnye stat'i i vospominanija* (New York, 1954).

2. Vladislav Khodasevich, *Nekropol'* (Brussels, 1939), p. 8.

3. In a 1912 poem addressed to Blok, Ivanov spoke of sharing with his younger soulmate a "mysterious baptism by Solovyov" (*zatem chto oba Solov'evym tainstvenno my kreshcheny*). Vyacheslav Ivanov, *Stikhotvorenija i poemy* (Leningrad, 1976), p. 251.

4. Samuel E. Cioran, *The Apocalyptic Symbolism of Andrei Bely* (The Hague, 1973). Bernice G. Rosenthal, "Eschatology and the Appeal of Revolution (Merezhkovsky, Bely, Blok)," *California Slavic Studies* XI (1980).

5. Fyodor Stepun, *Byvshee i nesbyvsheesja* (New York, 1956), p. 277.

6. Quoted in N. Valentinov, *Dva goda s simvolistami* (Stanford, 1969), p. 62.

7. See Andrey Bely's *Zapiski chudaka* (Moscow-Berlin, 1922).

8. Valentinov, *Dva goda,* p. 98.

9. Ibid., p. 67.

10. Andrey Bely, "Rodine," *Stikhotvorenija i poemy* (Leningrad, 1966), p. 382.

11. A. Blok, *Sobranie sochinenij,* V (Leningrad-Moscow, 1960), 121.

12. Ibid., 139.

13. Ibid., 168.

14. See Olga Deschartes, "Vvedenie," in *SS,* I, 94.

15. In a polemic with Valery Bryusov's harsh review of a 1906 miscellany, *Fakely,* whose editor G. Chulkov declaimed somewhat portentously on behalf of "mystical anarchism," Ivanov sought to salvage the notion by defining anarchism as a synthesis of individualism and *sobornost'*.

16. Vyacheslav Ivanov and Mikhail Gershenzon, *Perepiska iz dvukh uglov* (Petrograd, 1921).

17. Ibid., p. 11.

18. Ibid., p. 29.

19. Ibid., p. 56.

20. *Zolotoe runo* XI–XIII (1908).

POET

The Poetry of Vyacheslav Ivanov
Sergey Averintsev

The poetry of Vyacheslav Ivanov is not only a poetry of "symbolism," as the word was used by men of letters and is used today by historians of literature, that is, in the complex and secondary sense, but also a truly *symbolic* poetry in the simplest and primary sense: a poetry in which the symbol is not a decorative attribute that creates "atmosphere," but the foundation on which the edifice is erected. In the history of European and Russian Symbolism this is rather the exception than the norm. The self-designation "symbolist" on the lips of Ivanov is, to an unusual degree, etymologically literal.

It seems that no one who has written about this poet has evaded the responsibility of devoting at least a few words to the problem of the symbol. Nevertheless, too little attention has been given to the study of the *concrete* life of symbols in his poetry. The symbol as a "category" of poetics somewhat overshadows the symbol as a reality of poetry. There are reasons for this. Ivanov himself was too influential and productive a theoretician for us to avoid the temptation to follow closely his theoretical declarations in the interpretation of his poetic practice. The temptation is the stronger since he was not only an influential and productive theoretician, but also an intelligent one, and it is only natural that we rejoice at the abundance of opportunities to hear at first hand what the poet wanted from his poetry. Nevertheless, the temptation is a temptation, and for three reasons.

First, when Ivanov engaged in theory, he engaged precisely in theory, and not in his own self-portraiture. "This, to my mind, is the way a poet should write," and "This, according to my observation, is the way I write," are two different themes—comparable to each other, but different.

Second, the theory of Ivanov and especially the verbal expression of that theory are more marked by the epoch, and are therefore further from us than his poetry.[1] This is entirely understandable. In order to write the sort of poems that Ivanov wrote, it was necessary to cease listening to his fellow men of letters and go his own way, not looking around at the "milieu." For all its civilization and civility, Ivanov's poetry is obstinate and undomesticated—qualities that assure its strength of survival as the carnival time of the "Tower" recedes into the distant past. The young Mandelshtam had reason to write to Ivanov: "You are the most unintelligible poet of our time, the most obscure, in the ordinary use of the word—precisely because you, like no one else, are true to your element—having consciously entrusted yourself to it."[2] The internal choice which stands behind all Ivanov's poetry is expressed in the lines from a poem of 1915:

Human talk and everyday lies,
Don't trouble my flock under the clouds.

I know all, ascending to the hut in the air
And passing an indifferent glance over the town squares:

If I parted with my native dovecote
My song would be more intelligible to you.

If I said "farewell" to the ethereal region
And disbanded my white flock,

I would become necessary, and akin, and dear to you,
Ailing with the ailing, doleful with the doleful.

Ljudskaja molva i zhitejskaja lozh',
Podoblachnoj stai moej ne trevozh'.

Vse znaju, v vozdushnyj shalash voskhodja
I vzgljad ravnodushnyj po stognam vodja:

S rodnoj golubjatnej rasstalsja by ja,—
Byla by ponjatnej vam pesnja moja.

Efirnomu kraju skazhi ja "prosti"
I beluju staju svoju raspusti,—

Ja stal by vam nuzhen, i sroden, i mil,
S neduzhnym neduzhen, s unylym unyl. [3]

On the other hand, engaging in theory, that is, descending several
steps from the "hut in the air" and entering into explanations—no
longer with that "providential interlocutor" (Mandelshtam's expression) to whom the poet addresses himself, but with an entirely
predictable interlocutor, with the determinate, sociologically iden-
tifiable circles of the Russian and European intelligentsia of a certain
time—he necessarily reckoned, if not with "everyday lies," then with
"human talk." The codification of the Symbolist canon meant for
him, more than for any other poet of his epoch (except perhaps
Stefan George), a deliberate volitional act of cultural diplomacy,
cultural "politics," and such an act is subject to considerations of
prudence and the rules of etiquette. [4] Appearing as a theoretician,
Ivanov said to his contemporaries what he considered to be appropriate, τὸ πρέπον. If—let us imagine for a moment the impossible—
he saw before him not them but us, today's readers, what then? One
must assume that his poetic voice would not change in the least
(after all he promised not to disband his "white flock"); but it is
very possible that as a theoretician he would say something different
to us, something that it is not easy to imagine from his existing
works. [5] It is completely clear what he would not repeat today: all
those theoretical utopias which have been rendered impossible by
our historical experience. Among his poems time, as always, has
carried out an inevitable selection, [6] but those that survive the selection and have been cleansed *puritate ignium* reach us directly, right
on target, like a letter addressed to us; while his theoretical works
almost pass us by. To explain the poems by the theoretical works
today means to explain the closer phenomenon by the farther.

Third, the reality of any poetry, even such a conscious poetry
as that of Ivanov, by its very essence is not exhausted and cannot be
exhausted by any theory, even a theory so homogeneous with it as
Ivanov's; in poetry, there are many more secrets, hidden matters,
unexpected moments. According to the wise advice of Horace, it is

better for the seafarer to make his journey not holding too closely to
the "unreliable shore":

> . . . Neque, dum procellas
> Cautus horrescis, nimium premendo
> Litus iniquum.

For the interpreter, poetry is the open sea, the poet's theoretical
declarations are the shore, and an "unreliable" shore; not because
they are not adequate in their own way, but simply because they are
only theoretical declarations, and not the actual reality of poetic
practice. They may elucidate the latter but cannot explain it.

Before speaking of the system of symbols in Ivanov's poetry,
one must note that his symbols truly constitute a system in the full
sense of the word, a system that is closed to a greater degree than
that of any other Russian Symbolist.

A closed system of symbols means that in principle there are
no two symbols in Ivanov of which each would not require the other,
would not assume the other in the dialectical sense of the word
"assumption" (with varying degrees of insistence, of course); there
are no two symbols which would not be connected by a chain of
semantic couplings, in roughly the way that concepts are connected
in the idealistic dialectic of Hegel or especially Schelling (*Konstruk-
tion*).[7] It means further that each symbol occupies a precisely determined place in relation to the other symbols. It means, finally, that
each of the meanings of each symbol (which, as we know, is
polyvalent[8]) is turned in the direction of certain other symbols of
the same system, indeed, precisely to them and not to the others,
or if to the others, then only through them.

The symbolic lines, symbolic chains, and paired oppositions of
symbols which constitute the "working realm" of Ivanov as a poet,
could possibly be presented all together graphically in the form of a
very complex diagram. The author of this essay is not convinced
that there would be much use in such a diagram or that the under-
taking would be in good taste; therefore the essay will do without
a diagram.[9] But it is worthwhile to envisage the possibility of it.

Of course, the closed system of symbols cannot be mastered and revealed in the space of one poem, or even in the space of one poetic cycle or one poetic collection (a level of organization that is very important for all the Symbolists). No, for this system the entire sum of the poet's creation is needed, from the moment of its discovery by him to the very end. In other words, in order to be realized, a closed system of symbols must necessarily remain *stable* in the course of the poet's creative biography. It is indeed closed in still another and special sense: the poet closes it round himself like a magic circle from which he does not intend to exit. ("Making charms and closing circles. . . .")

The system also takes the reader *inside* itself, disposing him to a specific type of perception. Perhaps the most striking example is the *Tale of Prince Svetomir* (*Povest' o Svetomire Tsareviche,* 1928–1949): it is not "reading" at all—the sole means of contact with this work is to enter into it and let its verbal element close over one's head. (This, perhaps, relates it with *Romanzen vom Rosenkranz* by Clemens Brentano, and with *Ève* by Charles Péguy.) But there is no work by Ivanov that would not require a similar orientation on the reader's part. It is with good reason that in the letter cited above[10] Mandelshtam says that the reader agrees with Ivanov in roughly the same way that the traveler accepts the Catholic significance of Notre Dame—"simply by force of his being under those vaults." Ivanov's system of symbols is also conceived like vaults which close and come together from different sides, both over the poet and over *his* reader— the reader whom his poetry has in mind. The image of the closing circle appears in the same letter from Mandelshtam ("the astronomical circularity of your system"). The architecture of Ivanov's symbols, like the architecture of Hagia Sophia's cupolas, can be adequately perceived only by the view from within, not from without. Here is one parallel by way of elucidation: for the average Russian man of letters, German Romanticism is above all E. T. A. Hoffmann, but for Ivanov it is Novalis. One may regard Hoffmann as "reading" in the usual (by no means pejorative) sense of the word, but not Novalis. Hoffmann's world of images may be viewed from afar as a spectacle; one must enter into Novalis's world of symbols as into an especially dense reality, *realiora*—or else they are not necessary at all.

We have said that the closed system of symbols is a stable system; by this we have answered the question of why no other Russian Symbolist had a system of symbols that was or could be closed to such a degree, could be a *system* to such a degree, as that of Ivanov.

There is little point in dwelling here on the symbolism of *Skorpion* in contrast to the symbolism of *Ory*, on that symbolism which in Ivanov's terminology is called "idealistic" in contrast to "realistic," and which proceeded from Baudelaire's "Les correspondances" and not from the ideas of Novalis or of Vladimir Solovyov. If symbols have no ontological status, they cannot form a system and are connected only by the principle of "correspondences," which are reflected in each other like mirrors face to face. "Only fleeting things do I put into verse" (*Tol'ko mimoletnosti ja vlagaju v stikh*) is Balmont's motto. "I want the Free Boat to sail everywhere" (*Khochu chtob vsjudu plavala svobodnaja Ladja*) is the motto of Bryusov, whom Tynyanov called "a traveler in the realm of themes" (*puteshestvennikom po oblasti tem*).[11] The central task of the symbolism of Balmont and Bryusov is decorative.

Matters are more complicated with the "Solovyovians," Alexander Blok and Andrey Bely.

When we try to apply the phrase "closed system" to Blok, we immediately feel that the image behind these words would have evoked utter claustrophobia in him. One recalls his youthful lines, which could serve as an epigraph for his entire output:

> I have one friend—in the damp night fog
> The road into the distance.

> Mne drug odin—v syrom nochnom tumane
> Doroga vdal'.[12]

The road leads into the distance, and it lies in the fog, that is, it is impossible to survey it, to see in advance what its final goal is; however, one can see what it leads away from—from that which yesterday was home. The pathos of movement without looking back and without return ("no one will come back again"—*nikto ne pridet nazad*) which denies any stability and breaks any closedness, is for Blok's poetry simultaneously the most important objective characterization and just as important a subjective self-characterization, that is, a central theme.[13] Blok had always to retreat into the "lilac worlds" from the tower of his Tsarevna, from the chambers of his Beautiful Lady, in order to meet the Stranger in the restaurant, and he had to rebel, to revolt against the "lilac worlds" in order to see the Field at Kulikovo; there is not and cannot be a spiritual "space" which would gather his symbols together, unite them, make them compatible. This is not contradicted by the fact that there are image-emblems which traverse all periods of his lyric poetry (the same "road," "mother and son," etc.). D. E. Maksimov called such images "integrators."[14] It is precisely in their symbolic semantics, however, that these images are extremely unstable and subject to a radical reinterpretation that keeps them from identity with themselves. Each time, dramatic breaks with previous values lie behind the reinterpretation. The poetic biography of Ivanov, while of course by no means alien to movement, is characterized by a much greater immutability of its coordinates, its "pilot stars." Ivanov could say of himself, in the macaronic language of the polymath, what Blok could not have said in any form: "In truth, I am the same as always" (*semper idem*) although, of course, by force of law "everything flows" (πάντα ῥεῖ) and by force of the self-affirmation of my vitality "I also flow" (κἀγὼ ῥέω).[15] It is characteristic that for him historical time plays a limited role, and physical age plays a role still more limited (there are, for example, no "youthful poems" in the sense in which both of Blok's first cycles are characteristically "youthful"). In the organization of Blok's lyric poetry as a whole, the factor of temporal irreversibility works with great clarity. Blok himself understood the three volumes of his lyric poetry as a "trilogy of becoming a man" (*trilogiju vochelovechenija*);[16] this trilogy looks like the dynamic Hegelian triad of thesis, antithesis, and something like a synthesis— truly a "negation of a negation." When we speak of the poetry of Ivanov, Blok's "road" must be replaced by other metaphors: "source," "return," "seclusion." In the fullness of the "source" everything is given primordially, everything "flows out" from it, spreading and overflowing, but not changing its composition. On the personal level the "source" is "infancy," childhood as an image of eternal and immutable paradise:

> Immovable Eden, where anew
> We celebrate ancient love . . .
>
> Edem nedvizhimyj, gde vnov'
> Obrjashchem drevnjuju ljubov' . . .   [SS, I, 242]

On the level of poetic biography, the "source" is the first collection, *Pilot Stars* (*Kormchie zvezdy*, 1903), where in abridged, preliminary form, "everything is already there." (One cannot say anything of the kind about Blok's first collections; no one would begin to seek in *Ante lucem* and the *Poems about the Beautiful Lady* [*Stikhi o prekrasnoj dame*] for the content of "Iambs" [*Jamby*], "Garden of Nightingales" [*Solovinyj sad*], or "The Twelve" [*Dvenadtsat'*]). Finally, on the metaphysical level, the "source" is *realiora*: the Platonic "idea," the Aristotelian "entelechy," of which the poetry of Ivanov senses itself to be the gradual realization. But this means that the "source" is simultaneously the "goal": not only *causa formalis* and *causa efficiens,* but also *causa finalis*. Movement proceeds *from* the "source," but also—and this is still more important, still more secret—*toward* the "source," and this is "return."

> As to an unintelligible reed,
> Hearken to these speeches:
> The path is by a reverse course
> To the native springs . . .
>
> Kak trostniku neponjatnomu,
> Vnemli recham:
> Put'—po techen'ju obratnomu
> K rodnym kljucham . . .   [SS, III, 539]

In this theme of "return," "palirroia," "palirroj" is the esoterica of Ivanov's perception of time and life. For now, let us limit ourselves to the statement that the logic of this theme leads Ivanov, in essence, to the assertion of the malignant quality of everything transient in comparison with permanence:

> Have we not with our treacheries
> Forged the prison
> That mortal men
>   call time?
>
> Time whirls us away like wind,
> Divides us, separates us,
> It will bite its serpent tail
>   and die.

> Ne iz nashikh li izmen
> My sebe skovali plen,
> Tot, chto Vremenem zovet
>   Smertnyj rod?
>
> Vremja nas, kak veter, mchit,
> Razluchaja, razluchit,—
> Khvost zmeinyj v past' vberet
>   I umret.   [SS, III, 544]

In the context of this philosophical "accusation" of time as treachery, as a departure from memory and loyalty and so from existence, a symbolic meaning is acquired by preferring "seclusion" to "the road" (which, of course, also had a quite simple, literal meaning for the poet, who was close to 80 years old):

> "Go where your eyes are looking,
> Arrow-like the straight road flies!
> The wide expanse is a foretaste of God,
> And the turquoise of far eternity."

> The dry paths are trodden
> And the real disproves the fairy tale.
> The road is the run of a creeping serpent
> Cast down from the heights into the dust.

The far distance is Leah in a blue bridal veil
When love called Rachel.

And now as a free captive
I cherish my secluded enclosure,
The expanse is within me like a vast world,
By turning my gaze I'll not encompass it;
And to my homeless memory
Blueness shines beyond dark Lethe—
And I belong to myself.

"Idti, kuda gljadjat glaza,
Prjama letit streloj doroga!
Prostor—predoshchushchen'e Boga
I vechnoj dali birjuza" . . .

Iskhozheny tropy sukhie,
I skazku oprovergla byl'.
Doroga—beg polzuchij zmija,
S vysot nizrinutogo v pyl'.
Dal'—pod fatoj lazurnoj Lija,
Kogda ljubov' zvala Rakhil'.

I nyne tesnotoj ukromnoj,
Zatochnik vol'nyj, dorozhu,
V sebe prostor, kak mir ogromnyj,
Vzor obvodja, ne ogljazhu;
I svetit pamjati bezdomnoj
Golubizna za Letoj temnoj,—
I ja sebe prinadlezhu.   [SS, III, 626]

"The straight road flies like an arrow"—it is hard to resist the
temptation to recall a series of passages in Blok where the path is
likened precisely to an arrow, e.g.:

Our path—like an arrow of the ancient Tatar will—
    Pierced our breasts.

Nash put'—streloj tatarskoj drevnej voli
    Pronzil nam grud'.[17]

Ivanov feels he belongs to himself[18] in the "secluded closeness" of home, for it is to him the place and symbol of *gathering himself* ("whoever does not gather with Me is lost . . .")—the overcoming of that which in Hegel's philosophy is called "evil" or "negative" infinity. Such is the late, final sum of the experience of the man and the poet. The sum of Blok's experience, formulated scores of times in his poems and prose, is completely the opposite:

> I will never find a place in a quiet house
> By a peaceful fire!

> Ne najti mne mesta v tikhom dome
> Vozle mirnogo ognja![19]

In one of his articles Blok celebrates "flight from home" (from the composed and closed life cycle) and "flight from the city" (from culture, that is, historical memory) as a joyful and liberating oblivion, a way to simplicity. "Simplicity of lines, simplicity of solitude is outside the city. In flight from home the feeling of one's own hearth, one's soul, separate and barbed, is lost. In flight from the city the complicated measure of this once proud soul, with which it measured its surroundings, is lost. And the gaze, which has lost its memory of the straight lines of the city, is expended in space."[20] "To become like a path" for Blok means in a certain sense to "forget everything."[21]

A kind of echo of these motifs can be heard in the voice of Gershenzon, arguing with Ivanov in *A Correspondence from Two Corners* (*Perepiska iz dvukh uglov*, 1921). For Gershenzon the sole possibility of renewal is in forgetting, "plunging into Lethe," departing from the given of the cultural tradition. For Ivanov the vertical of ascent is opposed to the horizontal of the path leading away. Of the goal—true simplicity—he says: "It is not by exit from a given milieu or country that it is achieved, but by ascent. In every place—I again repeat and testify—there is a Bethel and a Jacob's ladder—in the center of every horizon" [*SS*, III, 412]. Of the cultural tradition he says: "Culture is the cult of ancestors and of course—even now it is dimly conscious of this—the resurrection of the dead" [*SS*, III, 412].

The cultural traditionalism of Ivanov ("filial respect toward history" in Gershenzon's expression [SS, III, 407]) bears the most immediate relation to that of which we speak, namely, the prerequisites for the closed nature of his symbolic system, for such a system could not be constructed by the efforts of a single man without entering into the rights of inheritance of the huge "thesaurus" of traditional symbolism. Here the poet needed not only all his polymathy,[22] not only the professional philologist's habit of patiently and slowly examining the significance of any signifier, but also the faith, which lay at the very heart of his poetry, in culture as the "resurrection of the dead," in the *reality* of his unity with the past, with the "fathers":

. . . Thus the crowd of the departed, the incorporeal
crowd, thinks and sings in those who live . . .

. . . Tak sonm otshedshikh, sonm besplotnyj
V zhivykh i myslit, i poet . . .   [SS, III, 234]

The point is not that Ivanov is a bookish poet; Andrey Bely is also bookish, but he is capable neither of a faith that would not immediately be washed away by a stream of nervous self-irony, nor of "filial" constancy, nor of patient scrutiny of any sort of objective fact, nor, finally, of the slackened pace of thought and emotion necessary for this. Bely tremulously takes symbols into his hands from the treasure-house common to mankind and has no time to look at them closely. Here is a very simple example:

. . . O, the radiant Hosanna
Of Matthew, Mark, and John!

O, osijannaja Osanna
Matfeja, Marka, Ioanna![23]

If these lines were by Ivanov, we would be obliged to ask ourselves why and on the basis of what special considerations and reflections Luke has been omitted from the list of Evangelists. This absolutely could not be without a reason, because for Ivanov the traditional name-symbols do not merge, as *from a distance,* into an indistinguishable series with an indeterminate meaning, but each of them

taken separately means what it means. In face of the lines by Andrey
Bely, though, such a question has no meaning. The utter fortui-
tousness of the choice of names—Matthew, Mark, John—is even
externally confirmed by the fact that immediately before this are
mentioned the bull, the lion and the eagle, i.e., the symbols of the
Evangelists Luke, Mark and John, with the omission of Matthew.
The choice is obviously dictated by phonetics and metrics; on the
semantic level the names "Matthew" and "Luke" are completely interchangeable for Andrey Bely. He is concerned with creating the
necessary mood and effective sound image: "Matthew" (*Matfej*) and
"Mark" are connected by alliteration, "Mark" and "John" (*Ioann*) by
the assonance of the stressed vowel, which has a particular force in
Russian verse; the feverish tempo of the poem allows neither the
author nor the reader to meditate upon more hidden shades of meaning. The three names are hurled at the reader by the rush of the
rhythm, and at the same moment all their diffuse meaning is given
away without a remainder; there is nothing left to scrutinize. Here
there is much "mysteriousness" but, strictly speaking, no real mysteries. It is the poetics of "glossolalia," not *philologia sacra.*
    Here is yet another example from the same poem:

You, sisters—
            —(You, Love, are like a rose,
            You, Faith, are trembling ecstasy,
            Hope is murmuring tears,
            Sophia is lofty Swedenborg!)—

Having united four forces
They were in a triple depth . . .

Vy, sestry—
            —(Ty, Ljubov'—kak roza,
            Ty, Vera,—trepetnyj vostorg,
            Nadezhda—lepetnye slezy,
            Sofija—gornij Svedenborg!)—

Soediniv chetyre sily
V trojakoj byli glubinoj . . .[24]

The numerical symbolism of the last two lines seems to express the pretension of this passage to a special spiritual significance. The names which figure in the fragment are taken from the church calendar: "Faith [*Vera*], Hope [*Nadezhda*], Love [*Ljubov'*]} and their mother Sophia [*Sofija*]"—according to tradition, Roman martyrs of the eleventh century, to whom the holiday of September 17, popular in Russia, is consecrated. At the same time, Sophia is the "Divine Wisdom" which plays such an important role in the Russian mystic tradition from the churches of St. Sophia in Kiev and Novgorod to the religio-philosophical conceptions of Vladimir Solovyov, Florensky and Sergej Bulgakov.

The poem "First Meeting" (*Pervoe svidanie*) stands in the shadow of Solovyov's image, and "sophiological" motifs are natural in it. But why is "Divine Wisdom" a characteristically Russian image that finds its embodiment on ancient icons,[25] so energetically connected with the name of the Swedish visionary and theosophist of the eighteenth century, the founder of a Protestant sect, the New Jerusalem Church, that was propagated mainly in England and America? What is "sophiological" about Swedenborg? Apparently, all the concrete connotations of the name "Swedenborg"—for instance, Swedish origin, or the sectarian and quasi-materialistic type of mysticism,[26] or whatever else—hardly exist for Bely. The semantics of the name is reduced here to a scant minimum ("something mystic, profoundly sagacious"); on the other hand, phonetics again triumphs. The accord of the consonants *n–r–g* and stressed vowel *o* bound the words "lofty" (*gornij*) and "Swedenborg" into a certain indissoluble semantic unit twice repeated in the poem.

But when the same name, "Swedenborg," appears in Ivanov—moreover, in a comic poem, written "for an occasion" and not included in a single collection—the name's meanings appear more concretely and fully. Describing, in a letter to Bryusov of January 3/16, 1905, his spending New Year's Day in the company of the still quite young V. F. Ern, Ivanov first speaks of their attempts to divine the military and revolutionary future of Russia in the coming year, that is, of efforts to perform, as it were, an act of clairvoyance (cf. contemporaries' accounts of the clairvoyance of Swedenborg who fore-

saw through space the fire in Stockholm, etc.). Secondly, he mentions the Swedish etymology of Ern's surname. After this there is
not the slightest arbitrariness when Ern is called "young Swedenborg."[27] Even here there is something to ponder; the question, Why
Swedenborg? is not meaningless. The historical name, transformed
into a symbol, is used in Ivanov's poetic joke with greater deliber-
ation and precision than in the pathetic and pretentious lines by
Andrey Bely.

As for the personifications of Faith, Hope, and Love, their use
by the two poets is also characteristic. In Andrey Bely, Love is "like
a rose" (the symbol of the rose is degraded into a simile—"like"),
Faith is "trembling ecstasy," Hope is "murmuring tears." The characterizations of the latter two do not reveal any distinction of nuances
in meaning and are semantically interchangeable, leaving meter and
phonetics aside. In Ivanov two examples may be given.
The first:

> . . . "I," grumbles Will, "do not accept the world."
> In reproach Wisdom tells her: "But the world is your
>   phenomena."
> But Faith whispers: "Await Epiphany!"
> And with her, Hope: "It's near, near—I hearken!"
> And with her, Love: "I will lift the cross of the Earth!"—
> And she weeps tears and weeps without alleviation . . .

> . . . "Ja,"—ropshchet Volja,—"mira ne priemlju."
> V ukor ej Mudrost': "Mir—tvoi zh javlen'ja."
> No Vera shepchet: "Zhdi bogojavlen'ja!"
> I s nej Nadezhda: "Blizko, blizko,—vnemlju!"
> I s nej Ljubov': "Ja krest Zemli pod"emlju!"—
> I slezy l'et, i l'et bez utolen'ja . . .   [SS, II, 266]

The second example:

> Wisdom has created "I am" in us,
> Love—"thou art." Over the abyss of darkness
> Faith has illumined God's city,
> Hope whispers: "I—am we . . ."

"Az esm'" Premudrost' v nas tvorila,
"Esi"—Ljubov'. Nad bezdnoj t'my
Grad Bozhij Vera ozarila,
Nadezhda shepchet: "Az—esmy" . . .   [*SS*, III, 238]

As early as 1904, Blok wrote of Ivanov: "There is the kind of
person . . . who is accustomed to reckoning with the whole multi-
storied edifice of human history."[28] In both cases this is precisely
what we see: the traditional symbols, while acquiring not only a
new but a very personal meaning (one must feel the passion the poet
invested in his thesis "man is united" in order to appreciate the
syntactic oxymoron of the words "I—am we" [*az—esmy*]), do not
become a private "myth" or a simple function of a momentary context; they do not fall prey to the author's self-will, they do not forget
their concrete historical past. Wisdom, which in the first example
exposes Will as the culprit for the transient world of phenomena[29]
and in the second teaches people self-consciousness, that is, in both
cases speaks of human freedom and responsibility, is truly Sophia or
Sapientia, as the most common tradition of Christian-oriented philosophical idealism, the so-called *philosophia perennis,* knows it. The
property of Faith is to oppose "epiphany"[30] (that is, *noumenon*) to
"phenomenon," that is, the lying manifestation of phenomenon—in
other words, to build the illuminated "city" of St. Augustine in the
face of dark chaos. This is a quite definite action with which one
may confuse neither the action of Love—to take upon itself the
common burden of all people, teaching self-exposure toward "Thou"
to the self-enclosed "I am"—nor the action of Hope—to affirm that
the fulfillment of promise is "near, near," exposing the meaning of
promise through the paradox "I—am we" as the imperative of ecumenicity (*sobornost'*), that is, of the *personal* unity of all humanity.[31]
Nothing is diffuse or arbitrary and hence nothing is interchangeable.
Each symbol taken separately preserves its inner adequacy and faithfulness to itself, which cannot be denied even by the reader for whom
the world view expressed in those symbols is unacceptable. The
correlation of the symbols has the precision of a mathematical prop-

osition which satisfies the mind. (Reading Ivanov, it is hard not to recall Aristotle, who explained the very existence of poetry by the fact that "to come to know is a most pleasant occupation."[32]) The intellectual satisfaction is all the fuller and broader since from the given realm of symbols proceed utterly necessary connections to neighboring symbols (in the first of the poems cited above, Will, Wisdom, Faith, Hope and Love appear as the five Wise Virgins of the Gospel parable, while the five Foolish Virgins are identified with the five senses in their uncleansed, unenlightened state), and disperse outward to the entire symbolic universe of the poet.[33]

Was the order of this "universe" identical throughout Ivanov's creative career? Of course not! The point is that from beginning to end it steadily grew and accumulated. The meaning of the symbols, for all its polyvalence, was not allowed to turn into its opposite under the destructive action of Romantic irony, which for Ivanov, in contrast to the other Symbolists,[34] played no role whatsoever.[35] The degree of stability in Ivanov's system of symbols is, by the way, perfectly apparent from the passages just cited in which Sophia and her daughters figure. As we ascertained, it is quite possible to interpret them together, bringing them into a certain concordance, despite the fact that more than a decade (1906 to 1918/19) lies between them. It would perhaps be more difficult to "harmonize" the symbolism of just one of Blok's cycles, *On the Field at Kulikovo* (*Na pole Kulikovo*), which originated in the second half of 1908, than to carry out this task for the sum of Ivanov's poetic texts. For the latter, the relations among symbols are organized so that biographical time has only reinforced the stability of the edifice, compacting more tightly the bricks which form it.

The poetry of Ivanov, which has so often been found to be obscure, in fact turns out to be unusually clear—a poetry of precise contour and firm, slowly unfolding significance. Perhaps it is not quite "lyric poetry" in that special sense to which the readers of Blok or Esenin or Marina Tsvetaeva have become accustomed, that is, it is not the "lyric element"; but it is nonetheless true poetry. In the world of poetry of our century, where there is too much opaque inarticulateness, mixing the author's overly personal idiosyncrasies with overly impersonal inculcations of "dynamic" rhythms, the voice of Vyacheslav I. Ivanov deserves renewed listeners.

Notes

1. Some time ago it was customary to accept Vyacheslav Ivanov more seriously as a theoretician than as a poet. Anna Akhmatova's well-known words are an expression of this: "an all-embracing intellect," but his poetry "no longer exists" (Anna Akhmatova, *Sochinenija,* vol. II, Mezhdunarodnoe literaturnoe sodruzhestvo, 1968, p. 340). It is somewhat strange to recall these words today. What comes to life once again is the poetry of Ivanov with its distinctive intimate sense of the cultural memory of humanity, of the "anamnesis" which struggles with oblivion. Poetry is necessary; theory is "interesting" or "instructive"—another hierarchical level.

2. Letter of August 13/26, 1909 (*Gosudarstvennaja biblioteka SSSR im. Lenina, Zapiski otdela rukopisej,* Issue 34, Moscow, 1973, p. 262). The word "element" as applied to Ivanov may seem unexpected; it is not as trite as when applied to Blok, but it is justified, for "philology" actually acquires the impetuosity of a lyric element in Ivanov's poems. The correlation of "artificial" and "elemental" is not at all simple here. As Andrey Bely once noted, "Vyacheslav Ivanov's artificiality is spontaneous in him" (*Russkaja literatura XX veka {1890–1910},* ed. S. A. Vengerov, Moscow, 1916, p. 123).

3. "Dovecote" (*Golùbjatnja*) (*SS,* III, 494). When we strive to comprehend the aspect of Ivanov as a poet, his human position in his poetry, a special problem is the correlation between cultural sociability and creative solitude. The "Tower" is a colorful and rather important fact of Russian cultural life at the beginning of the century; but when we think of poetry, it is better to forget about it for a while. The memoirists wrote what they remembered, and they remembered what they saw—the hospitable master of the "Wednesdays," "Vyacheslav the Magnificent," the tricliniarch and symposiarch in an environment of very lively but slightly feverish spiritual intercourse. "A door onto the street: crowds thronged," the irritable and impressionable Andrey Bely described it in *Beginning of the Century* (*Nachalo veka,* Moscow, 1933, p. 314). But even on a purely external biographical level, Ivanov's creative career begins with years of deep solitude and also ends with years of deep solitude; indeed the decisive turn in the middle of that career toward the new poetics of *Tender*

Mystery (*Nezhnaja tajna*), *Infancy* (*Mladenchestvo*) and *Winter Sonnets* (*Zimnie so-nety*) is also connected with seclusion. The contrast of these times with the sociable times of the "Tower" constitutes the theme of the seventh sonnet in the cycle *De profundis amavi* (1920). But even at the time of the "Tower," the hidden basis of sociability was, of course, solitude, which the memoirists could not see: a quite empirical solitude at the writing desk, but also an inner solitude—"in mundo solus."

4. Cf. for example the very revealing letter to Bryusov, January 14/27, 1905 (*Literaturnoe nasledstvo,* vol. 85, Moscow, 1976, pp. 471–72); it explains much about the psychological orientation of Ivanov, who appeals to the wisdom of the "public man." It is because of the observance of a peculiar etiquette, by the way, that it is so difficult to reconstruct with even relative completeness the range of reading of this *poeta doctus*: as a rule, in his articles he quotes authors who are painstakingly selected and accepted into a certain canon, avoiding the quotation of "non-canonical" authors. Dante is included in his canon, but not the medieval Latin poetry of sequences, in which, however, the poet must have been steeped for the sequence *Breve aevum separatum* to have arisen by itself out of his dream into waking life (*SS,* I, 130–31; II, 395). Except for Calderón, sixteenth and seventeenth-century European poetry, so dear to Ivanov, is excluded; or, to dwell on more recent examples, Nietzsche is included in the canon, but not Richard Wagner who remains at best on the borderline of the canon. It is interesting that the sole passage from Wagner's texts that is cited several times in Ivanov's articles (in his own translation) is Hans Sachs's monologue in *Die Meistersinger* about the essence of poetry, already cited in Nietzsche's *Birth of Tragedy* and thereby somehow attached to the canon. N. V. Kotrelyov, to whose generous help I am in general much obliged in my work on this subject, drew my attention to the connection of this selection of "canonical" authors and texts with the cultural-"diplomatic" mission and cul-tural-"political" wishes of Ivanov.

5. Ivanov's last pronouncement on Symbolism was, as we know, the 1936 article "Simbolismo" for the *Enciclopedia italiana,* and it is already, in essence, written differently from the theoretical articles of the preceding years: the tone is different.

6. Akhmatova found that there was much "of Balmont" in Ivanov's poems (see note 1 above). In itself this is a truism: any poet, no matter how original, uncompromising, or intractable a creator he is, is also the contem-porary of his contemporaries, and as such cannot be entirely protected from the diseases of the age. We are entitled to rejoin to Akhmatova's remark that we are interested in those of Ivanov's poems in which there is *no* "Balmont."

(Indeed, she herself said, "Now the *Winter Sonnets* I like."). A scholarly paper is not the place for categorical value judgments, but it can hardly be doubted that "Canzona I" in *Cor Ardens II*, almost all of *Tender Mystery*, the late sonnets, *Man (Chelovek)*, especially its second half, and *Roman Diary (Rimskij dnevnik)*, are much more vital today than are *Transparency (Prozrachnost')* or *Arcana*, "Eros" and "Golden Curtains" (*Zolotye zavesy*) in *Cor Ardens I*.

7. "Die Kunst construiren heisst, ihre Stellung im Universum bestimmen. Die Bestimmung dieser Stelle ist die einzige Erklärung, die es von ihr gibt" (*F. W. J. von Schellings Sämtliche Werke. I. Abtheilung*, vol. 5, Stuttgart and Augsburg, 1859, p. 373). R. Halbuzel, *F. W. J. Schellings Lehre von der menschlichen Erkenntnis. Dialektik und Einbildungskraft* (Basel, 1954).

8. "A symbol is only a true symbol when it is inexhaustible and boundless in its significance. . . . It is many-faced, polyvalent and always obscure in its furthest depths" (*SS*, I, 713).

9. Besides which, such a diagram would require not an article but a voluminous book for its substantiation and explanation.

10. See above, note 2.

11. Ju. Tynjanov, *Problema stikhotvornogo jazyka. Stat'i* (Moscow, 1965), pp. 278–79.

12. A. Blok, *Sobranie sochinenij*, (Moscow-Leningrad, 1960), I, 22.

13. Cf. D. E. Maksimov, "Ideja puti v tvorcheskom soznanii Al. Bloka," *Blokovskij sbornik* (Tartu, 1972), II, 25–121.

14. Ibid., p. 48.

15. Letter to Bryusov of June 3, 1906, *Literaturnoe nasledstvo*, vol. 85 (Moscow, 1976), 492.

16. In the well-known letter of June 6, 1911, to Andrey Bely.

17. Blok, *Sobranie sochinenij*, (Moscow-Leningrad, 1960), III, 249. Cf. these passages from his letters: "I know that my path is, in its basic aspiration, straight as an arrow . . ." (*Sobranie sochinenij*, VIII, 265); ". . . You go along the same highway, still unknown, but straight as an arrow" (ibid., p. 239).

18. Did he perhaps recall the words of St. Bernard: "Ubicumque fueris, *tuus esto*; noli te tradere"?

19. Blok, *Sobranie sochinenij*, III, 286.

20. Blok, *Sobranie sochinenij*, V, 73.

21. . . . And you won't understand the blue eye,
Until you yourself become like a path . . .

. . .

You will not forget everything and stop loving everything . . .

(Blok, *Sobranie sochinenij*, II, 84).

22. Ivanov's erudition was more substantial than that of any of the other Symbolists. He could not have permitted himself accidentally to confuse hermetics with hermeneutics, as did Blok (*Sobranie sochinenij*, V, 8), or include the seventeenth-century French philosopher Gassendi among the medieval Arab scholars, as did Bely (*Ofejra*, Moscow, 1922, p. 157), or involuntarily substitute the German *lügen* (to lie) for the Latin *lugere* (to mourn), as did Bryusov, who was proud of his high-school Latin (according to the testimony of S. V. Shervinsky).

23. Andrej Bely, *Pervoe svidanie* (St. Petersburg, 1921), p. 6.

24. Ibid., p. 53.

25. Cf. G. D. Filimonov, "Ocherki russkoj Khristianskoj ikonografii, I. Sofija Premudrost' Bozhija," *Vestnik Obshchestva drevnerusskogo iskusstva* (Moscow, 1874–1876); P. G. Lebedintsev, "Sofija Premudrost' Bozhija v ikonografii Severa i Juga Rossii," *Kievskaja starina,* December 1884, and others.

26. Let us note that Vladimir Solovyov, who displayed a certain interest in Swedenborg, rather sharply reproached the Swedish mystic for his "dry and sober intellect, with its formal-rational modes of thought," and for his "coarsely rationalistic polemics," as well as for his lack of philosophical culture (V. S. Solov'ev, *Sobranie sochinenij*, IX, [St. Petersburg, 1907], 242). He clearly would not have admitted Swedenborg as the embodiment of his Sophia. These facts have no connection with Andrey Bely: for him what is real and concrete is not the image of Sophia and not the image of Swedenborg, but the purely private "myth" about Nadezhda Lvovna Zarina—more precisely, his late "myth" about this youthful "myth" ("I wander before my very self . . ."). This arbitrariness is not at all like the symbolism of the *Tale of Prince Svetomir,* in which even the most intimate autobiographical *realia* (Georgievskij Lane and the Church of St. George, the poet's place of birth and christening, are turned into "the Egor boundary marker" and "the Egor spring"; Volkov [Wolves'] Lane, which intersects with Georgievskij Lane, becomes the packs of wolves before "Egor'e"; the return of the dead beloved Gorislava in her daughter Otrada is like Lydia Dmitrievna, who "returned" in Vera) are included in a strictly disciplined system and reconstructed with an orientation toward the objective facts of a suprapersonal—Russian national, Helleno-Byzantine, and omni-human—tradition. For Ivanov the suprapersonal is in principle *more real* than the mere personal: in the 1908 article "Two Elements in Modern Symbolism," he firmly opposed "objective truth" to "subjective freedom" (*SS*, II, 546) and demanded "self-restraint and renunciation of *ego* for the sake of *res*" (*SS,* II, 547).

27. *Literaturnoe nasledstvo,* 85, 470–71. It is worth recalling that contemporaries emphasize that Ern, who was of the Orthodox religion, had the

physiognomical and psychological traits of Protestant sectarianism. A. V. Kartachev wrote of him: "Tall, with a pale, beardless, never smiling face, in the black frock-coat customary at that time, he seemed to be a Protestant pastor of some moralizing sect, and was an example of the Protestant pathos in Orthodoxy" (*Pravoslavnaja mysl'*, 1951, VIII, 48). This shows the sort of concreteness of connotation there was even in such a comic and brief mention of Swedenborg's name by Ivanov.

28. Review of *Transparency* (Blok, *Sobranie sochinenij*, V, 538).

29. The world as a phenomenon of Will—this formula in itself, of course, inevitably brings to mind the philosophical language of Schopenhauer, and it would be unrealistic to assert that Ivanov was not thinking at all of the German metaphysician. The matter, however, is not so simple. First, this motif has correspondences in earlier thinkers than Schopenhauer, for example, Plotinus. Second and more important, it appears very often in the context of Ivanov's poetry and is subjected to interpretation in an ethico-Christian spirit like that of certain ascetic Orthodox authors; to me, precisely *to me* the world appears as a lie, "a dream," and "darkness," while not being such in its essence (in contrast to the "maya" of the Buddhists):

> . . . And the tender paradise, inherent in the earth,
> Has been covered with a fog, that races toward death

> . . . I nezhnyj raj, zemle prisushchij,
> Maroj pokrylsja, v smert' begushchej   (*SS*, III, 616)

and this action of *my* distorted will is my fault:

> . . . For a long time now my eyes have not cherished
> The pattern that cleverly wove darkness.
> That I was the weaver I will understand at the last moment;
> I will say: "You're right," to the judge without reservation.

> . . . Uzhe ne dorog
> Ocham uzor, khitro zatkavshij t'mu.
> Chto tkach byl ja, v poslednij srok pojmu;
> Sud'e: "Ty prav,"—skazhu bez ogovorok.   (*SS*, III, 574)

30. For Ivanov, to put the words of the same root *javlen'e* (phenomenon) and *bogojavlen'e* (epiphany) next to each other and bind them by rhyme means to reveal their philosophical contrast ("epiphany" as the transcendence of "phenomenon"). Such rhyming ranks with the punning rhyming of homonyms which is characteristic of the poet, but generally unusual anywhere but in

comic poetry: *lik*—"assembly, chorus, clergy" and *lik*—"face" (*Milost' mira*, "Mercy of the World," *SS*, I, 556); *trusu*—"earthquake" and *trusu*—"coward" ("An attack, like an earthquake [coward] . . ," *SS*, III, 598). It has its closest parallels in medieval poetry, in which punning rhymes are used in the most serious sacral context. For Ivanov the confrontation of words of the same root serves the same goal of reactualization of the etymological core of the word as it served for Plato. Cf. S. S. Averintsev, "Klassicheskaja grecheskaja filosofija kak javlenie istoriko-literaturnogo rjada," in *Novoe v sovremennoj klassicheskoj filologii* (Moscow, 1979), pp. 41–81.

31. Of course, this conception of humanity as a personality can be divorced neither from the ideas of Vladimir Solovyov nor from the trend of Christian personalism in twentieth-century philosophy. One must note, however, that it has parallels in ancient mysticism, especially the teachings of the Byzantine theologian Maxim the Confessor (662) about the "pleroma of souls" as a sort of multiple unity and suprapersonal personality.

32. *Poet.*, 4, 48b12.

33. One can see this very well in the example of two lines from *Man* (*SS*, III, 218):

The boundary river has no time for flesh,
Where for the *obolus* you give the *milot* . . .

Ne do plota reki predel'noj,
Gde za obol otdash' milot' . . .

The reader is obliged, first, to comprehend in one glance the image of the worlds divided by the river of the afterlife, an image which belongs among the fixed motifs of Ivanov's poetry and is, for example, given in one early poem (*SS*, I, 568):

With the soundlessly splashing Lethes
God divided his worlds . . ."

Bezzvuchno pleshchushchimi Letami
Bog razgradil svoi miry . . .

Second, his imagination is referred to the classical symbol of the *obolus* as payment to Charon for passage across this river. Third, still another line leads to the biblical symbolism of *milot* (μηλωτή —"goat's hide," the word which, by the way, designates the cloak of the prophet Elijah, given by him to Elisha at the River Jordan upon his parting with this world). All three symbolic aspects are given with characteristic conciseness.

34. Besides Ivanov, one may perhaps note the full absence of total irony (described, by the way, in Blok's frightful article "Irony," 1908) only in Balmont. A certain quality of wholeness in praising existence unites the two poets (cf. Ivanov's word to Balmont: "We are both glorifiers," cited in the article by Olga Deschartes, *SS*, I, 74). But in Balmont it is, first, bathed in the simplicity, if not inanity, of the general setting, and second, devalued by the essential denial of any coherent significance ("Only fleeting things do I put into verse . . .").

35. This does not at all mean that Ivanov lacks humor. Irony and humor are rather opposites: irony is pride, humor is humility. A quiet, "old man's" humor comes to the poet together with humility:

> To the neophytes by the threshold
> I prophesied as a mystagogue.
> I make fruit of repentance:
> I speak in common language.
>
> And what is there to say? A lot?
> Gogol's stopped being folksy,
> While making the fruit of repentance.
> But I repent, being folksy,
>
> Should I take a simile
> From Homer's garden?—like a cicada.
> To cicadas he (one himself!)
> Likened old men . . .

> K neofitam u poroga
> Ja veshchal za mistagoga.
> Pokajan'ja plod tvorju:
> Prostorech'em govorju.
>
> Da i chto skazat'-to? Mnogo l'?
> Perestal gutorit' Gogol'
> Pokajan'ja plod tvorja.
> Ja zhe kajus', gutorja,—
>
> Iz Gomerova li sada
> Vzjat' sravnen'e?—kak tsikada.
> On tsikadam (sam takov!)
> Upodobil starikov . . .   (*SS*, III, 593)

—Translated by Suzanne Fusso

Vyacheslav Ivanov the Poet:
A Tribute and a Reappraisal
Vladimir Markov

> But the pure treasure of lofty art
> Is too heavy for the people
>
> No vysokogo iskusstva
> Ljudjam tjazhek chistyj klad

One night back in 1940, the famous jack-of-all-literary-trades, Korney Chukovsky, came to the Philosophical Division of the University of Leningrad to read from his no less famous (and now recently, at last, published) *Chukokkala,* a visitors' book in which, for about thirty years, everybody who was anybody had left his or her impromptu contribution. The auditorium was packed with students; I was among them. Somewhere in the middle of the evening, he said: "Guess who wrote this?" And he recited a short *Gelegenheitsgedicht,* admirably crafted and rich in sound, with internal rhymes echoing toward the end of the poem. My fellow students began to shout out their guesses: Blok! Mayakovsky! Esenin! (My generation was not especially noted for either its taste or its imagination.) Chukovsky smiled slyly and kept saying, "No, better! No, greater!" and finally, after having teased those young barbarians to his satisfaction, he declared, "Vyacheslav Ivanov"—no doubt to everyone's disappointment.

The present generation is more sophisticated. They can discuss Pasternak, Akhmatova, Mandelshtam, Tsvetaeva and even Khlebnikov, but they still look at Ivanov's name "like a sheep at a new gate" (*kak baran na novye vorota*), or, to quote Mayakovsky, "like a goat at a poster" (*kak v afishu koza*). He is still little known, little read and little appreciated.

Genuine students of Russian poetry need neither proof nor reminder that Vyacheslav Ivanov was a major poet. Still, it is not too much of an exaggeration to say that he is the last great Russian poet of this century who remains to be established as such, who, in fact, is in need of a society to promote his work (similar, say, to the Gustav Mahler Society of only a decade and a half ago). What kind of a poet was Ivanov? Why do his admirers love his verse? Is there anything to love in it? What prevented his being recognized to the full extent until now? What is the critical consensus about him?

Twelve years ago, when I met the late and unforgettable Olga A. Shor in Rome and very cautiously ventured that I simply loved Ivanov's poetry but did not care much about Nietzsche, Dionysus, mystical anarchism, theurgy, mythopeia or ecumenicity (*sobornost'*), I fully expected to be shown the door. Instead, she smiled happily, saying, "that is exactly what Vyacheslav Ivanovich wanted." Having cited these two highest authorities, I proceed with more confidence, even if realizing that, often, while reading Ivanov, I listen to him "as a curious Scythian [listens] to an Athenian sophist" (*kak ljubopytnyj skif afinskomu sofistu*).

A description of Ivanov's poetry is a collective task for the future. In the meantime, Mandelshtam's words about another, quite different poet will suffice:

Nobody [has] these undulations of sounds . . .
And never [has there been] this murmuring of waves . . .

Ni u kogo—etikh zvukov izgiby . . .
I nikogda—etot govor valov . . .

The poet himself also helps us with his line:

Speak only gold and honey.

Tol'ko zolotom i medom govori.

But nothing helps as much as a poem read through from beginning to end. Let us choose one at random: the "Taormina" from *Pilot Stars* (*Kormchie zvezdy*, 1903):

> Beyond the darkness of Ausonia, the sky is reddening from the
>   East;
> Amber smoke rises above snow-peaked Aetna;
> The snow glows and burns, and flame-colored purple
> Flows from its head, like royal unction,
>
> Onto calm wooded slopes, onto peaceful fields
> And olive groves and the fore-dawn coast,
> Where the indistinct Pontus will soon glisten
> With a translucent blue amidst the ruins of the
>   sacred propylaeum.
>
> The theater sleeps in shattered pieces; the orchestra
>   has grown silent,
> But thy thymele smolders in the snows eternally,
> Thou who comest with the east of the day with the
>   triumph of the sacred!
>
> And from thy citadel, Evius, as in days of old,
> The mournful Melpomene espies a magic circle of wilderness
> And Tartarus breathing beneath a garden of captivity.

> Za mgloj Avzonii vostok nebes alej;
> Jantarnyj vskhodit dym nad snegoverkhoj Etnoj;
> Sneg rdeet i gorit, i purpur ognetsvetnyj
> Techet s ee glavy, kak tsarstvennyj elej,
>
> Na sklony tikhie dubrav, na mir polej
> I roshchej maslichnykh, i bereg predrassvetnyj,
> Gde skoro smutnyj pont golubiznoj prosvetnoj
> Sverknet v razvalinakh sviashchennykh propilej.
>
> V oblomkakh spit teatr, orkhestra onemela;
> No vechno kuritsja v snegakh tvoja fimela,
> Grjadyj v vostoke dnja i torzhestve svjatyn'!
>
> I s tvoego kremlja, kak drevle, Mel'pomena
> Zrit, Evij, skorbnaja, volshebnyj krug pustyn'

I Tartar, dyshashchij pod vertogradom plena![1]

This sunrise, ray after ray, is one of the finest crescendos in Russian poetry, worthy of the company of some of the Fet elegies or of that accumulation of cacophony in Nekrasov's "On Weather." The combination of colors is rare and remarkable: amber, white and dark red, which in a moment are to be joined by blue—the color which is not yet present. The allusions are subtle, too.[2] The poem echoes Pushkin's "The Dispersing of the Clouds" (*Redeet oblakov*) which, by contrast, describes evening; and a kremlin in Sicily should not surprise us: this metaphor of the jagged ruins of the amphitheater is another in a long series of Ivanov's "connections." Being a true symbolist, he tied things together; we may recall the unions of St. Francis and the sweet Cythera, of a knight and a tsarevna, Perun embracing Gaea, or the meeting, in one sonnet, of the Roman Coliseum, a Greek maenad, the New Testament lamb (*agnets*) and the Old Testament Eden (*vertograd*).[3]

I am far from suggesting that the marvelous "Taormina" is a tourist postcard (as most of Bunin's travel poems are), but it pays to begin to read it as such in order to experience the magnificent shock of seeing how a postcard becomes a metaphysical snapshot, how it is transfigured into a mythological landscape worthy of Tyutchev (or of Nicolas Poussin), with a beautiful sunrise ending in a premonition of an earthquake and with chaos throbbing beneath your very feet. A lesser poet would develop this into a sentimental sadness about the death of the gods. Ivanov's poem, however, ends on the precarious coexistence of the realm of terrifying, hidden noumena with a pleasing desolation in the phenomena. I have not even begun to admire the stately variety of the sonnet's sentences, the *o*'s of line 1, the *e*'s almost invariably ending the lines—with the stunning junction between lines 2 and 3—and a quantity of other beautiful things. To be sure, this relatively early poem does not demonstrate Ivanov fully. In a sense it is not even typical, although it does contain so many of his favorite ideas and themes; but it is as good a stepping-stone as any to his many other wonderful sonnets as well as to such small gems as "The Finger" (*Perst'*), "Subtile virus caelitum," "The Meeting" (*Vstrecha*), "The Sail" (*Parus*), "The Grave" (*Mogila*), "The First Purple" (*Pervyj purpur*), "A Siren" (*Sirena*), "The Sphinx is Looking" (*Sfinks gljadit*), "The Sorcerer-Cat" (*Kot vorozhej*) and "Taedium phaenomeni," as well as "Dryads" (*Driady*), "A Vision" (*Videnie*), "Chimeras" (*Khimery*), "Rainbows" (*Radugi*) and "Ad rosam."

If I were forced to do the impossible and to sum up in a short phrase what Vyacheslav Ivanov is about, I would say: the language of the gods. This language of the gods was, for centuries, considered to be the *sine qua non* of poetry, and it scarcely exists any longer. Many eighteenth-century Russian poets wanted to speak in it, few knew how to sustain it and only Derzhavin was truly bilingual: he could both soar and snore in his poems. But the death of the gods was imminent, and the nineteenth century sealed it. Perhaps the most important contribution of Russian Symbolism was its crazy, quixotic attempt to return the language of the gods to poetry. Ivanov's effort was the most consistent and, perhaps, the most successful.

The other party was stronger, however. Acmeism and Futurism are, in this instance, not enemies, but allies. Finally, Pasternak successfully filled the familiar five traditional meters with the spoken language, seemingly for good; and Akhmatova, in her old age, contemptuously dismissed Ivanov as unreadable.[4] (I am sure that she did not remember "Taormina" when she went there in December 1964 to collect her prize.)

The victory of the language of the mob created the greatest stumbling block on the reader's path to Ivanov. Firstly, it opened the doors for countless second-rate virtuosos of colloquial diction, such as Tvardovsky, Slutsky, Smelyakov (and I name the best), who managed to drown the organ of Vyacheslav the Magnificent with their balalaikas. Secondly, and more significantly, the process made us almost forget that Virgil, Dante, Milton and Derzhavin used the language of the gods to speak about lofty and significant things, and that, indeed, there is no other way to speak about them.

Ivanov moved easily in the world where Love and Beauty begin with capital letters; yet he was not the high-priest he is often made

out to be: he did not exchange an augur's smile with other high-
priests, as Bryusov was fond of doing;[5] and it obviously seldom
occurred to him that any of these lofty and significant things could
be inaccessible to anyone. In short, he is perfectly democratic and it
was not his fault that his world knew only brotherhood (*bratstvo*)
and not vulgar camaraderie (*panibratstvo*). Ivanov lacked the gift of
vulgarization and he never popularized. He knew full well that the
important meanings looming behind his lines could not avoid sounding oracular most of the time; he did not mind as long as his poetry
was heard:

> Even if the world finds what I sing obscure
> It will hear my sonorous lyre.

> Puskaj nevnjatno budet miru,
>   O chem poju,
> Zvonchatuju on slyshit liru.   [*SS*, III, 29]

If and when, however, the vulgarization of poetry is arrested or even
reversed, the name of Vyacheslav Ivanov will be written on banners
in large golden letters. Perhaps he foresaw this when he wrote, "My
lot is a golden one" (*Zolotoj mne zhrebij vypal* [*SS*, I, 763]), or when
he rhymed—tautologically, but so aptly—*-zlato* with *zlato* [*SS*, III,
33–34].

Russian criticism is partly responsible for the present lack of
interest in Ivanov. There is precious little of it, it is lacking in insight
and for the most part is on the trite side. It is simply astonishing
how uninformed criticism and judgments will often accumulate, take
on the appearance of a consensus and finally inundate textbooks and
reference works with worn phrases and arbitrary labels. Let us consider some of them: Ivanov is often seen as cold and bookish, an
intellectual poet who is difficult to understand and devoid of spontaneity, a poet for scholars. But cold intellectuals do not write poetry.
Even the verse of a mediocre poet originates in the subconscious.
The difference between Dante, on the one hand, and Surikov or
Surkov on the other, is that the subconscious of the former is immense, while that of the latter two is shallow and undeveloped.
Ivanov was a passionate and human being steeped in life. Reading

his biography, one can not help but realize that his love life was richer than that of many poets and he always responded sensitively to what was going on around him. This so-called "rationalist" (in the phrase of Ivanov-Razumnik) spent most of his life in visions and dreams, and voices dictated Latin poetry to him. It is certainly wrong to dub as "cold" the poet who "spoke gold and honey." What is more, coldness is not necessarily a poetical defect; a great poet can be cold, to wit, Alexander Blok: why else would he choose a blizzard to symbolize love? Those given to counting how many times a poet uses this or that color ought to consider the fact that when you read Blok's "The City, to the Red Limits" (*Gorod v krasnye predely*), with its orgy of the color red; you shiver. Ivanov's colors are not only warm by themselves (gold, red), but they communicate warmth. He is a poet of openness, roundness, fullness, mellowness and sweetness. It is not, however, the sweetness of sugar, but that of the slow-flowing, aromatic, sparkling and glowing, golden honey of poetry in which pipes "sounded out as did lyres and a sistrum, and a timbrel and a cymbal" (*zvuchali tsevnitsy i liry, i sistr i timpan i kimval* [SS, I, 541]). In short, it is no mere Pan-pipe; it is an orchestra with a Brahms-like density and opulence of sound.

This leads us to another quality of Ivanov's poetry, which renders it not only unique, but also desirable, relevant and even indispensable. It is the affirmative character of this poetry. Unique is, perhaps, the wrong word. After all, Russian poetry has Fet and Pasternak, who, even when in despair, wrote in a major key. Still, those two poets could not have written *Cor Ardens* (1911), a book born out of the death of a deeply beloved person, yet a positive and sweet book. This is why Ivanov is often, albeit mistakenly, deemed a non-tragic poet, a notion which only adds to his lack of popularity. Russians love what Dostoevsky called "lacerations"(*nadryv*), and so they feel uneasy in Ivanov's "expanses of divine never-ending plenitude" (*prostory bozhestvennoj, bezdonnoj polnoty* [SS, II, 428]). Was not Pushkin, someone may ask, no less life-affirming, indeed, the epitome of this very quality, and justly celebrated as such? Yes, indeed, but let us pursue the comparison. Ivanov could not have written

"My useless gift, my fortuitous gift" (*Dar naprasnyj, dar sluchajnyj*) or "Remembrance" (*Vospominanie*), and not because their themes were completely alien to him, but because, in his poetry, doubt and bitterness are overcome and transfigured.

Even the language of the gods consists of words, and so far we have neglected them. Who has not heard of Ivanov's predilection for rare words, his seven or more foreign languages, his Homeric epithets and the classical names which send us on yet another trip to the university library to consult Pauly-Wissowa? I cannot agree that these lexical features render Ivanov's poetry heavy and dry. Remember that he called Danaë a dark-bellied woman, open to the skies (*zhenoju temnolonnoju, otverstoj nebesam* [*SS*, II, 379]). What could be better? And is this dry? The point is, however, that not only the Old Church Slavonicisms and the other lexical curios,[6] but practically every word in Ivanov's poetry sounds new, strange and even odd. Sometimes he achieves this with a "wrong" stress that your dictionaries can tell you nothing about, as in "One generation after another on an ambush of eagerness" (*Za rodom rod na nakoval'nju rven'ja* [*SS*, III, 225]). And sometimes the effect is created by a most subtle intersecting of planes, as in the very first line of his *Man* (*Chelovek*, 1919): "When the azure is, like a giant fan" (*Kogda lazur' kak opakhalo . . .* [*SS*, III, 198]). I remember first reading this line and not immediately comprehending from where the pleasure derived. Later I saw, of course, that the cliché quality of *lazur'*, the neighbor of the unusual, and the very graphic *opakhalo*, simply and naturally is purified because its single -*u*- (and we all know that Ivanov knew a thing or two about this sound) is surrounded on both sides only by unstressed, half-stressed and stressed -*a*-'s; thus it stands out and is quite expressive. Even a hostile critic will fail to detect a trace of Ivanov's proverbial heaviness here; the line is as light as a feather.

We seldom realize how varied Ivanov is in his excellence. His poems seldom, if ever, resemble one another. Surprises await the reader at every step. The examples are numerous. I could point at the miracle of the verb rhyme in "Enthusiasm" (*Uvlechenie*); the Dantesque "Sphinx" (*Sfinks*) with its incredible ramifications of sentences; the marvelous diminuendo in stanza 6 of "The Morning Star"

(*Utrennjaja zvezda*); the fine Russian handling of the Alcaics in "Prayer of Camillus" (*Molitva Kamilla*). The anthologists have not yet created the "golden fund" of Ivanov: a selection of poems which ought to be in every anthology—except that they invariably select "The Sphinxes by the Neva" (*Sfinsky nad Nevoj*). In addition to the poems that I have mentioned earlier, my candidates for the "golden fund" would be Ivanov's difficult but rewarding masterpiece "The Dream of Melampos" (*Son Melampa*), his Gobelin-like "Theophilos and Maria" (*Feofil i Marija*) and his "Letter to the Caucasus" (*Poslanie na Kavkaz*)—so very different from the last two poems. Or his incredible ghasel "Rebirth" (*Vozrozhdenie*), or the name-studded "Cumae" (*Kumy*), or the color-filled "Sogno angelico." The list is endless.

If at least half of what I have said is correct and makes sense, then the problem is not whether to rediscover Ivanov or not, as some doubting Thomases still think, but to try to envisage how this rediscovery is going to unfold: which of his works might form a bridge to a future universal recognition and what segment of the community of *literati* could possibly initiate that rediscovery of Ivanov. The cultural historians and religious thinkers in Europe between the wars obviously viewed *A Correspondence from Two Corners* (*Perepiska iz dvukh uglov,* 1921) as the signal work here. Perhaps the Jungians should belatedly recognize the importance of Ivanov's concept of myth in connection with the ideas of their mentor. The narcissistic "peace and love" generation certainly missed its chance to discover in Ivanov the prophet of the universal Eros. Perhaps *Man,* with its intersecting planes, will prove such a starting point. Or Ivanov's prose? It may well be that the peaks of post-revolutionary Russian prose will, one day, form a triangle of unlikely bedfellows: Zoshchenko's stories, Bunin's *Life of Arseniev,* and Ivanov's *Tale of Prince Svetomir* (*Povest' o Svetomire Tsareviche,* 1928–1949). (This, of course, excludes Remizov, who is welcome at any time, but I do not know which of his post-war masterpieces to include.)

One thing is certain, Vyacheslav Ivanov's time is coming. His poetry, however, not only cries out for study, it needs crusaders. Millions knew—and forgot—Evtushenko; Brodsky may soon become a Nobel laureate, but Ivanov still has only a handful of admirers, although we all know that he is far more than a cult figure. To some of us his greatness is obvious, and we also know what a vast stretch of work lies before us. It is imperative, however, that we approach the poet without the critical clichés of the past, and not only with respect for his poetry, but with love as well.

Notes

1. *SS*, I, 623. Unfortunately there is a misprint in *SS*,I: the word *krug* in the next to the last line is absent.

2. See, for example, Fet's "Kogda medlitel'no ja predan tishine" or "O, dolgo budu ja, v molchan'i nochi tajnoj." For Nekrasov, see Part I of his "O pogode," section III ("Sumerki," the seventeen lines beginning with "V nashej ulitse zhizn' trudovaja").

3. "Old Testamental," courtesy of Pushkin, to be sure.

4. See her *Sochinenija*, ed. G. P. Struve and B. A. Fillipov, 2 vols. (Washington, D.C., 1965–68), II, 346.

5. It takes real courage, after Kozma Prutkov's famous fable, to use *prozjabshij/prozjablo* in its original meaning, as Ivanov does three times in *Prozrachnost'* (*SS*, I, 777, 781, 783).

6. Cf. also *SS*, III, 499.

Vyacheslav Ivanov's *Cor Ardens* and the Esthetics of Symbolism

Johannes Holthusen†

The term "esthetics of symbolism" is to be understood here as the Symbolists' conception of the literary function of their poetry as well as of the cultural function of Symbolist literature. Poetic techniques play a role here, as well as explicit statements on esthetic questions: these techniques may have not only a structural function in the individual poem, but may also have a specific function in the Symbolist literary system. It seems to me characteristic of Symbolist poetry that the poetic method functions in any given case on three levels: in the individual poem, in the cycle of poems, and in Symbolist poetry as a whole with all its cultural implications.

The cycle, indeed, would appear to me to constitute an appropriate subject for investigation. Here the framework of the individual poem no longer constitutes a limit. Thematic centers become visible that in turn highlight the role of important symbols and their corresponding semantic fields in the context of the personal and suprapersonal process of creation.

Quite early the Symbolists were united in broadly defining the cultural function of literature as prophecy. "Let the artist prepare himself as a prophet for the feat of life" (*k podvigu zhizni*), writes Bryusov in his essay "On Art" (*Ob iskusstve,* 1899). "Let him above all be wise. Years of silence lie ahead for the chosen ones."[1] The creative process, however, is at the same time an act of daring (*derzanie*), or, as Valery Bryusov puts it later in "Keys of the Mysteries" (*Kljuchi tajn,* 1904), "bold venturing beyond limits."[2] Vyacheslav Ivanov shares this notion. In his essay, "The Symbolism of Esthetic Principles" (*Simvolika esteticheskikh nachal,* 1905), dedicated to An-

drey Bely, Ivanov describes the emergence of the artist from the bog
of everyday life as follows: "Behind you is your sacred path which is
open to those who are daring" [*SS*, I, 824]. Two years later Ivanov
writes in "On the Gay Craft and Wise Gaiety" (*O veselom remesle i
umnom veselii*, 1907): "The symbol was that principle which had
undermined individualism, leaving as its only legitimate sphere of
activity the autocracy of bold ventures [*samovlastie derzanij*]" [*SS*,
III, 75].

On the other hand, Symbolist art, as Bryusov points out in
"Keys of the Mysteries," cannot abandon its unifying cultural function. "Art brings people into communion [*obshchit ljudej*], opens the
soul, allows everyone to share in the creative process of the artist."[3]
Ivanov later considerably developed this notion of the "social" function of art with an emphasis on religious matters. There is no question, however, that some of the basic ideas of Symbolism may be
seen emerging here. Bely set down similar thoughts quite clearly
and provocatively in his essay "Song of Life" (*Pesn' zhizni*, 1908).
He linked the idea of the "bold venture" of art to its context of
cultural activity. "Modern times, through the experience of daring
[*opytom derzanija*] has strengthened the innovators in art in their
efforts to find a form—through combining different art forms—that
would illumine the depths of the moving forces of life [*zhiznennykh
ustremlenij*]."[4] When Ivanov contrasts "art for life" with "art for art's
sake," he is arguing along the same lines. In "On the Gay Craft"
he calls for an art that "in the final analysis and in the deepest sense
of the word would create life, an art of seekers after a religious
synthesis of life" [*SS*, III, 66].

The process of rupture (*razryv*) and reunification (*vossoedinenie*),
of renunciation (*otreshenie*) and restitution (*vozvrat*), represented for
the Symbolists the most important law of the esthetic of the creative
process, while at the same time it meant a rhythm of life determined
by religion. In his essay "On the Boundaries of Art" (*O granitsakh
iskusstva*, 1913) Ivanov puts it this way: "Taking and giving: life is
the interaction of these energies. In spiritual life and creation they
correspond to ascent and descent."[5] Ivanov gave much thought to
the concepts underlying this esthetic of the creative process, begin-

ning with his study "The Poet and the Crowd" (*Poet i chern'*, 1904). Every Symbolist would surely have approved his statement that no great work of art can come into being before "great events in the spiritual life of the creator" have taken place [*SS*, II, 636].

As many able critics have noted, the Symbolist esthetic of literary reception is in contrast much less well-developed. We may recall Osip Mandelshtam's criticism of Balmont: "the rejection of an interlocutor" not only seriously devalues poetry as such, but also obliterates poetry's awareness of its "poetic rightness" (*soznanie poeticheskoj pravoty*).[6] Such criticism could hardly be directed at Ivanov. He had already defined the role of the poet in the "universal" process of communication in "The Poet and the Crowd." Ivanov's point of departure here is the concept of a "split" between poet and public, a split from which Lermontov and Tyutchev suffered, but one that Symbolism should overcome. Symbols lead the poet back to myth, to the forgotten and lost archetypal possession of the soul of a people: the poet himself becomes in this way the "instrument of the people's memory."[7] The inner freedom of the poet is at the same time the inner necessity of return and of becoming one (*priobshchenie*) with the ancestral element. The poet expresses this concisely. "He invents the new and discovers the ancient" [*SS*, I, 714]. The whole essay in its conclusion links up with Bryusov's "Keys of the Mysteries" in saying that these keys entrusted to the poet are above all the keys to the "inviolable recesses of the people's soul" [*SS*, I, 714].

Ivanov's short study "On the Lyric" (*O lirike*) in the collection *Sporady* (1908) tells us what techniques the lyric poet has at his disposal to bring about the esthetic effect. First of all, very specific esthetic demands are made, such as the "mastery of rhythm and number" as the "moving and structuring principles of man's inner life," as well as "order" (*stroj*), "harmony," and "consonance" (*sozvuchie*). In contrast to the epic with its temporal chain of events and to the drama with its resolution of conflicts "of opposing wills," the single happening (*sobytie*) of lyric poetry is the "chord of the moment" (*akkord mgnovenija*) that has touched the strings of the "lyre of the world" [*SS*, III, 19].

The transitions from one mental image to another constitute

the lyric style: they are the "lightning-like flashes of the imagination." It should be noted, however, that a unifying mood, that is, a "lyric idea," holds together the plurality of images evoked. To abstract the lyric idea from "visual and phonic elements," according to Ivanov, is "to experience it concretely" in the musical sense. He believes that the "natural movement of rhythm," as well as that of rhyme, should be brought to life through strengthening and refinement (*izoshchrenijem*): this is the most important task for the future. The energy of rhyme aims at "calling forth such an intense excitement of the phonic fantasy in the 'reader'" that the soarings and vibrations of the musical rhythm may be supported by an equivalent force [*SS, III, 120*].

Ivanov stresses further the importance of the "colon," or phrasal cadence, for vocal harmony and internal rhyme. The overarching principle for him, however, is the musicality of the verse; this is what is decisive for the listener's receptivity. "The poet was a 'singer' only metaphorically speaking and by virtue of his inherited title; he was not capable of creating out of his own personal convictions a universal experience and participation by means of the musical enchantment of communicating rhythm" [*SS, III, 121*].

This passage expressly deals with the esthetic side of poetry, and the notion of "communicating rhythms" is broadened to encompass a dancing quality and a bodily plasticity in the lyric. Ivanov, following Gogol as he himself admits, pleads in his essay for the "sacerdotal verse of conjurings and prophecies" (*zaklinanij i proritsanij*) [*SS, III, 123*]. This demand reflects the "magical" thinking through language of the Symbolists as well as their dynamic conception of language. Andrey Bely, for example, puts it this way in his essay "The Magic of Words" (*Magija slov,* 1909):

> The word, therefore, always reveals causality: it creates causal relationships that are only later recognized as such. In the earliest stages of the development of mankind, the explanation of ultimate causes lay in the creation of words. The magician [*vedun*] is he who most of all knows words, who most of all speaks and therefore the one who casts a spell. . . . Creating a living language is always

a struggle of man against hostile elements surrounding him. The word illuminates with victorious light the darkness that surrounds me.[8]

Cor Ardens as a whole is a "grand" poetic cycle symmetrically organized and consisting of five books in the final version (1911). The great cycle is divided into several smaller cycles, each with its own thematic and structural centers of gravity, which at times can be found outside any single poem or group of poems taken in themselves, for example, "Sun–Heart" (*Solntse–Serdtse*). The cycle *Eros* would seem to be the centerpiece in the architecture of *Cor Ardens*; it is especially closely tied up with the personal passions of the poet, was written in a very short period of time (autumn 1906), and was in print in early 1907 before the rest of the poems.[9] This centerpiece is bracketed by two books: "Cor Ardens" (Book 1) and "Speculum speculorum" (Book 2), on one side, and "Love and Death" (*Ljubov' i smert'*) (Book 4) and "Rosarium" (Book 5), on the other. While the two last mentioned were not written until after the death (October 17, 1907) of Lydia Zinovieva-Annibal, Ivanov's wife, Books 1 and 2 are more wide-ranging and represent a collection of poems over the years 1904–1909.

It was precisely during these years that the esthetic of Symbolism became the subject of heated debate, thanks partly to the journals *Vesy* and *Zolotoe Runo,* and it was at this point that it became possible to give final formulation to the esthetic. Ivanov played a particularly important part in formulating this esthetic and in applying it to a larger form—the lyric cycle.

During these years, to judge at least from the works of Blok and Bely, two intellectual stimuli that gave rise to much controversy were particularly important for the further development of Russian Symbolism: the doctrine of Dionysian "madness," of the Dionysian countervalence of life (*Gegenwertung des Lebens*),[10] as Ivanov understood it in his own scholarly terms and through his own particular reading of Nietzsche, and the doctrine of "peoplehood" as the supra-national vehicle of true culture, the universal Christian "ecumenicity" (*sobornost'*).

The preoccupation with Dionysian "ecstasy," which especially characterizes Russian Symbolism in the years 1908–1909, finds its roots essentially in Ivanov's understanding of Nietzsche's *Birth of Tragedy*. Ivanov begins his essay "Nietzsche and Dionysus" (1904) with a consideration of the myth of the Thessalonian military leader Eurypylos whose lot it was to receive the potent cult image of the god Dionysus as his share of the Trojan plunder. Ivanov compares the fate of Eurypylos, steeped in holy madness, with the fate of Nietzsche, and he develops the comparison: "Like that hero, he was in his lifetime a madman, and he rendered great services to the people he freed; he was a true hero of the new world, from the bosom of the earth. Nietzsche gave Dionysus back to the world: therein lay his calling and his prophetic madness" [*SS*, I, 716].

It is no accident, then, that the entire cycle "Cor Ardens" opens with the poem "Menada" in dancing homage to the god in the prayer of the water nymphs:

Liquid, liquid, liquid god! . . .
    Slaughter,
    Slash
With lightning tooth my stone, Dionysus!
    With sounding sledge pound out
From my congealed breast the springs of rejoicing tears . . .

Vlagi, vlagi, vlazhnyj bog!. . .
    Ty rezni,
    Polosni
Zubom molnijnym moj kamen', Dionis!
    Mlatom zvuchnym istochi
Iz grudi moej zastyloj slez likujushchikh kljuchi . . .
                                                        [*SS*, II, 227]

Likewise it is no accident that Ivanov concluded "Speculum speculorum" (Book 2) with the sonnet "To the Poet" (*Poetu*) as epilogue. This poem appeared in the first number of the journal *Apollon* (October 1909) under the title "Apollini" [*SS*, II, 742]. It is characteristic of the author's method that the two other epilogue poems devoted to the "poet" appeared in the last installment of the journal *Vesy* whose publication was interrupted in 1909. The cycle "Speculum speculorum" thus mirrors the entire range of the poet's personal inclinations, while the first two books of the cycle "Cor Ardens" represent as a whole a tension between Dionysian and Apollonian traditions. It is of particular interest that the "springs of rejoicing tears" in the poem "Menada" correspond exactly to the last sonnet's "springs of tears" with which love soaks the roots of the laurel trees in the place sacred to Apollo:

When Love soaks your buried root
With springs of tears, and bleak gloom
Like Death's canopy implants in the magic grove
Where Dante wandered a living trunk . . .

Kogda vspoit vash koren' grobovoj
Kljuchami slez Ljubov', i mrak surovyj,
Kak Smerti sen', volshebnoju dubrovoj,
Gde Dant bluzhdal, obstanet stvol zhivoj . . .   [*SS*, II, 359]

The name of the god is mentioned only at the end of the last tercet of this sonnet on the laurel, a plant sacred to Apollo, yet it is an exceedingly effective conjuring up of this divine energy that is the counterpart to that of Dionysus.

Who took soothsaying Daphnes into skyey captivity
And clad them in laurel, and reflected them in the well
of immortal transparency?—Apollo.

Kto veshchikh Dafn v efirnyj vzjal polon,
I v lavr odel, i otrazil v krinitse
Prozrachnosti bessmertnoj?—Apollon.   [*SS*, II, 359]

There is no need at this point to emphasize further the great importance that transparency had as an esthetic principle of Symbolism.[11] In making use of the word "transparency" (*prozrachnost'*), Ivanov is quoting himself, as this is the title of his second volume of poetry (1904).

Ivanov's Dionysus studies were very much in the foreground at the time *Cor Ardens* began to take shape. Bely's essay "Friedrich Nietzsche" (1904) which appeared in *Arabeski* (1911) was most certainly written under the strong influence of Ivanov. According to Bely, one should speak of the "crucified Dionysus in his bloody rags" rather than of the "teaching of Friedrich Nietzsche," and he asks Nietzsche the question: "Who can compare to this madman?" Bely comes to the significant conclusion that after Nietzsche there could no longer be any irreligious culture: "everything is encompassed in the religion of the creation of life (*religija tvorchestva zhizni*), even the ancient gods."[12] In "Song of Life" a year later, Bely expressly refers to Ivanov's "Hellenic Religion of the Suffering God" (*Ellinskaja religija stradajushchego boga*) that came out in *Novyj put'* in 1904 and *Voprosy zhizni* in 1905.[13]

Ivanov himself returns in *Cor Ardens* to the Eurypylos myth through which he related Nietzsche to ancient Greece. The myth of Eurypylos is told once more in the short poetic narrative "Judgment of Fire" (*Sud ognja*) in the first book: it is freely adapted here, to the effect that the fire that Eurypylos extols not only remains element and symbol of Dionysus—"Heady flame plows the field / Greedily harvests the harvest of life" (*P'janyj plamen' pole pashet / Zhadnyj zhatvu zhizni zhnet* [*SS*, II, 247]), but also acquires a universal meaning. The ballad-like poem appears under an epigraph from Heraclitus, πάντα τὸ πῦρ κρίνει (the fire will take care of everything), and the madness of Eurypylos relates the fire to the symbol of the phoenix that rises out of its ashes; this is a symbol which is important in *Cor Ardens* itself, but also relates it to the Slavic god Perun, a fact which can be explained by Ivanov's personal attachment to Sergey Gorodetsky to whom the entire poem is dedicated. Ivanov adds considerable weight to this dedication, as shown by the fact that "Judgment of Fire" is placed at the beginning of the cycle: it is the first of all the dedicatory poems in this work, apart from the dedication of the entire cycle to Lidija Dmitrievna Zinovieva-Annibal.

In any case, it is noteworthy that in the ecstatic song of Eurypylos, the myth of Gaea, the mother of creation, merges with the Slavic myth:

Perun plighted with Gaea
Will lick and judge all things.
Who dares to be shall be:
Ancient Phoenix is eternally young.

Alive through murdering thunderbolt,
By duel the world is red.
Discord in chordal pitch
And concord in strife of lyres.

Vse liznet i vse rassudit
S Geej spletshijsja Perun.
Kto prebyt' derznet—prebudet:
Vetkhij Feniks vechno jun.

Zhiv ubijtseju-perunom,
Poedinkom krasen mir.
Raznoglas'e v stroe strunnom,
I sozvuch'e v spore lir.   [SS, II, 247]

Esthetically it is important here that the semantic structure
conjures up an antithesis (even a near oxymoron): Zhiv/ubijtseju/:soz-
vuch'e/v spore—the force of which is increased by the "mythic" oxymoron (Vetkhij Feniks/vechno jun'.

The fire or the torch as symbol of purification and of rebirth
already brings into play the preceding "dithyramb" entitled "Firebearers" (Ognenostsy, 1906). The link to something outside the text
is disclosed by the fact that this cult-drama scene had already been
printed in the first annual Fakely (1906), a journal which was reputed
to be a manifestation of "mystical anarchism." It is not only the
tradition of Prometheus that is echoed in "Firebearers":[14] the burning torch also visits judgment on an earth that appears to be encir-
cled by an "evil ring" (kol'tsom nemilym). Ivanov attaches the poem
"Creation" (Tvorchestvo) from the cycle to his poetic manifesto: in
this poem the act of artistic creation is already compared to an
"uprising" (mjatezh) of the Promethiads. The chorus of "Firebearers"
addresses itself to the fire in dithyrambs—the chosen form is also
an echo of Nietzsche—beginning with the following strophe:

Of rebellious flames
The living streams!
O feathers of Phoenixes!
O harbingers
Signaling to stars
About the raging heart
Of earth stung
By holy conflagration!

Mjatezhnykh plamenej
Ruch'i zhivye!
O per'ja Feniksov!
O vestovye
Zvezdam glashatai
O serdtse jarom
Zemli, uzhalennoj
Svjatym pozharom!   [*SS*, II, 240 ff.]

The image of the phoenix inevitably reminds us of Bely's essay
"Phoenix" (1906) that appeared later in *Arabeski* (1911). After the
revolution of 1905 Bely too could only envisage society in the future
as faced with two alternatives: either the social mechanism of "socialism" as the embodiment of the "sphinx" with its empty and
"dark eyes" or the social dynamic of the "free community" (*obshchina*).[15] In the latter case it is not the "petrified sphinx on the
margin of national productivity" that regulates economic relationships, but rather the "high flight of the phoenix of life with its
wings like lightning [*na molnijnykh per'jakh*] rising from the scattered ashes of national life."[16]

The poems gathered together as "Sun-Heart" (*Solntse-serdtse*) are
of fundamental importance for the cycle *Cor Ardens* in the context of
Dionysian symbolism. In "The Treatment of the Sun" (*Zavet solntsa*)
the sacrificial fate of the "sun-heart" (the rising and setting of the
sun) is foreseen:

All of you is joy, early to early,
My brother, all of you is blood and wound
On the sacrificial brink.

Ves' ty—radost', rannim-rano,
Brat moj,—ves' ty krov' i rana
Na kraju vecherovom!   [SS, II, 233]

The central semantic field of *Cor Ardens* is marked out in this poem:
heart, flame, blood, wound, martyrdom, sacrifice, crown of thorns,
loss, and resurrection. The incantatory magic of the language reveals
itself in rhythm as well as in rhetorical techniques such as alliteration, rhyme, assonance, paronomasia, that is, in the lexical and
phonic dynamics.

Assonances and paronomasias in words with the same root
vowel or suffix rhyme ("echo") are particularly numerous in "The
Sun Psalm" (*Psalom solnechnyj*):

Net zharkomu Sertsu,
Bezyskhodnomu svetu,
Podspudnomu, skudnomu, trudnomy svetu,
Otzvuch'ja zemnogo: [SS, II, 234]

Or

Tsarstvennoj
Darstvennoj,
Zhertvennoj siloju . . .   [SS, II, 234]

These paronomastic repetitions can be traced directly back to
Nietzsche, who used them abundantly in *Thus spake Zarathustra.*
One example may serve for many others: "Einen goldenen Kahn sah
ich blinken auf nächtigen Gewässern, einen sinkenden, trinkenden,
wieder winkenden goldenen Schaukel-Kahn!" (I saw a gold bark
glittering upon dark waters, a submerging, surging, re-emerging
golden tossing bark!).[17]

The burning heart and the sun are of course closely related to
the theme of rebirth and fruitful sacrifice. Ivanov makes the same
allusion also in the essay he dedicated to Bely, "On the Descending"
(*O niskhozhdenie,* 1905), when, crossing the boundaries of esthetics,
he explains the religious symbolism of suffering and sacrifice. In this
connection, Ivanov paraphrases the biblical parable of the grain of

wheat (John 12:24) which Dostoevsky used as the epigraph for *The Brothers Karamazov*: "The sacrifice is the payment of the individual, through himself alone, for universal bail [*za vselenskuju poruku*]. He who isolates himself from the world for the world dies for the world. He must lose strength and die, just as the seed will not sprout unless it dies."[18]

For Ivanov the concepts of "bright" sun and "free" light complement those of the "dark, narrow, trapped" heart ("The Sun Psalm"), and so the heart becomes for him a winter-hard grain of seed:

> The heart, a winter seed of living fire!
> Serdtse, ozimoe semja zhivogo ognja!   [*SS*, II, 234]

The poet had already experienced the sense of remoteness from the sun in the winter of 1904–1905, when he wrote the beautiful poem "Winter Crop" (*Ozim'*). He will cite that poem again in his lecture "On the Russian Idea" (*O russkoj idee*, 1909). This poem, which belongs in the section "Year of Wrath" (*Godina gneva*), consists of only one sentence that unfolds in eight verses and two strophes by means of ingenious enjambments:

> Winter Crop
> As in foul autumn decays
> The sacred winter crop, the spirit secretly
> Ripens above the black grave
> And only the hearing of lightest souls
>
> Catches the not yet rustling quiver
> Among sluggish clods—so my Russia
> Contradicts mute death
> With unheeding pregnancy of life.

> Ozim'
>
> Kak osen'ju nenastnoj tleet
> Svjataja ozim',—tajno dukh
> Nad chernoju mogiloj reet,
> I tol'ko dush legchajshikh slukh

Nezadrozhavshij trepet lovit
Mezh kosnykh glyb,—tak Rus' moja
Nemotnoj smerti prekoslovit
Glukhim zachat'em bytija . . .   [SS, II, 251]

As we are attempting here to present an index of the structural and literary functions of symbols, it may also be pointed out that the image of sowing winter grain (*ozim'*) appears again in the second book ("Speculum speculorum"), namely in "The Scales" (*Vesy*), a poem first printed in the almanac *Severnye tsvety assirijskie* (Northern Assyrian Flowers). The winter grain acquires the concrete meaning of a spiritual sowing, since the poem concerns as much the constellation Libra as it does Bryusov's journal *Vesy*:

And not in vain, in corona of nocturnal beauty,
Above sowing of winter crops, burns the constellation
To which the spirit, having signaled world requital,
Gave in secret the name Libra.

I ne votshche gorit, v ventse nochnoj krasy,
Nad sevom ozimej sozvesd'e,
Chtò dukh, znamenovav vsemirnoe Vozmezd'e,
Narek tainstvenno: Vesy.   [SS, II, 289]

What is of course striking and interesting in this strophe is the relationship between the sounds in *sev* and *Vesy, sozvezd'e* and *Vozmezd'e,* and finally *vsemirnoe.*

Cor Ardens is an inexhaustible treasury of literary and universal symbols, religious emblems and Symbolist experiences. The symbolism of sun and heart that had already evolved in Ivanov's work by 1905 was later consolidated in Alexander Blok's cycle *Snow Mask* (*Snezhnaja maska,* 1907). While the images find their most intense and magical expression in "The Sun Chorus" (*Khor solnechnyj*), a poem Ivanov had already published in *Voprosy zhizni* in 1905 ("Sunheart, of suns of hearts," *Solntse-serdtse solnts-serdets* [SS, II, 231]), Blok later wrote in "Overtaken by the Snowstorm" (January 3, 1907) the two verses: "Yet beyond the distant pole roams / the sun of my heart" (*No bredet za dal'nim poljusom / Solntse serdtsa moego*).[19] This symbol remains fixed in the memory of the poet for the next few days: "Heart grown cold! Where are you, sun?" (*Ostylo serdtse! Gde ty, solntse?*).[20] Moreover, at the beginning of the poem "Away" (*Proch'*) of the same day (January 8) we find the verse, "And again they opened this door of the sun. / And again they draw from the heart this shade" (*I opjat' otkryli solntsa / Etu dver'. / I opjat' vlekut ot serdtsa / Etu ten'*).[21]

There are other parallels between *Cor Ardens* and *Snezhnaja maska* besides those of symbolism. The dance-like rhythm that plays such an important role in Ivanov's esthetic conception of the chorus is an expression of a Dionysian mood and emerges as early as the "Menada":

> Sacrifice, drink from the cup of peace
>   Silence,
>   Silence!—
> Blend of wine with heedless myrrh—
>   Silence . . .
>   Silence

> Zhertva, pej iz chashi mirnoj
>   Tishinu,
>   Tishinu!—
> Smes' vina s glukhoju smirnoj—
>   Tishinu . . .
>   Tishinu . . .   [*SS*, II, 228]

This folk dance rhythm (trochees and anapests) is taken up again in the poem "Dawn-dawning" (*Zarja-Zarjanitsa*), in the second book of *Cor Ardens* (first published in *Vesy,* 3, 1906), a poem whose language, too, is closely connected with that of folk poetry:

> With that sickle of cold potions
>   Mow down;
> On the dewdrops of sweet hops
>   Graze!
> I, O queen, some field brews
>   Will distill;

Or whip up meads of hops
For the king.

Tem serpom okhladnykh zelij
Nakosi;
Po rosam usladnykh khmèlej
Napasi!

Ja l', tsaritsa, zelij sel'nykh
Navarju;
Natvorju li medov khmel'nykh
Ja tsarju.   {*SS*, II, 320}

One can compare this in turn to Blok's poem "Her Songs" (*Ee pesni*,
January 4, 1907) which closes with the following verses:

With thread tangled in tow
I'll wind.
With light ale of snowy hops
I'll sing.

Prjazhej sputannoj kudeli
Obov'ju.
Legkoj bragoj snezhnykh khmelej
Napoju[22]

The stylized use of folk rhythms came into fashion particularly during the years 1906–1907. Sergey Gorodetsky also experimented with
this style in his poetry, a style that was quite popular for a time.
The fact that Blok's *Snow Mask* was strongly influenced by Ivanov
in style and theme is clearly indicated in a letter from Ivanov to
Bryusov dated January 28, 1906: "The literary event of the day is
Blok's *Snow Mask* which has already been printed in *Ory*. . . . Blok
reveals himself here for the first time, and for that matter in a new
way, as a source of truly Dionysian, demonic, and deeply occult
experiences. The sound (*zvuk*), rhythm, and assonances are captivating" [*SS*, II, 730 ff.]. We know too that Blok in his poem to
Ivanov expressly acknowledged their spiritual affinity at this time.

And shying till now
From your piercing eyes,
I glanced . . . And our souls chimed
Those days in the very same verse.

I ja, dichivshijsja dosele
Ochej pronzitel'nykh tvoikh,
Vzgljanul . . . I nashi dushi speli
V te dni odin i tot zhe stikh.[23]

Of all Ivanov's works, the cycle "Cor Ardens" certainly shares
to the highest degree the common strivings of Russian Symbolism
in the years after the disastrous war with Japan. In this connection,
the second book "Speculum speculorum" not only reveals the erudition of the poet, but also constitutes a signal effort to reflect as
fully as possible upon the esthetic of Symbolism. The large number
of personal dedications in this cycle seem to document convincingly
the poet's interrelationships with other people in the years 1905–
1906. The personal inclinations (*pristrastija*) of the poet are as evident in his concern with older poets as in his passionate disputes
with both his closer and his wider circle of friends (Bryusov, Blok,
Gorodetsky, Kuzmin, I. Annensky, Gumilev, Khlebnikov, and many
others).

Such dedications, of course, might also have a polemical side
as in the case of one poem dedicated to Sologub bearing the significant title "Apotropeia" (*Apotropej*), a warding-off. Here Ivanov is
replying to a poem of Sologub that he had just received (May 26,
1906) in which one finds the following verses:

The name Vyacheslav hovers.
    Magus? Divinator?
Or glorifying things?
    Council? Or crown?
Glory? Word? Or send?
How shall I decipher the signs?

Reet imja VJACHESLAV.
Vjaschij? Veshchij?

Proslovljajushchij li veshchi?
  Veche? il' venets?
Slava? slovo? ili slat'?
Kak mne znaki razgadat'?[24]

A comment on this poem may be found in Ivanov's notebook under the date June 2 of the same year: "Some sort of new attempt at sorcery. A game of riddles behind which is concealed something that he has experienced deeply" [SS, II, 326]. Ivanov answers Sologub with the poem "Apotropeia" from the section "Inclinations":

The secret of your counter feelings
And the sweetness of your twilight charms

Wish to capture with a magic ring,
To calm, like a muffled sound,
Him who with a song of praise
Was born to hymn the Greater Light.

Tvoikh protivochuvstvij tajna
I sladost' sumerechnykh char

Khotjat plenit' kol'tsom volshebnym,
Ugomonit', kak smutnyj zvon,
Togo, kto peniem khvalebnym
Vosslavit' Vjashchij Svet rozhdën.   [SS, II, 326]

Such rejoinders among the Symbolists often led to an entire poetic correspondence, and Sologub in this instance was not slow in replying. Since for him the sun had always remained a destructive evil dragon-serpent in the heavens, he forthwith fell upon this symbol, and in defense of his own "Dulcinea" unmasked Ivanov's "simplehearted'" Aldonsa (Dulcinea's "real" name in Don Quixote):

In vain do you glorify the Sun,
Chasing me down from your heights—
Aldonsa, laughing at your summons,
Shears the shaggy fleece.

Naprasno proslavljaesh' Solntse,
Gonja menja s tvoikh vysot,—

Smejas' na tvoj prizyv, Al'donsa
Runo kosmatoe strizhet. [25]

Ivanov dedicated this part of *Cor Ardens* to Bryusov in the name
of "Sancta sodalitas" (holy comradeship), and he explained the title
with a Latin commentary: "The image distorted by the mirror becomes a perfect representation by means of mirrors set opposite"
(Immutata dolo speculi recreatur imago adversis speculis integram
ad effigiem). [26]

The concept of "Speculum speculorum" emphasizes the basic
unity of an individual phenomenon in all its external contradictions
and plurality, that is, in terms of Ivanov's idea of *sobornost'*, and we
can see that this form of communication is an important element in
the esthetic of symbolism.

When Bryusov dedicated his volume of poetry *Stephanos* (1906)
to Ivanov, the latter took the sonnet relating to "Stephanos" of
January 1906[27] and placed it in the section of "Inclinations" from
the cycle "Speculum speculorum"; such an act is understandable after
years of almost completely harmonious and successful cooperation
between them. Ivanov renders Bryusov's two sides through the images "Pale magician" (*Volshebnik blednyj*) and "Triumphant singer"
(*Pevets pobednyj*); by making use of the structure of the central oxymoron from the preceding "Carmen saeculare"—"honey defiled with
hemlock" ("Vitiato melle cicuta")—he introduces the antithesis
"black poison" and "honeylike sun":

> From gold-bottomed cups sorrow's hostage
> Poured black poison. But now he scoops up charms
> Of honeyed suns in bright-faceted crystal.

> Iz zlatodonnykh chash zalozhnik skorbi
> Lil chernyj jad. A nyne cherplet chary
> Medvjanykh solnts kristallom jasnogrannym.   [*SS*, II, 327]

One may also cite here, by way of comparison, a poem that belongs
to the important section "Arcana" and whose title is a quotation
from Dante's *Inferno* (XXV, 4): "The serpents were my friends" (Mi
fur le serpi amiche). In this poem, Ivanov defines his own position

in contrast to that of Bryusov, but this considerably earlier reaction suggests similarities as well as differences between them.[28] Ivanov looks down from the snow peaks (*uzh ja topchu verkhovnyj sneg*) at his friend who finds himself still under the spell of decadence and its sweet poisons:

> You, in the sultry haze where wormwood's spirit is,
> Gather the poisons of bitter languors.

> Ty, v znojnoj mgle, gde dukh polyni,—
> Sbiraesh' jady gor'kikh neg. [*SS*, II, 290]

It is noteworthy that in its first publication in the almanac *Severnye Tsvety Assirijskie* (1905) this poem, together with several others, constituted the cycle "Serpents and suns" (*Zmei i solntsa*), to the effect that not only the poison, but also the serpents stand in opposition to the sun.

The snake, which plays an important role in Decadent and Symbolist art as a symbol of the head of Medusa and of the tempter snake of the Garden of Eden, represents in *Cor Ardens* a negative mythic force related to the symbol of the "evil ring" (*kol'tso nemiloe*). In the poem just cited, therefore, the poet's liberation from the power of the snake represents the decisive stage of occult experience. It is the last trial by fire before rebirth in the new light:

> And I was a slave in the knots of the snake
> And in spasms I called for the stigma of a sting;
> But fire of the final ordeal
> I conjured up, and by the sun of Emmaus
> My days were gilded.

> I ja byl rab v uzlakh zmei,
> I v korchakh zval klejmo ukusa;
> No ogn' poslednego iskusa
> Zakljal, i solntsem Emmausa
> Ozolotilis' dni moi.[29]

The "knots of the snake" (see also the adjacent poem, *Uzly zmei* [*SS*, II, 291]) and its "rings" represent at the same time symbolically the subjugation of man to the laws of cyclical time. The immediately preceding ghasel "Regeneration" (*Vozrozhdenie*), the poem that originally introduced the cycle "Serpents and Suns," expresses this very clearly:

> We, in the gold and rings of ductile snakes and suns
> Enrobed, officiate as priests and seers;
> Prophesying, we preside on the crags of snakes and suns.
> By centuple fate we are condemned to drag
> Recurrent scales of perennial snakes and suns.

> My, zolotom i kol'tsami moguchikh Zmej i Solnts
> Oblacheny, svjashchenstvuem, zhretsy i veduny,—
> Prorocha, verkhovenstvuem na kruchakh Zmej i Solnts.
> Sud'binoju stokratnoju vlachit' osuzhdeny
> My cheshuju vozvratnuju zhivuchikh Zmej i Solnts.
>   [*SS*, II, 290]

The rising and setting of the sun, as well as the ring of the snake that bites its own tail, symbolize causality, moving from past to future. Ivanov, however, proposes yet another causal movement, from the future into the past, which is called—in the notes to the important verse-tale "Melampos' Dream" (*Son Melampa*, 1907)—"the causality of coming to meet" (*vstrechnaja prichinnost'*). This kind of movement is also symbolically represented by means of snakes that are male and are characterized as "Snakes of Goals (*Zmijami Tselej*).

This philosophy of time is the central theme of "Melampos' Dream," an epic poem composed in hexameters that concludes the cycle "Arcana." Ivanov dedicated the text, which appeared for the first time in 1907 in *Zolotoe Runo*, to Maksimilian Voloshin, and he attributed great importance to its message.[30] Here Ivanov makes use, for his purpose, of the tale of the Greek seer Melampos to whom snakes have spoken in his sleep, so that after awakening he understands the language of animals. The myth of Melampos has a particular meaning for Ivanov's esthetic, namely, that the seer (*zrjashchij Melamp*) ties both chains of causality together as "Hymenaeus," so that the disunion (*razryv*) of the two vanishes and the true image of the "renewed Dionysus," as the son who belongs to the father (that is, as Christ), can appear:

It shall be: in maternal lap shall Dionysus' face be glorified
In its right image, on that day when mother's face grows faint.
Marriage icon will fuse the break, and wash away guilt
Of refraction, and revived Dionysus will imbibe father's heart.
For son's heart is in the Father; and fusion will be completed
In the Third of you severed ones, O Zeus-Persephone and Victim!

Budet: na maternem lone proslavitsja lik Dionisa
Pravym oblich'em—v tot den' kak roditelja lik iznemozhet.
Brakov svjatynja spajaet razryv, i vinu otrazhen'ja
Smoet, i otchee serdtse vop'et Dionis obnovlennyj.
Ibo synovnee serdtse v Otse: i svershitsja slijan'e
V Tret'em vas razluchennykh, O Zeus-Persefona i Zhertva!

[SS, II, 298]

Melampos himself becomes an "absolver" (*razreshitel'*) of souls from
the age of disunity, he becomes conductor of souls and harbinger of
what is to come:

Keen-Ear became the absolver of souls and the mixer,
Shadow of the future, eye in the night, unerring leader.
Thus the snakes made sleepy Melampos a seer.

Dush razreshitelem stal i smesitelem Chutkoe-Ukho,
Ten'ju grjadushchego, okom v nochi, nezabludnym vozhatym.
Sonnogo tak bogoveshchim sodelali zmei Melampa.

[SS, II, 299]

The "causality of coming to meet" is an important element of
the Symbolist esthetic: all prophecies of the Symbolists were built
on this idea of causality and without it Bely's novel *Petersburg* could
hardly be understood. Ivanov deals with this also in his famous essay
"Presentiments and Portents" (*Predchuvstvija i predvestija*, 1906).
Here the prophetic art of Symbolism is contrasted with Romantic
art. Romanticism, according to Ivanov, represents the "yearning for
that which cannot be fulfilled" (*toska po nesbytochnomu*), whereas
Prophecy is rather the yearning for that which is not yet fulfilled
(*toska po nesbyvshemusja*). Romanticism, therefore, would be *odium fati*

and Prophecy would be *amor fati*. Romanticism struggles against historical necessity, while Prophecy is in a "tragic pact" with necessity. The impossible (Ivanov speaks once of the "Eros of the impossible" as the "most divine legacy" of the human spirit),[31] the irrational, the miraculous—for Prophecy all of that is self-evident; for Romanticism, however, it is simply a pious desire (*pium desiderium*). Ivanov goes on to distinguish it from mere futurology: "By prophecy we do not mean necessarily the exact foretelling of the future, but we mean always a creative energy that conceives (*zachinaet*) and anticipates the future, fundamentally a revolutionary energy."[32]

From all that I have said, may this point remain: the constructive function of the conjurings, of the symbols, and of the myths of Russian Symbolism reaches far beyond the framework of individual works; it generates its own role in general literature; and it characterizes a rich culture that urgently and continuously calls for our scholarly understanding and endeavor.

Notes

1. Valery Bryusov, "Ob iskusstve," *Sobranie sochinenij* (Moscow, 1975), VI, 45.

2. Bryusov, "Kljuchi tajn," *Sobranie sochinenij* (Moscow, 1975), VI, 92.

3. Ibid., p. 91.

4. Andrey Bely, "Pesn' zhizni," *Arabeski* (Moscow, 1911), pp. 58 ff.

5. *SS*, II, 633. The essay "On the Boundaries of Art" (*O granitsakh iskusstva*) represents a significant elaboration of rise and fall, as this was first formulated in the article "On Descending" (*O niskhozhdenii*, 1909).

6. Cf. Osip Mandelshtam, "O sobesednike," *Sobranie sochinenij* (1966), II, 278 ff. Krystyna Pomorska puts it in a similar way about a particular tendency within Symbolism: "The speaker seems to ignore whether anyone is listening to him or not, because he knows that he is surrounded by emptiness (Gippius)." See Krystyna Pomorska, *Russian Formalist Theory and Its Poetic Ambiance*, Slavistic Printings and Reprintings, 82 (The Hague-Paris, 1968), p. 66.

7. *SS*, I, 713. This characterization of poetic perception is substantiated with the Platonic idea of "anamnesis."

8. Bely, "Magija slov," *Simvolizm* (Moscow, 1910), p. 431.

9. The sonnets of the cycle "Zolotye zavesy" appeared simultaneously with *Eros* and were printed separately in 1907 in the almanac *Tsvetnik Or, Kosnitsa 1-aja,* by the same publisher (Ory) as the book *Eros*. The two publications constitute the third book in *Cor Ardens* (Volume I, 1911, published by Skorpion). Books 4 and 5 appeared in the same year as Volume 8 of the complete edition of *Cor Ardens* in Moscow. See the commentary in *SS*, II, 698.

10. The expression "countervalence of life" is to be found in Nietzsche's own commentary on *The Birth of Tragedy,* which is entitled "An Attempt at Self-Criticism" (1866).

11. See Johannes Holthusen, *Studien zur Ästhetik und Poetik des russischen Symbolismus* (Göttingen, 1957).

12. Bely, "Fridrikh Nitsshe," *Arabeski,* p. 78.

13. Bely, "Pesn' zhizni," p. 54. Elements of the Dionysus theme are to be found throughout Bely's works, even in the novel *Peterburg* (see the segment "Dionis" in the sixth chapter of the novel, where Nikolay Appolonovich appears as "suffering Dionysus" [*Dionis terzaemy*]).

14. Parts of this dithyramb were later inserted in the tragedy *Prometheus* (*Prometej,* 1919). See the commentary to *Prometheus* in *SS*, II, 685.

15. In his manifesto of "mystic anarchism" (*Ideja neprijatija mira*) of 1906, Ivanov speaks of the ideal of *obshchina* as mystic union; see *SS*, III, 89.

16. Bely, "Feniks," *Arabeski,* p. 151.

17. This passage is taken from Part III of *Also sprach Zarathustra,* the chapter entitled "Das ander Tanzlied."

18. *SS*, I, 824. The same thought permeates Ivanov's discussion with M. O. Gershenzon; see *A Correspondence from Two Corners, SS*, III, 383–417, originally published in 1921.

19. Alexander Blok, *Snezhnaja maska, Sobranie sochinenij* (Berlin, 1923), II, 191.

20. *Golosa,* II (January 8, 1907), p. 203.

21. Ibid., p. 197.

22. Blok, *Sobranie sochinenij,* II, 193.

23. Blok, *Raznye stikhotvorenija, Sobranie sochinenij,* III, 131. See Ivanov's commentary in *SS*, II, 729 ff.

24. Fyodor Sologub, *Stikhotvorenija* (Leningrad, 1975), p. 331.

25. Ibid., p. 333.

26. *SS*, II, 284. In his treatise *Religioznoe delo Vl. Solov'eva* (1911), Ivanov characterized the correcting "other mirror" (*Speculum speculi*), that is, the other person, as important for mystic perception and for the mystic communion: for

man himself is only a "living mirror" that registers what is perceived inadequately (that is, backwards) (*SS*, III, 303).

Here one should also recall what Ivanov had written on art in "Zavety simvolizma" (published in the journal *Apollon*, 8 [1910]) in connection with the "inner canon": "Your mirror, which is set opposite the mirrors of the disjointed centers of consciousness, reestablishes the original truth of that which is reflected, in that it atones for the guilt of the first mirroring, which had distorted reality. Art becomes the "mirror of mirrors"—*speculum speculorum*—everything is, in its mirror-like quality, alone (*v samoj zerkal'nosti svoej*), the one symbolism of unifying being (*edinogo bytija*), in which every tiny cell of the living, fragrant fabric creates and celebrates its petal, and every petal is a shining forth and glory for the glowing center of the unfathomable blossom, of the symbol of symbols, of the flesh of the word" (*SS*, II, 601).

27. The letter to Bryusov of January 2, 1906, gives us an idea of Ivanov's enthusiastic reaction to Bryusov's "Venok." See the commentary, together with the letter, in *SS*, II, 727 ff.

28. Bryusov's correspondence with Ivanov shows how much he was impressed by this very poem. See the commentary in *SS*, II, 713.

29. *SS*, II, 291. For the significance of the concept "solntse Emmausa," see M. M. Bakhtin, "Vjacheslav Ivanov," *Estetika slovesnogo tvorchestva* (Moscow, 1979), pp. 380 ff.

30. See the commentary in *SS*, II, 716.

31. See Ivanov's "Simvolika esteticheskikh nachal," *SS*, I, 825.

32. *SS*, II, 87. With regard to this passage see also Igor Smirnov, *Khudozhestvennyj smysl i evoljutsija poeticheskikh sistem* (Moscow, 1977), pp. 60 ff., on the "chronogenetic organization of the universe" in Ivanov's works.

—Translated by Emily Robin Jackson

The Poetics of Vyacheslav Ivanov: Lectures Given at Baku University
Anna Tamarchenko

Vyacheslav Ivanov is not only a distinguished poet, but also one of the greatest thinkers of the Russian Silver Age. In the early 1920s, M. M. Bakhtin said of him: "As a thinker and a personality, Vyacheslav Ivanov had enormous significance. In one way or another the theory of Symbolism was created under his influence. All his contemporaries are only poets, but he was also a teacher. If he had not existed as a thinker, Russian Symbolism would probably have taken a different path."[1]

The course Russian Symbolism took under the influence of Ivanov's esthetic ideas was the most significant in Russian artistic thought of the time. The younger Symbolists were not just one school of poetry among many which had arisen: they attempted to oppose decadence and extreme individualism in art, combining the pursuit of poetry with a search for a way out of the general crisis of culture. In contrast to Bryusov or Balmont, as Bakhtin rightly noted, "they strive for understanding of the innermost life of existence. Symbol is for them not only a word that characterizes an impression of a thing, not just a product of the artist's soul and of his accidental fate: symbol signifies the real essence of the thing."[2] The high theoretical level of the esthetics of Russian Symbolism accounts for its great influence on all the schools and currents of Russian Modernism without exception both in poetry and in the other arts. The influence of Ivanov's theatrical ideas on the subsequent development of Russian theater was especially great.

It is necessary to emphasize the significance of Ivanov as an esthetic thinker not only in the name of historical justice (which is happening little by little even in Russia today) but in the interest of culture. None of the deadly forces of disintegration and rampant individualism against which Ivanov fought has yet been overcome. These forces have only become more widespread and dangerous.

Especially pertinent here is a course of lectures on poetics given by Ivanov at Baku University, where he was a professor in the Department of Classical Philology from November 1920 to June 1924. Reports about this course have begun to appear in specialized publications since 1968,[3] and in 1981 an article about it by Elena Belkind appeared in print. "The archives of Prof. V. A. Manuilov," she writes, "contain a synopsis of lectures on poetics read by Vyacheslav Ivanov in 1921–1922 (the synopsis was made by a student of Baku University, O. Ter-Grigorian; the whole volume consists of 175 pages of manuscript text; the synopsis has not been published)."[4] This synopsis, in E. Belkind's typescript, is in my hands.

Although it consists of notes by a student and is not a full stenographic transcript, the synopsis contributes much to the understanding of Ivanov's views in the realm of poetics. The sole systematic statement of his ideas, it is moreover an academically rigorous one: he sets forth here a system of views on poetry as a form of art, and proposes criteria for its esthetic analysis and evaluation. In the synopsis Ivanov also formulates his attitude toward various trends in university scholarship on poetry: the historical poetics of Aleksandr Veselovsky and the ideas of Humboldt and Potebnya on poetry and language. Finally, the course on poetics supplies a missing link in the evolution of Ivanov's esthetic ideas and his views on poetry. This link is all the more important since the Baku period, many indications suggest, was a turning point in the development of the writer's world view.

The course on poetics is divided into three major sections. The first consists of a definition of the subject of poetics (lectures 1–3), followed by a detailed and wide-ranging definition of poetry as a form of art (4–10). The second section (11–17) is devoted to the division of poetry into types and genres and to study of styles. The third section (18–22) is given over to problems of prosody.

The second most important theoretician of Russian Symbolism,

Andrey Bely, always strove to break down the subject of his studies analytically. He separates art from culture, poetry from art, and lyric from poetry. From Russian lyric poetry he chooses iambic tetrameter for further analysis, and in the innumerable variants of the iamb he distinguishes those elements that are connected with the unique poetic *rhythm*—with the rhythmic intonation of the poem. As a result, it appears that it is precisely the course of the intonation embodied and reinforced by the rhythm of the verse which is "decisive for form and context, amplifying both in a new direction."[5] In lyric poetry, rhythmic intonation is a structural factor which determines the dynamics of the artistic whole. Thus Bely arrives at his main conclusion in regard to the essence of poetry as an art form.

Probably the single most important feature of Ivanov's esthetic thought, on the other hand, is its constant striving toward integration, toward synthesis; and in his course on poetics Ivanov establishes first of all *connections* between things, the interdependence of various spheres of culture, and various elements of poetics itself. Historicism and a global perception of culture are especially characteristic of his thought. He presents poetry and poetics in the context of the universal development of culture. Ivanov traces every form, category, or term from its origin, from its sources. Thus, the synthetic nature of his thought does not lead him into abstractions or incorporeal categories. His thought is always concrete.

It is as though Ivanov sums up the history of culture in order to emerge on the threshold of its new stage, a stage, however, of which one can only have a presentiment; one can only ready oneself for it and prepare the consciousness of others, because it must be a new stage in the formation of man's spiritual nature. Thus the urge toward synthesis has a deep motivation.

The very definition of the subject of the course is a striking example of the tendency to synthesis. Ivanov sets forth three initial conceptions of poetics and of the methods proper to it: 1, historical poetics in the spirit of A. N. Veselovsky, understood as "the genetics and evolution of poetic forms"; 2, poetics as a part of esthetics and, consequently, as a philosophical discipline; 3, canon, that is, a code of norms, obligatory for poetic styles and forms, types and genres.

Not one of these varieties of academic poetics, in and of itself, satisfies the scholar: "Poetics, strictly speaking, does not exist" (2), and meanwhile "poetics is a discipline that is far from being completed" (5). For its transformation into a science, into "systematic knowledge about poetry," further elaboration is needed— first, of historical poetics, so that a theoretical poetics can be built on its foundation: "At the present time poetics, shunning canonicity, is a discipline that passes from the particular to the general, that studies literary monuments in an inductive way from an historical point of view, and strives only in this way to deduce general laws from the object under consideration" (5).

At the same time Ivanov is far from neglecting normative poetics. Relying on a theoretical understanding of the artistic experience of the great poets, he also deduces certain norms for what is "proper" and "improper" in various styles, types, and genres of poetic creation.

The principle of logical transition from an historical to a philosophical poetics is strictly observed by Ivanov throughout the entire course. General categories of esthetics as applied to verbal art, types and genres of poetry, verse meters and poetic tropes are all first considered with regard to the process of their origin and formation. Of the epic we learn how it arose from panegyric and singing at the funeral feasts of heroes; lyric poetry was born of incantations and charms or in the ecstatic states of "choral lyrics," in the syncretic rites of distant antiquity. Each term of poetics is traced to its inventor.

With the same firm consistency, the "genealogy" of poetic forms carries poetry to the moment when it becomes an art, and at the same time brings it within the categories of philosophical esthetics with Plato and Aristotle as its originators—their greatest successors being Lessing, Schiller, and Goethe. Thus, an integral framework for a synthetic poetics is gradually constructed.

At the beginning of the course history predominates; in the middle, esthetic categories in specific application to verbal art take precedence; in the "prosody" section, canonicity, connected with the requirement for unity of style, gains a certain preponderance: "To whichever type the poem is closest—romantic or classical—the poet must adhere to definite norms in the creation of his work. There can be no artist without law. The harmony of the entire work depends on those norms to which the poet adheres" (89–90).

Let us note in passing that in the prosody section the problem of the strophic organization of verse and the description of a great number of strophic forms occupy a place that might seem disproportionately large. For Ivanov, however, this emphasis has a theoretical basis: he considers the strophe to be the very element of verse that is coterminous with content and form in poetry. The strophe, according to Ivanov, is "the basis of metrical composition . . . the unit of metrical construction," and "simultaneously a finished syntactic and thematic whole" (87).

The isolation of the strophe as the most important factor in verse is due equally to the views of Ivanov the philosopher and to the artistic experience of Ivanov the poet. "All his poetry is a brilliant restoration of all the forms that existed before him. But this peculiarity, for which he has been reproached, flows organically from the essence of his poetry."[6] The striving to reproduce in Russian poetry "all forms" of strophe that ever existed in world poetry emanated from the urge for synthesis and summary, the desire to recreate in modernity all the beauty created through millennia of artistic culture.

The second important feature of Ivanov's course on poetics is the structural role of "recurrent ideas," which go back to his well-known pre-revolutionary articles. These ideas are revealed here in new aspects and become the frame for an integral system of esthetic views. For example, the motif of "Dionysian ascent" (epiphany) to a higher reality, intuitively grasped, and the subsequent "descent" to earth in order to make incarnate (in the image of one's art) what has been grasped.

This conception, already developed in detail in "Boundaries of Art" (*O granitsakh iskusstva,* 1913), serves in the lecture course as a key to the interpretation of many problems, especially those problems concerning the psychology of creation. It is set forth more fully than others in Belkind's article. More important for us is the direct application of these ideas to questions of theoretical poetics; this is only touched upon by Belkind.

Perhaps the most difficult question in general esthetics is that of criteria for artistic value in works of art and poetry. The theory of "Dionysian unrest" and "Apollonian shelter" appears in Ivanov's lectures as the key to the examination of this problem as well. He proposes a polysemantic and meaningful solution.

The prime factor determining the artistic value of a work is, in Ivanov's opinion, the weight of the design, which depends entirely on the height of the "ascent" and the force of "Dionysian restlessness." In poetry this "phonic agitation" or "Dionysian storm" is a state of uncontrolled ascent to the highest level accessible to a poet—an introduction to a higher reality. After this, only "descent" is possible.

The poet's main task in the process of "descent" is to hold on as fully as possible to what has been attained: to fix the original design in the images of his art without distorting it through arbitrary personal fantasy or excessive elaboration of the images of lower earthly reality. The brightness and strength of the "Apollonian dream" determine artistic value, especially in poetry; also determinant is the extent to which the moment of "mirroring" imagination corresponds to the design—to the height of the "spiritual impregnation."

For artistic value, those conditions and criteria specific to poetry as a verbal art are no less important: "If form is forcibly superimposed on language the work will not be artistic" (43). As "living material," language will not tolerate force: "language must be in agreement with the form superimposed on it" (43). This condition is connected in turn with the fourth condition for artistic value—perfect poetic technique. With the help of poetic technique one may attain the "consent of the language," so that "the language gladly accepts the form superimposed on it," and as a result "we have the impression of a perfect work" (43).

In this way Ivanov unfolds an entire hierarchy of conditions and criteria for artistic value in poetry, taking into account both spiritual significance and perfection of skill, both general esthetic requirements and the specifics of verbal art (tenth lecture).

In his course of lectures, Ivanov constantly turns to the opposition between the Dionysian and Apollonian principles. Thus in the lectures about the division of poetry into types and genres he explains that the epic is a predominantly Apollonian art, while lyric poetry is Dionysian. But in lyric poetry, in its turn, there are exclusively Dionysian genres, like the song, and more classical—that is, Apollonian—ones, like the sonnet and certain other strict strophic structures.

The same opposition recurs in the lectures on the "great styles" in world art. The classical style (first developed in ancient art and poetry) is based on Apollonian contemplation and is characterized by a rational clarity and formal fulfillment, by a reliance on visible shapeliness. The romantic style originating in the Middle Ages relies on creative intuition; here the expressive quality of sound predominates over distinctness and clarity of outline, arbitrariness of fantasy over earthly *realia*.

Certain important thoughts on Symbolism flowed from the pre-Revolutionary articles over into "Poetics," having undergone substantial evolution. For example, the view that Symbolism is called on to lead poetry beyond the confines of "art for art's sake" and turn it into a powerful force for transforming life itself, is constantly present in the course, but is nowhere directly formulated. Most likely, this springs from a realization that the hopes and aspirations among the younger Russian Symbolists for a speedy "transformation of life by art"[7] were essentially utopian. On the other hand, Ivanov systematically and convincingly leads his listeners to the notion that poetry, in the perspective of history, must inevitably go beyond the boundaries of "art alone," of pure "service to beauty," of "purposeless purposiveness."

The assertion that poetry is older than art, that it became "only art" after having separated from the syncretism of cult ritual, supports this conclusion. But even at this stage, the highest achievements of poetry could never be reduced to the "purposeless purposiveness" of pure art, but carried a spiritual and cognitive meaning inseparable from the genuinely beautiful. In this sense "any great art is symbolic" (47), a creative ascent from *realia* to *realiora*: "In the realm of *intuitio* we are confronted by a higher reality. Only truth [*istina*] is beautiful, untruth is not beautiful" (47), Ivanov affirms, citing Novalis at the conclusion of his lecture: "The more real, the more poetic, the more poetic, the more real" (47).

Avoiding excessively direct and categorical judgments, Ivanov carefully observes that Symbolism strove to synthesize the possibilities of both "great styles" of world poetry and to become a new phase, a new epoch of artistic development. This attempt, however, met with failure. "Symbolism, by setting itself against Classicism, does not draw closer to Romanticism," but like the oldest poets of antiquity, strives to convey those meanings that do not submit to precise verbal expression and clear logical consciousness. "The Symbolists," however, "did not know how to create a Symbolic style," and therefore "the stamp of artificiality lies on very many specimens of Symbolist poetry" (83). In summary, then, Symbolism remained a poetry for the few, the first attempt consciously and purposefully to break through to the creation of higher forms of life by means of poetry. "Mysticism is the outstanding feature of Symbolism. The poetry of Symbolism is accessible only to the initiated: this is its weak side, but also its merit" (83).

More than three lectures (the twelfth through the fifteenth) are devoted to dramatic poetry and in particular to the development of Ivanov's pre-Revolutionary ideas on tragedy, its historical fate and its great potential for spiritual influence on the souls of men.

Ivanov's lecturing manner was legendary. Not only his students at Baku[8] but also memoirs of the period refer to his charm. At a meeting of the Religio-Philosophical Society in the early teens he is described as follows:

> His wearily extended hand moved gracefully to his heart, and with this gesture, his facial expression held the audience fascinated. Thus the attention of parishioners in a Roman Catholic Church is focused at the sound of the handbell that marks the moment of

taking the symbolic wafer from the hands of the priest. This lecturer was a great magician.[9]

He knew how to affect even listeners to whom the high theoretical level of his discourse remained inaccessible, through the music of his speech and its magnificent solemnity, through the very sound of the word: "A movement, a musical movement carried the whole hall at once, in all its diversity, up a staircase made of magnificent dreams, not expressed in meaning and logic. . . . And along with this experience of mass hypnosis, the solid text of the same speech was taking form under the diligent pencils of the stenographers, genderless in their professionalism, preparing it for a journal where it became a literary model, rhetorically cold and, in its own way, splendid."[10]

Even less than a stenographic transcript, to be sure, can the student synopsis convey the action of "hypnotic" or parapsychological powers on an audience; indispensable to every oustanding orator, these powers served Ivanov for the communication of complex theoretical ideas.

Nevertheless, even the synopsis shows that in his Baku lecture course he renounced his earlier magnificence and solemnity of exposition presumably because of his own irreproachable feeling for the moment. The academic lecture demanded a more disciplined manner. Moreover, an evolution during these years toward greater rigor, naturalness and simplicity also characterizes his lyric poetry, beginning with *Winter Sonnets*. His manner of thinking, both philosophical and poetic, changed because the times had changed. Lofty solemnity and ornamentation of verbal forms were out of date; language now found this magnificence "uncongenial." He marks the beginning of almost every new theme with an unexpected statement to refute commonplaces and the pedantry of the educational tradition. Ivanov considers it useful to undermine them at the outset and only later to examine to what extent and in what sense they might possess a grain of truth.

Let us cite as an example a discussion on the essence of poetry. The definition of poetry is deduced in the first section of the course:

"Poetry is not an art that uses the word as its material, poetry is a natural function of language." The definition is expanded in the second lecture though at the same time Ivanov rejects the very possibility of such a definition. "Poetry is the incessant procreation of language. . . . It is impossible to give a definition of poetry; we can only describe its features. Language in poetry is not a tool and a means as in prose, but a goal."

The further exposition explains the antinomy between a poetry as a "function of language" and a poetry as an "art of the word." It turns out that poetry possesses primordial, eternal essence, which existed long before poetry became an art and personal craftsmanship of the poet, the essence which emerged simultaneously with the language: "Poetry becomes manifest in various forms as an eternal basic element; poetry is a unity, as language is also related to poetry and likewise emerges as a kind of living basic element. Poetry subsists together with language" (5). The main feature common to poetry and language is sound image, which is essential to both language and poetry. Poetry, like language, is a "type of energy," an exercise of will.

Speaking of poetry as an art form, Ivanov suggests that "the poet, insofar as he makes language his goal, surrenders to it his spiritual existence; language requires of him content; language requires logic." Language, furthermore, introduces into poetry the ethical element. And here Ivanov refers to the Neo-Kantian Rickert, who believed in the inherent ethical quality of language exemplified in the act of volition which connects the subject and the predicate. With the help of one of Michelangelo's sonnets (later in Rome, Ivanov made a verse translation of it) he explains that language is not the "material" of poetry just as a slab of marble is not "material" for a sculptor: both the one and the other are "living matter," an element imbued with spirit, which may or may not agree with the artist's intention.

As a result, after all these reservations, he gives a final definition of poetry. "An attempt at defining poetry from the point of view of form: Poetry is speech, consolidated and bound together by the external sound patterns of language, based on sound imagery, as the latter may be mined from the raw material of language where it is found in organic unity, and poetry is each time a new moment in the discovery of language and its energy" (10).

Dialectical complexity designed to provoke the listeners to think creatively may be found in Ivanov's discussion of tragedy of fate. "The idea of destiny is very rarely encountered in ancient tragedy. The tragedies of Aeschylus are all based on personal freedom; crime is the free act of a free personality" (71). Ivanov argues precisely the reverse of the usual scheme that would see the role of fate in tragedy decrease from the ancient tragedians to Shakespeare, and from Shakespeare to contemporary drama: "In Shakespeare there is a feeling of destiny. We perceive the personality as free on the one hand, and on the other, as causally determined." And in the later evolution of modern drama actual determinism assumes the role of fate in people's destinies: "Recently they have come to think of man in ways that annihilate the very meaning of personality (extreme materialism); the *I* itself goes unacknowledged. . . . But if the *I* is repudiated, if personality is completely repudiated, then personality cannot struggle even with itself and no agonist can exist; thus man becomes the passive object of active principles in the external world—in other words, none of the ingredients necessary to tragedy can be present" (71). Thus, though tragedy as a genre is expiring, the role of fate, paradoxically, has increased.

This kind of procedure trains listeners not to rely on preconceived notions and stimulates a demand for intellectual substantiation of received truths. It encourages students to think actively and conscientiously and shows the need to verify generalizations through the actual inspection of the text.

Nearly all of Ivanov's polemical and provocative discussions point out problems still unresolved, still in need of development and analysis. This course of lectures given sixty years ago is not outdated; it contains not only a succession of valuable innovative ideas but also a whole program for further research into the field of poetics. The course laid out by Ivanov in his Baku lectures could even now constitute a new direction in the development of a theoretical poetics.

Notes

1. M. M. Bakhtin, *Estetika slovesnogo tvorchestva* (Moscow, 1979), p. 374.

2. Ibid., p. 375.

3. N. V. Kotrelev, "Vjacheslav Ivanov—professor Bakinskogo universiteta," in *Trudy po russkoj i slavjanskoj filologii, XI, Literaturovedenie* (Tartu, 1968), pp. 326–39.

4. E. L. Belkind, "Teorija i psikhologija tvorchestva v neopublikovannom kurse lektsii Vjacheslava Ivanova v Bakinskom universitete (1921–1922)," in *Psikhologija protsessov khudozhestvennogo tvorchestva* (Leningrad, 1980), pp. 208–14. In this article, notable for its laconism, informative tone and analytical precision, Belkind, in keeping with the theme of the collection, defines the significance and place of Ivanov's lecture course in the elaboration of problems of the psychology of creative work; in addition, she describes the structure of the course, the lecturer's relationship with his predecessors and contemporaries in the field of theoretical poetics, and points out the significance of these lectures on poetics for understanding the evolution of Ivanov's views. Further references to this article are given in the text in parentheses.

5. Andrey Bely, *Ritm kak dialektika* (Moscow, 1929), p. 29.

6. Bakhtin, *Estetika,* p. 377.

7. There are also transcripts of conversations between Ivanov and one of his favorite students of that period, M. S. Altman, which testify to the deep changes in Ivanov's views and attitudes at this time. See M. S. Altman, "Iz besed s poetom Vjacheslavom Ivanovichem Ivanovym. Batu, 1921," *Trudy po russkoj i slavjanskoj filologii. XI, Literaturovedenie* (Tartu, 1968), pp. 304–25. In Belkind's article, the direction of the deep changes in Ivanov's views and moods is understood somewhat tendentiously: as a rejection of the concept of the role of mystical experience in creativity and a rejection of the "mystical role of symbolism"; as an endeavor to transform the course in poetics into a *practical discipline*; and, finally, as an elucidation of Ivanov's constant problems of the "boundaries of art" and the "incarnation" of the original conception. The author states that these problems now acquired for Ivanov a completely "earthly" character directed toward the practical, for helping beginning poets and critics. (See Belkind, "Teorija i psikhologija tvorchestva," p. 214. Italics mine.) Actually, the rejection of the utopianism of ideas about "art as life-building" was specifically connected with the intensification of historicism in Ivanov's understanding of the role and significance of art and poetry in the historical fate of humanity.

8. Aside from Altman's published transcripts, there are some very interesting reminiscences by other students of Ivanov at Baku: V. A. Manujlov and the late Elena Aleksandrovna Millior. All three memoirists read their reminiscences at a dinner at the Leningrad Writers' House, dedicated to Ivanov in connection with the publication of his poems in the *Maly* series of *Biblioteka poeta* (1976).

9. Olga Forsh, *Voron* (Leningrad, 1934), p. 63.

10. Ibid., p. 61.

V. I. Ivanov's Views on the Sound Fabric of Poetry

Edward Stankiewicz

Like many an outstanding modern poet, Vyacheslav Ivanov combined his work as an artist with that of theoretician and student of poetry. One of the recurrent themes of his theoretical writings is the pivotal problem of the relation between form and content in the production and perception of a work of art and, more specifically, of the role of sound in the structure of verse. Ivanov's ideas on the function of sound in poetic form are of considerable interest because they reflect the absorbing importance which the questions of sound-instrumentation came to occupy in modern poetry and poetic theory, and because, at the same time, they show Ivanov's own approach to these questions—an approach which departs in significant respects from the prevailing theories of the day and, in particular, from the views advanced by the Symbolists and later by the Russian Formalists. Ivanov's philosophical and classical interests, his historical sense and esthetic taste and, above all, his own poetic practice, enabled him to treat the question of the phonetic fabric of verse in a more profound and many-sided way than many of his contemporaries, including some of his Symbolist *confrères* and friends, such as, for example, Andrey Bely.

Unlike Bely, who tackled the questions of meter, sound-symbolism and sound-orchestration in a number of minor and larger theoretical studies (notable in this respect is his theory of glossolalia in "Poem about Sound" [*Poema o zvuke,* 1921/22]),[1] and unlike the Formalists for whom the sound fabric of poetry was of major theoretical concern, Ivanov never produced a work that dealt exclusively with the function and utilization of sounds in poetry. The most exhaustive treatment of the problem is given in his "About Sound-imagery in Pushkin" (*K probleme zvukoobraza u Pushkina,* 1913) which deals with the role of sound in Pushkin's poetry.[2] Remarks on the significance of sound and sound-texture in poetry are otherwise scattered in various of his theoretical and critical writings. This reserved and individual approach to one of the urgent problems of Symbolist theory stemmed, no doubt, from Ivanov's integral conception of verbal art; to him the question of sound was inseparable from that of the total composition of a poem as well as from its meaningful artistic expression.

Rather than isolate the question of sound as an autonomous and self-serving poetic dimension, Ivanov draws attention to other factors of verse which contribute to the perfecting of verbal art. In his "Thoughts on Symbolism" (*Mysli o simvolizme,* 1912 [*SS,* II, 604–12]), he reminds the reader that poetry has traditionally had a double link with its sister arts, painting and music. The Horatian formula (as reinterpreted) "ut pictura poesis," he writes, has lost none of its validity, inasmuch as one of the functions of poetry is to express and to interpret external reality. The descriptive and mimetic functions of poetry must, at the same time, be complemented by a euphonic quality, which, according to the precepts of the ancients, carries an immediate esthetic appeal and moves the soul of the listener ("non satis est pulchra esse poemata, sed dulcia sunto et quocumque volent animum auditoris agunto"). However, neither the descriptive nor the musical qualities of poetry are sufficient to produce a genuine work of art or true poetic "enchantment." Such a work, he argues, emerges only from the interpretation and transformation of amorphous experience by means of authentic artistic form [*SS,* II, 611].

By advancing his three requirements of genuine poetry, Ivanov departed from one of the cherished tenets of Symbolism which saw in the euphonic saturation of verse one of its principal goals and accomplishments. The one-sided emphasis on external form, and the cult of impressionism, were for him an invention of the radical or "subjective" wing of Symbolism that was initiated by Baudelaire and intensified by his followers. "With this trend of Symbolism," he wrote, "our poetry has neither a historical nor ideological affiliation" [*SS*, II, 611]. What is important for genuine or "objective" Symbolism, he continued, is not "the power of sound" (*sila zvuka*) but the "power of resonance" (*moshch' otzvuka*). The concentration on sound for its own sake, or as we would now say, the concentration on the signifier at the expense of the signified, cannot but lead to a fragmentation of the poem, to the reduction of its complexity to its most obviously sensuous aspect, and to the conversion of the poetic activity into a literary technique [*SS*, II, 606]. This, it would seem, straightforward position of Ivanov is, nevertheless, enmeshed in a number of concepts which Ivanov shared with his fellow Symbolists and which had become a commonplace of European esthetic thought.

In order to understand better Ivanov's views on the role of sound in lyrical poetry, it might be useful to consider more closely the significance which the Symbolists accorded to the problem and also the historical antecedents of their ideas.

In his well-known book *Die Struktur der modernen Lyrik* Hugo Friedrich[3] has drawn the main lines of the modernist tradition which have led from Baudelaire to all subsequent attempts at an autotelic, hermetic and difficult art. Like Ivanov, Friedrich, too, sees the beginnings of this tradition in the Symbolist quest for the musicalization of verse which was a part of their more general program to create a new poetic language, a "strange discourse" that would do away with the mimetic and rhetorical tendencies of older literature. This new and pure language was to be achieved by leaving the creation of a poem to the initiative of the words (Mallarmé's "rendre l'initiative aux mots") and by reclaiming from music its essential qualities ("reprendre à la musique leur bien").

The claim that poetry need not have any communicable meaning as long as it is imbued with sonorous, musical qualities became the leading motif of Symbolist poetics. Thus Verlaine required "de la musique avant toute chose." Valéry envied the musician who worked with a pure, ideal instrument "free from practical, changing and soiled language," while Nietzsche declared that "Lied heisst: Worte als Musik." It is clear that such an insistence on the phonetic and palpable aspects of poetry was not without profound consequences for the semantic structure of poetic works. The emphasis on the individual word at the expense of syntax, the call for *étrangeté* and the suggestive image ("où l'Indécis au Précis se joint") favored not only the dissolution of the unity of a poetic work, but also the breakdown of meaning and of everyday language.

The antecedents of this approach may, however, be found in an earlier tradition of the eighteenth and nineteenth centuries which posited the question of the sound-fabric of poetry in the context of such broad philosophical and esthetic issues as the mutual relation of the arts, the origin of language, and the role of the cognitive and affective faculties of man. A brief consideration of this tradition should help us recognize the complexity of our problem and the various ideas advanced toward its solution.

The recognition of the phonetic fabric of verse as one of its basic formal elements suggested from the beginning several lines of approach. Among the eighteenth and nineteenth-century theories of poetry we can identify at least three basic variants which have exerted an influence on the subsequent tradition and which are partly reflected in Ivanov's writings.

"Poetry," Lessing wrote in a letter to Nicolai (1769), "must try to raise the arbitrary signs of spoken language to natural signs; that is how it differs from prose and becomes poetry."[4] Such a requirement obviously stemmed from the belief in an original Adamic language which consisted of natural, iconic signs that were able to convey directly the true nature of things. Poetic language was then to aspire to this original condition in order to gain a deeper insight into hidden Reality, an insight that was presumably blurred through the use of ordinary speech. In poetic practice, however, this requirement could only amount to the use of onomatopoeia and semi-onomatopoeic words, for it is in such words that the natural function of the sign is most clearly pronounced.

Another and far more influential approach concerning the phonetic orchestration of verse was connected with the eighteenth-century speculations on the origin of language and the belief in the historical and logical priority of emotion over analytic and discursive thought. Primitive language was, in this opinion, primarily a tool of emotive expression, and poetry was the refuge and repository of that primitive state of affairs that had otherwise been suppressed by the advance of civilization and the development of man's rational faculties. The recognition of poetry as an art of emotion led then, in turn, to the rejection of the formula "ut pictura poesis," as they understood it, and to the recognition that music, the emotional art *par excellence,* provided the true analogue of poetic expression. "Sight," wrote Herder, "is the coldest of the senses, whereas hearing acts immediately on the soul," and provides the basic source of poetic imagination.[5] Just as primitive language was a language of song and of rhythm, so poetry was expected to perform its true task by exhibiting the musical quality of its forms. "A poem," claimed Ludwig Tieck, "needs neither sense nor content, because emotion is best expressed by sounds and by tones." Novalis, the most theoretical of the Romantic poets, makes the same plea: "Only good-sounding poems, even without any sense and connection" ("Gedichte—bloss wohlklingend, aber auch ohne Sinn und Zusammenhang").[6]

Another variant which exalted the role of phonetic orchestration is that which ascribes to individual sounds the capacity to evoke synesthetic associations or other kinds of sensual impressions. If the former variant leads to the spiritualization of the material aspect of a poem, this variant may be said to reduce its spiritual aspect to a sensual, physiological and ultimately hedonistic dimension. The content of a poem, it was said by some Formalists (Viktor Shklovsky), is merely a pretext for exhibiting its phonetic design. The appeal to synesthesia was, long before Rimbaud (in his sonnet on vowels), expounded by some Romantics (e.g., in the Jena lectures of A. W. Schlegel), whereas the association of sounds with the "dance" of the speech-organs was put forward by Bely in his "Poem about Sound."

This brief survey of the various approaches to the role of sound in poetry should enable us to see more clearly Ivanov's indebtedness to, and departure from, tradition.

As indicated above, Ivanov's fullest exposition of the subject is given in his "About Sound-imagery in Pushkin," a work that is couched in highly metaphoric language and charged with subtle philosophical allusions. But freed from the stylistic and metaphysical underpinnings (which one would find difficult to paraphrase) the basic arguments of the article seem to amount to the following: Pushkin is a master of poetic form, but at the same time he pursues the classical tendency to treat sound not as a surface phenomenon, but as an internally directed, translucent quality (*klassicheskoe stremlenie ne delat' narochito primetnym prosvechivajushchij, no kak by vnutr' obrashchennyj uzor zvukovoj tkani*).

The exploration of "sound instrumentation" is for Ivanov a poetic "device" only to the extent that it constitutes part of a poetic technique. The true nature of sound lies deeper and derives from a primordial striving for a magically effective verbal expression, an expression which has its roots not merely in euphony, but in the inseparable "consonance" (*sozvuchie*) of all elements of verse. Such a consonance characterized the primitive forms of verse, such as ritual hymns and incantations, which existed before the emergence of the various arts. This consonance is ingrained in the deepest layers of the word and is primary also in the psychological perception of verse. Its significance was underscored by Goethe, for whom the poet was the carrier of eternal melodies ("dem die ewigen Melodien durch die Glieder sich bewegen"), as well as by Pushkin. For the latter, the "awakening of poetry" was a moment of spiritual excitation in which the poet is overwhelmed by a stream of sounds pertaining to the realm of glossolalia and trans-sense language: "he runs wild and stern, full of sounds and confusion" (*bezhit on dikij i surovyj, zvukov i smjatenija poln*). In giving external expression to the initial lyrical impulse—when the soul is embarrassed by lyric agitation (*kogda dusha stesnjaetsja liricheskim volneniem*) the poet tranforms the primary diffuse and unstable rhythmic images (*dinamicheskij ritmo-obraz*, dynamic rhythm-image) into more permanent sound-images (*zvuko-obraz*) which lend sense and organization to fleeting experience. This is the initial stage of the creative act which has yielded the kind of poetry that we find in religious rituals (*obrjadovoe gimnotvorchestvo*) and in the works of the Futurists. Although such a poetry is wordless (*bezslovesnaja zvukorech'*), its phonetic material is drawn from everyday language. This phase of poetic creativity repeats philogenetically the process of primordial word-formation (*slovo-rozhdenija*). Trans-sense poetry is nevertheless incomplete, for its primary phonetic material remains devoid of image and meaning. Poetic representation is in such poetry subordinate to the play of homophones (including the play with rhymes). This type of poetry which utilizes vague and suggestive images suffused in a stream of sounds was cultivated by the Romantics and the early Symbolists, to whom it represented true poetic "inspiration." For Pushkin, on the other hand, this stage of the creative act was merely a form of "rapture," whereas by "inspiration" he meant a higher, more advanced stage of poetic creativity which required the participation of reason in the "structuring of the parts with relation to the whole." Pushkin was thus a representative of a classical art that tried to find a balance between the initial lyrical impulse and rigid poetic form.

The poems of Pushkin show, furthermore, the importance of sound-images which are endowed with symbolic value. The symbolic value of the sound-images stems from the presence of a central phonetic image which triggers the composition of entire poems and which yields "unity of melos, myth, and logos." The combination of the primitive poetic impulse and the symbolic sound-image is achieved in Pushkin's poetry in one of three ways:

(1) Through the use of onomatopoeia which lends symbolic content to sensual, acoustic impressions. This use is exemplified in Pushkin's "Stikhi sochinennye noch'ju vo vremja bessonnitsy." In this poem the "whispered" palatals *uch, ts, s, chu* alternate with the "quivering" and "fearful" cluster *tr,* with the "melting" *n* and the "fatal and ominous" syllables *ra, ar, re,* and *or.* These sounds suggest by themselves "the trepidation of the sleeping night" (*spjashchej nochi trepetan'e*) and the efforts of human consciousness to cope with the surrounding darkness and chaos.

(2) Through the conjunction of sound and image which has its roots in individual poetic apperception (e.g., the erotic charge of the "damp" syllable *ju* in Lermontov's *Pesnja rybki:* "*O, milyj moj ne utaju, chto ja tebja ljublju kak vol'nuju struju, ljublju kak zhizn' moju*") or from certain sensual associations which pertain to the realm of glossolalia. A case in point (cited by Bely) is the repetition of *r* in Pushkin's *ronjaet les bagrjanyj svoj ubor.* But unlike the Romantics and

the Symbolists, Pushkin valued the word not in and by itself, but rather for the conjunction of sound and meaning. The word in itself and its phonetic overtones are for Pushkin of secondary importance. The same is true of the above-mentioned *Stikhi sochinennye noch'ju* . . . where the interplay of consonants with the "whispering palatals" serves only a subordinate and secondary function.

(3) Pushkin's poetry is basically constructed on a third principle, a principle which draws its resources from everyday language, including the sound-texture of proper names. The name *Marjula* which rhymes with the words *gula* and *Kagula* provided, no doubt, the initial impulse for the composition of *Tsygany*. The syllable *da* is an all-pervasive element in the poem *Zaklinanie*. It appears in the word *sjuda,* which rhymes with the phrases *pravda chto togda, dal'njaja zvezda, bledna, khladna,* and it is foregrounded in the final exclamation *da*!, which affirms the power of faithful love and which is also the pivotal point of the poem. The sound-image of *obval* (in "Obval") is implied in its very form, which suggests the meanings of fall and thunder. The final syllable *al* is anticipated by its variant *ly* (in *valy*), and modified in a whole series of words ending in *ol* (such as *vol, vel, Eol, orel*) and in *ly* (in *orly*). The heavy sequence of *l* sounds is, in turn, relieved by the more "quiet" sounds of *kupets* and *zhilets* which terminate the poem and provide a sense of general relief. Thus it is apparent that Pushkin, like Virgil before him, attains the musical quality of his verse not by onomatopoeia or pseudo-onomatopoeia, but by variations in sound-texture which advance and organize the meaning of a poem. The symbolic value of sounds is most apparent in Pushkin's *Vospominanie*. In this poem the nasal consonants *m* and *n*, which are symbolic of memory (as in the Greek word *mneme*) occur in juxtaposition or in combination with the labials *p, b,* and *bd* (as in *tomitel'nogo bdenija, v bezdejstvii nochnom*; *tjazhkikh dum izbytok*), and with the spirants *s* and *z* (in such key words as *smert', zmeja* and *mest'*). Particularly characteristic are the lines *zhivej gorjat vo mne zmei serdechnoj ugryzen'ja,* which suggest an intimate link between recollection and remorse. A similar conjunction of these sentiments is suggested by the combination of dentals and spirants in the first chapter of *Eugene Onegin*: *Togo zmeja vospom-*

inanij / Togo raskajan'e gryzet. It should be obvious, Ivanov concludes, that the development of certain poetic ideas is carried and suggested by the combination of appropriate phonetic images.

External form and internal content make an inseparable unity which marks the highest achievement of poetry, inasmuch as poetry strives to reconcile external form with internal content. The true task of poetry is to convert form into content and content into form.

Now, what shall we make of Ivanov's arguments? In the first place we may notice that Ivanov is not so much concerned with the function of sounds in a literary work as with the very process of poetic creativity within which he distinguishes three discrete and ascending stages. This distinction permits him to evaluate poetic works in terms of their completeness and artistic perfection. The first two stages which involve the purely euphonic aspects of poetry, i.e., onomatopoeia and glossolalia, are clearly assigned to a different and lower order, since they are preparatory for the final stage which achieves integration of form and content and which was, according to Ivanov, attained in the works of such classical poets as Virgil and Pushkin. "For Pushkin," he writes, "the question of sound in itself was, in contrast to the Romantics and Symbolists, a matter of secondary concern."[7] Ivanov touches, as if in passing, on the question of glossolalia, which he more or less dismisses on the grounds that it had already been "masterfully" treated in a study by Bely.[8] The existence of a wordless, purely phonetic poetry, is, in fact, recognized, but with the qualification that such a poetry had a religious and magic significance, as we find it in the oldest ritual and religious chants which represent the earliest phases of man's poetic activity. The suggestion that these phases coincide with the early stages of the individual poetic process can be viewed as a bow to tradition which took for granted the coincidence of ontogeny with phylogeny. Ivanov's indebtedness to this tradition is further apparent in his discussion of the symbolic values of sound and sound-combinations. The different sounds of the Russian language, such as palatals and dentals, have, according to him, the power to evoke such emotional and physical states as the horror of the night, feelings of remorse or the trepidation of the heart. In this Ivanov is, of course, strictly in

step with Symbolist doctrines which recognized the symbolic capacity of sounds apart from (and above) the meanings of the words
in which they occur, though it is clear that without the envelope of
the word the putative symbolic powers of the sound would evaporate
into thin air. Far more persuasive are Ivanov's arguments concerning
the distribution of sounds in alternating and contrastive patterns,
for it is these patterns that carry the overall compositional structure
of a poem and which give shape and direction to its artistic content.

But before passing on to Ivanov's views on the relation of meaning and form, we may pause to consider his critique of the Formalist
theories of poetic form contained in his article "On the Latest Theoretical Research on the Artistic Word" (*O novejshikh teoreticheskikh
iskanijakh v oblasti khudozhestvennogo slova*, 1922).[9] In this article
Ivanov discusses specifically the views on sound-instrumentation advanced by such early Formalists as Jakubinsky, Polivanov, Brik and
Shklovsky. Ivanov applauds their attempts to define the distinctive
properties of poetry in opposition to prose, as well as their effort to
found a new, precise and scientific poetics. He treats, however, with
suspicion their tendency to consider poetic craft as a set of technical
devices and to absolutize the nature of the sound fabric in poetry.
Although the Formalists make use of such semi-mystical terms as
"trans-sense image" (*zaumnyj obraz*) and "internal sound-speech"
(*vnutrennjaja zvukorech'*) they ignore, in fact, the role of the poetic
image and poetry's perennial striving for "synthetic expression."
Their new positivistic stance and lack of historical perspective cause
them to mistake the part for the whole (*pars pro toto*) and to ignore
the complexities of verbal art. The importance of form in poetic texts
which was so clamorously proclaimed by the Formalists was also,
for Ivanov, one of the central problems of poetry, though he gave it
a totally different orientation. Form, he concludes (in his essay on
Pushkin's sound-imagery), strives forever to become content, and
content to become form (*Forma stala soderzhaniem, soderzhanie formoj:
takova polnota khudozhestvennogo "voploshchenija"*).[10]

The idea of interdependence of form and content is taken up by
Ivanov in a number of studies, most notably in his encyclopedic
article "Il simbolismo," in "Thoughts on Symbolism, Thoughts on

Poetry" and in "Forma formans e forma formata." Since the discussion of this problem would take us beyond the topic of this paper, I will limit myself to a few cursory remarks.

Ivanov's conception of the form-content relation may be summarized in the following terms: the question of whether poetry deals with the "how" or the "what" can be decided only in favor of the former. The essence of poetry is, indeed, artistic form, but form not in the sense of ornament and phonetic trappings, but form as the poet's peculiar perception and organization of reality. (It is another matter that, as a transcendental Realist, Ivanov believed that the true poet does not invent his own view of the world, but only discovers what is implicit in objective reality.)

Inasmuch as the poetic vision of reality is construed by means of images that require for their implementation artistic form, the putative opposition between the "inner" and the "outer" is indeed a misleading and illusory phenomenon. Consequently, some authors have come forth ("like some new Polonius") with the proposal to collapse the two aspects of art into one, i.e., either to banish the notion of content or to eliminate the concept of form. Both of these proposals are harmful to the artistic enterprise. The medieval Schoolmen (in particular, St. Thomas Aquinas) came closer to the truth when they declared that beauty is "resplendentia formae super partes materiae proportionatas," that is, "the splendor of form over the well-ordered parts of matter," or the meaningful arrangement of parts into a whole.

Form and content do not overlap, but remain in a relation of perpetual tension that derives from the interplay of the parts and the whole. And since the process of integrating the various parts into a whole is never complete, the proper definition of poetry is *energeia,* or that of open and evolving form (Goethe's "geprägte Form, die lebend sich entwickelt"), rather than that of closed and formally completed artifacts. It is this aspect of living form that determines the vitality of art and its persistent hold on our imagination.

A close reading of Ivanov's poetry will, I think, show that his poetic practice did not essentially differ from his theory. Although Ivanov is a master of form, his efforts were primarily directed toward the enrichment of the metrical and stanzaic possibilities of Russian verse. Thus he imitated the various types of classical meters, adapted the stanzaic forms of Old French and Provençal poetry, cultivated the terzina and elevated the Russian sonnet to new heights. The exploitation of sound-texture "for its own sake" was to him of secondary and peripheral interest. Thus we find in his poetry none of the "magical" combinations of sounds practiced by the Symbolists (such as Balmont's *Ja vol'nyj veter, ja vechno veju, / Volnuju volny, laskaju ivy*), the breathtaking euphonic experiments of a Tsvetaeva (*Drugie vsej plot'ju po ploti plutajut / Iz ust peresokhshikh-dykhanie glotajut*), or the metrical and linguistic innovations of the Futurists. Like his idol, Pushkin, Ivanov aims at classical compositional form that would harmonize and integrate the meaning of his poems. At the same time, he produced a number of poems in which the phonetic fabric is conspicuously foregrounded. Most typical in this respect are, however, his German *Gastgeschenke* [*SS*, II, 337–40] which he composed for his visitor, the poet and translator Johann von Gunther (in 1908) and which he patently treated as a kind of poetic entertainment.

Notes

1. Andrey Bely, *Glossolalija. Poèma o zvuke* (Berlin, 1922).
2. Vyacheslav Ivanov, "K probleme zvukoobraza u Pushkina" *Moskovskij Pushkinist,* II (Moscow, 1930), 94–105.
3. Hugo Friedrich, *Die Struktur der modernen Lyrik* (Hamburg, 1956).
4. Cited by René Wellek, *A History of Modern Criticism: 1750–1950,* vol. I (New Haven-London, 1955), 164.
5. Johann Gottfried Herder, *Sämtliche Werke,* vol. 4, B. Suphan, ed. (Berlin, 1878), 44.
6. Novalis, "Fragmente und Studien," in his *Schriften,* vol. 2, P. Kluckholn, ed. (Leipzig, 1929), 288.
7. Ivanov, "K probleme . . . ," p. 5.
8. Ibid.
9. See Ivanov, "O novejshikh teoreticheskikh iskanijakh v oblasti khudozhestvennogo slova," in *Nauchnye izvestija* (Moscow, 1922).
10. Ivanov, "K probleme . . . ," p. 9.

"Jazyk": An Analysis of the Poem
Tomas Venclova

Language

To a singer, his native speech is his native soil:
herein lies the unexchangeable treasure of the ancestors,
and the earthly mother of heaven-induced songs
divines according to the whisper of oak groves.

As it was of old, the sacred depth is waiting
for conceptions, and the spirit circles over it . . .
And the strength of the loins, being full, runs in the vine,
the juicy sweetness of verbal clusters.

Glorified, ringing with the reverberation of the spheres
resounding from afar, the element is lit
with the light of intelligent fire.

And the prophetic hymn is their nuptial encounter,
like coal that locked the sun of day into diamond,
the forerunner of spirit-bearing creation.

ЯЗЫК

Родная речь певцу земля родная:
В ней предков неразменный клад лежит,
И нàшептом дубравным ворожит
Внушенных небом песен мать земная.

Как было древле,—глубь заповедная
Зачатий ждет, и дух над ней кружит . . .
И сила недр, полна, в лозе бежит,
Словесных гроздий сладость наливная.

Прославленная, светится, звеня
С отгулом сфер, звучащих издалеча,
Стихия светом умного огня.

И вещий гимн, их свадебная встреча;
Как угль, в алмаз замкнувший солнце дня,—
Творенья духоносного предтеча.

The poem "Language" (*Jazyk*) was written by Vyacheslav Ivanov in Pavia on February 10, 1927, to commemorate the ninetieth anniversary of Pushkin's death. Originally, the poem bore the title "Poetry" (*Poezija*) and had a New Testament epigraph, "And the Word was made flesh" (*I Slovo plot' byst'*). In publishing the poem ten years later,[1] the poet abandoned the epigraph, or rather transformed a part of it into a title: the new redaction, with its many textual differences from the first, bore the name "The Flesh-Word" (*Slovo-plot'*). The third redaction was included in *Evening Light* (*Svet Vechernij*); its text was adopted as canonic in Ivanov's *Collected Works* as well as in the Soviet anthology of 1976.

Jazyk is essential to Ivanov's work in many senses. During his emigration, up to January 1, 1944, when he began his *Roman Diary* (*Rimskij dnevnik*), the poet had written only twenty-one poems. Like many a Symbolist, he regarded periods of prolonged silence as necessary for a poet, linking them with spiritual sobriety and with the muteness of "apophatic" ecstasy. "The holy language of silence" (*svjatoj bezmolvija jazyk*), hallowed by Ivanov, was more primary and important for him than any, even poetic, language.[2] The rare bursts of poetic speech, breaking this silence, are therefore all the more significant.

It is characteristic that at such moments, poetry, speech, language reflect upon themselves, as it were. The poem may be categorized as autothematic or, to use the term fashionable in recent years, metalinguistic. This is the poet's reflection on his material, on its innumerable possibilities and inescapable limitations, on its multifarious and antinomial nature, on the layers of the past imprinted on language, and on the possible future "as through a glass, darkly," anticipated by the language's very existence.

It is well known that Ivanov developed an original linguistic conception—to my mind, one of the most profound and solid in the history of Russian thought. Conceived as a crossing of the ideas of Humboldt, Schopenhauer and the early Slavophiles, it verges, on the one hand, upon Platonism and the mysticism of the Eastern Church and, on the other, upon such modern phenomena as Jungianism and even structuralism. In complex and indirect ways (through Mikhail Bakhtin in particular), it exerted some influence on present-day semiotics. One can easily find clear parallels to certain loci of the poem *Jazyk* in Ivanov's articles. Let me cite a few among many possible examples:

> Language is the earth; a poetic creation grows out of the earth. It cannot raise its roots into the air. Yet how can we strive onward in the rhythm of time which tosses and tears us, surrender to the call of universal dynamism while remaining "firm in the earth," faithful to the nurturing mother? The task is apparently impossible to fulfill, threatening poetry with ruin. But what is impossible for humans is possible for God, and the miracle may occur: a new knowledge of the Earth on the part of its belated children. If we lovingly press ourselves close to the bosom of our native language, the living verbal soil and our maternal flesh, we shall perhaps suddenly hear in them the pulsation of a new life, the trembling of the infant. This will be the new myth.[3]

> Language in general, according to Wilhelm Humboldt's profound view, is both the "act" and the "active force," the communal [*sobornaja*] milieu being created unceasingly by everyone together and both anticipating and conditioning each creative action in the very cradle of its conception; an antinomial combination of necessity and freedom, of the human and the divine; a creation of national spirit and God's gift to the nation. Language, according to Humboldt, is a gift fallen to the nation's lot as a predetermination of its spiritual being to come.[4]

The following quotation, from a much earlier article, is standard for Russian Symbolism:

Like an electric spark, the word is possible only in the contact of the opposite poles of a single creativity: the artist and the nation. What otherwise would be the purpose of the isolated *word, this means and symbol of universal one-mindedness?* . . . That cognition is memory, as Plato teaches, is verified through the poet, since, as the organ of national self-awareness, he is at the same time and thereby, the organ of national memory. Through him, the nation recalls its ancient soul and revives its ancient powers dormant for centuries. *Just as true verse is preformed by the element of language,* even so a true poetic image is predetermined by the national psyche. . . . The poet wishes to be solitary and aloof, yet his inner freedom is an inner necessity of return to and partaking of the native element. He invents the new and regains the ancient.[5]

These extratextual parallels are useful to keep in mind; however, they can in no way replace an analysis of the text. The sense and art of the poem are born from a complex intertwining of its phonological, grammatical and semantic themes. Only microanalysis can uncover this intertwining, and even then not entirely, for it occurs, as a rule, at an unconscious level. *Jazyk* not only states Ivanov's rather complicated linguistic conception within the condensed space of fourteen lines: the poem expresses it by its very matter, by the entire *flesh of the word,* by all its symmetry and balance. In so doing, *Jazyk* unites this conception with other philosophical and mythological planes of Ivanov's thought: its symbolism of the universal soul, Dionysianism, ecumenicity [*sobornost'*]. The literary-historical dimension of the poem is also significant, namely, its connection with Pushkin and his poetic tradition.[6] In its internal richness—its modesty of poetic means, rather atypical for Ivanov, and its very small compass notwithstanding—*Jazyk* stands out against the background of Ivanov's other poems, indeed against the background of the entire Russian Symbolist movement. Sergey Averintsev is quite right in reckoning the poem among those works of Ivanov "most alive" for a modern reader.[7]

Jazyk is a sonnet written in iambic pentameter, traditional for this form in Russian poetry; the sonnet is of the strictest type, the so-called Italian sonnet. Its pattern is *abba abba cdc dcd* (*a* and *d* rhymes are feminine, *b* and *c* masculine). This structure ("closed" quatrains and "open" tercets) is traditionally regarded as the most perfect. Most other characteristics of a strict sonnet are likewise maintained (except one to be discussed below): periods coincide with stanza boundaries; the last word may be regarded as the key to the entire poem. Ivanov's predilection for sonnet form is well known. The three volumes of his collected works contain 222 original sonnets (in approximately 1,000 poems), including two coronas, two unfinished sonnets and one sonnet in German.[8] In most cases, Ivanov's sonnets are written in iambic pentameter and their pattern frequently corresponds to the pattern of *Jazyk*. This form, infinitely variegated in all its strictness, evidently ideally reflected Ivanov's idea of art as ultimate freedom and ultimate obedience.

The form of the poem and its meter *per se* possess "sign" character: which means that it belongs to a certain European and Russian tradition—Pushkinian, to be precise—to a certain "elevated" type of poetic language. On the level of rhythm, the poem is devoid of any glaring individual characteristics: it is emphatically "unnoticeable," ascetic. Its iamb is without caesura; word boundaries after the fourth syllable are observed in seven out of fourteen lines (in the odd lines of the first quatrain, in the inner lines of the second quatrain, in the medial line of the first tercet and in the first two lines of the second tercet). This reflects the general tendency of the Russian poetry of the twentieth century quite well and cannot be considered specific to Ivanov.[9] The symmetry of word boundaries, however, is curious: an obvious analogue of the two outer and the two inner stanzas, supported also at some other levels. The rhythm of the poem is the regular alternating one;[10] stress omissions appear only on the weak feet: either on the second (line 2) or on the fourth (lines 5, 8, 10, 11, 12), or on the second and fourth (lines 3, 9, 14). Twelve out of the seventy possible pattern stresses are omitted (the average number of accented feet is somewhat higher than is characteristic of twentieth-century poetry). The brevity of the text does not allow one to draw any statistical conclusions. However, rhythmical movements, noticeable against the general background of saturation of the verse with accented feet, may in certain cases be related to the movement of semantic themes. On levels other than rhythm, symmetry and balance of structural elements are more noticeable. The poet spreads before us language with a wide range of possibilities, in the sphere of sound and in the sphere of sense, and, finally, in the sphere of style (archaisms, folk parlance and the like). Language is not only the philosophical theme of the sonnet, it is, at the same time, its "material theme." Vyacheslav Ivanov is not just *speaking about language*, he is also *displaying language* by turning its various facets; he is not just discoursing, *relating,* he is *showing* as well. The system shines through the text perceived by the reader (hearer), and behind the system of the Russian language, semiotic systems—"languages"—of myth and religion shine through.

The first quatrain is to a great extent built on sonorants: they constitute over a half (36) of the seventy consonant phonemes. The most frequent consonant of the quatrain is *n,* followed by *r* (and *m*). Among the scant plosives, *d* stands out.[11] Here one easily notices a consonantal theme, *n-r-d* (with its various permutations); i.e., the quatrain contains, anagrammatically,[12] the word *narod* ("nation"), which is quite essential to Ivanov's conception of language as an ecumenic principle.[13] The other word which is anagrammatized (not only in the quatrain but in the entire poem) is *rech'* ("speech"). In contrast with the word *narod,* this word actually appears in the text and does so in a very significant position, to wit, as the second word (the first noun and the first subject) of the sonnet; its resonance is heard in many lines (prédkov—drévle—sfér, zvuchashchikh izdalécha—vstrécha—tvorén'ja), up to the word predtécha ("forerunner"), which is the final predicate of the poem. Thus the sonnet runs a full cycle; the word *rech',* throughout the space of the fourteen lines, vibrates in consonance with the last, key word (the first subject, with the last predicate); *predtecha,* as it were, contains *rech',* both on the sound level and on the syntactic level, as well as on the semantic level.[14]

In the first quatrain, *a* is predominant among accented vowels (eight cases out of seventeen), including the first and the last accented vowel (rodn*á*ja—zemn*á*ja). The accented *a*'s frame the quatrain also in another sense: the syntagm *zemlja rodnaja* (end of the first line) mirrors the syntagm *mat' zemnaja* (end of the fourth line). One should also note the refined consonance of the third and the fourth line. The word *vnushennykh* which begins the fourth line contains phonemes of the three preceding words—*nash*eptom *du*bra*vn*ym *v*orozhit. Besides, it is connected with the beginning of the second line (*v nej*), as if forming a budding initial rhyme. On the grammatical level, the predominance of nouns is striking. Ivanov has been for a long time conventionally characterized as "the poet of the noun";[15] in this connection one speaks of his poetry as static, mosaical, abstract. Almost half (nine) of the twenty lexical units in the first quatrain are nouns (the entire sonnet has seventy-one lexical units, among which thirty are nouns). In addition, Ivanov's nouns are short, often monosyllabic. There are four adjectives in the first quatrain, all of them denominative (the total number of adjectives in the sonnet is thirteen). There are only two finite verbs (the total number of these in the sonnet is seven). However, both the verbs and the adjectives in the first (as well as in the second) quatrain are in a sense emphasized, since they carry rhymes. Ivanov's grammatical preferences are especially distinct in the first line which consists only of nouns (with the zero copula). Note that finite verbs are also absent in the five final lines of the sonnet.

The tense of the first quatrain is *present;* the past tense occurs only in the participle (aside from the subtext). Nominal inflection is represented sufficiently well; however, the nominative, the un-marked case, is by far the commonest. The quatrain consists of one coordinative sentence; syntactic subdivisions coincide with the rhythmic ones; the enjambment occurs only between the third and the fourth line, where the syntax becomes typically Ivanovian, confusing, "Latin" in character. It is difficult to disentangle the "many-storeyed" inversion: should one read the last sentence as "zemnaja mat' vnushennykh nebom pesen vorozhit dubravnym nasheptom" (the earthly mother of heaven-induced songs divines according to the whisper of oak groves) or as "zemnaja mat' vorozhit dubravnym nasheptom vnushennykh nebom pesen" (the earthly mother divines according to the oak grove whisper of heaven-induced songs); in other words, are the *pesen* governed by the word *mat'* (which is more probable)[16] or by the word *nasheptom?* The poet leaves us in ignorance and, apparently, intentionally so: this is part of his semantic enterprise.

The choice of structural elements, their interplay on different levels, helps create a complex semantic effect. The first quatrain introduces the semantic themes (topoi) of *zemlja* "earth, soil" and *pamjat'* "memory." *Rech'*, "speech" (*jazyk*, "language"), already in the first line is equated with *zemlja;* this metaphoric comparison, reinforced by the strictly symmetrical structure of the line and by the two identical epithets, turns into symbolic sameness. As is well known, in accordance with Ivanov's conception a symbol acquires different meanings and dimensions in different spheres of consciousness (and existence). *Zemlja*/Gaea/Demeter plays a very important role in Ivanov's symbolic system. She may be regarded as flesh—and soul—of the world, its feminine aspect, a dark reflection of the Eternal Virgin who gave birth to Dionysus.[17] In a Christian interpretation *zemlja* may be connected with the Mother of God; in a purely psychological interpretation, with the Jungian category of *anima;*[18] the sonnet "Jazyk" gives us yet another interpretation: in the creative—poetic—sphere, *zemlja* is *stikhija* (element) of the national speech, giving birth to *stikh* ("verse"),[19] already bearing it inside her, as it were. She embodies the moment of necessity, the communal experience and wisdom of the ancestors;[20] on her own, however, without the touch of the creative spirit she is passive and inert. It is precisely the semantics of *inertness* and *immobility* that is emphasized in the first quatrain. The "eternal present" reigns here—all is repeated, static, self-contained. On the plane of expression, this quality is, at least partially, reflected by the choice of tense, the intransitivity of the verbs, the passive construction, the heaping up of nouns in the unmarked nominative case, the difficult opaque syntax. Repetitions deserve special mention. The very first line is built in a mirrorlike fashion and is self-contained: it begins and ends with the word *rodnaja.* The initial position of this word, its feminine gender, as well as its phonetic and etymological connection with *narod* ("nation"), *rod* ("kin," "clan," "stock"), *rodina* ("native land"), *rozhdenie* ("birth"), *rodstvo* ("kinship"), make it uncommonly weighty in this context from the semantic standpoint. Ivanov emphasizes this word also by allowing himself to violate—only once in the entire poem—the rule of non-repetition of words in a sonnet. I have already noted certain similar instances (cf. the repetition with the characteristic morphological change and syntactic permutation *pevtsu zemlja rodnaja—pesen mat' zemnaja*). Metrically regular and "verbless" lines—the first and the fourth—also reinforce the effect of self-containment, of stasis, of full symmetry of the quatrain.

In the spatial semantics of the quatrain, the horizontal dimension (symbolically connected with the passive principle) is emphasized. There is a hint, however, of the vertical dimension: specifically, *dub* ("oak") is mentioned, indirectly in the word *dubravnym*. The symbolism of *dub* is multifaceted. First and foremost, this is one of the variants of the *world tree* which unites top and bottom, heaven and earth, light and darkness.[21] Ivanov used this symbol many times, emphasizing its ambivalent nature in every way: thus, in his poem "The Oak of Stone" (*Kamennyj dub*), written a year and a half before the sonnet under consideration, the image of *oak* neutralizes the oppositions *live/dead, spring/winter, birth/death* and some others. In this fashion, *dub* is linked with the complex of Dionysianism, the pivot of Ivanov's metaphysics. On the other hand, in the mythological vegetative code, *oak* as the tree of Zeus (and Cybele) forms the opposite of *vine* as the genuine tree of Dionysus. The contrast *dub/ vinograd (loza)* ("vine") is crucial to the entire sonnet (*loza* appears in the second quatrain approximately in the same slot as *dub* in the first quatrain). Third, the words of *nashept dubravnyj* ("oak grove whisper") refer to a specific philosophic conception. Human language and sign systems of culture are likened to the *language of nature*. This conception, going back to Schelling and the *ljubomudry*, was dear to Ivanov, as well as to Baratynsky, Tyutchev and Fet; we find tens if not hundreds of examples to that effect in Ivanov's verse, embodied now in somewhat worn-out metaphors, now in bold and original images. And, finally, *dub* and *dubrava* ("oak grove") are living signs of the Pushkinian tradition. They are connected with the introductory lines of "Ruslan i Ljudmila" (employed in the well-known poem from *Roman Diary* [*Rimskij dnevnik*, 1944]) and with *shirokoshumnyja dubrovy* ("wide-resounding oak groves") from the poem "Poet." Let us recall that the sonnet is dedicated to Pushkin's memory. Thus one word (one morpheme, to be precise) places Ivanov's verse in the broadest context—mythological, religious, philosophical and literary-historical.

The second quatrain is in many respects the opposite of the first. It shows other facets of language and myth. On the phonological level, the proportion of sonorants is decreased dramatically: *m* does not appear at all, whereas *l, n, r* constitute less than one third of all the consonants. There are significantly more plosive non-sonorants (twenty-three occurrences out of sixty-nine). While the first quatrain emphasizes sonority and harmony, the second presents language in its disharmonious aspect. However, the last two lines of the quatrain are based on repetitions of the non-plosive *s, l, v* (the anagram of the lexeme *slovo*, "word"). Front vowels *e, i* are predominant among accented vowels (nine out of eighteen), but the two accented *u*'s (*glub', dukh*) which occur in semantically loaded nouns, monosyllabic and situated in the same (third) foot in the neighboring lines, clearly stand out against that background. Ivanov's gravitation toward initial rhymes (or rhymoids) is noticeable as before; it becomes even stronger: while the second and the fourth line of the first quatrain echoed barely noticeably (*v nej*—*vn*ushennykh), the initial *kak bylo*—*i sila* in the second quatrain is striking (cf. the same tendency further: *slove*snykh—*prosla*vlennaja—i *ve*shchij, s ot*gu*lom—kak *ugl*'). On the grammatical level, one should note the decrease in the proportion of nouns (8 nouns per 23 words) and the increase in the proportion of verbs (4 verbs per 23 words); in addition, the past tense appears alongside the present tense (*bylo*, "it was"). Incidentally, while the first quatrain contains only imperfective verbs, the verb *bylo* (corresponding to the omitted copula in the first line) neutralizes the opposition *perfective/imperfective*. The second quatrain, in contrast to the first, consists of two sentences: the first sentence combines coordination with subordination, whereas the second sentence is an expanded simple sentence with inversions (it is, however, quite clear and transparent). The enjambment occurs in the beginning of the quatrain, not in its end. Rhythmically, the second quatrain is also, in a sense, the reverse of the first: regular lines are situated in its middle, not along its edges.

The semantic structure of the quatrain is noticeably connected with the choice and interplay of the elements of its expression plane. While passivity, inertness and "the eternal return" correlated with the *topos* of *zemlja* (feminine principle, *anima*) were emphasized in the first quatrain, the second quatrain affirms activity, motion and diversity correlated with the theme of *dukh* (masculine principle, *animus*). One is dealing here not with collective language but with its individual use by the poet; not with immersion into the primal element of the unconscious but with the next level, to wit, wilful individuation. Hence the replacement of the static with the dynamic. As I have said, the number of verbs is increased (two of them— *kruzhit* ["circles"] and *bezhit* ["runs"]—are verbs of motion); there appears an expressive enjambment underscored by a phonological and a morphological link (glub' *za*povednaja *Za*chatij zhdet—[the sacred depth is waiting for conceptions]); the "eternal present" is transformed into genuine time where there is both present and past. Similarly, the horizontal dimension is transformed into the vertical one (*glub'*—dukh *nad* nej—"*depth*—the spirit *over* it"); influence at a distance, inducement, turns into nuptial intimacy; containment, *closure,* into *openness.* As I have already mentioned, *dub* ("oak") is the opposite of *loza* ("vine") in the mythological vegetative code. *Loza* is also a mediator of top and bottom, heaven and earth, cosmos and chaos, life and death; in addition, *loza* entails connotations connected with the cult of Dionysus and, through it, with the Christian symbolism of *sacrifice* (cf. the category of *zhertvennoe iskusstvo* ["sacrificial art"], so important to many Symbolists). *Jazyk prirody* ("language of nature"), one of the themes of the first quatrain, is now shifted to a different plane: poetic language is likened to natural phenomena only metaphorically.

The first tercet again brings many changes. The sound-system of language turns about to show its new side. In the tercet, fricatives

(non-sonorants) are predominant (twenty out of forty-eight consonants). The consonantal theme of the tercet is based on the combinations *sv*, *zv* placed "diagonally" (*sv*etitsja—*sf*er—*sv*etom,
*zv*enja—*zv*uchashchikh; cf. also the reverse diagonal *o*tg*u*l*o*m—*u*m-
nogo *o*gnja). In this fashion, the poet introduces the semantic themes
of *svet* ("light") and *zvuk* ("sound") which were absent or almost
absent in the quatrains (there, *zvuk* was predicted by *nashept* ["whisper"]). The accented vowels *a* and *e* are virtually in balance. On the
grammatical level, the reflexive and the gerund appear for the first
and only time. The tercet is a single simple sentence saturated with
inversions. Rhythmically, it is particularly light, compared with the
other stanzas: it does not have accentually regular lines, and out of
fifteen possible stresses four are omitted.

On the semantic plane the orientation of the tercet differs from
that of the quatrains. *Temporal distance* established by the quatrains
turns into *spatial distance* (note the resonance of pre*d*kov, *drevle*—sfer,
iz*d*a*le*cha). The *horizontal* dimension of the first quatrain and the
vertical dimension of the second quatrain are transfigured into a
spherical world turned onto itself and linked to the tradition of medieval thought (particularly Dante).[22] Finally, *earth* of the first quatrain and *liquid* of the second quatrain are replaced by *ogon'* ("fire").
The poet, in sifting through the phonetic, grammatical, syntactic
and rhythmic possibilities of language, at the same time sifts
through fundamental structural elements of Mediterranean (and not
only Mediterranean) mythology. The completion of this sorting will
be seen in the next tercet.

Language, the main theme and the protagonist of the poem,
appears here in a new guise. It is still an element, as before, yet an
element transilluminated by the suprapersonal mind, the principle
of *umnyj ogon'* ("intelligent fire"). (Cf. *umnaja molitva* ["mindful
prayer"] in the tradition of the Orthodox church; note also the phonetic connections of *um*nogo—*ugl'*—a*lm*az). *Ogon'* is ambivalent and
in a sense "Dionysiac" in any mythology: it neutralizes the opposition *construction/destruction*, as well as *personal/impersonal*. Language
turns out to be an echo, *otgul* ("reverberation") of other remote

worlds, of another suprapersonal horizon of meanings; this theme is among those most fundamental to Ivanov (cf. e.g. the well-known poem "The Alpine Horn" [*Al'pijskij rog*] of 1902). In the traditional theory of the sonnet, the last tercet was always regarded as the key, the synthesizing stanza. Let us discuss some of its characteristics. Here the system of consonants comes into balance for the first time (numbers of consonants of different types being close). Accented syllables show no preference for either back or front vowels. Incidentally, the sonnet as a whole contains almost a complete set of Russian phonemes (and graphemes), which is far from expected in a short poem: in other words, the Russian language is quite fully *displayed* in its phonetic (and graphic) aspect.

On the grammatical level, the "verblessness" of the last tercet is remarkable; it correlates with the "verblessness" of the beginning of the poem. For the first time, a directional accusative appears (aside from it, there are only the nominative and the genitive). The shifting of grammatical genders in the sonnet is rather curious. In the first quatrain, the feminine (*zemlja, mat'*) is predominant; in the second, the masculine is underscored; in the first tercet, they are brought together; and last, the final tercet neutralizes the opposition: it contains the neuter gender (*solntse*, "sun," reminiscent of *nebo*, ["heaven,"] in the first quatrain and *zachatija*, "conceptions," in the second), and the concluding word of the poem—*predtecha*, "forerunner"—is grammatically androgynous.

On the syntactic plane, the tercet is a single sentence whose center is singled out by punctuation; it is singled out rhythmically as well: the inner line of the tercet, in contrast to the two outer ones, is accentually regular. In the middle of this line, "in the center of the center," Ivanov placed the word *almaz* ("diamond") which is a palindromic repetition of the word *zemlja* from the beginning of the sonnet.

The last tercet is highly significant semantically, as expected. It shifts the spatial orientation once again: the spheric world of the preceding tercet turns into a *point*. The diamond containing the sun is a symbol of unity signified by the point in many mystical systems. Space, in its dividing sense, no longer exists.[23] *Earth, liquid* and *fire* are followed by a superseding and a higher element. *Ugl'* ("coal") transformed into diamond is *matter transformed;* in it, firmness of the earth, translucence of liquid and splendor of fire are combined and strengthened; it contains the sun—i.e., Apollo, the mythic other-being of Dionysus.[24]

Svadebnaja vstrecha ("the nuptial encounter") of the creative spirit with the element of language has occurred; the extrapersonal and the personal have been reunited in the suprapersonal; the spirit has transformed *language* into *poetry;* the diamond evoked by the poet is the poem before us, Apollonically complete and Dionysiacally ecstatic, scintillating with its facets of sound and sense, speaking itself and not merely itself. Here Ivanov reveals a new and a final dimension. Language—and poetry—is just a portent, a prototype, a forerunner (*predtecha*) of a future universal ecumenic bond of people; at this stage, where all oppositions and contradictions are neutralized, language will overcome and obliterate itself; however, this universal communion may only be vaguely intuited and attempts to construct it arbitrarily are fraught with serious errors. In the words of a Western thinker, at first sight quite distant from Ivanov, "Whereof one cannot speak thereon must one be silent."

Notes

1. *Sovremennye zapiski,* 65 (1937), 165–66.
2. Cf. O. Deschartes' introduction in *SS,* I, 212–14.
3. *O krizise gumanizma* (1919). *SS,* III, 372.
4. N. V., "Vjacheslav Ivanov o russkom jazyke" (a publication of two fragments), *Grani,* no. 102 (1976), 151.
5. "Poet i chern' " (1904), *SS,* I, 712–14. Italics are mine.
6. It is known that Pushkin as an ideal example of a poet and of a poetic destiny played a prominent part in Ivanov's consciousness from his early childhood. Cf. O. Deschartes in *SS,* I, 8.
7. S. Averintsev, "Vjacheslav Ivanov" in Vjacheslav Ivanov, *Stikhotvorenija i poemy,* Biblioteka poeta, Malaja serija (Leningrad, 1976), p. 23.
8. It is significant that Ivanov's last piece of work is a sonnet (the third poem of the cycle *De profundis amavi* in "Svet vechernij").

9. See M. A. Gasparov, *Sovremennyj russkij stikh* (Moscow, 1974), p. 104.

10. Ibid., p. 105.

11. I join together the respective hard and soft phonemes *n* and *n'*, and the like.

12. See Jean Starobinski, *Les mots sous les mots. Les anagrammes de Ferdinand de Saussure* (Paris, 1971).

13. Cf. also the word *nedr* in the second quatrain.

14. The same can be said about the word *vstrecha*. On the other hand, the consonance of the word *predtecha* and the word *predkov* ("of the ancestors") is important (*future/past*).

15. Cf. Averintsev, "Vjacheslav Ivanov," p. 31.

16. In the 1937 redaction, line 4 was as follows: "The earthly mother of heavenly inspirations."

17. Cf. "O deistvii i deistve" (1919), *SS,* II, 165–66.

18. Cf. "Anima" (1934), *SS,* III, 269–93.

19. The famous connection of *stikhija* and *stikh* in Pasternak's "Tema s variatsijami" probably goes back to Ivanov (see the above quotation from the article "Poet i chern'").

20. Cf. the very modern-sounding definitions of culture as memory and as thesaurus in *Perepiska iz dvukh uglov,* and so forth.

21. See the numerous studies of V. N. Toporov on this topic.

22. The word *sfer* appeared only in the third redaction of the poem. Formerly line 10 read as follows: V lad muzyke, skhodjashchej izdalecha ("In tune with the music descending from afar"); Sozvuch'jam v lad, skhodjashchim izdalecha ("In tune with the consonances descending from afar").

23. Cf. Deschartes in *SS,* I, 159. Let us add that this refers to both *space* and *time.*

24. The absence of the fourth classical element, namely, air, is curious. *Almaz* ("diamond,") is a sort of anti-air, the opposite of air. However, air (*vozdukh*) to a certain extent is present in the word *dukhonosnogo* ("of the spirit-bearing") and is anagrammatically given in the last tercet.

The First Sonnet in Vyacheslav Ivanov's Roman Cycle

Alexis Klimoff

The nine sonnets written by Ivanov after his arrival in Rome from the Soviet Union in 1924 belong to a vast and venerable literary tradition. Practitioners of the art of *admiratio Romae,* that is, of lauding the Eternal City in verse or prose, have included some of the most celebrated poets and writers of the last two millennia—Virgil, Dante, Montaigne, Goethe, Byron, Gogol, and scores of others. As a rule this literature goes far beyond delight at the lavish spectacle that Rome presents to the visitor. The incomparably rich historical and cultural legacy that is everywhere evoked by the physical *realia* of the city made it almost inevitable that Rome should often have been perceived in historiosophic terms, as a symbol of the hopes, the achievements—or the failures—of human civilization itself.[1] Ivanov's *Roman Sonnets* (*Rimskie sonety*) of 1924 follow this pattern.

Vyacheslav Ivanov first set foot in Rome some three decades earlier, having just completed a lengthy course of studies in Roman history under the famous Theodor Mommsen at Berlin University. Some idea of his worshipful attitude toward the city can be gathered from a poetic epistle written soon after his arrival in Rome in 1892: "Having reached my sacred goal, pilgrim that I am, I have attained bliss."[2]

After an initial three-year residence in Rome, Ivanov returned on many occasions in the years before World War I, including an extended stay in 1912–1913. Although he gradually became more and more absorbed in the study of early Greek religious cults, Ivanov retained a deep interest in Roman history. In 1899 he took almost

an entire year from his research on Dionysus to gather data on the
religious and historical roots of the belief in the "universal mission"
(*vselenskaja missija*) of Rome.[3]

But beyond Ivanov's reverence for the city and its cultural heritage, his Rome was associated with powerful emotions of a different
order. It was here, in the summer of 1893, that Ivanov met Lydia
Zinovieva-Annibal, the gifted and intense woman who was soon to
become his second wife. Ivanov always looked upon this meeting as
especially providential: Lydia was to him the awakener and inspirer
of his gifts as a poet.

In 1924, long after the death of his beloved Lydia, after the
bitter privations of post-revolutionary Moscow had carried away his
third wife Vera, after years of increasing isolation as a poet and of
growing alienation from the values of the new regime, the return to
Rome must have seemed particularly poignant. It was not only a
journey to the healing source of culture and tradition, but also a
nostalgic trip in time to memories of love and happiness.

The first of the *Roman Sonnets* was written a few days after
Ivanov's arrival in Rome in September of 1924. The Italian origin
of the poetic format—the sonnet arose in medieval Sicily and was
made universally famous by Petrarch—makes it especially appropriate for a greeting to Rome. I quote the text in full:

A faithful pilgrim to the ancient arches, once again,
I greet you like the roof of my own home
With evening "Ave Rome" in my setting hour,
O haven of my wanderings, Eternal Rome.

We yield ancestral Troy up to the flames;
The chariots' axles splinter 'mid the thunder
And fury of the earthly hippodrome:
You, Tsar of Ways, behold how we burn on.

You too have burned and risen from the ashes,
And the retentive, recollecting blue
Of your deep skies did not go blind.

And in the soft caresses of a golden dream,
Your guardian cypress recollects how Troy grew stronger
As Troy lay burned to ashes.

(1) Vnov', arok drevnikh vernyj piligrim,
(2) V moj pozdnij chas vechernim 'Ave Roma'
(3) Privetstvuju kak svod rodnogo doma,
(4) Tebja, skitanij pristan', vechnyj Rim.

(5) My Troju predkov plameni darim;
(6) Drobjatsja osi kolesnits mezh groma
(7) I furij mirovogo ippodroma:
(8) Ty, tsar' putej, gljadish', kak my gorim.

(9) I ty pylal i vosstaval iz pepla,
(10) I pamjatlivaja golubizna
(11) Tvoikh nebes glubokikh ne oslepla.

(12) I pomnit v laske zolotogo sna,
(13) Tvoj vratar' kiparis, kak Troja krepla,
(14) Kogda lezhala Troja sozhzhena.[4]

Originally the sonnet bore the title "Regina Viarum" (Queen of Ways), a Latin phrase which, as Ivanov informs us in a note appended to the poem, used to be an ancient appellation for Rome [SS, III, 850]. In the final edition the title was removed and the Latin epithet is reflected in the phrase *tsar' putej* [8]. (The switch in royal gender is caused by a quirk of grammar: *Roma* is feminine in Latin, while *Rim,* the Russian equivalent, is a masculine noun.)

The journey to Rome is seen in the first quatrain as a symbolic homecoming and as the ultimate goal of a pilgrimage: to the "faithful pilgrim" [1], Rome is a sight as welcome as that of his own home [3]; moreover, the city is addressed as the "haven" of his wanderings [4]. The finality of the journey is further emphasized by the references to the persona's "setting hour" and his "evening" salutation [2]. This tone corresponds closely with Ivanov's declaration, on the eve of his departure from the Soviet Union, that he was going to Rome to die.[5] In this solemn context the term "pilgrim" [1] takes on added significance. One of the traditional Christian metaphors used in describing human life depicts man as a traveler (*homo viator*) or pilgrim who seeks to reach the ultimate haven of Paradise. The religious associations in Ivanov's sonnet gain further resonance from the reference to "Eternal Rome" [4]: on the symbolic level, the arrival in Rome is compared to the attainment of the kingdom of heaven.

Rome is greeted explicitly with an "Ave Roma" in lines [2–3] and the greeting is made to reverberate throughout the sonnet by means of an unusual device. The canonical rhyme scheme for the first octave of a so-called Italian or Petrarchan sonnet is *abba/abba*. Ivanov's sonnet more than fulfills this requirement: in seven of the eight lines, the rhymed units are either *rim* or *roma*, thus repeating the name of the city in both Russian and Latin. The pattern can be depicted as follows:

[1]	piligRIM	(a)
[2]	ROMA	(b)
[3]	(doma)	(b)
[4]	RIM	(a)
[5]	daRIM	(a)
[6]	gROMA	(b)
[7]	ippodROMA	(b)
[8]	goRIM	(a)

It is useful to recall in this connection Ivanov's theory of the "sound-image" (*zvukoobraz*) in poetry. The poet, Ivanov argues, does not primarily "think in images," as the conventional wisdom would have us believe. In truth, the poet "thinks above all in sounds," and Ivanov supports this contention with numerous references to Pushkin's use of sound symbolism.[6] Assuming that such considerations are relevant to the structure of Ivanov's sonnet, the pattern isolated above suggests that the name of the city is the core or germ around which the sonnet was formed. And this meshes well with W. H. Auden's definition of poetry as a rite which "pays homage by naming."[7] For it is clear that the recurring echoes of the name of Rome are extremely effective in dramatizing the pilgrim's pray-erful attitude. Repeated invocation of the object of worship is, after all, the central feature of all liturgical language.

The frame of reference is abruptly widened by the introduction of the Troy theme in the second quatrain. According to legend, Romulus, the founder of Rome, was a direct descendant of Aeneas, a refugee from the flaming ruins of Troy. In fact, as Ivanov informs us in another note, Rome was for this reason sometimes referred to as "New Troy" {SS, III, 850}. Ivanov's pilgrim is thus following an established—albeit mythical—pattern, since Rome has been a haven for refugees and exiles before. The use of the pronoun "we" in line {5} emphasizes this community of fate, since the reference is to all refugees, from the pilgrim back to Aeneas. It follows logically that the pilgrim (the "I" or persona) also has an "ancestral Troy" to consign to the flames. Troy, then, is evoked not only as a specific precedent, but also as a metaphor for any destroyed civilization. (The Troy-Russia analogy which emerges here will be considered at a later point.)

As the disasters and conflagrations of history thunder and rage around it, Rome seems to look on majestically [8]; it appears, at this juncture, to be somehow beyond time and history.

But the first tercet brings with it a characteristic twist.[8] Rome has not been outside history after all. It too has suffered destruction {9}. But more important, the city rose anew from its ashes, not once, but many times, as the imperfective aspect of the verb indicates (*vosstaval* {9}). This new theme is accompanied by a distinct phonetic shift. The second quatrain, which stressed destruction, was replete with the sound *r* (*TRoju, pRedkov, daRim, dRobjatsja, gRoma, fuRij, miRovogo, ippodRoma, tsaR', goRim*), while the first tercet has no *r*'s whatever, but is filled with *l* sounds: *pyLaL, vosstavaL, pepLa, pamjatLivaja, goLubizna, gLubokikh, osLepLa*. These contrasting key sounds are at the same time closely related, since both are liquid consonants. In this sense the link between destruction and renewal, central to the meaning of the poem, is prefigured in phonetic terms.

The resurrection of Rome from its ashes can be read as a strictly historical commentary. Rome not only survived its many disasters (destruction by the Gauls in 390 B.C., the great fire of Nero's time, the several sackings by barbarians, etc.), but acquired new splendor with the centuries and blossomed into the magnificent city of the Popes. However, the motif of regeneration through fire inevitably has other and more fanciful associations, above all the legend of the Phoenix, which was said to gain new life through periodic self-immolation.[9] This myth is substantially reinforced by the seemingly paradoxical ending of the sonnet: Troy grew stronger while Troy lay gutted and destroyed [13–14]. The Troy which gained strength here is of course the *New* Troy, that is, Rome, but from a structural perspective the Phoenix myth applies fully: destruction by fire is followed by regeneration.

It is important to note that the theme of fiery renewal is frequently encountered in Ivanov's earlier writings, usually in the sense of a radical spiritual rebirth. This is a major motif in his *Cor Ardens* collection (1911) and is reflected in the title itself ("The Burning Heart"). Ivanov's fondness for this theme was at times excessive, as for instance in the following lines written on the occasion of the catastrophic defeat of the Russian navy at Tsushima:

> Accept us, sacrificial fire,
>
> . . . .
>
> A Phoenix will arise! A Phoenix will choose
> The fateful sacrament of fire!
> Be baptized with fire, O Russia! . . .

> Primi nas, zhertvennyj koster,
>
> . . . .
>
> Kto Feniks,—vozletit! Kto Feniks,—izberet
> Ognja svjatynju rokovuju!
> Ognem krestisja, Rus'! . . .   [SS, II, 252–53]

The tone of liturgical celebration in this tragic context strikes at least one reader as disturbing if not downright perverse. It was precisely this tendency in Ivanov which prompted Ehrenburg's puckish comment:

> Vyacheslav Ivanov loves the traditional Orthodox way of life and the unhurried, harmonious world of the parish. But one should

not be deceived on this account. . . . When flames lick at the wooden fence [of the church], Vyacheslav Ivanov will come out not with a pail of water, but with a hymn to the purifying fire.[10]

Ivanov's attachment to this motif may be more easily understood if we note, with Tadeusz Zielinski, that there are important parallels between the concept of rebirth through fire and Ivanov's *idée maîtresse,* the theme of the suffering and resurrected god Dionysus.[11] The analogy between these concepts can be brought into sharp focus by referring to Mircea Eliade's groundbreaking study, *Cosmos and History: The Myth of the Eternal Return.* Eliade argues that when they are reduced to their structural elements, both concepts or myths are subsumed under the larger myth of eternal repetition, common in the ancient world. In both cases death and destruction are followed by resurrection, apparent defeat is transformed into a triumph.[12]

In each case we are dealing with a cyclical view of history. Such a theory, as Eliade stresses, is "unhistorical" in the sense that all real and concrete events are stripped of their autonomous value. They are all seen as mere reflections of an ideal pattern or archetype, as paradigmatic repetitions of a primordial event outside time and history. It is, in Eliade's words, a "supreme attempt . . . towards annulling the irreversibility of time."[13]

A cyclical theory of history is in its way a consoling philosophy. Apart from the promise of ultimate rebirth, the myth of eternal return provides an escape from the distressingly unpredictable sequence of events which is part of an "open-ended" view of history. All events—and all disasters—can be seen as reruns of similar, indeed identical, events in the past. Man need no longer view history as a terrible lurching through regions of the unknown.

Eliade's insights seem to be directly applicable to Ivanov's sonnet, especially in view of Ivanov's explicit conviction that the sonnet is a "philosophical and didactic" genre.[14] The hope and consolation offered to the pilgrim are summed up by the myth of the eternal return. Surrounded by events which are likened to a thunderous chariot race in the hippodrome—a cyclical symbol in itself—the pilgrim recognizes everywhere a familiar mythic pattern. His arrival in Rome parallels Aeneas's arrival from Troy, the fiery destruction of his homeland repeats Troy's archetypal fall. Rome itself has recovered many times from its disastrous conflagrations. He need not despair; his own "New Troy" will not fail to rise from the ashes of the "Troy of his ancestors." Aeneas's comforting words to his shipmates apply fully to Ivanov's pilgrim:

> Renew your spirit, and lay aside gloomy fear;
> perhaps one day it will be a pleasure to remember
> these trials. Through various mishaps,
> through many crises, we make our way to Latium
> where the Fates portend a peaceful settlement.
> There it is right for Troy to rise. Have courage
> and preserve yourselves for prosperous days. [15]

As he retreats before the terrors of history, Ivanov's wayfarer is offered refuge and consolation in myth and mythical time. And this is entirely consistent with the belief so frequently expressed by Ivanov that all poetry must attempt to create myth, where myth is defined as a reflection of a higher ("more real") reality. In any case, such a thrust was always a prominent feature of Ivanov's own work. As he noted with pride in 1921: "Not one of my contemporaries, I believe, is inspired by the sense of myth to the degree that I am. That is where my strength lies . . ." [16]

There is another aspect in this attempt to transcend time. The sonnet is most explicit in emphasizing Rome's ability to remember the past. The clear blue sky over Rome is endowed with the attributes of an eye {10–11} which has witnessed and retained in its memory the successive generations of the city {9–10}. Similarly, the cypress outside Rome remembers {12–13} how a mighty New Troy was founded by a handful of survivors from the original Troy {12–14}.

The "retentive" Roman sky and the "unforgetting" cypress are invoked by the poet to bear witness to the ultimate nature of things. Memory is the key to this "more real" dimension of ideal patterns where regeneration always occurs. Here Ivanov is once more following in the footsteps of the ancient Greeks. For them, memory was not merely a psychological function, but was identified with a vision of the truth, an insight into the original and archetypal realities. The truth, states Plato, is "a recollection of those things which our soul once saw while following God."[17] And since the cyclical nature of history was, to the Greeks, one of these realities, it follows that true memory could only speak of eternal regeneration and hence eternal life. Conversely, forgetting was equated with death; as Eliade has pointed out, Lethe, the river of forgetfulness in Greek mythology, was an indispensable feature of the realm of death. "The dead are those who have lost their memories."[18]

For the Greeks and for Ivanov, then, memory manifests and confirms the faith in eternal renewal. Memory offers refuge from the tyranny of time; in a sense, it even annuls death, as Ivanov proclaimed in an earlier poem:

He in whom eternal memory lives
Triumphs eternally over death.

Nad smert'ju vechno torzhestvujet,
V kom pamjat' vechnaja zhivet.   [SS, I, 568]

In the first sonnet to Rome, memory is the medium by which the Eternal City testifies to its regenerative powers. It is this aspect of Rome which gives strength to the pilgrim who arrives "in his setting hour" [2]. Through the agony of fire and destruction he passes into ultimate hope in the footsteps of Aeneas.

The hopeful conclusion noted above pertains to Ivanov's pilgrim-persona and his quest for meaning in a world gone mad. There remains, however, an unresolved ambiguity in another sphere. To the extent that the "Old Troy" of the sonnet can be identified with Russia, it is not at all clear what the concluding lines [13–14] imply for the future of the land Ivanov had left behind. In terms of the structural paradigm that operates in the sonnet, there would seem to be room for hope that a new Russia will emerge, Phoenix-like, from the crucible of the revolutionary epoch. Yet by identifying the

"New Troy" specifically and uniquely with Rome, as seems to be the case, Ivanov is sharply reducing the applicability of his paradigm to any other context. Pushed to a logical conclusion, this would imply that the "Old Troy" has been destroyed beyond resurrection and that the only hope for the future lies with Rome. But the poem resists such a conclusion, retaining a residual ambiguity which undoubtedly reflects an unresolved tension within the poet himself.[19]

Notes

1. The ancient period is surveyed in F. G. Moore, "On *Urbs Aeterna* and *Urbs Sacra*," *Trans. of the Amer. Phil. Assoc.*, XXV (1894), 34–60. The history of the evolving poetic image of Rome, with emphasis on the post-Renaissance period, is outlined in Walther Rehm, *Europäische Romdichtung*, 2nd ed. (Munich, 1960). See further: Camillo von Klenze, *The Interpretation of Italy During the Last Two Centuries* (Chicago, 1907); C. P. Brand, *Italy and the English Romantics* (Cambridge, 1957); Erika Schröter, *Beiträge zur Geschichte des russischen Italienerlebnisses* (Bonn, 1960).

2. Vyacheslav Ivanov, "Laeta" [Joy], *SS*, I, 636.

3. "Avtobiograficheskoe pis'mo," *SS*, II, 21.

4. *SS*, III, 578. First appeared in print as a complete citation in I. N. Golenishchev-Kutuzov, "Lirika Vjacheslava Ivanova," *Sovremennye zapiski*, No. 43 (1930), 466–67.

5. "Ja edu umirat' v Rim." Quoted in *SS*, III, 819. Cf. Ivanov's diary entry for December 1, 1924: *SS*, III, 852.

6. Ivanov, "K probleme zvukoobraza u Pushkina," in *Moskovskij pushkinist*, II (1930), 94–105.

7. W. H. Auden, *The Dyer's Hand* (New York, 1962), p. 57.

8. The tercets in a sonnet traditionally introduce a new theme or new perspective. See Johannes R. Becher, "Philosophie des Sonetts oder kleine Sonettlehre," *Sinn und Form*, VIII (1956), No. 3, 343.

9. It is interesting to note that the Phoenix was depicted on Roman coins in the period of the decline of the Empire. See Kenneth J. Pratt, "Rome as Eternal," *Journal of the History of Ideas*, XXVI (1965), No. 1, 30.

10. Ilja Ehrenburg, *Portrety russkikh poetov* (Berlin, 1922), pp. 92–93.

11. Faddej Zelinskij, "Vjacheslav Ivanov," in S. A. Vengerov, ed., *Russkaja literatura XX veka*, 3 vols. (Moscow, 1914–1916), III, 103.

12. *Cosmos and History,* trans. Willard R. Trask (New York, 1959), pp. 87–88, 100–102.

13. *Cosmos and History,* p. 123.

14. "Sonet—strogaja forma, on—ne lirika, on forma didakticheskaja, filosofichnaja." Quoted from an unpublished verbatim transcript of Ivanov's 1920 lectures on poetry in Moscow: *Kruzhok poèzii pod rukovodstvom poèta Vjacheslava Ivanova,* zapis' F. I. Kogan, 1920, p. 13. (Text is in the Roman archive.)

15. *Aeneid,* I, 202–207. I quote the translation by Kevin Guinagh (New York, 1953), p. 9.

16. M. S. Al'tman, "Iz besed s poètom Vjacheslavom Ivanovichem Ivanovym," *Uchenye zapiski Tartuskogo gos. univ.,* vol. 209 (1968), 321.

17. *Phaedrus,* 249c.

18. Mircea Eliade, "Mythologies of Memory and Forgetting," *History of Religions,* II, No. 2 (Winter, 1963), 333.

19. This essay is based on part of my dissertation on Vyacheslav Ivanov (Yale, 1974).

Roman Sonnets
Vyacheslav Ivanov
Translated by Lowry Nelson, Jr.

I

Again, true pilgrim of your vaulted past,
I greet you, as my own ancestral home,
With evening "Ave Roma" at the last,
You, wanderers' retreat, eternal Rome.

The Troy of your forebears we give to fire;
The chariots' axles crack from furious churning
In this hippodrome of the world entire:
Regina Viarum, see how we are burning.

And you went down in flames and rose from embers;
The mindful blueness could not blind the eye
Of space in your unfathomable sky.
Your cypress, standing sentinel, remembers

In the caresses of a dream of gold
How strong was Troy in ashes lying cold.

I

Вновь, арок древних верный пилигрим,
В мой поздний час вечерним 'Ave Roma'
Приветствую как свод родного дома,
Тебя, скитаний пристань, вечный Рим.

Мы Трою предков пламени дарим;
Дробятся оси колесниц меж грома
И фурий мирового ипподрома;
Ты, царь путей, глядишь, как мы горим.

И ты пылал и восставал из пепла,
И памятливая голубизна
Твоих небес глубоких не ослепла.

И помнит в ласке золотого сна,
Твой вратарь кипарис, как Троя сожжена.

II

Holding the reins their steeds untamely shun,
Strong with the dauntless ardor of the sky,
Naked in nakedness olympian,
Forward they strode, brothers, Diòscuri.

Quirites' fellow-warriors, bearing tale
Of victory, who, sagas say, unknown,
Beside Juturna's pool themselves unveil
Divine newcomers to the hub of Rome.

There they remained until the world should pass.
Of these huge youths a double effigy
Stood for millennia an unmoved mass,
And there they stand who stood primordially.

Six hills light up in blue surrounding air
As, from high Quirinal, a star shines fair.

III

Sang Pindar, poet-swan: "Beneath the sun
There's nothing more dear than water." From hills
Incline of aqueducts compels the run
Of water anciently from blessed rills.

It trickles into sarcophágous wells,
Now strikes the sky, a column, and, once shattered,
Far off now laps cool air; untamed, it swells
From marble threshold in the streams it scattered.

The babbling water makes the narrow lane
Come magically alive, and sea-gods leap
Beside it and lead on the dancers' train.
A chisel fused them. Old palazzi sleep,

Deserted, yet hear how waters rejoice,
How gently through the haze resounds their voice.

II

Держа коней строптивых под-уздцы,
Могучи пылом солнечной отбаги
И наготою олимпийской наги,
Вперед ступили братья-близнецы.

Соратники Квиритов и гонцы
С полей победы, у Ютурнской влаги,
Неузнаны, явились (помнят саги)
На стогнах Рима боги-пришлецы.

И в нем остались до скончины мира.
И юношей огромных два кумира
Не сдвинулись тысячелетья с мест.

И там стоят, где стали изначала—
Шести холмам, синеющим окрест,
Светить звездой с вершины Квиринала.

III

Пел Пиндар, лебедь: «Нет под солнцем блага
Воды милей». Бежит по жилам Рима,
Склоненьем акведуков с гор гонима,
Издревле родников счастливых влага.

То плещет звонко в кладязь саркофага;
То бьет в лазурь столбом и вдаль, дробима,
Прохладу зыблет; то, неукротима,
Потоки рушит с мраморного прага.

Ее журчаньем узкий переулок
Волшебно оживлен; и хороводы
Окрест ее ведут морские боги:

Резец собрал их. Сонные чертоги
Пустынно внемлют, как играют воды,
И сладостно во мгле их голос гулок.

IV

Turned to stone by the spell of water-sound
Of streams that run over the edge in swirls,
The ship-like fount Barcaccia lies half-drowned;
To it Campania sends flower-girls.

The great staircase goes stepping over mansions
And patterning the expansive way in twain,
It raises to the sky twin-pointed stanchions
And obelisk above the Piazza of Spain.

I love the sunburnt orange of the walls,
The crowds of people in the age-old square,
The rustling palms when parching noontide falls,
In dark of night an aria sighing there,

And, to the velvet zithers' strumming din,
The chirping of a roving mandolin.

V

Those tangled dolphins on their tails sustain
A mollusc shell agape; Triton stands there,
He blows into a giant snail; no strident strain,
It radiates and pierces the blue air.

How green from moss the daemon god's plicature
Amid hot slabs entreating clouds of pine!
The chisel's ancient dream resembles nature
In frenzied spontaneity of line.

Bernini—ours anew—your playful skill
Makes me rejoice as from Four Fountains' knoll
I wander to the Pincio, memory's hill,
Where Ivanov to Gogol's cell would stroll,

Where Piranesi's fiery needle heightens
Rome's sadness and her masonry of Titans.

IV

Окаменев под чарами журчанья
Бегущих струй за полные края,
Лежит полу-затоплена ладья;
К ней девушек с цветами шлет Кампанья.

И лестница, переступая зданья,
Широкий путь узорами двоя,
Несет в лазурь двух башен острия
И обелиск над Площадью ди-Спанья.

Люблю домов оранжевый загар
И людные меж старых стен теснины
И шорох пальм на ней в полдневный жар;

А ночью темной вздохи каватины
И под аккорды бархатных гитар
Бродячей стрекотанье мандолины.

V

Двустворку на хвостах клубок дельфиний
Разверстой вынес; в ней растет Тритон,
Трубит в улиту; но не зычный тон,
Струя лучом пронзает воздух синий.

Средь зноя плит, зовущих облак пиний,
Как зелен мха на демоне хитон!
С природой схож резца старинный сон
Стихийною причудливостью линий.

Бернини,—снова наш,—твоей игрой
Я веселюсь, от Четырех Фонтанов
Бредя на Пинчьо памятной горой,

Где в келью Гоголя входил Иванов,
Где Пиранези огненной иглой
Пел Рима грусть и зодчество Титанов.

VI

Over their backs they let the turtles slip,
Those humped captives at basin's edge aground,
Within they dive and freely splash and dip,
Forget their fear, crawl torpidly around;

The adolescent boys dance on each head
Of snub-nosed monster. Wondrous pranksters they.
Those goggle-eyed gargoyles beneath their tread
From rounded jaws are spouting powdery spray.

The four of them, on dolphins romping, play.
Now on their shins of bronze, on their bronze backs,
Sparkles the greenly rippling laugh of day,
And in this languor, indolently lax,

I catch an echo of your cheering folly,
Echo, Lorenzo, of your melancholy.

VII

The autumnal pool lies sleeping, gently blown
With beggared purple's tattered majesty,
Asclepius with snake mid moss and stone
Beholds beneath an arch the maple tree.

The azure vault is framed, as if in bronze,
By trappings of a dark resplendent show,
The foliage untouched by deadening bonds
Of frost or glint of any shroud of snow.

The Blessed gaze on us and smile abashed
As they would contemplate a platan tree
That wilts in sunlight. Sound of crystal splashed:
The rippling form flows upward radiantly.

And on the mirrored surface calm, capsize
Asclepius, maple, fountain, and the skies.

VI

Через плечо слагая черепах,
Горбатых пленниц, нá мель плоской вазы,
Где брызжутся на воле водолазы,
Забыв, неповоротливые, страх,—

Танцуют отроки на головах
Курносых чудищ. Дивны их проказы:
Под их пятой уроды пучеглазы
Из круглой пасти прыщут водный прах.

Их четверо резвятся на дельфинах.
На бронзовых то голенях, то спинах
Лоснится дня зелено-зыбкий смех.

И в этой неге лени и приволий
Твоих ловлю я праздничных утех,
Твоих, Лоренцо, эхо меланхолий.

VII

Спит водоем осенний, окроплен
Багрянцем нищим царственных отрепий.
Средь мхов и скал, муж со змеей, Асклепий,
Под аркою глядит на красный клен.

И синий свод, как бронзой, окаймлен
Убранством сумрачных великолепий
Листвы, на коей не коснели цепи
Мертвящих стуж, ни снежных блеск пелен.

Взирают так, с улыбкою печальной,
Блаженные на нас, как на платан
Увядший солнце. Плещет звон хрустальный:

Струя к лучу стремит зыбучий стан.
И в глади опрокинуты зеркальной
Асклепий, клен, и небо, и фонтан.

VIII

Tidings of mighty waters will be given
In wafting of cool air as roaring mounts.
Walk toward the sound: palazzi will seem driven
Aside, disclosing Trevi, queen of founts.

Cascading silver from façades will spout,
Marine steeds, brightly fierce, will leap aside;
Glad welcome nymphs from grottos will come out
As Neptune greets the maiden of the tide.

How many times, a fugitive from Rome
Against my will, I have beseeched return,
Over my shoulder casting coins in foam.
The vows have come to pass as they were sworn.

This day again, enchanting fount, you bless
The pilgrim you restore to holiness.

IX

Slowly I savor the sun's honeyed glow
Thickening like the valley's farewell chime;
With careless care the spirit is aglow,
All plenitude, whose name is paradigm.

This wedding cup of Day, does it not brim
With honey of resuscitated past?
Did not Eternity, beyond time's rim,
Plight troth with Day and give a ring to last?

Sky's glory, in likeness to the glassy sea,
Sparks molten fusion, casts celestial gleam,
Where sun's disk melts and drowns colossally.
With dazzled fingers groping, the last beam

Felt pine-top and its eye went out. Left there
In liquid gold the blue Dome circles air.

VIII

Весть мощных вод и в веяньи прохлады
Послышится, и в их растущем реве.
Иди на гул: раздвинутся громады,
Сверкнет царица водометов, Треви.

Сребром с палат посыплются каскады;
Морские кони прянут в светлом гневе;
Из скал богини выйдут, гостье рады,
И сам Нептун навстречу Влаге-Деве.

О, сколько раз, беглец невольный Рима,
С молитвой о возврате в час потребный
Я за плечо бросал в тебя монеты!

Свершались договорные обеты:
Счастливого, как днесь, фонтан волшебный,
Ты возвращал святыням пилигрима.

Iё

Пью медленно медвяный солнца свет,
Густеющий, как долу звон прощальный;
И светел дух печалью беспечальной,
Весь полнота, какой названья нет.

Не медом ли воскресших полных лет
Он напоен, сей кубок Дня венчальный?
Не Вечность ли свой перстень обручальный
Простерла Дню за гранью зримых мет?

Зеркальному подобна морю слава
Огнистого небесного расплава,
Где тает диск и тонет исполин.

Ослепшими перстами луч ощупал
Верх пинии, и глаз потух. Один,
На золоте круглится синий Купол.

CRITIC

Vyacheslav Ivanov and Dante
Pamela Davidson

Throughout his literary career, Vyacheslav Ivanov maintained a lively and profound interest in Dante. This interest found its expression in Ivanov's poetry and prose writings, which contain numerous references to Dante's works. There is another extremely important although virtually unknown area in which this interest also manifested itself; this is the ambitious program of translations of Dante's major works which Ivanov embarked on and partially completed. It is worth noting that the essential character of the interest which both these areas reflect is symbolically foreshadowed at the very outset of Ivanov's literary career; Ivanov's first published work, *Pilot Stars (Kormchie zvezdy,* 1903) is prefaced by an epigraph from Dante's *Purgatorio*:

> Poco potea parer lì del di fuori:
> Ma per quel poco vedev'io le stelle
> Di lor solere e più chiare e maggiori.[1]

This epigraph describes Dante contemplating the stars. The image of the *kormchie zvezdy* or "pilot stars" was chosen by Ivanov as the title of his first book of poetry in order to reflect his central preoccupation with the eternal transcendent truths which rule the universe.[2] It is clear that by taking up and developing the image of the stars introduced in the title within the context of Dante's spiritual experience, Ivanov wishes to emphasize the central importance of Dante's teachings to the spiritual questions with which he is primarily concerned; this is the clue to the source and essential character of Ivanov's interest in Dante throughout his literary career; it is always rooted in Ivanov's own preoccupation with spiritual matters.

In this respect, Ivanov was a typical representative of his age.

Indeed, Ivanov's interest in Dante is one of those fascinating questions which are key issues for the understanding of the intellectual history of an epoch as well as of the spiritual outlook and works of an individual. As is well known, the Symbolist movement arose in Russia at the end of the nineteenth century in response to a tremendous new flowering of interest in spiritual matters. Dante was taken up in this context as a writer whose works offered a vision of the universe as a spiritual entity, and of man's life as a mystical journey. In particular, the younger, more mystically orientated generation of the Symbolists—writers such as Blok, Bely, Ellis, Sergey Solovyov and Vyacheslav Ivanov—turned to the figure of Dante as a model for the understanding and expression of their own spiritual searchings. In the *Vita Nuova* they found an account of the experience of mystical love as the origin of a spiritual journey, and in the *Divina Commedia* they found a record of the mystical journey of the soul towards its final union with the divine essence. In both these works the author's spiritual experience is paralleled by an account of his literary experience as a writer seeking to find adequate expression for his vision in words. Dante's works were thus a particularly rich source for the Symbolist writers, providing them not only with a possible model for their spiritual experience, but also for its literary expression, and ultimately even for an esthetics of symbolism.

Within this general framework, each of the Symbolists naturally invested Dante with the characteristics of his own particular spiritual outlook. In the spiritual development of one of the younger Symbolists, Ellis, one can see a particularly striking example of the way in which the figure of Dante corresponded to the spirit of the age and could be accommodated to fit its various manifestations. Ellis was of a passionate, indeed fanatical nature; his example is an instructive one, because his enthusiasms reflected in an extreme form the typical tendencies of his age and interests of his contemporaries. During a period of just over ten years, from his emergence on the Moscow Symbolist scene in the early 1900s until his disappearance from it towards the middle of the teens, Ellis went through a succession of dramatic metamorphoses; he was in turn a committed Marxist, a Baudelairian Symbolist, a decadent mystic, a fervent disciple

of the anthroposophist Rudolf Steiner, and finally, a dedicated up-
holder of the Catholic faith. It is extremely characteristic of the spirit
of the times that, throughout these various metamorphoses, Ellis
should have remained obsessed with the figure of Dante, whom he
advanced at each stage of his spiritual development as an exponent
of the particular ideology to which he was at the time committed.[3]

It is also clear from Bely's memoirs of Blok that Dante was a
figure of central importance in the context of the mystical mood
which prevailed at the beginning of the twentieth century. Bely
records the questions which he and Blok discussed in their correspondence of 1903, and which were at the time regarded as burning
issues of the day by the Symbolists; these questions included the
problem of the relation of the teaching of the philosopher Vladimir
Solovyov on the nature of "Sophia" or Divine Wisdom to the figure
of Beatrice in Dante's works. Bely regarded Dante as a leading authority who had reflected for decades on the very questions which
were of such vital importance to the Symbolists; he lamented the
fact that many of the Symbolists, instead of turning to Dante for
guidance on these questions, were led astray by popular leaders of
the day such as Bryusov and Merezhkovsky; they were consequently
unable to do justice to the importance of these questions which, like
Dante, proved too profound and complex for their young and im-
mature minds.[4]

From Bely's comments we can see exactly where Ivanov's approach to Dante differed substantially from that of the majority of
his contemporaries. Although the Symbolists' references to Dante
had an important significance in relation to the mood of the times
and to the Symbolists' own individual spiritual interests, they were
often superficial in terms of the knowledge of Dante's works or ideas
which they betrayed. Not all the Symbolists could read Dante in
the original, fewer still studied him in any depth. Dante was more
often invoked as a source of poetic images than as one of philosophical
or religious ideas. Ivanov's approach to Dante, while arising out of
the same general context as that of his contemporaries, differed in
two major respects: first, it was based on a much closer knowledge
of Dante's works and deeper understanding of his ideas; and second,

Ivanov turned to Dante for guidance in the context of his own spiritual outlook on a much more profound level than the other Symbolists did; for both these reasons Ivanov can be regarded as exempt from the castigatory remarks to which Bely subjected his contemporaries.

Both of these areas of difference can perhaps be best accounted for by the strong intellectual strain in Ivanov's character. If we turn first to the question of Ivanov's knowledge and understanding of Dante's works, we will see that his academic background played an important role. Although Ivanov is always grouped with the younger generation of the Symbolists because of the mystical orientation which he shared with them, he was in fact many years their senior; before establishing himself as a poet and returning to Russia to take up an active part in the Symbolist movement in 1905, Ivanov had already spent several years conducting research into classical antiquity in Berlin, Paris, Rome, London, and Athens.[5] During these years, Ivanov acquired a solid grounding in classical antiquity and European culture, as well as a conscientious thoroughness and depth of approach characteristic of scholarly work. This academic seriousness is an important element in Ivanov's approach to Dante, which rested on a proper scholarly knowledge of the poet's main works.

In the Manuscript Department of the Lenin Library in Moscow, we find evidence of Ivanov's close scholarly study of the *Divina Commedia*; there is for example a plan of the nine circles of the *Inferno*, and a detailed canto-by-canto summary of the *Purgatorio* and *Paradiso*.[6] These notes and the passages from the *Divina Commedia* which Ivanov has chosen to copy out reveal a particularly strong interest in the *Paradiso* and in the spiritual significance of Dante's light imagery, a theme which finds many echoes in Ivanov's own poetry.

We know that Ivanov lectured on Dante and Petrarch during the first academic year which he spent at the University of Baku from 1920 to 1921.[7] In Ivanov's archive in Moscow, we find the draft of the beginning of a lecture entitled "Dante, Petrarch and Boccaccio";[8] in this draft Ivanov places great emphasis on the importance of Dante for world culture as the creator of the Italian language and of new poetical forms, and describes in detail the historical background to Dante's epoch. We also know that Ivanov introduced an Italian language course for beginners at the University of Baku;[9] one of Ivanov's former students who attended this course, Viktor Andronikovich Manuilov, recalls that Ivanov used the *Vita Nuova* as his basic language teaching text during this course; the students would read aloud and translate from the *Vita Nuova* into Russian, and Ivanov would correct their Italian pronunciation and improve their translation.[10]

Ivanov's scholarly study of Dante was firmly grounded in a close knowledge of Dante's works in the original. Indeed, we can see from Ivanov's unpublished papers that he translated parts of Dante's three major works, the *Vita Nuova*, the *Convivio*, and the *Divina Commedia*. Although none of these translations was in fact ever completed, they are nevertheless extremely important projects and testify to the closeness of Ivanov's knowledge of Dante's works.

In 1910 the publisher M. V. Sabashnikov decided to start a new series entitled *Monuments of World Literature* (*Pamjatniki mirovoj literatury*); the plan for the series shows that Dante was to be represented among its authors.[11] In 1911 Ivanov agreed to translate Aeschylus's tragedies for this series.[12] Two years later, in a business letter to M. V. Sabashnikov, Ivanov mentioned that he would be interested in doing some more translations for the series, and not just in the sphere of classical literature; Ivanov wrote that he would for example be happy to translate at some point the *Purgatorio*, and particularly the *Paradiso*, as well as the *Vita Nuova*.[13] The outcome of this suggestion was a contract which Ivanov signed in Rome on April 21, 1913, committing himself to completing his translations of Aeschylus's tragedies, of poems by Sappho, and of Dante's *Vita Nuova* within the next two years.[14]

Ivanov did not, however, keep to this deadline. Four years later, in an autobiographical letter dated January–February 1917, he wrote that his main current occupation was working on his translations of Aeschylus's tragedies and of Dante's *Vita Nuova* [*SS*, II, 22]. It is not clear whether Ivanov ever succeeded in finishing his translation of the *Vita Nuova*, since only fragments of the translation survive.

In 1914 Ivanov published his translation of almost the whole of the third chapter of the *Vita Nuova* in the Moscow journal *Trudy i dni*. Ivanov's translation forms the first part of his celebrated essay "On the Boundaries of Art" (*O granitsakh iskusstva*, 1913) and is the basis on which Ivanov builds up his theory of the esthetics of religious symbolism [*SS*, II, 627–51]. Apart from this passage, the rest of Ivanov's translation was never published, and survives only in the form of unfinished drafts which are located in the Manuscript Department of the Lenin Library in Moscow.[15] These fragments are drawn from five different chapters of the *Vita Nuova*, and include several versions of three sonnets as well as passages of prose. These are prefaced by an introductory note in which Ivanov attempts to set out his own understanding of the nature of Dante's work. The rough drafts of certain sonnets and passages of prose enable one to see the nature of Ivanov's working methods and, in particular, the meticulousness of his attempts to find the right word in Russian for conveying key concepts of medieval philosophy.

The Sabashnikov publishing house was also responsible for the translation of another major work of Dante's, the *Convivio*. This translation was embarked on by a friend of Ivanov's, the philosopher Vladimir Ern. Unfortunately, Ern had only managed to complete the translation of half of the *Convivio*—its first two books—when his work was interrupted by the outbreak of war in 1914.[16] Ern's death in 1917 prevented the continuation of the work, which was never completed. Ern evidently asked Ivanov to translate the poetry in the *Convivio* for him; we find that the canzona which occurs in the first half of the *Convivio*, "Voi che 'ntendendo il terzo ciel movete," is not in Ern's but in Ivanov's translation; the first line of the translation reads "O vy, chei razum dvizhet sferu tret'ju!" The manuscript of Ern's translation of the first two books of the *Convivio*, together with Ivanov's translation of the first canzona of the *Convivio*, are preserved in the Manuscript Department of the Lenin Library.[17] The translation is a finished version; Ivanov's part of it is highly polished and extremely accurate, preserving the images, archaisms and scholastic intricacies of the original with remarkable success.

Finally we come to the question of Ivanov's translation of the

Divina Commedia. We have seen that M. V. Sabashnikov did not take up Ivanov's suggestion that he should translate the *Purgatorio* or the *Paradiso.* Ivanov did not however abandon the idea, and we find that he returned to it again seven years later. On May 12, 1920, Ivanov wrote an official application to the Society of Lovers of Russian Literature (*Obshchestvo ljubitelej rossijskoj slovesnosti*) requesting the society to provide official support for his intention to go abroad in order to finish translating Aeschylus's tragedies, write a monograph on Aeschylus and translate the *Divina Commedia.*[18]

Two days later Ivanov signed a contract with the publishing house Izdatel'skoe Delo byvshee Brokgauz-Efron, in which he committed himself to producing a translation of the *Divina Commedia* in two versions, poetry and prose, by the end of 1923.[19]

It is clear that Ivanov got down to work on his translation immediately. We know from *A Correspondence from Two Corners (Perepiska iz dvukh uglov,* 1921) that Ivanov was translating Dante's *Divina Commedia* while he was staying at a sanatorium near Moscow in June 1920; Ivanov would read out passages of his translation of the *Purgatorio* to his roommate Mikhail Gershenzon, who would check Ivanov's translation against the original text and, if necessary, dispute it.[20]

There is further confirmation of this fact in the notes made by Feyga Kogan on the poetry circle run by Ivanov in Moscow during the summer of 1920. Feyga Kogan records that Ivanov read out some of his recently composed sonnets at a meeting of the poetry circle in June 1920. These sonnets had been written by Ivanov while he was at the sanatorium, and later became part of the cycle entitled "De profundis amavi" [*SS,* III, 574–78]. When Feyga Kogan commented to Ivanov that she sensed a Dantesque influence in one of the sonnets, Ivanov replied that this was not at all surprising since he had always loved Dante and felt a great affinity with him, and was at the present time translating the *Divina Commedia.*[21]

In 1923, in an essay on Dante's fortune in Russia, Ettore Lo Gatto, the pioneer of Slavic studies in Italy who subsequently became a close friend of Ivanov, wrote that Ivanov's translation of the *Purgatorio* was about to be published.[22] When Ivanov left Baku in 1924, he was accompanied on his journey to Moscow by one of his students, Viktor Andronikovich Manuilov. Manuilov recalls very clearly having seen the manuscript of Ivanov's translation of the *Divina Commedia* on a desk in Moscow before Ivanov's departure for Italy.[23]

We have mentioned a number of indications which, when taken together, do suggest that Ivanov had translated the *Divina Commedia* or, at any rate, a substantial portion of it. However, the fact remains that the whereabouts of this translation is not known, and one cannot therefore say with any certainty how much of the work Ivanov was able to complete. The only fragment of the translation which it has been possible to locate is in the Rome archive and consists of the first canto of the *Purgatorio,* written out in Ivanov's hand in a neat, finished version, with only a few corrections.[24] Like Ivanov's other translations from Dante's works, it is of an extremely high standard.

From these examples we can see that Ivanov's approach to Dante was grounded in a thorough knowledge of Dante's works, based on a combination of the academic study and translation of parts of these works. None of the other Symbolists had a remotely comparable knowledge of Dante's works. However, the fact of Ivanov's greater knowledge and understanding of Dante's works is not in itself sufficient to explain the different quality of Ivanov's approach to Dante from that of the other Symbolists. It is only an outer manifestation of the fundamentally intellectual character of Ivanov's approach to Dante on a deeper level. Ivanov was never simply a poet, he was always at the same time an intellectual. It is perhaps for this reason that he became the acknowledged leader and most important theoretician of the religious Symbolists. Because of his academic background, superior learning, and greater intellectual bent, Ivanov sought to provide a definition of the spiritual outlook and esthetics of symbolism in terms of certain intellectual and philosophical concepts drawn from other currents in literary and spiritual history to which he felt that the phenomenon of symbolism was related. It is in this context that Dante became a figure of such importance in Ivanov's spiritual outlook and esthetics. Dante, like Ivanov, was a writer whose mystical vision rested on a complex intellectual and philosophical basis. This inner affinity between Ivanov and Dante was noted by a number of Ivanov's contemporaries, including the religious philosopher Sergey Bulgakov; in an essay written in 1915, Bulgakov dwelt at some length on the strong intellectual element in Ivanov's poetry, and compared Ivanov in this respect to Dante, using the term "poet-thinker" (*poet-myslitel'*) of both writers.[25] This inner affinity is one of the most important factors which caused Ivanov to turn to Dante in the context of his own spiritual searchings, and to find in him such a rich source of guidance and inspiration; Dante's works, and the medieval tradition in general, offered a certain structure of intellectual and philosophical concepts for the comprehension and description of a mystical, spiritual reality; Ivanov felt a similar need to express his mystical intuitions intellectually, and drew on the medieval tradition extensively for the understanding and formulation of many of the elements of his own spiritual outlook and esthetics.

Dante was a natural model for Ivanov to turn to for other more obvious reasons. Dante is the chief poet of Italy, of the Middle Ages, and of the Christian tradition. Ivanov regarded Rome as his spiritual fatherland from the time of his first visit to Italy in 1892,[26] and Italy subsequently became his real fatherland when he emigrated in 1924; Ivanov regarded the Middle Ages as a period in history which exemplified the spiritual and poetic ideals to which he aspired;[27] finally, as a spiritual thinker and poet, Ivanov placed himself firmly within the Christian tradition. For all these reasons, it is natural that Ivanov should have turned to Dante. However, it is important to remember that, as in the case of Ellis and the other Symbolists, Ivanov's approach to Dante is an entirely subjective one; it exists only as part of his general spiritual outlook and cannot be understood outside this context.

Ivanov's approach to Dante reflects the problems which are inherent in his own spiritual outlook, namely the problem of the incorporation of the legacy of pagan classical antiquity into the Christian tradition. This problem is a complex one which cannot be easily resolved; there are certain conflicts and incompatibilities at the heart of Ivanov's world view, and these emerge particularly strongly in the case of his approach to Dante. Ivanov's spiritual ideal

was a form of Christian mysticism based on an endlessly self-renew-
ing cyclical experience of sacrifice and ecstasy, death and resurrection,
which in Ivanov's view constituted the essence of the cult of Dionysus
and the eternal mystical core at the heart of all religious experience.
Ivanov regarded the Middle Ages or early Renaissance as the period
in history which came closest to his own understanding of the mystical nature of the Dionysian religion, and which provided the most
perfect expression of his spiritual ideal.[28] Dante, as the chief representative of the Middle Ages, was naturally regarded by Ivanov as
the main exponent of this ideal.

It is true that the Middle Ages did experience a revival of
interest in pagan antiquity; it was during the Middle Ages that a
permanent place was secured for many Platonic and Aristotelian notions in Latin Christian philosophy. Virgil was regarded as a prophet
of Christianity on the basis of his "Messianic" Fourth Eclogue. This
partial Christianization of pagan antiquity is reflected in Dante's
works; we find that Dante draws on the mythology of classical antiquity as well as on the Bible for illustrations to his arguments; the
great philosophers of classical antiquity are placed by Dante in a
special Limbo on the periphery of the *Inferno,* and Virgil plays an
important role as Dante's guide through Hell and Purgatory. However, within Dante's scheme, there are firmly defined limits to the
place which classical antiquity can occupy in the Christian tradition.
The philosophers of classical antiquity are in the *Inferno* for all eternity and have no hope of revelation;[29] Virgil may have been a prophet,
but he was no participant in the Christian revelation, and could only
serve as Dante's guide as far as the Earthly Paradise; after this point
natural reason can no longer suffice, and Beatrice, enlightened by
divine revelation, must take over.[30]

Ivanov on the other hand sees the Dionysiac religion of classical
antiquity as the mystical *core* of Christianity; he therefore sees in
Dante—a Christian mystical writer—a carrier of the Dionysiac
spirit. Ivanov's desire to synthesize Christianity and the religion of
Dionysus leads him to invest Dante with Dionysiac traits. Indeed,
Ivanov explicitly declares this to be his intention in "Ad Rosam"

[SS, II, 44–50], the opening poem of the last book of *Cor Ardens*, "Rosarium". In this poem, Ivanov makes a plea for the mystical rose of the Middle Ages, which we find in Dante's *Paradiso* to be joined once more to its earthly Hellenic roots.

We can see an example of this tendency in a passage from *The Hellenic Religion of the Suffering God* (*Ellinskaja religija stradajushchego boga*, 1917), in which Ivanov attempts to relate Dante to Dionysus by drawing a direct line from Dionysus, a god who in some of his guises inhabits trees, through Virgil to Dante's description of the souls of the suicides imprisoned in the trees of the dolorous wood in *Inferno* XIII.[31] It is true that Dante based his passage on a similar episode in Virgil's *Aeneid*,[32] but to carry the line back through Virgil from Dante to Dionysus is a clear instance of the distortions to which Ivanov's desire to see Dionysiac elements in Dante can lead. The same association between Dante and Dionysus occurs again in the third part of "To the Poet" (*Poetu*) [SS, II, 358–59], the final poem of the second book of *Cor Ardens*. In this poem Ivanov links Dante's wood to Daphne, who was changed into a laurel; Ivanov had mentioned Daphne in the passage discussed above as one of the masks of Dionysus, and he uses the image in this poem together with that of the wood as illustrations of the Dionysiac meeting between life and death, the source from which poetry is born.

There are two poems in Ivanov's 1904 collection of verse, *Transparency* (*Prozrachnost'*), which reflect the same general tendency to give a Dionysiac coloring to Dantesque images. In one of these poems, "Transcende te ipsum" [SS, I, 782–83], Ivanov uses the biblical figures of Rachel and Leah as symbols of the contemplative and active ways of life; in following this usage, Ivanov is consciously adopting the interpretation given to the figures of Rachel and Leah which was current in the Middle Ages and which was used by Dante in the *Purgatorio* (XXVII.94–108).[33] Ivanov uses the images of Rachel and Leah in this Dantesque sense in order to illustrate two different ways of achieving the Christian ideal of self-transcendence advanced by St. Augustine. However, it is clear that the ideal described by Ivanov is primarily a mystical, Dionysiac ideal rather than a purely Christian one, and that the Christian and Dantesque images which Ivanov has used are given a new Dionysiac meaning within this context.

The second poem, "Gli spiriti del viso" [SS, I, 785], uses a term taken from Dante's *Vita Nuova* (II, 5; XI, 2; XIV, 5), the "spirits of the eyes," translated into Russian as *dukhi glaz*. However, Ivanov does not use this term of medieval physiology in the sense in which it occurs in Dante's text; he uses it in the context of a vision of the Dionysiac mystical essence of the universe, and we find that the *dukhi glaz* lead up to the final revelation in the last line of the poem "That the world is the face of the suffering God" (*Chto mir—oblich'e strazhdushchego Boga*).

The same tendency can be observed in Ivanov's love poetry. The Dionysian ideal of achieving ecstasy through sacrifice is based on a central experience of erotic love.[34] This was revealed to Ivanov through a profound personal experience, his love for Lydia Dmitrievna Zinovieva-Annibal, whose sudden death in 1907 introduced an element of sacrifice into Ivanov's experience of ecstasy.[35] Dante's *Vita Nuova* was an obvious model for the literary expression of an experience of mystical love involving ecstasy and sacrificial death, and in 1908 Ivanov recorded in his diary that the poet Mikhail Kuzmin had suggested to him that he should write an explanatory text in prose, according to the model of Dante's *Vita Nuova,* linking together the canzonas and sonnets of the fourth book of *Cors Ardens,* "Love and Death" (*Ljubov' i smert'*) dedicated to the memory of Lydia Zinovieva-Annibal [SS, II, 772]. Ivanov did not take up the suggestion in this particular form, but he did make extensive use of Dante's *Vita Nuova* and of Petrarch's *Canzoniere* as models for the literary expression of his own spiritual experience. As usual, however, Ivanov infuses Dante with elements of the Dionysiac experience which are alien to Dante; we find that Dante's *Amor* becomes invested with the characteristics of Dionysian eros. We can see an example of this in a poem from the last book of *Cor Ardens,* "Crux Amoris" [SS, II, 492–93]. The poem opens with the line "Amor e cor gentil son una cosa"; this is a slightly amended version of the first line of a sonnet from Chapter XX of the *Vita Nuova.* Ivanov continues to address Dante as a poet to whom the secret of the divine transformation of earthly love and of temporary loss through death was revealed. From the rest of the poem it is clear that the connection between love and death which Ivanov is celebrating in this poem has its deepest roots in the Dionysian cult of death and resurrection, for which the example of Dante's *Vita Nuova* serves only as an illustration.

Ivanov's approach to Dante reflects a typical tendency of the Symbolist age in a highly original and individual form which brings out the complexities of Ivanov's own spiritual outlook. His tremendous interest in Dante as the foremost poet of the Christian tradition conflicted with his attempt to invest Dante with his own Dionysian-inspired mystical version of Christianity.

Notes

1. The quotation from Dante comes from *Purgatorio*, XXVII.88–90. It is given in the form cited by Ivanov on the cover and title page of *Kormchie zvezdy* (St. Petersburg, 1903); see also *SS*, I, 513.

2. Preface to *Kormchie zvezdy* (Carmel, May 1901), Gosudarstvennaya biblioteka SSSR imeni Lenina, Otdel rukopisei (hereafter GBL), *fond* 109. This preface appears in the 1901 proofs of *Kormchie zvezdy* but has not been subsequently published.

3. See Ellis's letters to E. K. Metner, 1907–1914, GBL, *fond* 167, 7–8.

4. Andrei Belyj, "Vospominanija ob Aleksandre Aleksandroviche Bloke," *Zapiski mechtatelej*, 6 (1922), 5–122 (pp. 22–24). Reprinted Letchworth, 1964.

5. Vyacheslav Ivanov, "Avtobiograficheskoe pis'mo S. A. Vengerovu," in *Russkaja literatura XX veka (1890–1910)*, ed. S. A. Vengerov, 3 vols. (Moscow, 1914–1917), III, pp. 81–96. Reprinted in *SS*, II, 5–22.

6. GBL, *fond* 109.

7. N. V. Kotrelev, "Vjach. Ivanov—Professor Bakinskogo Universiteta," *Trudy po russkoj i slavianskoj filologii*, 11, *Literaturovedenie* (1968), 326–339.

8. GBL, *fond* 109.

9. See Kotrelev, p. 327.

10. Conversation with Viktor Andronikovich Manuilov, Leningrad, April 30, 1978.

11. M. V. Sabashnikov, "'Vechnye knigi'—pervonachal'nyj proekt serij 'Pamjatniki mirovoj literatury'" (1910), GBL, *fond* 261, 9/105.

12. M. V. Sabashnikov, Letter to V. I. Ivanov, April 6, 1911, GBL, *fond* 109.

13. Letter to M. V. Sabashnikov, January 20, 1913, GBL, *fond* 261, 4/25.

14. Izdatel'stvo M. i S. Sabashnikovykh, "Dogovor s V. I. Ivanovym," April 21, 1913, GBL, *fond* 261, 8/7.

15. GBL, *fond* 109.

16. See V. F. Ern, Letter to A. S. Glinka, July 14 and August 21, 1914, Tsentral'nyj gosudarstvennyj arkhiv literatury i iskusstva, *fond* 142, 1/313.

17. GBL, *fond* 261, 10/10.

18. GBL, *fond* 207, 32/12.

19. V. Ivanov Archive, Rome. I am very grateful to Dmitry Vyacheslavovich Ivanov and to Lydia Vyacheslavovna Ivanova for showing me the material in V. Ivanov's Rome archive.

20. V. Ivanov and M. O. Gershenzon, *Perepiska iz dvukh uglov* (Petrograd, 1921), pp. 14–15. Reprinted in *SS,* III, 383–415.

21. F. I. Kogan, "A record of V. Ivanov's comments at the meetings of the poetry circle which met under Ivanov's direction from February to August 1920, at the Literary Section of the Moscow State Rhetorical Institute," Typescript notes, dated October 12, 1953; Institut mirovoj literatury i iskusstva, fond 55, 1/6.

22. Ettore lo Gatto, *Saggi sulla cultura russa* (Naples, 1923), p. 169.

23. Conversation with V. A. Manuilov, Leningrad, April 30, 1978.

24. V. Ivanov Archive, Rome.

25. Sergej Bulgakov, *Tikhie dumy* (Moscow, 1918), p. 138.

26. In the poem "Laeta" (*SS,* I, 636–40), composed in 1892 after his first visit to Rome, Ivanov wrote, "Rodine veren, ja Rim rodinoj novoju chtu."

27. See for example the section "Antichnyj idealisticheskij kanon i srednevekovyj misticheskij realizm" in Ivanov's essay, "Dve stikhii v sovremennom simvolizme," first published in 1908 (*SS,* II, 535–61).

28. See Vyacheslav Ivanov, "Ellinskaja religija stradajushchego Boga," *Novyj put',* 2 (1904), 48–78, and "Religija Dionisa," *Voprosy zhizni,* 7 (1905), 122–48.

29. Virgil describes his own situation and that of the other spirits of

Limbo to Dante in the following words: "semo perduti, e sol di tanto offesi /
che sanza speme vivemo in disio" (*Inferno*, IV, 41).

30. See Virgil's parting words to Dante in *Purgatorio*, XXVII. 127–42.

31. Vyacheslav Ivanov, "Ellinskaja religija stradajushchego Boga," *Novyj
put'*, 9 (1904), 47–70.

32. See *Inferno*, XIII, 48, in which Virgil refers to the fact that the scene
of the bleeding twig which Dante has just witnessed was already known to
Dante from Virgil's verses (*Aeneid*. III).

33. See Ivanov's note (*SS*, I, 861) to an earlier reference to Rachel and
Leah in "Sfinks," a long poem written in Dantesque terzinas and included in
Kormchie zvezdy (*SS*, I, 643–60).

34. Vyacheslav Ivanov, "Religija Dionisa," *Voprosy zhizni*, 6 (1905), 187.

35. Vyacheslav Ivanov, "Avtobiograficheskoe pis'mo S. A. Vengerovu,"
SS, II, 20.

Translatio Lauri:
Ivanov's Translations of Petrarch
Lowry Nelson, Jr.

Переводчику

Будь жаворонок нив и пажитей—Вергилий,
Иль альбатрос Бодлэр, иль соловей Верлэн
Твоей ловитвою,—все в чужеземный плен
Не заманить тебе птиц вольных без усилий,

Мой милый птицелов,—и, верно, без насилий
Не обойдешься ты, поэт, и без измен,
Хотя б ты другом был всех девяти Камен,
И зла ботаником, и пастырем идиллий.

Затем, что стих чужой—что скользкий бог Протей:
Не улучить его охватом ни отвагой.
Ты держишь рыбий хвост, а он текучей влагой

Струится и бежит из немощных сетей.
С Протеем будь Протей, вторь каждой маске—маской!
Милей досужий люд своей забавить сказкой.

To the Translator

Lark Virgil of the fields and meadowlands,
Albatross Baudelaire, or nightingale
Verlaine ensnared? Surely alien hands
Cannot entice free birds without travail,

My dear birdcatcher—even though you may refuse,
As poet, to betray, to force amain,
Or though you be the friend of every Muse
And evil's botanist and idyll's swain—

Because it's not your poem: in slippery jet
God Proteus, despite your pluck and flail,
Can flee by flowing through your feeble net

And leave you holding a mere fish's tail.

Be Proteus to Proteus, set mask to mask!
Or else amusing idlers is your proper task.

(Translated by Lowry Nelson, Jr.—brazenly
by way of epigraph.)

Both Francesco Petrarch and Vyacheslav Ivanov were passionate poets, passionate scholars, and passionate believers. Yet both men disciplined themselves through form, through history, and through religion. The positive tensions generated by their individual modes of conceiving and living their lives were, in both, the source and the means of their poetic expression. Parallels could be drawn between their views of scholarship: in the most general terms, they set out to know the past, to understand it, and to retrieve it in some way for the present. For Petrarch, the past was largely ancient Rome and the barely knowable barbarism that succeeded it. For Ivanov— Hellenist, Latinist, historian, and philosopher—the past was naturally much vaster and the range of reference incalculably greater. Yet both found their alpha and omega and their center in eternal Rome, and both as exiles: Petrarch was born in Arezzo in familial exile from Florence and grew up near the exiled Roman Church in Avignon; Ivanov, born in the "third Rome," Moscow, became for the last twenty-five years of his life, an exile in the first and only Rome. It is tempting to dwell on the differences and the ironies of their destinies, but my purpose here is merely to suggest that a large-scale comparison is not incongruous or unfruitful. What brings them together in history is poetry. Though of vastly disparate provenience in time, place, and culture, they share a skill which each practiced in such a way that I am not shy of calling them both great poets. Here, then, are my precise terms of comparison: we have the unusual case of one great lyric poet translating another great lyric poet, and doing so across a gap of some 570 years. My comments and generalizations leave entirely out of account epic and dramatic and didactic poetry, not to mention epyllia, epistles, and the rest: I am concerned with lyric poetry and its translation into lyric poetry. Both the greatness of the poets Petrarch and Ivanov and the greatness of the gap of time are thus to me unusual and remarkable.

As the first lyric poet to be translated Petrarch has had an extraordinary impact on the whole enterprise of poetic translation itself. When did it begin? Almost automatically one thinks of Catallus' translation-with-a-difference of Sappho, but can one think of any other lyric instances before the Renaissance? It is one of those obvious questions which no one I know of has before now even asked. Implicit in the question itself is the need to define "translation," as distinct from "version," "imitation," and "re-elaboration,"not to mention matters like form, content, influence, and whatever else enters into this kind of intertextuality. But I arbitrarily invoke, for my present purposes, the rule of rigor, with enough play to make the game interesting. If it be granted that there is such a thing as translation and that it properly aspires to fidelity, the questions that seem central are these: Who does it and how? Who reads it and why? And, What relation does it bear to its original? I would say, simply, that it takes a poet to translate a poem, that the poet-translator must know the language from which he is translating, and that equivalent or reasonably modified formal patterns should be observed. These are of course sticking points, since Ezra Pound's example, for Anglo-American aspirants who all too often take ego-trips on another poet's ticket, usually in a now-dated Modernistic vein, but now and then also in the old fake-antique vein. The question of *how* translators do it may for the moment be deferred or perhaps reverently referred to their several muses. It is an act of craft or art. The first readers are naturally the poet-translators themselves, who must sense an affinity, a challenge, and a peculiar sort of inspiration. Translations of lyrics, though, are usually offered to a readership without a knowledge of the original in its own native idiom. On the most pragmatic level, the translation is supposed to give a feeling (notion-emotion) of what the original is *like*. That is a modest and proper goal. English idiom is here peculiar, and differs from any other language I know: What is it like? is the form of a question we ask on all sorts of occasions. Not *How is it?* But *What is it like?* We are asking for a comparison, a simulacrum, a simile, a metaphor perhaps, or even a symbol. And what could be more challenging to our powers of equivalence and analogy or to our poetic imaginations? In ordinary speech our responses are often trite, but in formal verse translation the tension between fidelity and equivalence is acutely focused. A successful translator should be able to say to the reader, in effect, This is *not* the original, this is not a plain-prose rendering, this is not an imitation or a version or a set of variations, but simply, That is what it's like. Granted then that there is an original poem and a poetic translation of it into another language, my last general question is, What relation do the two texts bear to each other? First, they are both poems and can be read and enjoyed and evaluated quite separately. Their separateness is, for better or worse, one of the staple assumptions of national literary histories. The versions or translations of Petrarch produced by, say, Sir Thomas Wyatt or Joachim du Bellay are sometimes not even acknowledged as such or if they are so acknowledged they are seldom compared with their originals. Such a comparison might seem merely the province of a pedant or a comparatist. That there is something positive about this I would not deny: the translations are correctly, however partially, viewed as poems in their own right.

Currently there is a general linguistic and practical concern with translation within various contexts: comparative syntax and contrastive grammar; construction of computerized translating machines; and official political and diplomatic conventions of equivalence. In the West there has been only sporadic concern with theory of translation as related to practice; some major monuments would be the essays of Friedrich and August Wilhelm Schlegel on Ludwig Tieck's translation of *Don Quixote,* the pronouncements and practice of Ezra Pound, the volumes *The Craft and Context of Translation* (1961) edited by William Arrowsmith and Roger Shattuck and *On Translation* (1966) edited by Reuben Brower, the views of Vladimir Nabokov as elaborated in his multifarious edition of Pushkin's *Evgenij Onegin,* and such a specialized yet theoretically grounded work as Anna Kay France's *Boris Pasternak's Translations of Shakespeare* (1978). Elsewhere, especially in the Soviet Union, unusual attention has been paid to the theory of literary translation by such notable practitioners as Elfim Etkind and Korney Chukovsky, who not only theorize, but also minutely and interestingly evaluate and often masterfully ex-emplify. I know of no attempt, however, to consider and evaluate Ivanov's translations of Petrarch. In my own sketch of a theory, I first fix boundaries of definition by setting apart the otherwise es-timable enterprises of paraphrase, imitation, re-elaboration, and par-ody (sacred or profane). Poetic translation, in my view, attempts to transmute into the target language as much of the content and the form of the original as a translator possibly can. His task is literally a kind of re-presentation or, in terms of painting, a copying of the original. The ruling principle is fidelity. The operational principle is equivalence. In translation, as distinct from other forms of inter-textuality, a sonnet should be rendered as a sonnet, an ode as an ode, a rimed poem as a rimed poem. The level of language should be matched. But it would be quite unreasonable to demand that in some mechanical way nouns should be rendered as nouns or adjectives as adjectives or verbs as verbs, even within the Indo-European family of languages. Casting a Petrarchan sonnet in a Shakespearean mold seems to me within the bounds of fidelity. Where a poem has marked alliteration, marked assonance may do. For a hendecasyllabic line a pentameter may be more natural. A general pattern of caesura or enjambment may be honored generally. My principles might well be denounced as too binding and prescriptive, yet a free-for-all is not translation: it can go its own way and find another label.

Since I shall make judgments as to success or value, I should be explicit in naming possible, even actual dilemmas. It has been wittily observed that a good poem which is a translation of a poor poem is by that fact a poor translation: it has violated the principle of fidelity. Balmont's brilliant translations of Edgar Allen Poe are, then, failures as much as is Baudelaire's ridiculous "Peace Pipe" extract from H. W. Longfellow's *Song of Hiawatha*. The usual situ-ation is, of course, quite different: the translator aims at approxi-mating an impossible target and may, with luck, come close; he could only succeed under J. L. Borges's dispensation for the utterly unique Louis Ménard. More to the point is the following pedestrian scheme of permutations: a good translation of a good poem; a poor translation of a good poem; a good translation of a poor poem; a poor translation of a poor poem. Fortunately these extreme and schematic possibilities are narrowed by my insistence that both Petrarch and Ivanov are great poets, not day in and day out perhaps, but the level is high. Ivanov, in his translations, always plays the game of translating Petrarch according to the rules and definitions I have proposed. If he falls short as translator, he does so on his and our terms.

Writing a poem of one's own is a remarkably complex process: it involves language with a history, a tradition of usage, a host of predecessors, an awareness and multiple sorts of self-awareness, a gift of craft, a flash or flashes of inspiration, and hard labor. Poets almost always revise and rework and even recast. Every change reverberates through the whole poem; every change requires adjustment of other elements, or, alternatively, the other elements conspire to force the change. Besides, the result may be more likely poor than good. In translating someone else's poem a writer must necessarily adopt some sort of allegiance or fidelity to an *original* and in doing so he naturally restricts his range of choices. Revising and recasting, which for an "original" poet can be sources of fresh, unexpected inspiration, are for the translator like the feats of a straitjacketed escape artist. He can of course give up approximating the target and settle for a version, an imitation, or a parody—but that becomes a different matter. Yet I would insist that the translator is also a poet with his own linguistic historical repertory. Before examining the nature of Ivanov's translations and versions of Petrarch I shall attempt briefly to characterize the peculiar, native, free-valenced lyrical strain in each one.

Petrarch has, in my view, great limitations as a poet. His range, though spanning life and eternity, is nonetheless rather narrow in its moods and insights. He is a poet of love and conscience, of sensuousness and asceticism, of political passion and spiritual anxiety. Generally he qualifies and mutes his contrasts and outbursts. He is incapable, at one extreme, of solemn grandeur and, at the other extreme, of playful wit or humor. He is never sublime or witty.

Yet he can evoke both pathos and joy. Though he often laments to the point of querulousness, he is at times successful in expressing quietly a moving quiet irony. This irony, this understated plaint or elation is, I think, his greatest gift of expression. He can indeed compose a masterpiece, though there are not 366 masterpieces in his *Canzoniere*. No poet has ever had that luck. Perhaps also no poet has ever so boldly challenged the reader to savor and judge quality as did Petrarch in stringing so many poems into an ambiguous continuity and equality of setting. As inheritor and progenitor of the most durable lyric strain in history, he caught up in his work aspects of Provençal and Siculo-Tuscan poetry and became himself the model and motive for about three succeeding centuries. For the lyric his place is as crucial as Virgil's is for the epic. On the bad side, he unwittingly spawned a school of tyros and poetasters as well as emulators and reactors. That Russian literature had no Renaissance such as in the West was in some ways a blessing as well as a handicap. Ivanov, scholar-poet, could set out on his own to recover in an original way an older past that, unlike the Enlightenment and Romanticism, never really happened in Russia.

Ivanov had, however, the resources of Old Slavonic and the language and example of Derzhavin and Pushkin, as well as the fully ripened fruits of Western European poetry since Dante and Petrarch. (Obviously, for my limited purpose, I leave out any consideration of Ivanov's profound involvement with ancient Greece.) Long before he published in 1915 his translations of 27 sonnets from Petrarch's *Canzoniere*, Ivanov had mastered the sonnet to a degree and in a plenitude far surpassing any previous Russian poet. *Pilot Stars (Kormchie zvezdy*, 1903) and *Transparency (Prozrachnost'*, 1904)—his first two collections of poetry which in the complete edition occupy 275 ample pages—contain 49 sonnets in various thematic groupings in the midst of other poems of the greatest formal variety. *Cor Ardens* (1911)—more than 300 pages in the complete edition—contains in its vastness all of 98 sonnets, again in groupings. Indeed, Book Four of *Cor Ardens* is called "Life and Death" and has as its epigraph a passage from Petrarch's first canzone on Laura's death: the parallel is thus explicit between Laura and Lydia Dmitrievna Zinovieva-Annibal. All this original sonneteering precedes the translations from Petrarch, and of course does not bring to an end Ivanov's mastery of the sonnet, as witness his greatest examples of that form in *Evening Light* (*Svet Vechevnij,* 1962), his final and posthumous volume of poems. Quite early, it would seem, Ivanov fashioned for himself a range of style that is astonishing in its suppleness and variety. Much of his poetry is difficult for its compression of grammatically linked words and phrases more than for any syntactical participial involution. In other terms, he takes more artistic advantage of prefixes and suffixes than of periodic sentence structure. Yet in his versification he follows, naturally, the established tradition of Russian syllabotonic poetry, strict in observance of line-length and rime-pattern. This is indeed in considerable contrast to Petrarch's native freedom in the use of apocopation, elision, and synalepha. Oftentimes in Petrarch the sense and sound vie with each other for prominence, as in the sonnet of 23 rivers (no. 148) in which their exotic names flow fluvially into each other. Perhaps the two poets are equal in their syntactic prowess, that is, in the difficulty, the *esthetic* difficulty, they often present on first reading. Lexically they are at once equal and different: equal, in the sense that they both draw on various levels of style and use what may be perceived as unusual, exotic, or archaic words; different, in the sense that Petrarch for us is often truly archaic with respect to modern Italian, while Ivanov often uses words and forms that are Slavonic or obsolete or even dialectal. A finer parallel could be drawn between the two poets and their lexicon, but I save that for my examples instead of generalizing here. Ivanov's style is perhaps more learned than Petrarch's, yet its tonal range is broader. Seldom is Petrarch in the *Canzoniere* hieratically solemn, however insistently contrite and weary of the earthly world. He can be serious, intimate, tender, laconically ironic, and quietly joyful. Ivanov, in his original poetry, stretches the range of Petrarch greatly, from the mystical and rhapsodic at one extreme, to the playfully witty at the other. Both took poetry seriously enough to covet in earnest the laurel or the thyrsis. For the Augustinian Petrarch, heir of a Christianized Plato and cultivator of the moral Romans, lyric poetry was eschatologically *vanitas*. For the Hellenic Catholic Ivanov,

heir to Byzantium and cultivator of Mnemosyne and Dionysus, poetry, as nature, was immanently divine and earthly love and its poetic
memorials were *realia* empowered to lead to *realiora*. Hence a difference in mission and in cultivation of verse. As child of his time,
Petrarch wrote his poems within a figural view of fulfillment of life
in the life after death. For Ivanov, symbolist-realist, this earthly life
is infused and inanimated with divinity, and this life and the life
to come, in their individual embodiment, exist in a fusion for which
the term "symbol" was the most potently descriptive. Though different in "manner, person and style" they share enough traits to
make their compresence on Ivanov's writing-table congenial and momentous. Both were *vates*.

After so many centuries and between two so diverse tongues,
equivalence in key vocabulary becomes a prime criterion for *re*-pre-
sentation. So much of Petrarch's lexicon had become trite, especially
at the hands of his latter-day heirs, the Romantics: beautiful, dear,
sweet, pale, weary; eyes, mouth, hair; love, sorrow, joy, virtue—not
to mention the objects of external nature, such as birds, meadows,
rivers, sun, stars, and moon. But such signifiers are, of course, the
continuing givens of our experience. How to freshen, vary, recast,
or adapt them without traducing sense and subject? Petrarch himself
faced up to this in often avoiding the Provençalisms and Siculisms
of his immediate predecessors. For Ivanov what must have been a
besetting preoccupation was to avoid the shop-worn words and for-
mulas of *his* immediate predecessors in their lyrics of love and death,
nature and introspection, earthly and celestial forms of common
experience—ever new in individuals but ever obsolescing in expression. Nothing like a computer lexicon will do. Love is not love in
all cases of *amore* or *ljubov'*. The Christian words in the Vulgate—
caritas and *dilectio*—became one with pagan Latin *amor,* first in Provençal and then in Italian. But Petrarch inherited both traditions in
his poetry and uses *amore* in ways that Ivanov carefully distinguishes
by using not only *ljubov'* but also *amur* or *bog* or *bog ljubvi* or on one
occasion *kumir* and, on another, omitting translation. That wide-
ranging word *dolore,* and its cognates *duolo* and *doglia,* are variously
rendered by *bol'* (most commonly) and *skorb'*. I think I detect here

a strong tendency to avoid the nouns *gore, pechal'*, and *grust'*, as well as *tomlenie* and *toska* (used once each) and of course *skuka*, as well as their adjectival derivatives. Petrarch's emblematic word *pensero* (modern form, *pensiero*) is rendered either as *dukh* or less commonly as *dumy*. *Smorto* and *impallidire* are inevitably some form of *blednyj*, just as *stanco* is usually *ustalyj*, though once *iznemog*, and once omitted. *Dolce* is almost always forthrightly *sladkij* or (I must say, understandably) either omitted or paraphrased, as in the case where Petrarch contrasts *alcun dolce* with *tanti amari* (57) and Ivanov writes *mëd skupoj* contrasted with *ne sladok pozdnij mëd*. It surely is significant that for *dolce* we seldom find either *milyj* or *nezhnyj* (though in other connections these words do rarely appear). Such instances as these could be multiplied, yet to do so would run the risk of distorting the translator's task, which is of course not simply to render noun by noun and adjective by adjective. What I hope to have shown in this preliminary comparison is that Ivanov has taken some care to break out of conventionalized nineteenth-century equivalencies like those familiar to English-readers in versions of Rossetti and his epigones working in the wake of the great English Romantics.

It should come as no surprise that Ivanov does not equally succeed in all of his 27 translations from Petrarch. In a more ample context it would be a worthy and enlightening enterprise to take up each sonnet in turn and mark their qualities, deficiencies, remodelings, and misses. I feel my own understanding and enjoyment of *both* poets have been greatly enhanced by my private and fairly exhaustive study of these texts. What I propose, within narrower public bounds, is to choose—I trust not tendentiously—a few whole poems and passages for the purpose of showing high achievement, honorable failure, local triumphs, some free variations, and a few clashes of sensibility.

First I consider Ivanov's translation of Sonnet 156, which in the original has a certain sustained rapture and gentle solemnity but which in Russian takes on something like a Rossettian or early Yeatsian, indeed a pre-Raphaelite, portentousness. Petrarch, in this sonnet, celebrates the harmony of his beloved's demeanor on earth that reflected her heavenly origin and destination. Terrestrial nature was so hushed by the harmonious heavens that not a leaf stirred. The first quatrain goes thus:

> I saw on earth angelic ways and heavenly beauties unique in the world, such that remembering pleases and pains me, for whatever I look upon seems dreams, shadows and vapors [smokes].

> I' vidi in terra angelici costumi
> e celesti bellezze al mondo sole,
> tal che di rimembrar mi giova e dole,
> ché quant'io miro par sogni, ombre e fumi.

Ivanov singles out for his exordium the sense of the word "dole" (which is coupled in the original with its antithesis "giova") and makes from the attributive "angelici" an actual substantivized angel twice mentioned in the first three lines. "Celesti bellezze" is omitted; "dreams" become "a dream"; "shadows" become "a cloud of charms"; and "fumi" or "vapors" are either subsumed by "cloud" or are simply omitted. (One learns by the way what a trial to the poet is the English word "smoke" and its plural.) The classical echo of phrases like "pulvis et umbra" or "umbra, cinis, nihil" is lost in the selective questioning: was it a dream? or a cloud?

> Ja litsezrel nebesnuju pechal',
> Grust' angela v edinstvennom javelen'e.
> To son li byl? No angela mne zhal'.
> Il' oblak char? No sladko umilen'e.

(I beheld heavenly sorrow, an angel's sadness in a singular vision. Was it a dream? But I grieved for the angel. Or a cloud of charms? But sweet was the emotion.)

And the manner continues, as in the second pair of lines in the second quatrain. Petrarch's words are simple and his hyperbole traditional:

> e udi' sospirando dir parole
> che farian gire i monti e stare i fiumi.

(And I heard words spoken sighing that would make mountains move and rivers stay.)

In considerable contrast, Ivanov, with languorous elaboration, adds and ornaments:

> Krotkikh ust molen'e,
> chto val skovat' moglo b i sdvinut' dal',—
> iznemoglo, istajalo v tomlen'e.

(The supplication of her gentle lips, which could fetter the billow and shift distance, grew faint, melted with lassitude.)

Perhaps in an effort to shun triteness and at the same time to fulfill his uncharacteristic scheme of easy, mostly grammatical, rimes, Ivanov chooses to be consistent in his fin-de-siècle and mannered rendition. Petrarch ends his poem with great artistic control, describing the stillness of heaven and earth in which "no leaf on a bough could be *seen* to move." In Ivanov we read:

> i vozdukh byl raznezhen eju—stol',
> chto ni listka v vetviakh ne shelokhnulos'.

Petrarch's breathless silence and immobility suggest, inappropriately, to Ivanov all those Romantic rustlings and murmurings we *hear* with crashing frequency in his immediate and earlier predecessors.

For the reasons I have given, Sonnet 156 in its Russian vesture is a fascinating failure. It is a good example of what many poets of Ivanov's generation, both in Russia and elsewhere in Europe and in America, coped with in their practice and in some splendid instances—Yeats, Pound, Rilke, Blok, and Ivanov—overcame on their way to a less edulcorated new style that we may now call Modernism. It is also a good example of Ivanov's own independence, however wilful, in confronting and transmuting his brother poet. There are notable examples of intriguing failures of fidelity also in a few translations that in effect "out-Petrarch" Petrarch at his most mannered. In one of Petrarch's most imitated sonnets (199) he addresses with fancy fervor that most metonymically coveted appendage, the female hand:

> O bella man che mi destringi 'l core
> e 'n poco spazio la mia vita chiudi . . .

(O beautiful hand that grips my heart and encloses my life in such little space . . .)

That hand is an artwork on which nature and heaven have lavished every skill. The fingers are orient pearls that, naked, can "enrich" when they are not probing love's wounds. Even the white glove that covers the coveted hand is dear as a token he has snatched; it makes him wish he had also some of her veil. But such is the inconstancy of life that this is theft and he must be deprived. One might irreverently call this a pretty poem and wonder idly about the *other* hand. It is trivial and at the same time a bit solemn, a combination that had enormous and continuous vogue for five or six centuries: let me call it "proto-baroco-rococo." Ivanov cannot resist further prettifying the poem, but to his credit he adds a touch of sly drama and humor of which Petrarch was temperamentally incapable. Reference to the inconstancy of life is simply dropped and supplanted with an airy exclamation "In vain! The brief delight is over: the culprit must return his booty":

> Votshche! Nastal konets uslady kratkoj:
> Vernut' dobychu dolzhen likhodej.

Even this slight poem in its Russian version is a worthy cultural appropriation: it contains and emblematizes with inventive grace a whole long European tradition of coy clever poetry from the Alexandrians to Petrarch and his imitators down to polished album verse of the nineteenth century. Suffice it to cite, along that way, Romeo's words of wonder:

> See how she leans her cheek upon her hand!
> O that I were a glove upon that hand,
> That I might touch that cheek!

But to follow this would conjure up the *blason* and all its precious body-parts.

A considerable achievement of Petrarch in the sonnet was to make its slender and articulated form capable of dramatized passion. His means are often visions, some dialogue, and understatement or Petrarchan irony. Sonnet 336 is an especially interesting example in that the dialogue goes on inside his own mind, in that the vision is presented as a memory and not an outward fiction or allegory, and in that the crushing reality of her death takes the form of the dry, spare, precise citation of its hour and date. In paraphrase the poem goes thus:

> She returns to my mind (whence Lethe cannot banish her) just as I saw her in flower lit up with the rays of her star. I see her as in our first meeting, pure, lovely, solitary, and demure. I cry, "It is she, still alive!" and beg the gift of her sweet speech. Sometimes she answers, sometimes not. As if coming to my senses I tell my mind, "You are deceived; you know that her blessed soul left her body at the first hour on April 6, 1348."

It is something of a stroke of genius to versify the calendar. Ivanov shows in his fine translation that he deeply respects the tone and modality of Petrarch's poem, occasionally heightening and condensing, yet observing essential fidelity. The solemnity of Petrarch's interruptive parenthesis on Lethe in the first quatrain is naturalized in a normal flow of syntax and rendered forceful by the word *neprestannoj*. The sequence of typical adjectives in the second quatrain is summarized creatively:

> dushoju obajannoj
> Lovlju v chertakh zastenchivost' priveta.

(In my captivated mind I catch in her features a shyness in greeting.)

The word "greeting" does not occur in the original, but it is latent in Petrarch's world of the beloved's momentous *saluto-salute*. And she does speak later, most mysteriously, as would a memory:"Talor risponde e talor non fa motto" (at times she answers and at times says not a word). Ivanov here heightens the necessarily imprecise memory: "Poroj molchit,—poroju . . ." (at times she is silent, at times . . .). The phrase falters movingly. Again, in this first tercet, Ivanov condenses the lightly sententious lines of Petrarch,

> i', come uom ch'erra e poi più dritto estima,
> dico a la mente mia . . .

(I, like one who errs and then reckons more justly, say to my mind . . .),

into a heightening of the mental state from a wandering brought back along the straight and narrow path to a raptness or even intoxication followed by regaining sober consciousness. Ivanov invents the phrase "Serdtsu dorog / Takoj vostorg" and continues:

> A posle, kak ot khmelja
> Ochnuvshijsja, skazhu: "Znaj, obmanula
> Tebja mechta.

"The dream-vision has deceived you" as compared to Petrarch's phrase, "I say to my mind: thou art deceived." The final lines in Petrarch would translate: "You know that in 1348, the sixth day of April, at the first hour, that blessed soul issued from the body":

> Sai che 'n mille trecento quarantotto,
> il dì sesto d'aprile, in l'ora prima,
> del corpo uscìo quell'anima beata.

To put that into another language without sounding like a bureaucrat or anchor-man is a greater achievement than may seem plausible to those who have not had the often hopeless and thankless experience of a poet-translator. Ivanov manages to naturalize that dry direct simplicity, using the customary three rimes in the sestet: dorog / sorok, khmelja / aprelja, and obmanula / usnula. The last sentence reads:

> V tysjacha trista sorok
> Os'mom godu, v chas pervyj, v den' aprelja
> Shestyj—mezh nas blazhennaja usnula.

This is the sort of triumph a translator must keep to himself or share only with those in the know. As a whole this sonnet radiates and resonates authentically and artistically in its Russian glow and echo.

At times, between these two systems of texts, there is something like an antiphonal correspondence from two corners: dissonance that resolves into harmony; a musical "third" that rings true; a coincidence of perfect pitch; or even a cadence that improves. In tone, as I have said, Ivanov's range is wider than Petrarch's: he can be more intensely passionate and truly witty; he can more easily avoid insistent complaint and near bathos. For example, Petrarch's lovely sonnet (190) "Una candida cerva sopra l'erba / verde"—also well known from Wyatt's very free adaptation "Whoso list to hunt, I know where is an hind"—relates the appearance of a golden-horned doe with a necklace inscribed in diamonds and topazes: "Let no one touch me; it pleased Caesar to set me free." After so dazzling a vision and so enigmatic a motto, the poet fell into the water and the doe disappeared:

> Et era 'l sol già volto al mezzo giorno,
> gli occhi miei stanchi di mirar, non sazi,
> quand'io caddi ne l'acqua, et ella sparve.

This is very close to bathos, if I am not mistaken, though the poet's sudden plunge, presumably in full dress, can be of course attenuated by pious commentary. Ivanov in his translation shows great discretion. *His* poet is said to "forget all" in his enchantment and a hint of danger or violence is added in the phrase "Ne ran'!" that follows the canonical "Ne tron' menja!" Besides, the doe is called a "splendid-headed wanderer on magical shores" whose "collar of diamantine words was sparkling on her neck." By such added enhancement Ivanov suffuses a fairytale atmosphere. The fall thus can become delicately mythic as it is circumstantial in the last lines:

> No ne byl syt moj vzor, kogda v rechnye
> Zatony ja upal—i skrylas' lan'.

(But my gaze was not sated when into the river eddies I fell, and the doe vanished.)

Yet on the other hand some fine touches of Petrarch's laconic irony go unacknowledged in the Russian texts of these poems. In Sonnet 285 Petrarch celebrates the tender and solicitous tutelage he receives from his beloved in heaven to keep him on the right path, and he does so with a continuous rhetorical sweep that leads up to the climactic last line:

> E sol quant'ella parla ò pace o tregua.

(And only so long as she speaks do I have peace or truce.)

The word "tregua" (truce) is more than a pleonasm or afterthought; it gently or ironically reminds us that on earth peace is never a permanent state. Ivanov chooses to render "l'alma," which has in Petrarch its religious sense, as both "dukh" and "serdtse," and expands the single Italian line to two:

> I mir mne dan s molitvoj legkokryloj,
> kogda svjataja serdtsu govorit.

(And peace is given me with light-winged prayer when the blessed one speaks to my heart.)

In this otherwise admirable and welcome rendition the most delicate effect is, for whatever reason of craft, lost. Likewise in Sonnet 364, which comes just before the last sonnet and the final canzone directed in prayer to the Virgin, the humble supplication to God in the conclusion undergoes in the Russian version a change in tone. Indeed Ivanov heightens the mood of repentance throughout the poem. Petrarch's final lines are thus:

> Signor che 'n questo carcer m'ài rinchiuso
> tramene salvo da li eterni danni,
> ch' i' conosco 'l mio fallo e non lo scuso.

(Lord who hast enclosed me in this prison, draw me from it safe from eternal ills, for I know my guilt and do not excuse it.)

It is late contrition, end of the whole drama of the *Canzoniere,* for which he tallies his sins and waits in hope for God's absolving grace. In Russian, however, it takes on a rather Dostoevskian tone or, perhaps more accurately, a Davidian tone echoing the Book of Psalms, and thus more Old than New Testament:

> k tebe moj vopl' iz sej temnitsy strastnoj,
> gde ty menja zamknul, i chrez ogni
> vvedi v Svoj raj tropoju bezopasnoj!

(But mark my cry to Thee from this suffering prison where you enclosed me, and through fires lead me to Thy paradise by a safe way.)

Petrarch's tone of utter humility, which cannot of course in any way *demand* God's grace, becomes a cry *de profundis,* with almost a touch of Christopher Marlowe's Doctor Faustus, for safe-conduct through Purgatory to Paradise. Here there is a notable dissonance of tone between the two poems. To put it more positively, these are two poems whose differences are as interesting as their resemblances.

A true chiming of both poets occurs with Sonnet 312, my last example. In a long enumeration of the attractive shows of nature and of mortal life, Petrarch leads up to the sad reality that the beloved has buried them all for him, since she was his light and mirror. The last three lines are movingly measured in the understated irony he found consolatory.

> Noia m'è 'l viver sì gravosa e lunga
> ch' i' chiamo il fine per lo gran desire
> di riveder cui non veder fu 'l meglio.

(For me living is an anguish so burdensome and prolonged that I call out for the end in my great desire to see her again, *not* seeing whom had been best.)

The sense is not easy to render exactly; it is, with its own emotional exactitude, appropriately *uneasy.* (Latin usage, in proverbial and sententious utterances, is the model here.) In his beautiful translation

Ivanov achieves true artistic fidelity and yet retains a measure of creative independence, as exemplified here in his final tercet:

> Zhizn' odnozvuchna. Zrelishche unylo.
> Lish' v smerti vnov' uvizhu to, chego
> Mne luchshe b nikogda ne videt' bylo.

(Life is monotonous. Its pageant is melancholy. Only in death will I see again that which it would have been better for me never to see.)

English idiom allows this slightly uncommon rendering of the tenses. The present in the past is normal in Russian, and gives a fairly close approximation of the original Italian. Petrarch is not saying flatly that it would have been better if he had never seen his beloved at all. He is, in classical idiom, stressing the pain of loss sustained over so many years and the even greater desire to see her, if possible, again and forever. "Noia" suggested to Ivanov not its true archaic meaning of "anguish" but rather its modern meaning of "boredom" or "nuisance." Yet he chose the right word by his lights: "odnozvuchna." The usual modern equivalence, "skuchna," would have perhaps inappropriately evoked shades of Pechorin and Onegin. "Zrelishche unylo," though not exact, is proper in the context of the whole poem. Petrarch's "gran desire" goes unrendered, but it is there implicitly. Most important of all, the sense and tone live viably in the Russian words. When free, as in other places I have not mentioned, Ivanov's version has its own further function as a mediation of traditions. But that is a very complex matter for which neither the present context nor the present writer is adequate.

Ivanov as Russian Petrarchist came far too late to found a lineage. Yet he succeeded in showing once again, in these 27 Russified sonnets from the Tuscan master, how vital his sense of poetic mission was: to retain and renew memory and make Mnemosyne, mother of the Muses, respond to his artful, mediated invocations. The scholar-historian reconstructs and interprets the past, recovering it from dormancy and oblivion and freshening it for new contemplation. The poet or poet-translator weaves himself a pattern from and among the patterns already in the fabric of memory and so changes and re-orders it, however slightly. Both Petrarch and Ivanov as profoundly religious men were, above all, concerned with anagoge, the escha-tological way to God; but that way can pass by and through poetry and can be known through presage and memory. For Ivanov, Pe-trarch's "cult" of the laurel was "revolutionary." It was something of which Petrarch himself was in no way aware. To quote from Ivanov's essay on "Il lauro nella poesia del Petrarca" (1933):

> [In Petrarch's love poetry] for the first time Parnassus is completely separated from religion, for never in the ancient world was it set up in opposition as a sovereign, independent, intellectualist realm, nor had the separatism of art ever been previously so radically asserted. No retraction [such as Petrarch made] could any longer deprive humanism of its charter of freedoms, its privilege of hav-ing, on the same footing as any religion, a paradise of its own.

Perhaps there is a touch of mischief in Ivanov's summation: it is a high tribute in the name of poetry and secular learning, but it might well have given Petrarch, so pious and yet so anxious to become *laureatus,* both pang and pleasure and made him burn in ice and freeze in fire. Both poets are now, we trust, in the same true Par-adise, beyond all passion and repentance, beyond earthly schism and syncretism. For us, the heirs of their common humanism, it is, I hope, an instructive pleasure to overhear their parnassian colloquy in these sonnets in the paradisiacal region of our own memorial poetic minds.

*   *   *

Sonnets Cited

156

I' vidi in terra angelici costumi
e celesti bellezze al mondo sole,
tal che di rimembrar mi giova e dole,
ché quant'io miro par sogni, ombre e fumi;

e vidi lagrimar que' duo bei lumi
ch'àn fatto mille volte invidia al sole,
et udi' sospirando dir parole
che farian gire i monti e stare i fiumi.

Amor, senno, valor, pietate e doglia
facean piangendo un più dolce concento
d'ogni altro che nel mondo udir si soglia,

ed era il cielo a l'armonia sì intento,
che non se vedea in ramo mover foglia:
tanta dolcezza avea pien l'aere e'l vento!

199

O bella man che mi destringi 'l core
e 'n poco spazio la mia vita chiudi,
man ov' ogni arte e tutti loro studi
poser natura e 'l ciel per farsi onore;

di cinque perle oriental colore,
e sol ne le mie piaghe acerbi e crudi,
diti schietti soavi, a tempo ignudi,
consente or voi, per arricchirme, Amore.

Candido, leggiadretto e caro guanto,
che copria netto avorio e fresche rose,
chi vide al mondo mai sì dolci spoglie?

Così avess' io del bel velo altrettanto!
O inconstanzia de l' umane cose:
pur questo è furto, e vien ch' i' me ne spoglie.

156

Я лицезрел небесную печаль,
Грусть ангела в единственном явленье.
То сон ли был? Но ангела мне жаль.
Иль облак гар? Но сладко умиленье.

Затмили слезы двух светил хрусталь
Светлейший Солнца. Кротких уст моленье,
Что вал сковать могло б и сдвинуть даль,—
Изнемогло, истаяло в томленье.

Все—добродетель, мудрость, нежность, боль—
В единую гармонию сомкнулось,
Какой земля не слышала дотоль.

И ближе небо, внемля ей, нагнулось;
И воздух был разнежен ею—столь,
Что ни листка в ветвях не шелохнулось.

199

Прекрасная рука! Разжала ты
И держишь сердце на ладони тесной.
Я на тебя гляжу, дивясь небесной
Художнице столь строгой красоты.

Продолговато-вежные персты
Прозрачней перлов Индии чудесной,
Вершители моей судьбины крестной,
Я вижу вас в сиянье наготы.

Я завладел ревнивою перчаткой!
Кто, победитель, лучший взял трофей?
Хвала, Амур! А ныне ты ж украдкой

Фату похить иль облаком развей!..
Вотще! Настал конец услады краткой:
Вернуть добычу должен лиходей.

336

Tornami a mente, anzi v' è dentro, quella
ch' indi per Lete esser non po sbandita,
qual io la vidi in su l' età fiorita
tutta accesa de' raggi di sua stella;

sì nel mio primo occorso onesta e bella
veggiola, in sé raccolta e sì romita,
ch' i' grido: «Ell' è ben dessa, ancor è in vita»,
e 'n don le cheggio sua dolce favella.

Talor risponde e talor non fa motto;
i', come uom ch' erra e poi più dritto estima,
dico a la mente mia: «Tu se' 'ngannata:

sai che 'n mille trecento quarantotto,
il dì sesto d' aprile, in l' ora prima,
del corpo uscìo quell' anima beata».

190

Una candida cerva sopra l' erba
verde m' apparve, con duo corna d' oro,
fra due riviere, all' ombra d' un alloro,
levando 'l sole a la stagione acerba.

Era sua vista sì dolce superba
ch' i' lasciai per seguirla ogni lavoro,
come l'avaro che 'n cercar tesoro
con diletto l' affanno disacerba.

«Nessun mi tocchi» al bel collo d' intorno
scritto avea di diamanti e di topazi,
«libera farmi al mio Cesare parve».

Et era 'l sol già volto al mezzo giorno;
gli occhi miei stanchi di mirar, non sazi,
quand'io caddi ne l' acqua, et ella sparve.

336

Я мыслию лелею непрестанной
Ее, чью тень отнять бессильна Лета,
И вижу вновь ее в красе расцвета,
Родной звезды восходом осиянной.

Как в первый день, душою обаянной
Ловлю в чертах застенчивость привета.
«Она жива,—кричу,—как в оны лета!»
И дара слов молю из уст желанной.

Порой молчит,—порою... Сердцу дорог
Такой восторг!.. А после, как от хмеля
Очнувшийся, скажу: «Знай, обманула

Тебя мечта! В тысяча триста сорок
Осьмом году, в час первый, в день апреля
Шестый—меж нас блаженная уснула».

190

Лань белая на зелени лугов,
В час утренний, порою года новой,
Промеж двух рек, под сению лавровой,
Несла, гордясь, убор златых рогов.

Я все забыл, и не стремить шагов
Не мог (скупец, на все труды готовый,
Чтоб клад добыть!)—за ней, пышноголовой
Скиталицей волшебных берегов.

Сверкала вязь алмазных слов на вые:
«Я Кесарем в луга заповедные
Отпущена. Не тронь меня! Не рань!..»

Полдневная встречала Феба грань;
Но не был сыт мой взор, когда в речные
Затоны я упал—и скрылась лань.

285

Né mai pietosa madre al caro figlio
né donna accesa al suo sposo diletto
diè con tanti sospir, con tal sospetto,
in dubbio stato sì fedel consiglio,

come a me quella che 'l mio grave esiglio
mirando dal suo eterno alto ricetto
spesso a me torna co l' usato affetto,
e di doppia pietate ornata il ciglio,

or di madre or d' amante; or teme or arde
d'onesto foco, e nel parlar mi mostra
quel che 'n questo viaggio fugga o segua,

contando i casi de la vita nostra,
pregando ch' a levar l' alma non tarde:
e sol quant'ella parla ò pace o tregua.

364

Tennemi Amor anni ventuno ardendo
lieto nel foco e nel duol pien di speme;
poi che Madonna e 'l mio cor seco inseme
saliro al ciel, dieci altri anni piangendo;

omai son stanco e mia vita reprendo
di tanto error, che di vertute il seme
à quasi spento, e le mie parti estreme,
alto Dio, a te devotamente rendo,

pentito e tristo de' miei sì spesi anni:
che spender si deveano in miglior uso,
in cercar pace ed in fuggir affanni.

Signor che 'n questo carcer m'ài rinchiuso
Tramene salvo da li eterni danni,
ch' i' conosco 'l mio fallo e non lo scuso.

285

Не слышал сын от матери родной,
Ни муж любимый от супруги нежной
С такой заботой, зоркой и прилежной,
Преподанных советов: злой виной

Не омрачать судьбы своей земной,—
Какие, малодушный и мятежный,
Приемлю я от той, что, в белоснежный
Одета свет, витает надо мной

В двойном обличье: матери и милой.
Она трепещет, молит и горит,
К стезе добра влечет и нудит силой,—

И, ей подвигнут, вольный дух парит;
И мир мне дан с молитвой легкокрылой,
Когда святая сердцу говорит.

364

Лет трижды семъ повинен был гореть я,
Амуров раб, ликуя на костре.
Она ушла,—я дух вознес горе.
Продлится ль плач за грань десятилетья?

Страстей меня опутавшую сеть я
Влачить устал. Подумать о добре
Давно пора. Твоей, господь, заре
Я старости вручаю перволетья!

Зачем я жил? На что растратил дни?
Бежал ли я змеи греха ужасной?
Искал ли я Тебя? Но помяни

К Тебе мой вопль из сей темницы страстной,
Где Ты меня замкнул, и чрез огни
Введи в Свой рай тропою безопасной!

312

Né per sereno ciel ir vaghe stelle
né per tranquillo mar legni spalmati
né per campagne cavalieri armati
né per bei boschi allegre fere e snelle,

né d' aspettato ben fresche novelle
né dir d' amore in stili alti ed ornati
né tra chiare fontane e verdi prati
dolce cantare oneste donne e belle,

né altro sarà mai ch' al cor m' aggiunga:
sì seco il seppe quella seppellire
che sola agli occhi miei fu lume e speglio.

Noia m' è 'l viver sì gravosa e lunga
ch' i' chiamo il fine per lo gran desire
di riveder cui non veder fu 'l meglio.

312

Ни ясных звезд блуждающие станы,
Ни полные на взморье паруса,
Ни с пестрым зверем темные леса,
Ни всадники в доспехах средь поляны,

Ни гости, с вестью про чужие страны,
Ни рифм лубовных сладкая краса,
Ни милых жен поющих голоса
Во мгле садов, где шепчутся фонтаны,—

Ничто не тронет сердца моего.
Все погребло с собой мое светило,
Что сердцу было зеркалом всего.

Жизнь однозвучна. Зрелище уныло.
Лишь в смерти вновь увижу то, чего
Мне лучше б никогда не видеть было.

Vyacheslav Ivanov and Russian Poetry of the Eighteenth Century
Ilya Serman

In his review of Vyacheslav Ivanov's article "The Poet and the Mob," Alexander Blok wrote in 1905 that the poet "amazingly" transmuted a long chain of literary influences within himself."[1] This remark ought to be examined, but in the meantime I will venture to offer a first attempt at analyzing one of these "transmutations," that is, how Vyacheslav Ivanov resurrected in his art the forgotten—and therefore new for the twentieth century—achievements of eighteenth-century Russian poetry.

In the history of Russian poetry of the beginning of our century, Vyacheslav Ivanov has the reputation of being a "difficult" poet. Not only the hidebound contemporary journal critics raised on the epigonic verse of the 1880s complained of his incomprehensibility, of his difficulty, but so did Ivanov's colleagues in the new literature, such poets as Bryusov and Blok. Bryusov accompanied his otherwise rather favorable review of Ivanov's verse collection *Pilot Stars* (*Kormchie zvezdy,* 1903) with a characteristic reservation: "This book will be beloved by all who want to take the *trouble* to understand and accept the poetry of Vyacheslav Ivanov."[2] In other words, for Bryusov, Vyacheslav Ivanov is a "difficult" poet, whose comprehension demands mental and emotional effort, demands work, even from a reader of the early twentieth century experienced in reading poetry.

Alexander Blok regretted that Vyacheslav Ivanov, "thanks to certain features of his particular style, presents difficulties of comprehension";[3] while Bely recalled in his memoirs a characteristic episode which reveals that Ivanov well knew how difficult his readers found him. In one of his first visits to Bely's Moscow apartment,

Ivanov gave his host an exam: "He took his book *Transparency,* which had just come out and was lying on my desk, and shook it at me, questioning me as though I were a schoolboy. 'Of course you know what "A pipe of seven separations" means?' What the hell! So help me! And I blurted out hoarsely, 'A pipe with seven apertures.' . . . 'Well, of course! There's nothing hard to understand here!'"[4]

Konstantin Erberg made a note in a similar vein. "I received this book for review from a certain journal. It made a great impression on me because of its high cultural level, its impossible style, and the forceful talent of its author. However, several poems in this book seemed like riddles to me, for I was then inexperienced in reading poetry. Reading *Pilot Stars* with the purpose of publishing a critical review of it, I made . . . a whole series of marginal notes expressing my bewilderment, sometimes indignation, and often delight. But, I didn't write the review after all. . . . About five years later, when I had gotten to know Vyacheslav Ivanov well, I told him about my impressions of this book of his and about my notes, which somehow caught his interest. He asked me to bring him my copy. A short time later he returned the book to me, having written on the first page his poem 'Kak mnogo myslennykh borenij' ('How many mental struggles')."[5]

Vyacheslav Ivanov himself knew that his readers were not always acquainted with the proper nouns and mythical allusions which he introduced into his verse. In the poem "Beauty" it is stated in the third and last stanza:

Radostno po tsvetonosnoj Gee
Ja idu, ne vedaja—kuda.
Ja sluzhu s ulybkoj Adrastee,
Blagosklonno-devstvenno-chuzhda.   [*SS,* I, 517]

(Joyfully I walk about flower-bearing Gaea, not knowing whither. With a smile I serve Adrastea, benevolent-virginal-alien.)

Having made a certain effort, that is, having translated the unfamiliar metaphor "flower-bearing Gaea" into the usual image—Earth—a reader is still unable to understand who Adrastea might

be without turning to special reference sources. Bryusov, for example, thought it meant Death.[6]

The author explains the name in a complicated note. "According to the Stoics and Orphics, Adrastea is inescapable, inevitable
Fate, world Necessity" [SS, I, 859]. Vyacheslav Ivanov felt that he
had to instruct and train his readers, cultivating in them the appreciation of conventions and devices new to Russian poetry. The
name Adrastea had not entered the sphere of classical allusions with
which Russian poetry had been providing its readers for almost two
centuries.

The poem "Terpander" [SS, I, 575, n. 860] was provided with
a note in the form of a complete translation by Vyacheslav Ivanov
himself of the Byzantine retelling of a legend from the lost books of
Diodorus, previously unknown to Russian readers:

> When the Lacedaemonians were waging internecine wars, there
> was an oracle that the citizens would return to concord if Terpander
> of Methymnia would play the cithara to them. And when he played
> a certain *melos* to them, Terpander, the skillful lyre-player, returned
> the insurgents to friendship and attunement—tuning a song, as
> Diodorus relates. And the men turned, embraced one another,
> wept, and lovingly kissed.

But even this seemed insufficient. And the poet explains that the
seven-stringed cithara was considered to have been Terpander's invention, while the "Theban architect" Amphion and "the Horae
(Dike, Eunomia and Eirene) are also the patrons of civic harmony."
For the line "Cheretom venchannyj khor" ("the reed-crowned
chorus") Vyacheslav Ivanov gives a bibliographical reference to a
particular German study: "'Cheretom venchannyj': See O. Müller,
Die Dorier, II, 334."[7] As a matter of fact, *cheret* is a reed (Ukrainian
or South Slavic), and it would have been easy to have identified this
little-used word.

Another, more complex instance is the poem "Pietà" [SS, I,
702]:

> The yearnings of the stars are allowed to glimmer out of the

dark depths of the ether: And we—the dust of the earth—are
placed so as to contemplate the Separation of the World.

Universal Isis, leader of yearnings, Love! We will come to
know you in the ways of your seekings, sorrowing with you,

Seeking with you the incorruptible trace of the God torn to
pieces. . . . Oh! The Single Light has been separated into many
broken lights!

Oh, sistrum of the worlds, and plectrum of lamentations!
All Beauty, One Soul of innumerable breaths—Pietà, Pietà! . . .

For ages he has been lifeless in the bosom of your anguish,
oh Dark One on the starry horizon! Oh, Mother of Sorrows!

And I, the shade of sleep, the tribe of the violent Titans,
their living ashes, carry the divine seed in my breast—Mother, I
am yours!

Hear (and His torments took place here, and He died!) my
passionate wail of severance and separation, my mortal moan!

Alkan'jam zvezd iz temnykh nedr èfira
    Dano mertsat':
Da—prakh zemli—vmestim Razluku Mira
    My sozertsat',—

Vselenskaja Izida, vozhd' alkanij,
    Ljubov'! tebja
Da poznaem v put'jakh tvoikh iskanij,
    S toboj skorbja,
Ishcha s toboj rasterzannogo Boga
    Netlennyj sled . . .
Akh! rasluchen v netsel'nykh svetov mnogo
    Edinyj Svet!

O, sistr mirov, i plektron vozdykhanij!
    Vsja Krasota,
Odna Dusha beschislennykh dykhanij—
    Pietà, Pietà! . . .

Ot veka On, bezzhiznennyj,—na lone
    Toski tvoej,

O, Temnaja na zvezdnom nebosklone!
  O, Mat' Skorbej!

I ja, ten' sna, Titanov bujnykh plemja,
  Ikh pepl zhivoj,—
Nesu v grudi bozhestvennoe semja,—
  Ja, Mater', tvoj!

Uslysh' (i zdes' Ego svershilis' muki,
  I umer On!—)
Moj strastnyj vopl' razryva i razluki,
  Moj smertnyj ston!   [*SS*, I, 702}

For the line "O, Temnaja na zvezdnom nebosklone" the poet gives
the following note: "'Dark' is one of the epithets of Isis. Isis seeks
the body of Osiris, who was torn to pieces, just as Dionysus was,
and whom the Greeks identified with Dionysus" [*SS*, I, 861}. And
he then gives a general commentary for the poem: "Just as the
depiction of Isis with Horus in her arms recalls the artistic type of
the Madonna and Child, so the Pietà type was anticipated by the
ancients in their portrayal of Eos and Cephalus, and of Niobe (Stark,
Niobe 203, Taf. V)."[8] This factual and precise commentary explains
much that is incomprehensible at first reading.

     But there is nothing in the commentary to explain what *sistr
mirov* and *plektron vozdykhanij* mean, although this is not the main
obstacle to understanding the poem. The main difficulty for the
reader is created by the shift from "we" to "I" and the deliberately
obscured relationship between the man, the "I" who pronounces the
lyrical monologue, and the god who has perished (Osiris), over whom
he grieves and sorrows. Thus, in the very text of the poem there
arises another category of difficulty which the poet does not explain,
hoping to make his reader become accustomed to it. Bryusov approved of the poet's having added a "small commentary" to his book
"which would explain the most difficult passages," and felt that "it
would not be superfluous to enlarge this commentary."[9]

     A note to a poetic text is always a signal, an indication of the
particular acuteness of the given literary situation. In Russian literature such notes first appeared in the eighteenth century, at its

beginning, in Kantemir, and at its "end," in Derzhavin. As the first poet of the new Europeanized type, Kantemir had to operate in a time of a complete literary vacuum and a conscious break with the entire pre-Petrine cultural tradition. He had to teach and train his readers, accustom them to the perception of a system of conventions and devices completely new for Russian literature, for which they had no preparation. Kantemir's notes explain the novelty of his poetical system to his readers and at the same time form the literary consciousness of the epoch, creating the literary context obligatory for the new poetry.

At the beginning of the nineteenth century Derzhavin felt very keenly that a change of literary eras was taking place and that he was losing his readers, since, as he wrote bitterly to Merzlyakov, "many people" now, especially the young, did not understand his verse. Derzhavin felt that he was being squeezed out of literature and that the system of poetic meanings which he himself had created was becoming "incomprehensible," that is, was being eliminated from the literary context of the new era.

Very different literary processes were reflected in the work of these two poets in similar ways. We can thus propose here the action of a certain general law, according to which at a particular moment in the evolution of literature a given system of texts falls into the position of having to explain itself, thereby defending its right to participate in the living literature. The poetic text by itself is not perceived by readers as its author had expected. Either the anticipated mode of perception has not yet come into being, or it has already disappeared. The given poetic system finds itself in a dangerous border area between literature and non-literature, between that which is perceived esthetically and that which is either being cast out of the esthetic realm or cannot enter it. [10]

Vyacheslav Ivanov's notes are analogous in function to Kantemir's: they are intended to clear the way for his poems and make it easier for them to penetrate the literary context of the epoch.

But it is not only Vyacheslav Ivanov's own commentary to his poems that recalls the eighteenth century in his poetic legacy. The poem "Terpander" is divided into two parts (emphasized by the

change from iambs to trochees). The second part tells how Terpander's song brought peace and tranquility to the life of Thebes, how
it conquered Discord. This part depends stylistically on words which
Bryusov calls "outworn," that is, those which have long since fallen
out of use and therefore have "all the freshness of novelty." Moreover,
what is characteristic of Vyacheslav Ivanov is not the insertion of
individual "old" words, but combinations of them, word blocks, so
to speak.

> And *coldness pierces* the hearts . . .
> He flings *ringing thunderbolts* . . .
> The *calves are prepared* for the greedy *altar flames.*
> And *fresh garlands* wind among the *amber temples.*

> I serdtsa *pronzaet khlad* . . .
> Meshchet *zvonkie peruny* . . .
> Zhadnym *plamenjam altarnym*
> *Ugotovany tel'tsy.*
> I po *kapishcham jantarnym*
> V"jutsja *svezhie ventsy.*   [*SS*, I, 576]

The examples given do not contain any insurmountable difficulties
of meaning, although it is not altogether clear why *svezhie ventsy*
wind among *kapishcha,* but the penultimate quatrain demands a
more detailed commentary than that which the poet gives for the
names of the Horae (see above):

> And the rejoicing council,
> increasing with the dance of the light-footed Horae;
> in the distance resounds the reed-crowned chorus
> of sportive maids.

> I likujushchee veche
> Mnozha pljaskoj legkikh Or,
> Rezvykh dev zvenit daleche
> Cheretom venchannyj khor.   [*SS*, I, 576]

What does "mnozha pljaskoj legkikh Or" mean? Neither from the poem's text nor from the notes are we able to obtain a meaningful explanation, although emotionally this is rather expressive.

Characteristic of Vyacheslav Ivanov's poetry in general and for this poem in particular is the introduction of Old Russian words and concepts into the portrayal of ancient (in this case, Greek) life— for example, *peruny* and *veche*. In the Russian literary consciousness these concepts are marked with a specific national and historical meaning. It was extremely daring to recall *peruny* after the poetry of the eighteenth century, or after the historical ballads of Aleksey Konstantinovich Tolstoy to recall the *veche,* which is one of their main conceptual symbols; but it was even more daring to transfer both *peruny* and *veche* to a poetic account of the exploits of Terpander, little known to anyone in Russia. Moreover, while *likujushchee veche* is perfectly understandable, *zvonkie peruny* "sounds" rather strange. Russian poetry of the eighteenth century had initially assimilated the word *perun* in the meaning "thunder." Thus, Lomonosov wrote:

Terrible thunderbolts are flung by the swinging of powerful Russian arms.

Uzhasnye peruny meshchut
Razmakhi sil'nykh rosskikh ruk. [11]

And Derzhavin wrote: "That his thunder suddenly falls silent" (*Chto vdrug ego perun molchit*),[12] "And the echo of his thunder has already shaken in the midst of the earth" (*I otzyv ego peruna / Uzh potrjas sredi zemli*).[13] In all these examples there is retained the meaning of *perun* as thunder. But in Vyacheslav Ivanov *peruny* become musical sounds, the accompaniment to dance.

The poem "Oceanides" is curious in that it makes it possible for us to determine precisely where Ivanov got his arsenal of "old words" and archaic forms. Speaking to the "female friends" of Prometheus, the poet says:

And may it not be you, restless maidens, who resolve the discord of *eternal laws*; and may you not recast the *statute of time* with magnanimous anger.

I pust' ne vam, mjatezhnym devam,
Reshat' razdory *vechnykh prav;*
I pust' velikodushnym gnevom
Ne prelozhit' *vremen ustav* . . .   *[SS, I, 526}*

These lines refer directly to Lomonosov, to his "Evening Meditation
on the Greatness of God" (1743):

O vy, kotorykh bystryj zrak
Pronzaet knigu *vechnykh prav,*
Kotorym malyj veshchi znak
Javljaet *estestva ustav.*

Oh, you, whose quick sight pierces the book of *eternal laws,* to
whom the *statute of nature* appears as a small prophetic sign.

It is not only the rhyme that corresponds here but also the epithet
vechnye, so that we cannot consider this an accident; moreover, every
gymnasium student knew Lomonosov's "Evening Meditation" by
heart.

Ivanov also took from Lomonosov the use of the plural form of
nouns where they are not found in everyday language: this is a very
rare device, found for the most part only in these two authors.
Lomonosov:

Veselyj vzor svoj obrashchaet
I vkrug dovol'stva ischisljaet.[15]

He turns his joyful gaze and enumerates *contentments* all around.

Ikh slave, *bedstvami* obil'noj
Bez brani khishchnoj i nasil'noj
No mozhno razve ustojat'?[16]

To their glory, abundant with *poverties,* without predatory and
violent battle, but is it really possible to resist?

Ivanov:

Almaznye grezy
Pomerknuvshikh *slav.*

Diamond dreams of faded *glories*.

No kak solntse drevnee vsekh *utr.*   [*SS*, I, 774]

But like the sun more ancient than all *mornings*.

In both cases, the device has the same stylistic purpose—to give an abstract, general, or, more precisely, universal character to the poetic statement.[17]

There are other instances of direct correspondences between Vyacheslav Ivanov's poetic thought and that of eighteenth-century Russian poets. For example, in his recasting of the 103rd Psalm, Lomonosov replaced the biblical metaphor which compares the sky to a *skin* by the image of a tent:

Ty zvezdy rasproster bez scheta
Shatru podobno pred toboj.[18]

You spread out the stars without number like a tent before you.

Derzhavin knew Lomonosov's version when he wrote his own recasting—and took from Lomonosov the tent image not present in the original:

Ty svetom, slavoj, krasotoj
Kak budto rizoj, oblachilsja
I, kak shatrom, ty osenilsja
Nebes lazurnoj vysotoj.[19]

You arrayed yourself with light, glory, and beauty as though with a chasuble, and you shaded yourself with the azure heights of the heavens as though with a tent.

Vyacheslav Ivanov uses the image of the sky-tent in the poem "Morning Star":

Ty odna, v ventse rassveta,
Klonish' vzory, chado sveta,
K nam s *vozdushnogo shatra*   [*SS*, I, 524]

You alone, in the crown of dawn, incline your gazes to us, child
of light, from the *airy tent.*

And he probably also took the image of Leviathan from Lomonosov:

The silence keenly harks to the distant murmur of the ocean . . .
We are carried on the back of the tamed Leviathan!

Dal'nij ropot okeana
Chutko vnemlet tishina . . .
Nas neset Leviafana
Ukroshchennogo spina!   [*SS*, I, 594]

Of course, the examples given are only single instances which
enter into a general system of conscious use of the style of the high
poetry of the eighteenth century. Here we can also mention complex
compound epithets which Tredyakovsky first used in Russian poetry
and to which Derzhavin gave full literary value. As Yury Tynyanov
noted, compound epithets "were an essential part of the archaizing
style: from Lomonosov and Derzhavin they came to the Shishkov
group (Shikhmatov, Bobrov)."[20] Here are several examples, characteristic in structure, of Derzhavin's compound epithets: whitely-
crimson fingers (*belorumjany persty*),[21] black-fiery glances (*cherno-og-
nennye vzory* [85]), gold-edged thunderclouds (*kraezlaty tuchi* [86]),
silvery-rose steeds (*srebro-rozovye koni* [101]), golden-shining phaeton
(*zlatozarnyj faeton* [101]), silvery-scaled ocean (*srebno-cheshuinu
okeanu* [122]). Compare several of Vyacheslav Ivanov's compound
epithets: sun-splintering star (*solntsedrobjashchaja zvezda*), brightly-
inclined (*svetlosklonnym*), grittily-sawing (*skrezhetopil'nye*), fiery-pow-
erful (*ognemoshchnyj*), fiery-resounding day (*ognezvuchnyj den'*), fiery-
eyed delirium (*ogneokij bred*), fiery-streamed (*ognestrujnyj*), keenly-
leaved (*chutkolistnyj*).

Derzhavin's compound epithets are mainly coloristic. There are
some of these in Vyacheslav Ivanov—for example, silvery-smokey
hearth (*srebrodymnyj ochag*); but in his verse another category predominates. An epithet such as fiery-resounding (*ognezvuchnyj*), applied to day (*den'*), brings together distant concepts, fire/sound (*ogon',
zvuk*), and is explicable only in the context of the poem as a whole.

A compound epithet is a situational device, in contrast to a qualitative (simple) epithet, which can be used over and over in various contexts.

It might be enough to note the above correspondences between Ivanov's poetry and that of the eighteenth century; but another instance of such continuity in his verse can be mentioned, one to which his contemporaries and comrades-in-arms gave particular attention. Bryusov wrote, "The constant use of adjectives as nouns, of prepositions and conjunctions as semantically significant words, the frequent omission of the predicate, the replacement of *kotoryj* by *chto,* and so forth, make reading [Ivanov's poetry] all the more difficult."[22]

The replacement of *kotoryj* by *chto* is a characteristic feature of the poetry of the eighteenth century and to varying degrees is found in both Lomonosov and Derzhavin. For example, from Lomonosov:

> He spreads like a tree that grows beside flowing waters.

> Kak drevo on rasprostranitsja,
> Chto bliz tekushchikh vod rastet.[23]

> May the persecutors who seek evil in my soul be ashamed.

> Goniteli da postydjatsja,
> Chto ishchut zla v dushe moej.[24]

from Derzhavin:

> He has already stepped into the glorious footsteps that the ancient orator laid down.

> Uzhe vstupil on v slavny sledy,
> Chto drevnij vitjaz' prolozhil.[25]

> He looks at the opulent rich men, who are idols in gold and silver.

> Gljadit na pyshnykh bogachej,
> Chto v zlate i srebre kumiry.[26]

and from Vyacheslav Ivanov's verse:

> Oh, Fantasy! You are like a miser who, having saved up his pennies, increases them with interest.

O, Fantazija! ty skuptsu podobna,
Chto, lepty skopiv, ikh rastit likhvoju   {SS, I, 580}

When your soul saw with its eyes in the darkness those images
that hover behind bodies.

Kogda tvoj dukh ochami zrel vo t'me
Te obrazy, chto za telami rejut   {SS, I, 647}

In the general return of the 1880s to the Golden Age of Russian
poetry, to the Pushkinian era, Vyacheslav Ivanov took a particular
and well-founded position. He declared not Pushkin but Tyutchev
to be the ancestor and teacher of the new Russian poets. He noted
that in Pushkin's poetry a break or "schism" between the poet and
the people had come about. The poet had nothing to say to the
people because he was too far removed from popular consciousness,
from the popular religious and mythmaking spirit. Tyutchev carried
out what was to Ivanov the poet's main mission: "Through him,
the people recalls its ancient soul and resurrects the potential that
has slumbered in it for centuries. As true verse is determined by the
spirit of a language, so the true poetic image is determined by the
psyche of a people. . . . The poet . . . depicts the new—and discovers the very old."[27]

But Ivanov understood that Tyutchev was closer to him than
Pushkin also because he was oriented toward pre-Pushkinian poetry,
toward the poetic language worked out in the odic verse of the
eighteenth century. "The discovery of the very old" in the language
of poetry is the main idea, the main focus of Vyacheslav Ivanov's
theory of poetic language. "In all epochs," he wrote, "when poetry
as art blossomed, poetic language was opposed to the conversational
and generally accepted language, and both bards and people loved
these differences and peculiarities and were proud of them, the bards
as their privilege and priestly or kingly attire, and the crowd as a
treasure and object of worship of the people."[28] Hence his focus on
those eras of the development of the Russian language and Russian
poetry which were closest of all to the spirit of long ago, when the
"broad, powerful billows of sounds purely Russian in their free and

all-encompassing majesty"[29] were heard. It was Ivanov's conviction that this "is required by our language itself (the only one among the living languages so deeply imprinted by the spirit of ancient languages)."[30]

Faithfulness to the forgotten spirit of a language closest of all in type to that of the ancient languages—what is this but an almost literal repetition of Lomonosov's well-known words from his "Introduction on the Use of Church Books"?

> The exceptional beauty, richness, majesty, and power of the Hellenic language is held in very high regard, as sufficiently witnessed by the amateurs of the philological sciences. . . . One can see clearly if one contemplates the Church books in the Slavonic language to what extent we, thanks to the translations of the Old and New Testaments, the discourses of the Fathers, the hymns of the Damascenes and other composers of canons, see Greek richness in the Slavonic language, and thus we increase the plenitude of the Russian language, which is great enough by its own abundance, and for which it is natural to absorb the Greek language through the intermediary of the Slavonic.[31]

This coincidence in the two writers' concept of the language and its structure helps us to understand the genesis of those features of Ivanov's poetry in which we demonstrated the reflection of the poetry of the eighteenth century. The practical result of Ivanov's view of the poetic language is the conscious archaization of his style. Thus, disputing Belinsky's opinion of the style of Pushkin's *Gypsies,* Ivanov writes:

> The critic is free to prefer the forged and weighty verse of "Poltava" to the harmoniously tender verse of "Gypsies"; but to speak in a haughty manner of "errors of style," about certain peculiarities of literary form whose artistic purpose and intent are incomprehensible to him, is a mistake in esthetic judgment. The verb *rek* which precedes the old gypsy's concluding speech is apparently intended to prepare the listener for something exceptionally trium-

phant and holy; while for Belinsky it simply "connotes heavy book-
ishness."[32]

The poet himself used this verb readily:

And from the sky fell a bloody fire, and having descended into it,
Love spoke . . .

I s neba spal ogon' krovavyj,
I, v nem soshed, rekla Ljubov' . . .   [SS, I, 540]

Intentionally or not, Vyacheslav Ivanov chose for himself the
position of a "difficult" poet with a "heavy," i.e., strange or even
incomprehensible style. Despite the great originality of his position
for his time, from the perspective of the by then three-hundred-
year-old development of Russian poetry, in matters of poetic language Ivanov belongs to those poets who were set apart from time
to time—to the perplexity, and sometimes to the consternation, of
the *dominant* current in literature. Fifty years ago, using material
from the poetry of the Pushkinian period, Yury Tynyanov demonstrated what a leavening effect the literary activity of those he called
"archaists" had on the poetic development of that period, and brilliantly showed that it was in fact they who were the "innovators."[33]

Recent studies have shown that "difficulty" as a value category
appeared by the middle of the eighteenth century, and that Tredjakovsky was not alone in this regard. He was followed by Vasily
Petrov, Alexander Radishchev and Semyon Bobrov, to name only the
most important poets with the reputation of being "difficult." But
in discussions of critics and literary historians about the poetry of
the post-Pushkinian era one rarely meets the concept of "difficulty."
Therefore, one must define more precisely whether the "difficult"
poets had a common goal, a common focus.

A comparative analysis shows that Petrov, Tredjakovsky before
him, and after him Bobrov and Radishchev were occupied with a
like task—testing the "durability" of Russian poetic semantics.
They simultaneously tested both the Russian language and the pa-
tience of their readers, overloading their style with almost unpron-
ounceable consonances and syntactic cryptograms. The victory of the

school of harmonious precision (Zhukovsky, Batyushkov, Pushkin), a victory that seemed final, materially changed the standard of "difficulty," and writers were threatened with literary ostracism for exceeding it. Thus, for example, the young writers of the early nineteenth century considered Derzhavin's late verse to be "difficult" and "incomprehensible" when under the influence of the Society of Amateurs of the Russian Word he turned to the legacy of Vasily Petrov and wrote with an obscurity no less mannered than that of Tredjakovsky. The following lines were written in 1807:

> Do we not see in Europe the image of Andromeda; in the Russians' martial spirit the glorious traces of Perseus; in the Destroyer the fable of the living Salamander, not sated with blood?

> Ne zrim li obraza v Evrope Andromedy,
> Vo Rosse brannyj dukh—Perseja slavny sledy,
> V Gubitele my basn' zhivogo Salamandra,
>   Nenasytima krov'ju?[34]

Shevyrev battled valiantly against Pushkinian smoothness and in the era of Pushkin's unmitigated triumph dreamed of the appearance of a new "difficult" poet, a new Derzhavin: "We already have Lomonosov, we had an uneducated Derzhavin; but since his death we have not so much created verse as prepared material for a poet of the future: that is, we have purified the language, divined the secret of its harmony, enriched it with various meters, turns of phrase, sonorous rhymes, in a word, prepared everything for a new genius, a new, educated Derzhavin, who may already be hidden somewhere in Russia."[35]

The most penetrating critics understood or guessed that the "difficulty" and "heaviness" of Vyacheslav Ivanov's poetry revealed or mapped out completely new paths for Russian poetry as a whole. Bryusov promised Ivanov's readers unexpected rewards for the labor which it would be necessary to expend in reading him: "The reader of Vyacheslav Ivanov must approach his poems with a penetrating and sober attitude, scout out, divine their hidden sonority, examine his art, bore into these ruddy, often inhospitable, sometimes fanciful rocks, knowing that out of them will spurt the silver springs of pure poetry."[36]

There were such readers, and they were rewarded for their efforts. Of course, there were not only readers, but also new poets, for whom Vyacheslav Ivanov was no longer either heavy or difficult. But this does not mean that they followed him obediently. Gumilev, while admiring Ivanov's style, writes of the dangers of his path for others: "The style is the man—but who does not know Vyacheslav Ivanov's style with its solemn archaisms, sharp enjambments, emphatic alliterations, and an arrangement of words which assiduously obscures the general meaning of the sentence. . . . But for others to follow him, lacking his essential qualities, would be a risky, even fatal exploit."[37]

Acmeism's battle against Symbolism was above all a battle against Vyacheslav Ivanov, against his theory and his poetic practice. When the Acmeists announced that in their poetry a Rose had become a living and beautiful flower, not a symbol of something from the Beyond, they meant in part Book Five of *Cor Ardens,* "Rosarium," in which several dozen poems were dedicated to the various forms of the symbolic conceptualization of the Rose, and also the commentary in which were given detailed quotations from Alexander Veselovsky's article "Poetics of the Rose," without which the poems would be largely or completely incomprehensible.[38] But battles and polemics do not preclude assimilation and elaboration of the poety of the repudiated school.

Vyacheslav Ivanov's poetry has not yet been studied from the standpoint of its immediate influence on Acmeism and Futurism. I will not even mention here the subject of Vyacheslav Ivanov and Khlebnikov, a special and important topic.[39] I will only note here that, freed from the burden of erudition and on soil prepared by Vyacheslav Ivanov's verse, there appeared the antiquity of Mandelshtam, with its original elaboration of the Terpander theme. On the other hand, Pasternak, with his animation of nature, with his landscapes that gaze at each other, owes much to such pieces of Vyacheslav Ivanov as "Tramontana," in which the wind says of itself:

I rush down among the olive trees like a brightly-inclined water-fall, carrying blueness to the gulfs, clearing the heavens.

Ja nizvergnus' po olivam
Svetlosklonnym vodopadom,
Sinevu nesja zalivam,
Raschishchaja nebesa.   [*SS*, I, 773]

Thus, once again in the history of Russian poetry the path of an archaist showed the way for the innovators.

—Translated by Jean Laves Hellie

Notes

1. Aleksandr Blok, *Sobranie sochinenij* (Moscow-Leningrad, 1962), V, 7.

2. Valery Brjusov, *Dalekie i blizkie* (Moscow, 1912), p. 122. Emphasis added here and elsewhere.

3. Blok, *Sobranie sochinenij,* V, 7.

4. Andrej Bely, *Nachalo veka* (Moscow-Leningrad, 1933), p. 311.

5. Konstantin Erberg [K. A. Sjunnerberg], "Vospominanija," S. S. Grechishkin and A. V. Lavrov, eds., *Ezhegodnik rukopisnogo otdela Pushkinskogo Doma na 1977 god* (Leningrad, 1979), pp. 129—30.

6. Brjusov, *Dalekie,* p. 135.

7. Karl-Otfried Müller (1797–1840), *Die Dorier,* 2 vols. (Breslau, 1844; 1st ed., 1824). Vyacheslav Ivanov counted Müller among those "frontiersmen of science" who paved the way for Nietzsche. According to Ivanov, Müller discovered the "spirit" of the Dionysian people. See Vyacheslav Ivanov, *Po zvezdam* (St. Petersburg, 1909), p. 5.

8. Ivanov's reference is to K. V. Stark, *Niobe und die Niobiden* (Leipzig, 1863).

9. Brjusov, *Dalekie,* p. 123.

10. See I. Serman, *Kantemir i problem literaturnogo konteksta* (in press).

11. M. V. Lomonosov, *Polnoe sobranie sochinenij* (henceforth *PSS*) (Moscow-Leningrad, 1959), VIII, 635.

12. G. R. Derzhavin, *Stikhotvorenija* (Moscow, 1958), p. 95.

13. Ibid., p. 277.

14. Lomonosov, *PSS*, VIII, 121–22.

15. Ibid., p. 222.

16. Ibid., p. 122.

17. See I. Z. Serman, *Poeticheskij stil' Lomonosova* (Moscow-Leningrad, 1965), pp. 179–82.

18. Lomonosov, *PSS*, VIII, 228.

19. G. R. Derzhavin, *Sobranie sochinenij*, ed. Ja. K. Grot (St. Petersburg, 1868), p. 605.

20. Jurij Tynjanov, *Arkhaisty i novatory* (Leningrad, 1929), p. 215.

21. Derzhavin, *Stikhotvorenija*, p. 85. The bracketed numbers in the text refer to pages in this edition.

22. Brjusov, *Dalekie*, p. 123.

23. Lomonosov, *PSS*, VIII, 369. (The 103rd Psalm in the Russian Bible is numbered 104 in the English-language Bible. Translator's note.)

24. Ibid., p. 375.

25. Derzhavin, *Stikhotvorenija*, p. 191.

26. Ibid., p. 6.

27. Ivanov, *Po zvezdam*, pp. 40–41.

28. Ibid., p. 355.

29. Ibid.

30. Ibid.

31. Lomonosov, *PSS*, VII, 587.

32. Ivanov, *Po zvezdam*, pp. 174–75.

33. Tynjanov, *Arkhaisty*, pp. 87–106.

34. Derzhavin, *Stikhotvorenija*, p. 254.

35. S. P. Shevyrev, "Obozrenie russkoj slovesnosti za 1827 god," *Moskovskij vestnik* 7 (1828), p. 66.

36. Brjusov, *Dalekie*, p. 125.

37. N. S. Gumilev, *Pis'ma o russkoj poezii* (Petrograd, 1923).

38. Vyacheslav Ivanov, *Cor Ardens* 2 (St. Petersburg, 1909), p. 207.

39. N. L. Stepanov, *Velemir Khlebnikov, Zhizn' i tvorchestvo* (Moscow-Leningrad, 1975), pp. 13–16, 29, 45–53.

Ivanov and Bely's *Petersburg*
Carol Anschuetz

In a comparative review of Ivanov's *Transparency* (*Prozrachnost'*) and Bely's *Gold in Azure* (*Zoloto v lazuri*), both of which appeared in 1904, Bryusov observed, "The poetry of Bely and the poetry of Ivanov rather exclude than complement each other, and only our 'eclectic' era, which knows how to pray to all the gods, is ready not only to 'accept' both the one and the other, but to recognize both poets as proponents of one and the same literary school."[1] We know from Bely's published memoirs that Ivanov's name reached him by way of Bryusov, who attended Ivanov's lectures on the religion of Dionysus in Paris; and that, although they met briefly in the spring of 1904, when Ivanov visited Moscow on his way to Petersburg, Bely became close enough to Ivanov to reflect his influence only in the autumn of 1905, when Ivanov had established the famous Wednesdays in his Petersburg "Tower." Ivanov was thirty-eight years old when they met, whereas Bely, who confidently pronounced him as "an out-and-out theoretician" (*sploshnoj feoretik*), was only twenty-three. Nevertheless, when Bely dedicated a short prose work of 1904 entitled "The Masque" (*Maska*) to Ivanov as "preacher of Dionysianism" (*propovednik dionisiazma*), Ivanov repaid Bely's tribute with a major theoretical article of 1905 entitled "The Symbolism of Esthetic Principles" (*Simvolika esteticheskikh nachal*). In nearly twenty years of mutual association, Ivanov patronized Bely and his work whereas Bely, always the *enfant terrible,* did not hesitate to attack his patron in return. To wit, he attacked the position of mystical anarchism, which Ivanov declared together with Georgy Chulkov shortly after the revolution of 1905, and what Bely considered the expression of Russian chauvinism in *The Native and the Universal* (*Rodnoe i vselen-*

skoe), a collection of Ivanov's essays published shortly after the revolution of 1917. Both these polemics have been intelligently discussed, the first one by Olga Deschartes in her notes to volume III of Ivanov's works; and the second by Heinrich Stammler in an article of 1974.[2] Until Nikolay Kotrelev, the Soviet scholar, has published his edition of Ivanov's correspondence with Bely, it would be rash to venture beyond their discussion.

The interval between the two polemics is recorded in Bely's published memoirs as the period of closest association between Ivanov and Bely. Whether this is because Bely sided with Ivanov against his former ally Bryusov in *Apollo* (*Apollon*) No. 11 for 1910 is debatable. The two years after 1910 are, however, the period in which Bely wrote the most cogent and powerful of his novels, to which Ivanov gave the title *Petersburg* (*Peterburg*).[3] I do not propose to explain why Bely wrote this novel in 1911 and 1912 rather than in 1905 and 1906 when its action took place. But I do intend to suggest that its cogency, if not its power, derives from a vision of Hellenic culture which Ivanov imparted to the younger poet. Central to this vision is the concept of the poet as the organ by which the people remember their original nature and awaken the mythopoeia latent within it. Thus, insofar as the poet has the gift of memory, he also has the gift of prophecy; the development of his art anticipates the evolution of culture as described in Nietzsche's *Birth of Tragedy*. "He may be either an Apollonian artist in dreams or a Dionysian artist in ecstasies or, finally—as in Greek tragedy—at once an artist in both dreams and ecstasies" (*The Birth of Tragedy,* §2). Bely's "symphonies" reflected Nietzsche's influence two years before Ivanov's name reached him from Paris but, although *Petersburg* also reflects Nietzsche's influence directly, certain facets of the novel become clear only when viewed through the prism of Ivanov's influence. Consequently we shall have to distinguish Ivanov's influence on Bely from Nietzsche's as we move from Ivanov's concept of the poet to the structure of Bely's *Petersburg,* and from Ivanov's essays on Dostoevsky to Bely's image of revolution as tragedy.

The structure of Bely's *Petersburg* is based on an analogy between the city of Petersburg and the city of Atlantis described in Plato's late dialogues, the *Timaeus* and the *Critias*. The analogy between Petersburg and Atlantis is Bely's own but the idea of Atlantis is the one proposed by Ivanov in an article of 1909 entitled, "Ancient Terror" (*Drevnij uzhas*) after Bakst's oil canvas, "Terror antiquus."[4] The waters which flooded Atlantis evoke the same profound terror and Dionysian ecstasy that overwhelm man whenever he gazes into what Ivanov, in reference to Nietzsche, calls the "abyss." This bottomless sea is Nietzsche's symbol for the ultimate reality into which the principle of individuality normally veils man's gaze. In *The Birth of Tragedy,* the abyss is personified by Dionysus, god of music, whereas the principle of individuality is personified by Apollo, god of sculpture. Only at brief intervals does the opposition between these two antagonistic gods find mediation in the birth of tragedy. "Ancient Terror" represents the flood of Atlantis as the victory of Dionysus over Apollo, that is, the end of an Apollonian period of history and the onset of a Dionysian one. The story of how the memory of the flood was preserved in Egypt becomes a metaphor for anamnesis, the half-conscious memory of ultimate reality, which men forget, as it were, when they are born into this world. Now, if we keep in mind that Ivanov conceives the poet as the organ by which the people remember their original nature and awaken the mythopoeia latent within it, we shall see that the analogy between Petersburg and Atlantis links Bely's novel with Ivanov's theory of poetic creation.

Nietzsche maintains that, inasmuch as the epics of Homer turn the war of those pre-Hellenic barbarians known as Titans into art, they also mark the victory of Apollo over what he calls the "titanic-barbaric" nature of Dionysus or, in short, the victory of order over chaos. Between the epics of Homer and the tragedies of Aeschylus, however, there elapses a period in which Apollonian order gradually becomes rigidified. Thus, the epics of Homer are merely a prelude to the tragedies of Aeschylus, which, by reintroducing the Homeric myths into poetry, mark the victory of Dionysus over the beautiful but now rigid order of Apollo. It is clearly just this victory of chaos over order that we find in Bely's novel where, in 1905, a Dionysian tide of revolution is about to flood the Apollonian dream city founded by Peter the Great. Nietzsche would have said that, with this tide of revolution, the age of the Titans would be recovered from Tartarus and once more brought to the light (*The Birth of Tragedy*, §10). Bely makes the age of the Titans into the age of the Mongols, who, in his novel, are recovered from oblivion and once more felt in the Ableukhov blood. The novel captures just that moment in time when the Atlantes of Petersburg, who, like petrified Titans, support the city's architecture, threaten to collapse.[5] When they do collapse, Hellenized Mongols like the Ableukhovs will be swept away in the tide of revolution to make way for un-Hellenized Mongols like the terrorist Lippanchenko. As the victory of Dionysus brings one generation of Mongols to an end, it engenders another: Bely describes what this means for politics with tongue in cheek, but he is serious about what it means for esthetics.

Nikolay Apollonovich turns out to be descended from the Titan Atlas when, in a dream, he remembers that the collective past of his race began with Atlantis. The Titan Kronos (Saturn) appears to him in the guise first of his forefather, the Mongol Ab-lay, and then of his father, who brings him to the discovery that "Saturn's reign has returned" (*Saturnovo tsarstvo vernulos'*). The consequences of his offer to murder his father, the tsarist minister, plunge him into a Dionysian ecstasy in which he finds himself literally "beside himself" (*vne sebja*). If his patronymic Apollonovich characterizes him as a son of Apollo, his Dionysian ecstasy underscores the victory of Dionysus over the theoretical man, Socrates, who is the post-tragic surrogate for Apollo. All this confirms Horst-Jürgen Gerigk's thesis that Bely wrote *Petersburg* with *The Birth of Tragedy* in hand, although, as I understand Professor Gerigk's recent essay in *Nietzsche Studien*, he reads *Petersburg* as a novel about the victory of Socrates over Dionysus and not of Dionysus over Socrates.[6] This is a crucial difference because the victory of Socrates over Dionysus means that art has entered a period of decline whereas the victory of Dionysus over Socrates means that Russia is about to witness the rebirth of tragedy.

Nietzsche devotes the last nine chapters of *The Birth of Tragedy* to the proposal that a rebirth of tragedy is about to take place in Wagner's operas. These operas mark the victory of Dionysus over Socrates just as the tragedies of Aeschylus once marked the victory of Dionysus over Apollo. Moreover, they reintroduce German myths into poetry just as the tragedies of Aeschylus reintroduced Homeric myths into poetry at the end of the Doric period. "What power was it that freed Prometheus from his vultures and transformed the myth into a vehicle of Dionysian wisdom?" asks Nietzsche. "It is the Heracleian power of music: having reached its highest manifestation in tragedy, it can invest myths with a new and most profound significance" (*The Birth of Tragedy*, §10). This quotation raises the problem of how the power of music at work in Wagner's operas can be said to affect Bely's novel: the solution to that problem is, I believe, to be found in Ivanov's reinterpretation of one particular thesis from *The Birth of Tragedy*. Nietzsche singles out the novel as the art form which most clearly exhibits the reduction of the Apollonian principle to mere logical schematism. In the novel as in the Aesopian fable, poetry functions as an ancilla to philosophy; hence the novel and the fable are, in Nietzsche's opinion, the only art forms comprehensible to a logician like Plato. The novel would thus seem an unlikely cradle for the rebirth of tragedy yet, in the very chapter where Nietzsche treats the novel, he holds out the possibility that the birth of an artistic Socrates may not be altogether a contradiction.

If the birth of an artistic Socrates is not altogether a contradiction, then neither, perhaps, is the birth of a truly poetic novel. It is on this possibility that Ivanov seizes when he comes to write his essays on the Russian novel and on the novels of Dostoevsky in particular. To understand Ivanov's essays on the novels of Dostoevsky one must first, however, understand his lectures on the religion of Dionysus. Like *The Birth of Tragedy*, those lectures put scholarship to the service of mythopoeia but, unlike *The Birth of Tragedy*, they make Dionysus a prefiguration of Christ and the ecstasy which inspires tragedy a prefiguration of Christ's Passion. In "Dostoevsky and the Novel-Tragedy" (*Dostoevskij i roman-tragedija*), the first of his essays on the novels of Dostoevsky, Ivanov sums up the reasons why Western esthetics traditionally classifies the novel as an epic genre; he then goes on to find the "epics" of Dostoevsky uniquely dramatic in both form and content.[7] The conception of Dionysian ecstasy as a prefiguration of Christ's Passion leads him to identify them, in their deeply Christian spirit, with the Dionysian principle, and thereby to classify them not as Aesopian fables but as epic tragedies. His reinterpretation of Nietzsche's thesis about the novel casts Dostoevsky in the role of a Russian Aeschylus, whose myth of Petersburg Bely's novel might be expected to reintroduce into poetry. This would in turn cast Bely in the role of a Russian Wagner and, in his mind's eye, Bely probably did play such a role, but, whereas Ivanov viewed Dostoevsky as the Russian Aeschylus, Bely viewed him as a Russian Socrates.[8] The difference in their respective views of Dostoevsky explains why Bely parodied Dostoevsky in *Petersburg,* and why Ivanov, in his review of it, wrote that, for Bely, Dostoevsky would forever remain a book with seven seals. Nevertheless, the glorification of Aeschylus in the spirit of *The Birth of Tragedy* and the consequent search for a Russian Wagner are common to both poets. In *Petersburg* and later, again, in *Kotik Letaev,* Bely attempts to do for the novel what, in his tragedies *Tantalus* and *Prometheus,* Ivanov attempts to do for the drama. He attempts to translate Aeschylus into that peculiar idiom of the Russian Symbolists which expresses the iconoclastic philosophy of Nietzsche in terms of the religious philosophy of Solovyov. The fact that Bely's novels, like Ivanov's tragedies, were conceived as parts of trilogies is only further evidence that the conception for all of them originates in Nietzsche's view of Aeschylus.

Ivanov provided Bely with a classical education that brought both Aeschylus and Aeschylus's sources in Homeric myth to life for him. Homer and especially his younger contemporary Hesiod show the genealogy of the gods as a bloody struggle in which barbaric punishments are meted out for barbaric crimes. The Titan Kronos castrates his father Uranos because Uranos has cruelly locked his children by Gaia in her womb. Zeus in turn dethrones and banishes his father Kronos because Kronos devoured his children by Rhea as she gave birth to them. The hero of Aeschylus's tragedy *Prometheus Bound* forewarns Zeus that, unless he relinquish his tyranny over mankind, one of Zeus's own sons will dethrone him just as he dethroned Kronos. Thus the sins of the fathers against the sons continually provoke the sins of the sons against the fathers. History

becomes a vicious circle that one could describe, in a phrase from
Nikolay Apollonovich's dream, as "an ancient Mongolian business"
(*starodavnee mongol'skoe delo*) or, more loosely translated, "the same
old Mongolian affair." The genealogy of the tsars includes Ivan the
Terrible and Peter the Great who, as fathers, are roughly analogous
to Uranos and Kronos; in Peter's son Alexis and in Alexander I it
also includes sons who sought, like Kronos and Zeus, to overthrow
the tyranny of their fathers. The prototype of the son who desires
his father's death yet does *not* murder him is Dostoevsky's hero, Ivan
Karamazov, whose Russian tragedy *Petersburg* works out again in
terms of the *Oresteia*.

The hero of the *Oresteia* murdered his mother Clytaemnestra
because she murdered his father Agamemnon; but Clytaemnestra
murdered Agamemnon because he sacrificed their daughter Iphigeneia to the gods. In fact the whole Trojan War, on which Agamemnon was about to embark when he sacrificed Iphigeneia, can be said
to result from Thyestes's curse on the house of his brother Atreus,
who murdered Thyestes's children and served them up to him at
dinner because Thyestes had seduced Atreus's wife. What is important for *Petersburg* is that the Erinyes, also called Furies, pursue
Orestes relentlessly as a matricide even though he murdered Clytaemnestra at Apollo's command. They also pursue Nikolay Apollonovich as a parricide even though he, like Ivan Karamazov, has
stopped short of murder. At the end of the *Oresteia,* the Furies are
transformed by Athena's justice into Eumenides or, in other words,
"Kindly Spirits." At the end of *Petersburg,* the furies of Nikolay
Apollonovich's conscience are softened by repentance when he hears
the cranes of Ibykus, an allusion to Schiller's ballad by that title.
The ballad tells how Furies in the form of cranes fly over the performance of a tragedy at Olympia and thereby provoke the murderers
of the poet Ibykus publicly to betray their guilt. In *Petersburg,* however, the cranes are heard not as the voice of the Furies but as the
voice of childhood, and thus, in *Petersburg* as in the *Oresteia,* not
retribution but reconciliation sounds the final note. If Nikolay Apollonovich is a Prometheus *manqué,* unready to defy Zeus's tyranny,
this is partly because he, like Orestes, is a hero inexorably drawn

by his patrimony into a struggle between justice and terror. Ivanov gave his review of *Petersburg* the title "Inspiration by Terror" (*Vdokhnovenie uzhasa*), which evidently refers to Bely's own terror as he gazed into the abyss. In that review Ivanov wrote that Bely originally meant the end of *Petersburg* to be far less conciliatory and benevolent than it is. One is tempted to speculate whether Ivanov himself might not have reminded Bely that the tragedies of Aeschylus put an end to history's vicious circle.

Literary comparisons are fully valid only when, having shown how one writer influenced the other, they also show how those two writers differ, and that is what must here be attempted in a few words. If Ivanov can be said to have provided Bely with a classical education, this does not mean either that Bely read Plato and Aeschylus as Ivanov read them or that he alludes to them directly in *Petersburg* as he does to Russian and German literature. It rather means that Bely's association with Ivanov led him to draw analogies between Hellenic and Russian culture that parallel the analogies between Hellenic and German culture in *The Birth of Tragedy.* The analogies between Hellenic and Russian culture in *Petersburg* confirm that Bely, like Ivanov, was responsive to the young Nietzsche; they also confirm that, unlike Ivanov, he was sympathetic with the mature Nietzsche, whose critique of Judaeo-Christian morals becomes most provocative in *The Antichrist.* Although Dionysus plays a central role in *Petersburg,* Bely does not make him a prototype of Christ for the simple reason that Christ, for Bely, is the so-called "idiot" Jesus, whom Nietzsche believes Dostoevsky would have understood. This anti-Christian Christ Bely equates with Nietzsche's Antichrist, and so it is that we have two Antichrist figures in *Petersburg*: the white domino, whom Sofya Petrovna mistakes for her husband* and the Bronze Horseman, who destroys Dudkin. It is the Bronze Horseman who embodies the Antichrist of the Apocalypse, once described by Nietzsche as "the most wanton of all literary outbursts that vengefulness has on its conscience" (*The Genealogy of Morals,* §16). Both

---

*Her so-called "idiot" husband rises from the dead after his botched suicide attempt.

these Antichrist figures pursue the main characters of *Petersburg*: the white domino pursues them with the hope of reconciliation, and the Bronze Horseman with the threat of retribution. Reconciliation and retribution are, however, the same two themes of Aeschylus that, as we have seen, Bely derived from Nietzsche by way of Ivanov, and with them Bely attempts, like Aeschylus, to put an end to history's vicious circle.

Even where Ivanov and Bely are both readers of *The Birth of Tragedy,* they read it differently: Ivanov as a treatise on the history of culture, and Bely, with his more positivistic turn of mind, as a treatise on the history of language. Bely maintains that the word is first of all a sound, and that metaphor begins to evolve when that sound evokes a poetic image. The image gives rise to myth, which leads to religion, which leads in turn to philosophy, and there the word ultimately becomes a scientific term without sound or image. But no sooner has metaphor degenerated into mere scientific terminology than it begins its evolution again through the sounds and images of poetry, so that periods of degeneration and regeneration alternate cyclically with one another like the periods in *The Birth of Tragedy.* Apollonian periods tend towards the formalization of myth; Dionysian periods tend towards the destruction of form which precedes mythopoeia. Bely's goal in *Petersburg* is to usher in an era of transition from one cycle to the next, for "such eras," he writes in words that could be Nietzsche's, "are marked by the intrusion of the spirit of music into poetry: the musical force of sound is resurrected by the word."[9] *Petersburg* is not, however, the story of a young man who learns to use words, as the novels of Bely's contemporaries Proust, Joyce and Mann so often were. Nor does it deceive its readers with the sleight-of-hand by which a novel turns out to be written by one of its characters. This is the way Nabokov, a novelist much enamored of Bely, might have written *Petersburg,* but not the way Bely wrote it: *Petersburg,* as Bely wrote it, is an attempt to induce the rebirth of tragedy. It turns the revolution in politics into a metaphor for revolution in esthetics, just as it turns the city of Petersburg into a metaphor for Atlantis, the city of myth. Surely this is why, at the end of the novel, Nikolay Apollonovich leaves

Russia for Egypt, where Plato tells us the memory of the flood was preserved, and where Ivanov would therefore also bid us look for a prophecy of the flood to come. Thus, when Bely chose the art form of the novel to express his own response to Nietzsche, his choice was determined by certain basic tenets of Ivanov's esthetic, which help to fuse *Petersburg* into a cogent whole.

Notes

1. Valerij Brjusov, "Vjacheslav Ivanov. Andrej Belyj," *Dalekie i blizkie* (Moscow, 1912), p. 124.

2. *SS,* III, 724–31. H. Stammler, "Belyj's Conflict with Vjačeslav Ivanov over War and Revolution," *Slavic and East European Journal,* XVIII, No. 3 (1974), 258–70.

3. Ivanov alludes to this fact in his review of *Petersburg,* "Vdokhnovenie uzhasa," *Rodnoe i vselenskoe* (Moscow, 1918), p. 92; and Bely confirms it in his memoir *Nachalo veka* (Moscow, 1933), p. 326. For a thorough discussion of how *Petersburg* was written and published, see L. K. Dolgopolov, "Andrej Belyj v rabote nad 'Peterburgom'," *Russkaja literatura,* No. 1 (1972), pp. 157–67. The first, "Nekrasov" redaction of *Petersburg* was written late in 1911; the "Sirin" redaction in 1912 and 1913. Ivanov tells us that Bely read him the unfinished manuscript of *Petersburg,* presumably in the "Nekrasov" redaction ("Vdokhnovenie uzhasa," p. 92); Olga Deschartes maintains that Bely actually wrote "a significant part" of *Petersburg* in Ivanov's "Tower" (cf. *SS,* III, 729). If we cannot take this on the sole authority of Olga Deschartes, who did not then belong to the Ivanov circle, there is reason to suppose that Bely *might* have written a significant part of *Petersburg* in Ivanov's "Tower," for we have it on his own authority that he and Asya Turgeneva lived there for part of 1912 (cf. Bely, *Nachalo veka,* p. 327).

4. Vjacheslav Ivanov, "Drevnij uzhas. Po povodu kartiny L. Baksta 'Terror antiquus'," *Zolotoe runo,* No. 4 (1909), pp. 56–65; reprint: *Po zvezdam* (St. Petersburg, 1909), pp. 393–424. On Bakst's oil, see André Levinson, *Bakst* (New York, 1922), pp. 107–09, and I. N. Pruzhan, *Lev Samoilovich Bakst* (Leningrad, 1975), pp. 114–18. Levinson approaches "Terror antiquus" in terms of Nietzsche; Pruzhan, and other Soviet critics, in terms of the revolution of 1905.

5. "Atlantes" (in Russian, *atlanty*) is the architectural term for male

caryatids; in Russian, it is homonymous with the word for citizens of Atlantis. It is derived, like the word "Atlantis," from the name of the Titan Atlas, brother to Prometheus, who is the central figure in Nietzsche's conception of tragedy. Bely uses it to link the imagery of Petersburg and its founder, Peter the Great, with the imagery of *The Birth of Tragedy,* and thus to make of Peter the Great a Russian Prometheus, whom Pushkin, the Russian Aeschylus, immortalizes in "The Bronze Horseman" (*Mednyj vsadnik*).

6. Horst-Jürgen Gerigk, "Belyjs 'Petersburg' und Nietzsches 'Geburt der Tragödie'," *Nietzsche Studien,* IX (1980), pp. 356–73.

7. Most relevant to *Petersburg* are two essays published by Ivanov while Bely was at work on his novel: "Dostoevskij i roman-tragedija," *Russkaja mysl'* (May 1911), pp. 46–61, and (June 1911), pp. 1–17; reprint: *Borozdy i mezhi* (Moscow, 1916), pp. 3–60; and "L. Tolstoj i kul'tura," I (1911), pp. 167–78; reprint: *Borozdy i mezhi,* pp. 73–93. "Dostoevskij i roman-tragedija" was occasioned by the thirtieth anniversary of Dostoevsky's death; "L. Tolstoj i kul'tura" was occasioned by Tolstoy's death in 1910. The relevance of both essays to Bely's view of Dostoevsky is outlined in footnote 8 below; however, Dostoevsky figures in most of Ivanov's work at this period, the lectures on the religion of Dionysus.

8. Although Ivanov calls Dostoevsky a "Russian Shakespeare" (cf. Ivanov, "Dostoevskij i roman-tragedija," p. 28), he does not actually call him a Russian Aeschylus. His essay follows a Nietzschean thought pattern, which, if taken to its logical conclusion, inevitably leads to the notion of one. Dostoevsky represents to Ivanov a "latter-day Zarathustra" (ibid., p. 8), who tempted Russians to eat of the fruit of the tree of individualism. In section 3 of his essay Ivanov compares the work of Dostoevsky with that of Aeschylus on grounds that it fulfills the tragic potentialities of the nineteenth-century novel just as the work of Aeschylus fulfilled those of Homer's *Iliad.* The notion of Dostoevsky as a Russian Aeschylus becomes fully evident where Ivanov compares Dostoevsky with Tolstoy and Tolstoy with Socrates as follows. "Dostoevsky did not, like Tolstoy, follow the path of Socrates in search of a norm of the good that would concur with true knowledge, but, like the tragedies of Greece, kept faith with the spirit of Dionysus" (ibid., p. 35). The notion of Tolstoy as a Russian Socrates provides the topic of Ivanov's essay, "L. Tolstoj i kul'tura," mentioned in footnote 7 above.

9. Andrej Belyj, "Magija slov," *Simvolizm* (Moscow, 1910), p. 434.

The Literary Criticism of Vyacheslav Ivanov
René Wellek

Victor Terras's discussion of Ivanov's esthetic thought and its sources allows me to assume a knowledge of it and to concentrate on the literary criticism understood as the interpretation and judgment of concrete works of literature. I realize that the critical essays cannot be divorced from his esthetics, his theory of poetry, and ultimately his religious thought which implies also a philosophy of history. Still, it may be of interest to look at these writings from a point of view which may be that of an outsider, of a literary historian and critic who believes in the evidence of the text, in some consensus of common sense in interpretation, in the value of factual information and even in a "common pursuit" of judgment. I may at times appear as an *advocatus diaboli* who, I understand, always precedes the canonization.

Ivanov's literary criticism ranges very widely and uses several distinct styles or manners. There are some sober, expository discussions full of solid information written for an encyclopedia or a handbook: they do not shirk judgment but preserve a tone of detachment and objectivity. The late contributions to the *Enciclopedia italiana Treccani,* dating from 1936, on symbolism and realism, are a case in point. The piece on symbolism provides accurate information on the French school, its antecedents and its spread abroad. It distinguishes between two kinds of symbolism: one Ivanov calls "realistic" (which in his scholastic terminology refers to a transcendent and even supernatural reality) and subjective symbolism. Ivanov traces this distinction to Baudelaire's early sonnet "Les Correspondances," in which the first eight lines evoke the forest of symbols while the concluding six concern individual psychic complexes and synaes-thesias. Ivanov approves of realistic symbolism, of the idea of a signature of things and of the poet as the decipherer of the great alphabet of nature, and he disapproves of subjective symbolism, which he associates with decadence, art for art's sake, extreme in-dividualism, even solipsism, and thus with the breakdown of com-munication, obscurity, hermeticism. Ivanov had long before praised Verlaine as a "realistic" symbolist and Huysmans at the stage he considered the right symbolist (see *By the Stars* [*Po zvezdam,* 1909]). He sees subjective symbolism in Swinburne and Oscar Wilde and praises the late stage of Ibsen as that of a "realistic" symbolist. I cannot here enter into Ivanov's polemics with his Russian contem-poraries: obviously this distinction played a major part in the split of the Symbolist movement.

The article on realism is of less interest: it gives information about the French debate and the association of realism with sociology and positivism. Condemnation emerges only at the end: "Realism," Ivanov says, "as an ideology (a sure sign of its anti-artistic nature) has overstepped the limits of art." Only Maupassant and Verga are praised: they knew how to free themselves from a bad theory.

The long (42 large pages) article on Goethe for *A History of Western Literature,* edited by Batyushkov in 1914, is a well-informed survey of Goethe's life and writings. Ivanov read widely in Goethe, drawing even on recondite corners of his enormous *oeuvre.* He must have studied some of the huge literature on Goethe: once he refers to an article in the *Goethe-Jahrbuch* (p. 145) and to the life of Goethe by Richard Moritz Meyer (1894, p. 148). Ivanov gives short but substantially accurate accounts of Goethe's esthetics and his interest in the natural sciences; he describes *Iphigenie auf Tauris* as a "sermon of eighteenth-century humanism" (p. 129) and *Torquato Tasso* as a masked confession, and alludes to and quotes from *The Roman Elegies* and some of the hymns, either in literal translation or in his own verse translations. If this were all, the piece would be no more than an excellent handbook article. But it bears the stamp of Ivanov's personal views in his emphasis on the classical and late period of Goethe and in his playing-down and sometimes downright ignoring

of the period usually called "Storm and Stress." There is not a word
about Herder or Spinoza, and the full account of *Faust* barely mentions the Gretchen tragedy. Ivanov admires Goethe's victory over the
Werther mood and his turn to antiquity. Much is made of the trip
to Italy, of Winckelmann, German classical scholarship and the
friendship with Schiller. Ivanov speaks of Goethe's objectivism, his
rejection of what he calls, with Husserl, "psychologism." But the
admiration for the classical Goethe is overshadowed by his admiration
for the symbolism of his last works. "His poetics," he states at the
outset, "appears, in general, to be our poetics of the last
years" (p. 114). The interpretation of *Faust* is slanted toward the last
scene of the second part: the glorification of the Eternal Feminine.
The line, "Alles Vergängliche ist nur ein Gleichnis . . . ," is considered to be written under the influence of Schelling (p. 138) and
to anticipate Vladimir Solovyov, the two main sources of Ivanov's
own esthetics. Much of the reading of *Faust* seems to me forced, as
is the attempt to deny pantheism in Goethe by quoting theistic
phraseology in his pronouncements. Still, the article contains many
shrewd remarks. Ivanov's view that "Goethe was much more of a
historian than he is ordinarily considered" and that "at least, he
thought historically" (p. 132) has been elaborated by Friedrich Mei-
necke in his *Entstehung des Historismus* (1936), and the reflections on
Goethe's avoidance of tragedy have been developed in Erich Heller's
Disinherited Mind (1952). Ivanov's view that the second part of *Faust*
and *Wilhelm Meisters Wanderjahre* are underrated and still speak to
our time has been amply vindicated, at least with respect to the
second part of *Faust*.

Another group of essays could be called occasional. An article
on "Shakespeare and Cervantes" was written in 1916 for the tercen-
tenary of their deaths. (Incidentally, Ivanov repeats the old idea that
they died on the same day, April 23. But Shakespeare's death is
recorded according to the Julian calendar still in force in England
while Spain already used the Gregorian, then ten days ahead.) The
essay assumes a conception of history which considers the Renaissance
as a decline from the Middle Ages into modern individualism and
secularism. Shakespeare—in a way most modern scholars would not

accept—is described as having broken with the tradition and the old faith. His cultural "knapsack" was light: it contained only the Bible, two or three chronicles and Plutarch (see p. 105). But Ivanov grants that Shakespeare felt the mystery of life yet denies that there is true catharsis in his tragedies, as it can be achieved only on the ground of a religious synthesis of the tragic contradictions of life. Shakespeare makes his protagonists (Lear, Hamlet) escape into madness, reducing the power of reason to absurdity. Birnam Wood approaching the castle of Macbeth is used as a symbol for the victory of belief over reason—a far-fetched allegorization which is the main flaw in Ivanov's criticism.

Cervantes is interpreted as exposing the irrational to ridicule. Don Quixote is a loving saint crucified by Reason. But Cervantes himself was saved by his faith in the Church: something of the mystical Spanish soul remained burning in him.

The essay on Schiller written for the centenary of his death in 1905 shows much more sympathy and personal engagement. Ivanov deplores the way Schiller was seen as an abstract idealist who became a classic for the German middle classes and schools and could be called a "Moraltrompeter" by Nietzsche. Ivanov discovers in some of Schiller's lyrics something "mysterious and inward," a "sibylline murmur" which makes him "a priest and a mystagogue" (p. 78). Ivanov quotes poems such as "Sehnsucht" and "Der Pilgrim," whose conclusion, "Und das *Dort* ist niemals *Hier*," Ivanov considers "pure mysticism." He finds Christian symbolism in "Das Berglied": the door, the valley, the four streams and the Queen (who seems to me merely a trite personification of the mountain, possibly *Die Jungfrau*). Besides, argues Ivanov, Schiller anticipated the future choric drama and wrote the dithyramb, the "Hymn to Joy," used in Beethoven's Ninth Symphony. Dmitry Karamazov quotes it and "Das eleusische Fest." The essay ends with a reservation: Schiller, in his dithyrambs, says "yes" to the world but it is a "yes" from need and not from plenitude, a distinction drawn from Nietzsche. Schiller called himself a "sentimental" poet and this is also Ivanov's conclusion. In spite of celebrating the gods of Greece, Schiller was a deeply Christian poet, and a poet of community, as he revives the Greek chorus in

The Bride of Messina, and depicts the nation as a totality in the Switzerland of *Wilhelm Tell.* Schiller is thus seen as a precursor of what Ivanov himself hoped for: a new drama as national festivities. The essay hardly pretends to a total view: the main plays and theoretical writings are ignored. Ivanov presses casual metaphors to discover mysticism for which I see no evidence, and ignores Schiller's deep *malaise* and even distrust of life and his willed assertion of freedom. But it would lead too far to defend a different image of Schiller's person and work.

Ivanov admired Byron greatly. In 1909 he translated Byron's last long poem, *The Island,* based on Captain Bligh's story of the mutiny on the *Bounty,* and wrote an introduction on "Byron and the Idea of Anarchy." He argues there that Byron was torn between his pride, his individualistic titanism as in *Childe Harold, Manfred,* and *Cain,* and a passion for the freedom of suppressed nations which led him to support the *carbonari* and finally die for the independence of Greece. *The Island* envisages a utopia which combines anarchy with community. A later essay, "Byronism as an Event in the Life of the Russian Spirit" (1917), argues unconvincingly that Byronism in Russia did not mean pessimism, *Weltschmerz,* but only the revelation of personality. Byron's concept of freedom is quite different from that of the French Revolution, which Ivanov considers to be purely negative. Byron believed in a personal and living God, in "the religious idea of man as the Son of God," a questionable assertion as Byron was rather a deist who doubted personal immortality and condemned all churches.

The most interesting single literary essay is "Gogol's *Inspector General* and the Comedy of Aristophanes" (1925). Ivanov argues that Gogol's play is a radical innovation in the history of comedy. It harks back to the Old Comedy of Greece, to Aristophanes, where a commune acts and speaks, rather than to the New Comedy of Menander and Terence, which is concerned with private affairs. Ivanov sympathizes with Gogol's much later allegorical interpretation of his comedy as a "drama of the soul," though he recognizes that this was an attempt to make it sound innocuous and could not have been his original intention. The town is, however, a collective as in a

morality play. The last speech of the Mayor, addressed to the townspeople and implicitly to the audience, and culminating in his shout-
ing: "What are you laughing at? You are laughing at yourselves!"
is seen as a revival of the Aristophanic *parabasis,* as the address of
the chorus to the people. The Mayor appears as the voice of the
chorus, the town. The impostor Khlestakov is not, Ivanov argues
somewhat too ingeniously, an outsider but the protagonist of the
place, "the very flesh and bone of the town (though it may be some
other just like this one)." Khlestakov, after all, originally had no
intention of impersonating the Inspector. The role is forced upon
him. Still, Ivanov must recognize that at the end the Mayor turns
against his fellow townsmen, but he tries to show that the Mayor is
still tied to them. When the Mayor asks the others to throw off
their masks ("I see only pig's snouts instead of faces—nothing else!")
it becomes clear that the Mayor and the town are one and that the
town is one with the laughing spectators.

This is a brilliant essay. I can only doubt whether Gogol's
procedure has no antecedents except in Aristophanes. There are mobs
with speakers sometimes called Citizen 1 and Citizen 2 in Shakespeare. Most strikingly in Lope de Vega's *Fuenteovejuna* (1618?) the
village of this name forms a collective and even under torture answers
chorally, "Fuenteovejuna," to the questioners who want to know who
killed the commander, who abducted Laurencia. Also in Calderón's
El alcalde di Zalamea (1636) the village forms a collective supporting
the mayor in his defiance of authority. Addresses to the audience are
common in *Commedia dell'arte,* and even Molière's *L'Avare* appeals
at the end of the play to the audience for the return of his pink box.
August von Platen composed Aristophanic comedies, complete with
parabases, in German before Gogol's play (1836). I don't know
enough of Goldoni and Gozzi or the minor comedy writers Gogol
may have read or seen on the stage in Italy to suggest anticipations.
Gogol may not have known any of these plays. I only want to argue
that Ivanov overstates his case for the novelty of Gogol's communal
or choral presentation.

By far the most extensive studies of a single author were, however, Ivanov's writings on Dostoevsky. One must distinguish several

stages. There is a long essay on Dostoevsky dating from 1911; there is a short piece on *The Possessed* dating from 1914: both were published in the collection *Furrows and Boundaries* (*Borozdy i mezhi*) in 1916. There is an essay "The Face and Masks of Russia" (*Lik i lichiny Rossii*), mainly on *The Brothers Karamazov*, written in 1916, published in the collection *Matters Native and Universal* (*Rodnoe i vselenskoe*) in 1917; and there is finally a German book, *Dostojewskij. Tragödie-Mythos-Mystik* (1932), which was translated as *Freedom and the Tragic Life* into English in 1952. I am told that the Russian original of the German book has been lost. It would be an interesting task far exceeding my purpose to compare the different versions: to see what Ivanov eliminated in the final book, what he added and what he changed.

One must see Ivanov's essays as part of the trend to interpret Dostoevsky in religious terms, in contrast to the rival view which sees him mainly as a depth psychologist, an existentialist, and a social historian. It began with Vladimir Solovyov's three speeches in 1883, in which he hailed Dostoevsky as a "prophet of God," a "mystical seer." V. V. Rozanov then examined "The Legend of the Grand Inquisitor" (in 1890) almost as sacred text. Dmitri Merezhkovsky's *Tolstoy and Dostoevsky* (1901) then drew the famous contrast between Tolstoy, "the seer of the flesh," and Dostoevsky, "the seer of the spirit." Merezhkovsky argued that Dostoevsky is not a realist but a symbolist. Leo Shestov juxtaposed *Dostoevsky and Nietzsche* (1903), the pessimistic visionary of catastrophe and decay to the optimistic prophet of the superman. Ivanov belongs to this group: he shares their view of the transcendent importance and ultimate truth of Dostoevsky's doctrines consonant with Russian Orthodoxy, but he differs from them by focusing on the figures and actions in the novels rather than on some abstract doctrines extracted from them. He conceived of the four great novels (*Crime and Punishment, The Idiot, The Possessed* and *The Brothers Karamazov*, hardly referring to other works) as myths on the analogy of the plots of Greek tragedy. Thus *Crime and Punishment* is interpreted as showing the rebellion of human pride and presumption (*hubris*) against the holy laws of Mother Earth, the fatal derangement of the senses of the culprit (his *até*), the anger of the earth at the bloodshed, the ritual purgation of the murderer chased by the inner Fury, kissing the earth in front of the assembled people, and finally the recognition of the right way through suffering—*padeimados* (German ed. 1932, pp. 64–65). The book is reduced to the bare outlines of a myth. The model of Gilbert Murray's scheme and the work of the other "Cambridge anthropologists" is obvious, not to speak of the inspiration of Nietzsche's *Birth of Tragedy* (1871).

The early 1911 essay had not gone that far. There Dostoevsky's innovations are rehearsed, the history of the novel is sketched, Dostoevsky's immediate antecedents—Rousseau, Schiller, Balzac, Dickens, George Sand, E. T. A. Hoffmann, and Gogol—are briefly considered. Gogol could have influenced Dostoevsky only in the period of *Poor People*, as he is the polar opposite of Dostoevsky: Ivanov states that his characters have no soul while Dostoevsky's are nothing but soul. Then Ivanov makes the proposal that a Dostoevsky novel should be called a "novel-tragedy," the kind of hyphenation common in Russian. It has been widely accepted, though it says no more than the old "tragic" novel, contrasted with the commonly used "comic" novel. Ivanov considers the *Iliad* a tragedy in epic form and argues that Dostoevsky simply reintroduced tragedy into the epic. *Catharsis,* Ivanov explains, had a purely religious meaning in Greek tragedy. Aristotle made it psychological. Dostoevsky returned it to its religious meaning. He wants us to become different beings. Later, Ivanov expounds the difference between idealism which leads to solipsism and his kind of realism which assumes the existence of other selves. Ivanov gives it a Latin version "Es, ergo sum," parodying Descartes, and he assumes that it contains a postulate of God and Christ. The source is in Schopenhauer's citation of the Sanskrit *Tat tvam asi* ("I am you"). (See also Ivanov's poems and the section *Ty esi* in *Chelovek* [*SS,* IV, 207] and an article [*SS,* III, 262, cf. 745], published in 1907.) Schopenhauer, of course, would not have drawn the theistic consequences from the identification of "I" and "thou." At least Ivanov returns to something strictly literary, distinguishing three planes in Dostoevsky's novels: the fabulistic, the psychological, and the metaphysical (the decision for or against God). Men have an

"empirical" and a "metaphysical" character. The four brothers Karamazov are characterized in these terms. Smerdyakov has no metaphysical character at all, Ivan knows God but cannot accept him,
Dmitry is divided. For a time he wished his father's death, but then
returned to God: not speaking but singing his hallelujah, his "yes"
and "amen" to the Creator of the world. The injustice of his sentence
becomes an instrument of divine justice. Alyosha has a metaphysical
character, he is a saint. Ivanov then distingishes between different
kinds of guilt, first in Greek tragedy and then analogously in Dostoevsky. Guilt is either the will of Fate or is due to the hero's wrong
preference for one god only, and finally it is the guilt of existence,
of merely appearing on earth. The first idea of fate appears in Dostoevsky as the irrevocable choice between God and the Devil: the
struggle between these two kinds of men as it is depicted in *The
Possessed*. The preference for one God, that is, an exclusive passion
which leads to guilt, is rare in Dostoevsky: the Raw Youth, Rogozhin and Dmitry qualify. The third guilt, the mere fact of incarnation is Myshkin's. He comes into the world as a stranger, a guest,
and does not understand and forgive the world.

    All the emphasis in Ivanov's interpretation falls on the purifi-
cation, the redemption, so much so that the crime of Raskolnikov
is treated as a temporary aberration. Raskolnikov has an inborn
knowledge of the sacred realities of being. He killed the pawnbroker
to prove idealism but discovered it to be false, and resurrects his
soul by love and contact with Mother Earth, "the vision of primitive
pure days" when the nomads roamed the steppes of Asia. The earth
is in Dostoevsky the symbol of communion. Not that Dostoevsky
has much concern for nature, Ivanov admits: there are the steppes
in the Epilogue of *Crime and Punishment,* there is Alyosha seeing the
starry sky, there is the little star and the "tender emerald sea" in
the *Dream of a Ridiculous Man* and there is the dark rustling park
in which Shatov is killed. That is all. But Marya Timofeevna, the
Cripple, whose soul has the "substantiality of mystical depths,"
proclaims that "God and Nature are one," that "the Mother of God
is the great Mother Earth," that "our tears should water the earth."
In Ivanov's interpretation the Cripple reflects the soul of the Great

Mother Damp Earth, waiting for the sunny Bridegroom, the Russian *hypostasis,* the soul of the Russian earth. To Ivanov she expresses the mystical psychology of the Russian national element which is love, longing, faith and hope, and not the battlefield of history. The Cripple looks for the face of Christ in all humanity.

These sixty pages are an impressive statement of the parallelism between Greek tragedy and Dostoevsky's novels and their underlying myths. The account of Dostoevsky's innovations, of his historical position and antecedents is generally accurate. Also the motifs of tragic guilt are well distinguished, though I think that Ivanov over-emphasizes the Epilogue of *Crime and Punishment,* making Raskol-nikov's murder a mere episode in a story of redemption, and that he inflates Marya Timofeevna to a mythic figure of Mother-Earth which is at the same time the Mother of God.

The long essay dating from 1911 was supplemented in 1914 by an article on *The Possessed.* In *The Possessed* Dostoevsky conceives of the nation as a person, a unity which has two principles: the feminine and the masculine. The first is represented by the Mother Earth, the World Soul; the second, the masculine, by the hierarchy of heavenly powers, by allegiance either to God or to Satan. In *The Possessed* the masculine element chose to close itself against God and Christ while the feminine element, the Soul-Earth, sighs and waits for the Bridegroom but discovers that he is a Pretender and curses him. The Eternal Feminine suffers under the demons. Even the Mother of God is insulted in the symbolic episode of the live mouse in the icon, though the demons cannot reach her fully. When the burned house is searched after the murder of the Cripple, the silver setting of the icon of the Virgin Mary has not been touched. Ivanov draws an elaborate parallel to Goethe's *Faust.* The Cripple takes the place of Gretchen. Stavrogin is a negative Faust, negative because he has ceased to love and strive. The role of Mephisto is taken by Pyotr Verkhovensky. The terror of the Cripple at the sudden ap-pearance of Stavrogin in her room is anticipated by the scene with Gretchen in the jail. The Cripple's ravings about a child are almost the same as the hallucinations of Gretchen. The Cripple's song is the song of the Russian soul like Gretchen's song of the "King of

Thule" and his goblet. The Cripple is a medium of the Mother-Earth, the Soul of the Russian Earth. She is Stavrogin's legal wife though she remains a virgin. "The Prince of this World" thus lords it over the Soul of the World but cannot really touch her—just like the sixth husband of the Woman of Samaria in the Gospel of St. John. The Cripple knows that she is guilty before the other Prince, the Prince of Glory. Her lameness signifies her secret guilt, the guilt of original incompleteness, of opposition to the Bridegroom who abandons her as Eros abandons Psyche for her sin. The Cripple curses Stavrogin, as the Pretender, the false Dmitry, the ally of Satan. Stavrogin was, after all, disloyal to Satan, betrayed the revolution and returned to his mountain retreat. Still, he had ruled the herd of the demons. Two of them separated from the crowd: Kirillov and Shatov. Ivanov explains them well: Kirillov loves Christ, but wants to become God and commits suicide. Shatov wavers as his name suggests. He had a false relation to Christ: he did not know the Father through him. He thought that the Russian Christ was the nation itself: he elevated the nation to divinity. Shatov believed in the soul of the Earth: he is thus kindred to Marya Timofeevna, a guardian of the Female Soul in its sin and humiliation. Shatov is torn to pieces (hardly literally—Peter kills him with a shot from his pistol) by the demons because he did not give himself to them unreservedly. Dostoevsky in this novel raises the question whether Russia can become holy Russia. He began to dream of the mysterious mission of the elder Zosima, one of the "pure and elect," a forerunner of a "new kind of people and a new life."

The article makes many true observations and characterizes some of the main figures well. But it suffers from inflation of the role of the Cripple and of her worship of Mother-Earth. Dostoevsky himself could never have agreed with her saying: "God and Nature are one." The parallel with *Faust* limps badly. To say that Stavrogin is a negative Faust without love and striving means that he is no Faust. The crowded, even overcrowded novel becomes unfocused, distorted by the emphasis on the Mother-Earth motif.

The 1932 book reprints with many cuts, small additions and changes the two essays just discussed and uses the 1916 essay on

The Brothers Karamzov. The passages on literary history are dropped,
the tone has become more ecstatic. Sometimes details are added
which seem to be based on only vague memories of the texts. Thus,
as the parallel between Marya Timofeevna and Gretchen is reproduced, we are told that "similarly Gretchen turns, in her song, from
the old King of the farthest West, of *Ultima Thule,* and from his
sun-goblet, to the distant beloved, and touchingly adjures him to
keep faith—by returning as a new sun" (p. 61). The 1914 essay
contains no such statement. There is nothing in *Faust* to suggest it:
Gretchen sings the song in which there is no word of a sun or a new
sun (only of gold) before she sees the casket of jewels Mephisto had
left in her bedroom. She has just been accosted by Faust in the street
and merely wonders who he may be. He is not distant, nor does she
adjure him to keep faith, as he had not and could not yet have
pledged it.

    This strange loss of contact with a text becomes obtrusively
obvious in the new parts. Some comments lifted from the 1916 essay
on the *Brothers* are still defensible. Ivanov distinguishes between two
kinds of devils: Lucifer and Ahriman (Dostoevsky never uses the
second, Zoroastrian term). Luciferian figures are full of pride, rebels
against God; the captives of Ahriman are simply evil: Svidrigailov
imagining eternity as a bathhouse full of spiders, Fyodor Karamazov
with his grudge against God. Also Dmitry has nothing of Lucifer
in him. Ivan is a vassal of Lucifer but Ahriman's darkness thickens
around his Luciferian light and brings forth Smerdyakov and the
shabby devil. Much is made of Alyosha ruling the community of
boys and of Ilyusha and his transformation by death. The brotherhood of the boys foreshadows the coming hagiocracy, the government
of the saints, the reign of Christ forming invisibly in this world. In
1916 Ivanov apparently believed that the triumph of Christ is fatefully ordained and that Dostoevsky is the great prophet of his victory.

    But the interpretation of the novels shows an increased forcing
of the allegory. The view that Dostoevsky's works all deal "with
man's revolt against Mother Earth" makes Ivanov say that the
money-lender killed by Raskolnikov is "the female avenger," "the
emissary of Mother Earth" (p. 76). Both Raskolnikov and Hermann

in Pushkin's *Queen of Spades* are guilty of killing the Fate, and must suffer her posthumous revenge. The old countess is identified with the money-lender and both are, somehow, Earth goddesses. Poor Sonya is considered a "great sinner" as she takes upon herself "not only suffering but also the curse of another's deed, by making it her own" (p. 82). Raskolnikov is a scapegoat who has consented to carry out "the will of the many which is directed toward the elimination of the repulsive old woman" (p. 84). Surely there is no hint that the loner Raskolnikov is the instrument of a collective will, nor can I see the old money-lender as an "emissary of Mother Earth" (she seems particularly far removed from it) or see the sin of Sonya in knowing Raskolnikov's guilt and sharing his Siberian exile.

The *Idiot* is even more completely allegorized in defiance of the text. Myshkin, we are told, "is, above all, the type of a spirituality that descends, that seeks the Earth: rather a spirit that assumes flesh than a man who rises to the spiritual. All his glory lies behind him in the past . . ." (p. 90). Ivanov ignores the description of "the complete breakdown of his mental faculties," his imbecility, the visit of Mrs. Yepanchin, who "wept bitterly when she saw the prince in his sick and humiliating condition." In Ivanov's reading, Myshkin longs for incarnation. Aglaya wants to "enfold him in her primitive darkness," an odd characterization to apply to that beautiful girl with nihilistic sympathies whom Ivanov calls "festively resplendent" on the very same page (p. 98). Myshkin's pity for Nastasya proves, however, stronger than his love for Aglaya. But the famous last scene—Rogozhin and Myshkin keeping vigil at the bed of the dead Nastasya—is completely misread. Ivanov tells us that "Myshkin, knowing nothing of the bloody deed that has been wrought, stations himself at the murderer's bidding beside the virginal-nuptial bed, close by his murdered bride, who is hidden by a curtain, while Parfyon (Rogozhin) lies on the other side" (p. 104). But from the text it is perfectly obvious that Myshkin not only suspects but knows that Rogozhin killed Nastasya. He asks Rogozhin: "Was it you?" and Rogozhin answers, "Yes, me." Shortly afterward they both speak of the smell of the corpse. Myshkin asks: "What did you kill her with? The knife? The same one?" and Rogozhin obliges with the information that "the knife went in three or four inches—just under the left breast—and no more than half a tablespoon of blood came out under the nightshirt."

One has to conclude that Ivanov is expounding a book which he would have wanted Dostoevsky to have written, rather than the one he actually wrote. We can imagine the scheme: the Christ-like man who descends from the upper world to seek incarnation through Love, but fails and is received back into Heaven. Yet it seems to me a proof of Dostoevsky's honesty and artistry that he wrote a very different book, where Nastasya's corpse is to smell "by tomorrow morning," where Rogozhin put four uncorked bottles of disinfectant next to it, where a fly, awakened from its sleep, starts buzzing, and where Myshkin is returned to Switzerland in a state of complete imbecility, and Aglaya marries a fake Polish count and is converted *terribile dictu* to Roman Catholicism.

The interpretation of *The Idiot* shows the dangers of arbitrary allegorizing which has damaged criticism not only of Dostoevsky but of almost any author, ancient and modern, one can think of. It is a prime example of how a mistaken interpretation can be refuted by appeal to a text which is unambiguous on all essential points at issue. In their later stages Ivanov's readings of Dostoevsky are misreadings explainable and excusable by his religious preoccupations, but misreadings nevertheless. It is a recent superstition that misreadings cannot be corrected. Ivanov's case demonstrates the truth of the old wisdom that there is a difference between correct and incorrect reading, however difficult it may be to decide on it in some cases.

Tolstoy must appear to Ivanov as the antipode of Dostoevsky. In an article, "Tolstoy and Culture" (*Tolstoj i kul'tura*) published in 1912 in *Logos,* the Russian and German philosophical periodical where in the same volume Georg Simmel, Heinrich Rickert, Georg von Lukács (still "von" at that time) and others published substantial essays. Ivanov, after a tribute to the flight and death of Tolstoy, describes him as a "terrible simplifier" who found only words of prohibition: don't drink, don't smoke, reject sensuality, don't swear, don't fight wars and do not resist evil. Tolstoy, Ivanov states, had an *odium generationis,* a hatred for the origin of forms, a deeply anchored rejection of Dionysus, or rather of his world. The pathos of the artist Tolstoy is a pathos of unmasking and accusation, an antinomian and hence totally anti-artistic pathos. Tolstoy's religion is supposed to be similar to Buddhism, but he thought of it as essential Christianity. Yet if Christianity means what Ivanov considers it—a belief in God's descent into the world, the will to restore and justify the earth in God, a belief in the resurrection of the body, and in the mystic marriage of the heavenly Bridegroom with his earthly Bride—then Tolstoy's worldview is immeasurably remote from Christianity and the Christian Church. His views imply also the abandonment of a belief in the superempirical reality of the national existence. Tolstoy, in short, is a Westerner though he does not want Russia to fuse with Western Europe. Rather, with him the genius of the nation extends its hand to America. In Tolstoy's doctrines there are traits of Anglo-Saxon sermonizing. Tolstoy is not an expression of the Russian national soul but a product of Russian cosmopolitan education, of the highest strata of society and not of its national depths. Tolstoy is a phenomenon of "culture," understood, I assume, as the opposite of nature and nation. Tolstoy's situation and outlook are similar to those of Socrates, interpreted in terms of Nietzsche's denunciation of him as a rationalist who identifies religion with morality and denies the creative and instinctive depths of life. Tolstoy shares his illusion—denying heredity, the influence of environment and education—that if we once understand what is the Good, we shall act as a morally consistent personality. Ivanov distinguishes between three types of attitudes toward culture: the relativistic, the ascetic, and the symbolistic. The first abandons the religious foundation of culture and conceives it as a system of relative values. The second (which is Tolstoy's) emphasizes the moral basis of cultural production and subjects it to a moral utilitarianism. It is based on a deep distrust of nature. The third type, the symbolistic, seems to Ivanov the only correct and sane one. It asks us to change culture into a symbology of spiritual values corresponding to the hierarchies of the divine world and to justify all human doings and creations by their symbolic relations to the Absolute; in other words, it defines its task as a transfiguration of all culture and with it of all nature into a mystic Church. Tolstoy was never a symbolist. In Ivanov's essay, *War and Peace* is not mentioned, *Anna Karenina* is only alluded to as leading up to *The Kreutzer Sonata*. It is hardly *literary* criticism.

We see the norm with which Ivanov judges Tolstoy and all other writers: it is religious in the specific sense of a belief in a system of doctrines and salvation history. This is why Dostoevsky is for him the central writer. Ivanov managed in his own mind to reconcile this norm with an admiration for Greek tragedy, which outlined, he assumed, the same basic myth of salvation. Extravagantly, Ivanov assimilates Dostoevsky, rooted in Eastern Orthodoxy, to ancient Greek exuberance. "The Muse of Dostoevsky," Ivanov states fancifully, "resembles a Dionysiac Maenad, the daughter of Darkness, the hunting dog of the Goddess of Night, the innately learned Fury, with a torch in one hand and a scourge in the other." Ivanov had to devalue writers like Shakespeare or Cervantes who did not conform to this norm, and he can praise poets like Goethe, Schiller, and Byron for glimpses of the higher world. The criticism even of plots or figures is thus always a criticism of ideas, or rather of religious attitudes and beliefs. No doubt Ivanov felt that this was his highest obligation.

Mandelshtam's "Silentium":
A Poet's Response to Ivanov
John E. Malmstad

In a 1913 essay, "On the Addressee" (*O sobesednike*), Osip Mandel-shtam reproached the Symbolists for never troubling to ask them-selves whom they were addressing. Mandelshtam himself was always conscious of his "addressee" and made his verse a kind of constant dialogue ("*Net liriki bez dialoga*") with contemporaries, figures from the past, and, ideally, the readers he would find in the future.[1] Over the last few decades much work has been done to elucidate this complex of "addressees," yet much remains unclear in our efforts to acquire, as it were, Mandelshtam's culture and thus the ability to "read" the texture of his art. No area has been more unjustly ne-glected than his relationship with Symbolists such as Sologub and particularly with Vyacheslav Ivanov, who, along with Annensky and Tyutchev, "exerted a strong influence" on him, in the words of one of the leading authorities on his work.[2]

Akhmatova asserted that "by 1911 Mandelshtam had no rev-erence at all for Vyacheslav Ivanov."[3] There is much evidence to the contrary which suggests that she and the poet's widow (in her mem-oirs) let literary and personal animosities get the better of the facts. We know from Sergey Kablukov's diary, for example, that Mandel-shtam made several visits to Ivanov (two as late as 1916), and that Ivanov's "recognition" (*priznanie*) of the second edition of *Stone* (*Ka-men'*) meant a great deal to him, as did Ivanov's efforts on his behalf with publishers.[4] His letters to Ivanov reveal deep admiration for the older man, as well as the care and attention with which he read and absorbed Ivanov's verse and critical writings. We also know that Mandelshtam twice inscribed copies of the first edition of *Stone* to

Ivanov in 1913, after the young poets of the "Tsekh poetov" had publicly announced their allegiance to Acmeism. The two dedications show no lessening of his feelings for Ivanov: "To Vyacheslav Ivanov with joyous admiration. The author. May 13, 1913." "To Vyacheslav Ivanovich Ivanov with profound gratitude and real love. The author. October 2, 1913. Petersburg."[5] Studies by Kiril Taranovsky and G. A. Levinton have proven the presence of "enciphered" lines from Ivanov in poems of 1919–1920 (and, no doubt, later ones as well), which make clear that after 1911 Mandelshtam read *Cor Ardens* (1911), *Tender Mystery* (*Nezhnaja tajna*, 1912), and the translations of *Alcaeus and Sappho* (*Alkej i Safo*, 1914).[6] The poet and his wife also stopped to see Ivanov in 1921 on their way through Baku.

In the last letter we have from Mandelshtam to Ivanov (No. 10, August 21/September 3, 1911), the young poet "rushed" to relate a piece of news which he believed would excite Ivanov as much as it had him: the possibility that new poems by Tyutchev had been discovered.[7] Ivanov's articles attest to his love for his nineteenth-century predecessor. Tyutchev's considerable influence on his verse, evident in allusions and intonational patterns, for example, has yet to receive critical attention. The impact of Tyutchev on Mandelshtam, on the other hand, has been much studied. Several articles have been devoted to a specific instance of it, the 1910 poem "Silentium." Yet the exclusive concern with Tyutchev has in the case of this particular poem obscured the no less profound influence of Ivanov. It is on this poem that I want to focus, first by establishing (and expanding) the context in which it should be read and then, to borrow the terminology of Taranovsky, by indicating a specific subtext for it.

Let me quickly summarize previous comment on Mandelshtam's poem. Kiril Taranovsky has called it a "poetic polemic with Tyutchev."[8] Jan Meijer has gone further, stating that the poem "is both a case of quoting of and polemics with Tyutchev and thereby with symbolism," and Ryszard Przybylski even further: "Mandelshtam's poem is an Acmeist reply {sic—in 1910 there was, of course, no Acmeism} to Tyutchev's famous 'Silentium!' At the same time it polemicizes with the Symbolist perception of the Tyutchev tradi-

tion."[9] Nikolaj Khardzhiev, in his notes for the *Biblioteka poeta* edition of Mandelshtam, writes: "The poem recalls Tyutchev's
'Silentium!,'" but is even more connected with the poetic declarations
of the Symbolists, in particular with Verlaine's 'Art poétique' ('De
la musique avant toute chose . . .')."[10] Khardzhiev, one notes, mentions unspecified "Symbolist declarations," but, following Gumilev,
focuses on French, not Russian antecedents.[11] Przybylski does refer
to Ivanov in his article, but only in a general (and highly tendentious)
discussion on Mandelshtam and Symbolist notions of music.

If the poem is a polemic with the Symbolist view of Tyutchev,
then why was it written in 1910 and not later, when the younger
generation was openly stating its differences with Symbolism? And
why does the poem take the form of a myth, the first in Mandelshtam's *oeuvre*? The poem has elements in common with earlier Mandelshtam texts, and the theme of silence is central in this period of
Mandelshtam's art.[12] However, the key words *slovo* (word) and *muzyka*
(music) appear together in this poem for the first time, and much
of its other vocabulary, including the colors, appears nowhere else
in Mandelshtam. One should also add that while a close reader might
have detected the presence of Tyutchev in the poem's oppositions
(*zvuchanie-tishina* [sound-silence], *dvizhenie-pokoj* [movement-stasis],
or *more-muzyka, zvuchanie* [the sea-music, sound], as for example in
"There is melody in the waves of the sea" [*Pevuchest' est' v morskikh
volnakh*]), the poem did not acquire the title "Silentium," the feature
which most vividly betokens a connection with Tyutchev, until its
publication in the first edition of *Stone* in 1913. It was therefore far
more ambivalent, even cautious, in its first appearance in print, and
direct connections with "Silentium!" were far more tenuous. This
fact is quite appropriate, given that it is, in my view, primarily a
response not to Tyutchev or Verlaine, but to Ivanov, whom Mandelshtam in 1910 still revered, yet from whom he was beginning
to distance himself as he developed his own poetic method. It is not
a polemic but the beginning of a serious dialogue with Ivanov which
would become polemical only in later essays.

On March 17, 1910, Ivanov gave a lecture entitled "On New
Literary Groupings" (*O novykh literaturnykh gruppirovkakh*) at a meet-

ing of the Moscow Society for Free Esthetics (*Obshchestvo svobodnoj estetiki*). He read an expanded version in Petersburg on March 26 at a meeting of the so-called Academy (*Akademija*), i.e., the Society of Adherents of the Artistic Word (*Obshchestvo revnitelej khudozhestvennogo slova*), in the editorial offices of the new journal *Apollon.*[13] We do not know whether Mandelshtam was present on either occasion, although he regularly attended the Petersburg gatherings of the Academy. But he could not have been unaware that these two meetings had taken place. Ivanov himself wrote to Blok on March 25 that his talk "on the contemporary state of symbolism and whether symbolism still exists" had caused a "sensation" in "our circles" in Moscow.[14] On April 13, Anna Mintslova reported to Bely from Petersburg that the "Academy" reading had provoked a similar reaction there (*vyzvalo bol'shoj povorot i volnenie*).[15] Mandelshtam paid close attention to what was happening in Petersburg literary circles, and must have heard of the lecture, even if he did not attend it. It is simply inconceivable that he did not *read* the lecture when it appeared, in a radically reworked form, as a programmatic article under the title "The Testaments of Symbolism" (*Zavety simvolizma*) in the eighth issue (May-June) of *Apollon,* together with Blok's equally well-known reply "On the Present State of Russian Symbolism" (*O sovremennom sostojanii russkogo simvolizma*). The next issue (No. 9, July-August) contained Bryusov's reply to both Ivanov and Blok; and it was in this very issue that Mandelshtam made his debut as a poet. Among his five poems published there was the one we now know as "Silentium." In fact, this was yet another response (albeit a poetic one) to Ivanov's article, but was overlooked in the noisy polemics which followed the appearance of the articles by Ivanov and Blok.[16]

Mandelshtam's poem responds primarily to the first two sections of Ivanov's article and it is to them that I will confine my discussion. Ivanov opens by citing Tyutchev's famous "A thought that is uttered is a lie" (*Mysl' izrechennaja est' lozh'*).[17] He then sets forth a reading of "Silentium!" and several other Tyutchev lyrics in much the same way as he had in 1904 in the essay "The Poet and the Mob" (*Poet i chern'*), included in *By the Stars* (*Po zvezdam*). In both contexts Ivanov emphasizes the gulf between the "spiritual growth of the personality" (*dukhovnyj rost lichnosti*) and the "external means" of communication. The word is no longer "equally matched" with the more developed internal world of the poet; language has lagged behind spiritual growth. Thus, attempts to express the internal world must result in a "lie." Yet the creator must express himself, and therefore has recourse either to indirect communication (*priobshchenie,* a word with sacramental overtones), which disappoints his audience, or fails to resist the temptation of "direct communication" (*soobshchenie*), which gives the audience only the "lie." Ivanov refuses to accept defeat and sees hope in the "purely symbolic or mythological energy" of a special poetic language which alone can "restore the truth of the expressed thought" now, as it once did in a Golden Age when poets were priests.

"In the poetry of Tyutchev," Ivanov continues in the opening of the second section, Russian Symbolism first recognized the "need for a new poetic language." But Tyutchev, and Ivanov's fellow Symbolists, are at present locked in a dualism of consciousness and art, or in "antithesis," as he put it in the actual speech. Ivanov cites the famous "Oh my prophetic soul!" (*O, veshchaja dusha moja!*) as Tyutchev's expression of his divided consciousness, and views art (*tvorchestvo*) as equally split between the external world of Day, which envelops us in the "full brightness" of its "manifestations" (*projavlenija*), and a mysterious but terrifying world of Night. But this symbolic dualism of day and night, of a world of "perceptible 'manifestations'" (*chuvstvennye projavlenija*) and a world of "supersensible revelations" (*sverkhchuvstvennye otkrovenija*) only *seems* to be irreparably divided: "They are both together in poetry. Now we call them Apollo and Dionysus, we know their non-fusion (*neslijannost'*) and indivisibility, and sense in every true work of art their realized two-in-oneness (*dvuedinstvo*)." Tyutchev's divided soul experienced the pull of Dionysus, that craving to merge with the infinite (*I s bespredel'nym zhazhdet slit'sja*), more powerfully than the pull of Apollo. Therefore, to "preserve his individuality," to curb this craving, the "artist turns to the clear forms of diurnal existence," to those "patterns" (or "designs"—*uzory,* a favorite word in early Mandelshtam) of that veil

(Tyutchev's *pokrov*) which the gods have thrown over the "'nameless abyss,' i.e., that which does not find its name in the language of diurnal consciousness and external experience." Fearing absorption by Chaos (Dionysus), the artist turns to Cosmos (Apollo), external forms and instruments of expression—words. And yet, Ivanov continues, "the most precious moment in experience and the most prophetic in creation is the immersion in that contemplative ecstasy, when 'there is no boundary' between us and the 'naked abyss' yawning—in Silence.

> There is a certain hour of worldwide silence
> And in that hour of vision and marvels
> The living chariot of the universe
> Openly rolls through the sanctuary of the heavens.

> Est' nekij chas vsemirnogo molchan'ja,
> I v onyj chas javlenij i chudes
> Zhivaja kolesnitsa mirozdan'ja
> Otkryto katitsja v svjatilishche nebes."

Ivanov had himself undergone the experience Tyutchev had expressed in his "A Vision" (*Videnie*). And he knew the temptation of "ineffable silence" (*neizrechennoe molchanie*), as he put it in his poem "Silence" (*Molchanie*—"V tajnik bogatoj tishiny . . ,*" 1904–1907) in *Cor Ardens*. Nature, although itself without voice, could communicate with man. The artist-creator cannot communicate in this way and must break the Silence, that state of noumenal openness when the *realiora* are fully revealed and when "that art which we call Symbolic becomes possible." Poetry must give both the "external, phenomenal and the internal, noumenal" ("Macrocosm and Microcosm. 'As above, so below.'"), and its means of giving full and truthful expression to that for which there are "no words"—the *realia* and *realiora*—is the "word-symbol" (*slovo-simvol*) in its fullest form, Myth. As Ivanov had earlier written in "Premonitions and Portents" (*Predchuvstvija i predvestija*, 1906),

> In the sphere of symbolic art, the symbol reveals itself naturally as the potential and the embryo of myth. The organic course of

development turns symbolism into mythmaking. . . . The symbol
is supra-individual by its very nature, and that is why it has the
power to transmute the most intimate silence of the individual
mystical soul into an organ of universal collective thought (*edi-
nomyslie*) and collective feeling (*edinochuvstvie*) in a way similar to
the word and more powerfully than the ordinary word.

It is not hard to see that Mandelshtam's "Silentium" has far
more in common with the imagery of Ivanov's article, his notion of
Silence, and his general view of Tyutchev, than with the Tyutchev
poem "Silentium!" itself. Apollo and Dionysus, Cosmos and Chaos,
"formative" and "visionary" certainly underlie Mandelshtam's opposition of Word and Music; and the poem takes place in that moment (*svetel den'*) when the artist turns, as Ivanov puts it, to the
"clear forms of diurnal existence," i.e., words, in the face of the
"dremljushchij mir" out there. One also recalls Ivanov's expression
"ocharovanie *garmonii*" and his citation of Tyutchev's "V sej *zhivot-
vornyj okean*" near the end of the second section of the article. Mandelshtam's *svjaz'* might also be seen in Ivanov's discussion of the
essential syncretic unity which marked the Golden Age before that
division which has marked consciousness and art up to this present
fateful moment when it may be overcome. Even the poem's multiple
inversions are reminiscent of Ivanov's poetic style.

The second stanza of the poem has colors that never again
appear in Mandelshtam: "And the pale lilac of the foam / In the
cloudy azure vessel" (*I peny blednaja siren' / V mutno-lazorevom sosude*;
cherno-lazurevom [dark azure] in the later revised version). They may
have been suggested by Blok's response to Ivanov. In "On the Present
State of Russian Symbolism" Blok writes of the "purple-lilac" (*pur-
purno-lilovyj*) color of the ecstatic moment of inspiration, the "purple
of the lilac worlds" (*purpur lilovykh mirov*), and the world's opposing
"blue-lilac" (*sine-lilovyj*) shade. These colors, Blok notes, have been
best captured in Vrubel, who is also mentioned by Ivanov: "Peace
to your . . . shade, *madman* Vrubel" (*Mir tvoej . . . teni, bezumets
Vrubel'*).[19] We should also note the following from Ivanov's earlier
essay "Premonitions and Portents":

and in *music* itself the plastic *form* of a *radiantly* outlined melody suddenly arises from the *harmonious waves* and stands like an Apollonian vision above the *dark purple* depths of the orgiastic *swells*.

i v samoj *muzyke* vnezapno voznikaet iz *garmonicheskikh voln* plasticheskaja *forma solnechno*—ocherchennoj melodii i stoit apollinijskim videniem nad *temno-purpurnymi* glubinami orgijnykh *zybej*.[20]

But we should not, I think, force comparisons of individual elements. Mandelshtam's is a poetic response, not a point-by-point commentary on the Ivanov, which—and this is the poem's most distinctive feature—follows Ivanov in taking the form of *mythic* expression. It does so not so much to polemicize with Ivanov's view of symbolic art, but to express a longing for a pre-historic existence when there was no duality to overcome, no opposition of Music and Word, no Chaos or Cosmos, no myth itself (for if Aphrodite is not born, there can be no myth of the goddess), but an immense tranquil ocean, a crystalline "note" (*nota*), a "primordial muteness" (*pervonachal'naja nemota*) (note the two feminine *singulars* in rhyme position), the "indestructible bond of everything living" (*nenarushaemaja svjaz' vsego zhivogo*) which "birth" will only disrupt. There existed then no "two-in-oneness" (*dvuedinstvo*), but only the "oneness" (*edinstvo*) of Beauty or Love—also two central concepts in Ivanov.[21]

Ivanov's reading of Tyutchev's "Silentium!" challenges those of the first generation of Symbolists who used the poem to argue the impossibility of communication and art. Ivanov disagreed with this view all his life. In 1904, he had observed ironically that "Our most recent poets do not weary of celebrating silence" ("The Poet and the Mob").[22] And as late as 1938 he returned to the matter in his "Thoughts on Poetry" (*Mysli o poezii*), where he remarked in a humorous aside that Tyutchev "had, fortunately, forgotten his vow of silence" [*SS*, III, 663]. Ivanov reads Tyutchev's *molchanie* in another way, and argues not only the possibility, but the necessity of art. Here Mandelshtam in part follows Ivanov: there is nothing in his poem which can be read as suggesting the impossibility of communication or art. But Mandelshtam departs from Ivanov in his desire to reach a *pervonachal'naja nemota*, to surrender to that "merging" which Ivanov, following Tyutchev, had called the "thirst for merging" (*zhazhda slijanija*), the "striving to blend with the sleeping world" (*stremlenie . . . smesheniju s dremljushchim mirom*), that state of contemplative ecstasy which Ivanov called Silence.[23] Even more fundamentally Mandelshtam departs from Ivanov in his call (*Ostan'sja!*) for that state in which art itself is unnecessary, since all things are One. The poet's awareness that such a state is impossible is the source of the poem's tension ("not yet, but . . ."—"*eshche ne, no . . .*") and anxiety, in marked contrast to Ivanov's feeling of confidence. In its nostalgia for a past when there existed the "indestructible bond of everything living" (*nenarushaemaja svjaz' vsego zhivogo*), the poem seems implicitly to question the possibility of the *recreation* of that state which is called for in the conclusion of Ivanov's article: "The integral world-outlook of the poet will discover it [a "living bond"—*zhivaja svjaz'*] within himself, integral and unified. The poet will find religion within himself if he finds within himself the bond."[24]

As Taranovsky has written, the music of "Silentium" is "not our human music, but rather metaphysical music: the spontaneous language of being. In this poem Mandelshtam is still a symbolist."[25] (The "word," one should also add, is the *logos*, not ordinary speech.) None of the Symbolists wrote more eloquently of this Music than did Bely or Ivanov. Mandelshtam would have been well aware of Ivanov's many statements about it not only in the 1910 article ("lyric poetry . . . like music, is a motive art" [*lirika . . . podobno muzyke—iskusstvo dvigatel'noe*; *SS*, II, 600]), but in such articles in *By the Stars* as "Two Elements in Contemporary Symbolism" (*Dve stikhii v sovremennom simvolizme*), where Ivanov discusses Verlaine's "De la musique avant toute chose," and, most notably, in "Premonitions and Portents."[26] In that essay, where both *molchanie* and *muzyka* are discussed in the space of two pages, Ivanov writes:

> In every work of art, even the plastic arts, there is a hidden music. . . . the very soul of art is musical . . . aspiration for the ineffable [*neizrechennoe*—a Tyutchev allusion, of course] which con-

stitutes the soul and life of esthetic enjoyment: and this volition, this transport is music [*SS*, II, 92—93].

And in the same essay we also find: ". . . for from the Dionysian sea of orgiastic agitation arises the Apollonian vision of myth" [*SS*, II, 99].

But in none of these articles, nor in "The Testaments of Symbolism," is Aphrodite connected in any way with Music; nor is she in any version of the myth known in the ancient world. Of course, she is the goddess of Beauty. In the conclusion to "The Symbolism of Esthetic Principles" (*Simvolika esteticheskikh nachal*, 1905), Ivanov had written:

> In the image of Aphrodite "born from foam" ancient acumen combined all three principles of the beautiful. From foaming chaos arises . . . the goddess.—"Aphrogeneia," "Anadyomene." . . . she ascends—and already embraces the heavens—"Urania," "Asteria."[27]

Three paragraphs earlier, he speaks of "the most potent of the arts—Music" (*mogushchestvennejshee iz iskusstv—Muzyka*), and writes of its Siren-like call to us to merge ourselves in Chaos, the realm of the "bisexual, masculofeminine Dionysus" (*dvupolyj, muzhezhenskij Dionis*), of Night, to which he opposes the sunny realm of Cosmos with the male Apollo and the female Aphrodite, from which we rise to Beauty. Ivanov also writes there of the realm of Chaos: "Only the *white foam* covers the avid tumbling of the waters" (*Belaja kipen'* odna pokryvaet zhadnoe rushen'e vod [*SS*, I, 829]—compare the *peny blednaja siren'* in Mandelshtam).

However, Ivanov had in fact made a specific connection between Aphrodite and Music in the first part of the poem "Music" (Muzyka). There the birth of Music is imaged in terms of the myth of Aphrodite (note too the color gold, traditionally associated with the goddess):

Music
Music's Voice

My father is
That hungering god who desired to bear

The color-woven destiny of blind incarnations,
A much-suffered, suffering fate.
And he drenches, and *being's vessel foams*
And, uncontained, golden rims pour
Inexhaustibly seething Will.
But like a gilded cloud
Am I born from the foam spilt in thunderclaps
And I soar, and bear
The muffled storm of inescapable blazings,
And I sob in the wilds of upper air.

Muzyka
Golos Muzyki

Moj otets—
Onyj alchushchij bog, chto nesti voskhotel
Voploshchenij slepykh tsvetno-tkanyj udel,
Mnogostradnuju, strastnuju dolju.
I poit on, i *penit sosud bytija,*
I lijut, ne vmestiv, zolotye kraja
Neischerpno-kipjashchuju volju.
No, kak oblak zlatoj,
Ja razhdajus' iz peny, v gromakh prolitòj
I nesus', i nesu
Neizbytykh pylanij glukhuju grozu,
I rydaju v pustynjakh èfira . . .[28]

In a letter of August 13/26, 1909, Mandelshtam had asked Ivanov to send him a copy of *Pilot Stars* (*Kormchie zvezdy*), where "Muzyka" appeared in the cycle "To Dionysus" (*Dionisu*).[29] We do not know how Ivanov responded, but we may be sure that Mandelshtam, on his return to Russia from Switzerland, read the volume, and that "Muzyka" provided the specific subtext for his own response to Ivanov in 1910. (Note specifically *"penit sosud bytija,"* as well as *"Ja razhdajus' iz peny"*; for Aphrodite is derived from the Greek *aphros,* foam; and "Aphrogeneia" means "born of foam" [*penorozhdennaja*], and "Anadyomene" means "appearing on the surface of the sea," [*pojavivshajasja na poverkhnosti morja*]).[30] The conclusion of the beautiful "Italian Sonnet," "The Sistine Chapel" (Sikstinskaja kapella), in *Pilot Stars* may also have echoed in Mandelshtam's mind: *I khram ispoln' gromov i reva*— / *Javlennoj* muzyki koleblemyj sosud.[31]

Seen in the context of the "Symbolist Debate" and of Ivanov's poetry, Mandelshtam's poem takes on new resonance. His "dialogue" with Ivanov did not end there. Two years later, in 1912, he would again allude to Ivanov's programmatic article (and his own response) in the poem which begins "We cannot endure *silence full of tension* . . ." (My *naprjazhennogo molchan'ja* ne vynosim . . .).[32] In 1913, in "The Morning of Acmeism" (*Utro akmeizma*), Mandelshtam would make his declaration of poetic independence, and it is natural that he would there allude specifically only to the one Symbolist who had had the greatest impact on his early art by writing "Acmeism makes it [the law of identity] its slogan and proposes it instead of the dubious *a realibus ad realiora*."[33] Yet in the later essay "On the Nature of the Word" (*O prirode slova*), he could assert:

> The *tastes,* not the *ideas,* of the Acmeists turned out to be fatal for Symbolism. The ideas turned out to be, in part, copied from the Symbolists, and Vyacheslav Ivanov himself assisted greatly in the formulation of Acmeist theory.[34]

In the 1920s he included Ivanov among those Russian poets who were "not only for yesterday or today, but for all time."[35] And in another essay, "Storm and Stress" (*Burja i natisk*), published in 1923, he wrote:

> The complex Byzantine-Hellenic world of Vyacheslav Ivanov fares somewhat better. Being essentially the very same kind of pioneer and colonizer as all the other Symbolists, he did not, however, look at Byzantium and Hellas as foreign lands destined for conquest, but rightly saw in them the cultural springs of Russian poetry. But, owing to the lack of a sense of proportion, something characteristic of all the Symbolists, he overburdened his poetry to an incredible degree with Byzantine-Hellenic images and myths, which depreciated it considerably.[36]

Only two pages later, however, Mandelshtam added (and the remarks

show that the roots of Mandelshtam's own "Hellenism" lie in part
in Ivanov):

> Vyacheslav Ivanov is more national (*naroden*) and more accessible
> in the future than all the other Russian Symbolists. A significant
> portion of the fascination of his solemnity relates to our philolog-
> ical ignorance. In no other Symbolist poet does the noise of the
> lexicon, the mighty rumble of the bell of national speech, swelling
> up and waiting its turn, sound so distinctly as in Vyacheslav
> Ivanov. His sense of the past as the future makes him akin to
> Khlebnikov. Ivanov's archaism stems not from his choice of
> themes, but from his incapacity for relative thinking, that is, for
> the comparison of different periods of time. The Hellenic poems
> of Vyacheslav Ivanov are written not after and not at the same
> time as Greek poems, but before them, because never for a mo-
> ment does he forget himself as he speaks in his barbarian native
> idiom.[37]

Obviously Mandelshtam's view of Ivanov and his legacy was as complex (and inconsistent) as many other of his statements.

These remarks can only suggest that Ivanov served as something
more than merely the "filter" for Mandelshtam's "Hellenism," a topic
which in itself deserves study. By ignoring Ivanov, as has been the
case for too long, we impoverish Russian verse. By ignoring his
impact on other poets of his time we seriously distort the history of
Russian verse. The time is long overdue to take the right measure
of both.

Notes

1. Osip Mandelshtam, *Sobranie sochinenij,* II (Washington, D.C.,
1971), 239. Hereafter references will be to the volume and page number of
this four-volume edition.

2. N. I. Khardzhiev in the notes to O. Mandelshtam, *Stikhotvorenija*
(Biblioteka poeta, 1973), pp. 254–55.

3. Anna Akhmatova, "Mandelshtam (Listki iz dnevnika)," *Sochinenija,* 2 (Washington, D.C., 1968), p. 169.

4. "Mandelshtam v zapisjakh dnevnika S. P. Kablukova," ed. and introd. A. A. Morozov, *Vestnik R. Kh. D.*, 129 (III-1979), 151–52.

5. Cited in A. A. Morozov's publication of "Pis'ma O. E. Mandelshtama k V. I. Ivanovu," *Zapiski otdela rukopisej GBL*, 34 (1973), 261.

6. Kiril Taranovsky, *Essays on Mandelshtam* (Cambridge, Mass., 1976), p. 83. For Levinton see *Russian Literature*, V, 2–3 (1977).

7. See "Pis'ma . . . ," pp. 273–74.

8. Taranovsky, *Mandelshtam*, p. 122. E. Toddes, in his exhaustive "Mandelshtam i Tjutchev" (*International Journal of Slavic Linguistics and Poetics*, 17 [1974], 59–85), must consider the connection between the two poems so obvious and, perhaps, "over-commented" that he does not even mention them.

9. Jan Meijer, "The Early Mandelshtam and Symbolism," *Russian Literature* VII, 5 (1979), 529. Ryszard Przybylski, "Osip Mandelshtam i muzyka," *Russian Literature*, 2 (1972), 111. Przybylski's hostility to the Symbolists here and in other articles has blinded him to their impact on Mandelshtam. Przybylski insists on seeing him at war with them in all respects.

10. Mandelshtam (Biblioteka poeta), p. 256.

11. In his review of the second edition of *Stone* in *Apollon*, 1 (1916), Gumilev called "Silentium" a "bold completion" (*smeloe dogovarivanie*) of Verlaine's "Art poétique," (*Sobranie sochinenij* IV (Washington, 1968), 363.

12. See poems like Nos. 457d, 457e, 457o, 457p, 457v in Mandelshtam II (1971). Mandelshtam sent all these poems to Ivanov in his letters.

13. Blok registered a detailed summary of the Petersburg version in his notebook (knizhka tridtsataja, 26 marta); see *Zapisnye knizhki 1901–1920* (Moscow, 1965), pp. 167–69.

14. "Iz perepiski Aleksandra Bloka s Vyach. Ivanovym," publikatsija N. V. Kotreleva, *Izvestija Akademii nauk, serija literatury i jazyka,* vol. 41, 2 (Moscow, 1982), p. 170.

15. *Literaturnoe nasledstvo (Aleksandr Blok. Novye materialy i issledovanija)* 92, book 3 (Moscow, 1982), 365.

16. Kablukov noted in his Diary on August 18, 1910: "Iz napechatannykh v 'Apollone' luchshee; 'Ona eshche ne rodilas' . . .'" (*Vestnik,* 129, 135). In the same diary entry he mentioned that he had met Mandelshtam in July at Hangö (Finnish Hanko), near Helsinki, where both were vacationing, and that they had discussed Ivanov. Mandelshtam had read Ivanov's and his own poems aloud to him.

17. All citations from "The Testaments of Symbolism" will be from the

text published in volume II of the Brussels *Sobranie sochinenij* (1974), 589–603. The article was republished in *Borozdy i mezhi* (1916) after its appearance in *Apollon* in 1910.

18. *SS*, II, 90. The essay was first published in *Zolotoe runo* 5–6, (1906), and republished in *Po zvezdam*.

19. Blok, *Sobranie sochinenij v 8-i tomakh*, V (Moscow, 1962), 428; *SS* II, 599. My italics.

20. *SS*, II, 92. My italics. The colors of Ivanov's "Bogini" (*Kormchie zvezdy, SS*, I, 587), in which "penorozhdennaja Kifera" appears, could also be noted (1. 3: "I gonit zvonko jakhont sinij"; 11. 5–6: "Tkan' Oread—lazurnyj dym / Okutal krjakh lilovo-seryj"), especially line ten: "Nad sinevoj neizrechennoj." Note too lines 3–4 of "Uvlechenie" (*Kormchie zvezdy, SS*, I, 610): "Lazurnye valy, gorja, preobrazhalis' / I rizu purpura prozrachnogo vlekli," and lines 5–6 of "Poety dukha" (*Prozrachnost', SS*, I, 737): "My—vspleski rdjanoj peny / Nad blednost'ju morej."

21. The grammatical referent for *ona* in the poem's first line is highly ambivalent when first encountered and could refer to *Krasota* (Beauty) or *Ljubov'* (Love) or both, both of which Aphrodite represents.

22. *SS*, I, 712. See also his later letters in *Perepiska iz dvukh uglov* (1921).

23. *SS*, II, 591. The conclusion of Ivanov's poem "Molchanie" (which begins "Vsja gorit—i bezmolvstvuet roza . . .") offers suggestive parallels with Mandelshtam's poem: "Poljubi [an imperative] *soprirodnuju* s neju [rozoj], / *Serdtse solntse*, svoju *nemotu* (*SS*, II, 508). I cannot say, however, whether Mandelshtam knew the poem or not. It was included in *Cor Ardens*, and the editors of the collected works give no indication whether or not it was published before 1911. Mandelshtam could certainly have known the other "Molchanie" ("V tajnik . . .") of *Cor Ardens*, as it had appeared in the fifth issue of *Pereval* in 1907 (not 1904, as the note to the poem on p. 704 of *SS*, II states). Mandelshtam's locution "Da obretut usta moi" alludes directly, however, to a much earlier text, Pushkin's *Evgenij Onegin*, One, 49, ll. 13–14: "S nej [Venetsianskoju mladoj] obretut usta moi / Jazyk Petrarki i ljubvi."

24. *SS*, II, 601–602. Victor Terras described "Silentium" as "the poet's nostalgia for primordial unity with the cosmos" expressed in his theme of the "reversed flow of time" in "The Time Philosophy of Osip Mandelstam," *The Slavonic and East European Review*, XLVII, 109 (1969), 351.

25. Taranovsky, *Mandelshtam*, p. 122.

26. Mandelshtam had enthusiastically greeted the publication of *Po zvezdam* in 1909. His letter to Ivanov of August 13/26, 1909, shows that he had read the volume carefully (see "Pis'ma," pp. 262–63).

27. *SS*, I, 830. First published under that title in *Po zvezdam*; in *Vesy*, 5, 1905, the article was entitled "O Niskhozhdenii." In Tyutchev's early poem "Uranija" Urania is represented not so much as the muse of astronomy as the incarnation of Beauty and thereby linked with Aphrodite (ll. 22–25: ". . . Kak luna iz-za oblak, vstaet / *Uranii* ostrov iz srebrjanoj peny; / Razlilsja vokrug nemertsajushchij svet, / Bogin' ulybkoju rozhdennyj . . ."), but not with Music.

28. *SS*, I, 542. My italics. The poem is among the first in the collection *Kormchie zvezdy.*

29. "If you have an extra, a completely extra copy of *Kormchie Zvezdy*, could it not by some means or other make its way into my careful hands? . . ."—"Pis'ma," p. 263.

30. See the entry *"Afrodita"* by A. F. Losev in *Mify narodov mira* I (1980), p. 132.

31. *SS*, I, 622. My italics. The image of the sea in a *sosud* also appears in the poem "Kassandre" (III, 2) in *Prozrachnost'* (1904): "A More zhdet v nedvizhimom sosude" (*SS*, I, 790).

32. The poem was included in the third edition of *Stone*, but first published in *Giperborej* 9–10 (1913). All editions of *Stone* contain the "architectural" poems "Notre Dame" and "Aija-Sofija," both from 1912. The imagery of "Notre Dame" obviously prefigures the architectural metaphors in which Mandelshtam set out an Acmeist esthetic in "The Morning of Acmeism" (1913). "Aija-Sofija" salutes another great monument of sacred architecture. It stands in sharp contrast to the Paris cathedral both in terms of architectural style and faith. The Gothic and Latin Notre Dame *overcomes* chaos in the thrust of its spire and multiple tensions. The Byzantine and Greek Hagia Sophia *harmonizes* chaos, and in the image of its great cupola sailing through the world like a ship Mandelshtam finds the very symbol of *sobornost'* (a central concept in Ivanov as well as Orthodoxy). As such, despite its "Acmeist precision," I would argue (although I cannot prove) that the poem "Aija-Sofija" represents a kind of salute to Ivanov as well as to the building. There is a distant textual parallel to Mandelshtam's "Aija-Sofija" in Ivanov's lines "Eony dolgie, svetilo, ty plyvesh'; / Ty moj letuchij vek, kak den', perezhivesh'" from the poem "Pokornost'," II, 1–2, in *Kormchie zvezdy* (*SS*, I, 523). But I think more of the terms in which Mandelshtam expressed his admiration for the collection *Po zvezdam* in the letter to Ivanov of August 13/26, 1909, which emphasizes its harmony and *kruglost'*: "When a person steps under the vaults of Notre Dame does he really ponder the truth of Catholicism, and does he not become a Catholic simply by virtue of being under those vaults? Your book

is excellent because of the beauty of its great architectural creations and astronomical systems. . . . Only it seemed to me that the book is too—how to say it?—too circular, without angles. . . . And only the breathing of the Cosmos fans your book, imparting to it a charm it shares with *Zarathustra*— compensating for the astronomical circularity of your system. . . ."— "Pis'ma," pp. 262–63. By 1912 Mandelshtam had begun to derive from his sense of the "otherness" of Ivanov's view of art a corresponding sense of his own identity. What better way to assert it than to close the first edition of *Stone* with these two poems?

33. Mandelshtam, II, 324. When the article was published in 1919, Mandelshtam included a specific footnote: "A formula of Symbolism given by Vyacheslav Ivanov. See 'Thoughts on Symbolism' in the volume *Borozdy i mezhi.*"

34. Mandelshtam, II, 257. My italics. In the same essay Mandelshtam cited Tyutchev's "Silentium!" and his remark that "Skorost' razvitija jazyka nesoizmerima s razvitiem samoj zhizni" is close to Ivanov's "nesootvetstvie mezhdu dukhovnym rostom lichnosti i vneshnimi sredstvami obshchenija" in "Thoughts on Symbolism."

35. "Vypad," Mandelshtam, II, 228.

36. Mandelshtam, II, 341.

37. Mandelshtam, II, 343.

Vyacheslav Ivanov's Reflective Comprehension of Art: The Poet and Thinker as Critic of Somov, Bakst, and Čiurlionis

Aleksis Rannit†

Vyacheslav Ivanov was neither an art critic in the modern sense nor an impressionistic writer-on-art of Rilke's, Hofmannstal's or Pater's type. He was many things: a classical philologist, a specialist in the history of ideas, a thinker interested in the philosophic side of mysticism, an exuberant language-maker, an inventor in metrics, an Alexandrian lyrical poet, and a pan-European *poeta doctus* whom Vladimir Markov has termed the only Russian man of letters able to converse at his ease with Dante and Goethe.[1] Ivanov, however, was neither an art historian like Wölfflin (with his pioneering studies of stylistic change in art) nor a regular reviewer of art exhibitions as was Baudelaire. As a thinker primarily interested in theories of the ultimate nature of things, he seldom wrote about the visual arts, only occasionally exploring the region of purely esthetic knowledge. We have from his pen only three essays on the subject: "The Spear of Athena" (*Kop'e Afiny,* 1904), on the problems of art in general; "Ancient Terror" (*Drevnij uzhas,* 1909), on a specific painting, "Terror Antiquus," by the decorative, calligraphic Russian artist Lev (Léon) Bakst (1866–1924); and a third, a panoramic philosophical and analytical article on the enigmatic Lithuanian painter Mikalojus Konstantinas Čiurlionis (1875–1911), one who was the first to apply several levels of musical time and purely musical rhythms, meters, and structures to painting. The essay "On Joyous Handicraft and Wise Rejoicing" (*O veselom remesle i umnom veselii,* 1907) deals primarily with literature. Nonetheless, we may cite two short fragments

of this treatise in which Ivanov spoke his mind about the purpose
of art. The essay opens with a long and labyrinthine sentence:

> Argument about the purpose of art—whether it justifies itself in
> its own terms as "art for art's sake" or needs the further justifi-
> cation of life as "art for life's sake," an argument advanced as
> conclusive, but for all that, never decided in the depths of our
> souls—such an argument never entered men's minds during those
> times (happy times for art) when creative genius, one way or
> another, was the joint creativity of the artist as tradesman and of
> his customers—whether those customers served as authorized rep-
> resentatives of the public (for example, the magistrates of the an-
> cient republics or the archbishops of the medieval church), or, like
> the Medici, arbitrarily expressed the tastes and demands of the
> times; whether they were innovators who rose out of the crowd
> but were still of the crowd in spirit, or, like Louis XIV, were
> masters of the crowd who, while not losing their connection with
> it even in their domination of it, ensured themselves of the crowd's
> imitative submission.[2]

Later in the same essay, as he contemplates art and artists of all
kinds, Ivanov is ethical earnestness itself; he writes specifically of
poets, but certainly could be speaking of the practitioners of the
plastic arts as well:

> Every kind of "playing at genius" ("genialisches Treiben") and
> Romanticism is but the haughty idle wandering of arty Bohemia
> constrained to work not otherwise than for storage and for emer-
> gency: all this Bohemia immediately elevates into a principle and
> in its own presumptuous jargon terms "art for art's sake." If,
> however, some people finally begin to listen to these "holiday
> revellers," "priests of the one and only beautiful," the artists view
> this attention they have aroused as a perfect surrogate for paid
> commissions, regard "the epoch" or "life itself" as their customers,
> and willingly agree to "create" for the vague promise of future
> glory as leaders and liberators of humanity. Thus they turn out to
> be not averse even to the formula "art for life's sake" as long as

they are allowed to consider as life their dreams about life and to imagine themselves its organizers or even outright creators. In this way, Byron overthrows tyrants and Heine liberates Germany.

Artists are particularly inclined to subscribe to the "art for life's sake" pact on condition that life is understood as something very broad and cosmic, and not fully intelligible . . . [SS, III, 63]

In addition to these essays Ivanov composed poems to and about artists and single works of art. Konstantin Somov (1869–1939), an influential member of the World of Art group, was one of the few Russian artists with whom Ivanov became associated. Their meeting took place in 1905 through Lydia Zinovieva-Annibal, a friend of Somov. The artist actively participated in the poet's famous Wednesdays in St. Petersburg, and Ivanov celebrated him in a special poem called "Terzine to Somov" (*Tertsiny k Somovu,* 1906). It is a poem of considerable energy composed of eleven iambic tercets, wrought in the manner of modernist stylization and rhythmically enriched by the use of enjambments. Its intricate harmony is achieved by Ivanov's mastery of form, producing a structure at once massive and subtle. The poem includes reminiscences of Somov's well-known painting "Isle of Love" (*Ostrov ljubvi*), now in the Tretyakov Gallery in Moscow, and of Lermontov's "Meditation" (*Duma*), of Calderón and of *Ecclesiastes;* it may also refer to Byron's *The Island,* translated into Russian by Ivanov, and to Watteau's *Embarkment for Cythera* and Baudelaire's "A Voyage to Cythera." To understand the poem, one needs to be acquainted with the middle period of the artist's work, when he changed his early realist style to a poetic, sentimental manner full of *passéism* and retrospectivism, achieving both an expression of nostalgia for the eighteenth century and a delicate ridicule, even satire, of the etiquette and vanity of those times. Exaggerating, the Symbolist poet and critic Andrey Bely called the subject of these paintings "comic terror." Bely, one of the very few early critics who understood Ivanov's style and philosophy, likewise called him "the most refined of Russian poets," and recognized "Terzine to Somov" as one of the ten best poems of *Cor Ardens.* [3]

Somov's art, the art of self-conscious illusion, was rich in mellowness; everything pointed to a consummate perfection of technique. Ivanov might well appreciate the worldly enchantment of
Somov's subjects, the courtly beauty of his colors, the exquisiteness
of minor forms, the Beardsleyan capriciousness of the graphic line.
Looking at Somov's pictures, he also understood that as Somov presented it, life is an entrancing game with a strange beginning, then
a long mystery of inspiration and divination, and at last a discon-
solate, gloomy end. Ivanov, I believe, at least hinted his own regret
that Somov had willfully deserted the strong world of his pure,
painterly landscapes (the artist was especially fond of the landscapes
of northern Estonia and of the area surrounding St. Petersburg) and
could probably no longer liberate himself from the illusion-making
of art and return to those fresh forests and untilled meadowlands
that had been his first love. Ivanov's poem, written in 1906 and
published in *Cor Ardens* in 1911, is a philosophical and psychological
essay in itself, and must be read in its entirety.

Terzine to Somov

Ah Somov, magus! Why with such malicious pleasure
Are you hastening to degrade your magic dream
And make a mockery of your own proper treasure?

And conjuring a wayward beauty all your own
From your forefathers' graves with such inconstancy,
Why rush to show the naked and the overblown

In what you clothed yourself with dainty finery?
Is it from envy of those shades in olden times
Who knew happiness under powdered prudery?

Your avid spirit is tormented by a yearning
For those "Amorous Isles" to which, as years ago
They auctioned off that creaky world, there's no returning.

The Graces are no more, nor delicate debauch
Nor rendezvous nor those adventurous exploits
In which their childish lives were so profusely rich . . .

Nor primly proper gardens nor their sportive flurry,
And we, encumbered by cognition and by doubt,
Are old in youth, so life for us is toil and hurry . . .

When will your genius then from this captivity
Break loose to freedom, to the meadows and cool woods
Where you may catch the changeable proclivity

Of heavens with their fleeting clouds, their rainbow spectrum.
Or you may paint the vivid shades of sumptuous evenings.
And secretly some sort of demon feeds your tedium

At your festivities of lavish idleness,
And in your ear it whispers this: "All life is play.
And all things change in primal variableness

Of lovely vanity. To everything give way!
And all is dream and shade in dream. All smiles and talk,
All patterns and all colors (now, as yesterday)

Flow past, each pestering in turn—and far away
They falsely beckon. Over all an empty sky.
Life plays with dolls. Such playing is not worth one's breath.

And from behind a hundred masks is smiling . . . Death."[4]

The other poem in *Cor Ardens* on a Somovian subject is "Fireworks"
Feerverki) inspired by Somov's painting and pen drawings of the same
title, produced between 1904 and 1908 {*SS,* II, 312]. It is not
lacking in imagination, but nonetheless is reflective in only a simple
way, and we must return to the previous, much more profound poem,
"Terzine to Somov" to ask ourselves why Ivanov was so taken with
Somov. Was the source of enthusiasm the friendship between Somov
and Lydia Zinovieva-Annibal, or the portrait of Ivanov—a drawing
of precision and lightness—made by the artist in the same year the
poem was written? Was it the philosophy of joyous playfulness
which, strangely enough, was not foreign to Ivanov? Later in 1922,
it will be recalled, Ivanov even wrote the text for Mikhail Popov's
operetta "Love—A Mirage" (*Ljubov—mirazh*), an enterprise that led
him to give considerable attention to artists really quite alien to his

taste. The poet and the artist were acquainted for a decade or so. It is difficult for us today to understand why Ivanov asked Somov in 1911 to design the cover of his important book of poems *Cor Ardens*. This conspicuously embellished and superficial cover design, composed in the style of the so-called *belle époque,* illustrates only one segment of Ivanov's work of that period, namely the decorative aspect. It is true that *Cor Ardens* has elements of ornateness (or, as Olga Deschartes said so beautifully, it is "reminiscent of a Byzantine gown"),[5] yet Ivanov's poetry is not based on ornament for ornament's sake; in his case, the romantic and intellectual synthesis of heart and head does not break down, as happens in Victorian poetry. The decorative romanticism of the Victorians and of some Symbolists is actually an impossibility in Ivanov's case, because even his richest verbal orchestration is deeply saturated with inductive and deductive thought. As with Plato, one of Ivanov's dominant motifs is a persistent faith in the faculties of mind. He had a clear feeling for the relation between the senses and the intellect, the active and the contemplative powers. This is the first of two essential differences between Ivanov and his fellow Symbolists in Russia, Balmont, Bely, and Blok, or, for that matter, between Ivanov and the Austrian poet Rainer Maria Rilke (the Rilke of the early verses). The second difference is that these poets sometimes apply ornament as a purely sentimental and mannerist, decorative, euphonic device, which occasionally leads to a divorce of being from becoming and to a certain hypnotic *melomania,* especially in Balmont and in Blok. The music in Ivanov, however, is always functional. In this he may be compared with, for example, the German Symbolist poet Stefan George, whom he calls the "great master" or with Osip Mandelshtam who for some years was Ivanov's follower and admirer. A balanced ornamental, spatial form is present in Ivanov's metrically linear verse, but it is an ornamental form of depth, not of the surface.

Bearing all this in mind it is difficult to comprehend Ivanov's deep interest in Somov's art, not because Somov was an amateur—on the contrary, he was a master, especially as a draughtsman—but because Somov's rococo kind of artificiality, his inner skepticism, his indecisive hovering between various meanings and dimensions, did not correspond at all to the core of Ivanov's regulative principles of significant art. Ivanov expressed his own ideas on art in his combative essay "The Spear of Athena," a title possibly suggesting that the war-goddess Athena (who, we must not forget, was also a patroness of the arts and crafts) guided her hero Diomedes' spear into Ares' flank.[6] Was she now guiding Ivanov's own spear against unimportant art, in favor of art resplendent and universal in its meaning? Ivanov's mention of Mozart and Velázquez in this essay as men of intimate, limited appeal stuns us now. Velázquez, notwithstanding the so-called "impressionistic" caprices of his palette, has nobility and dignity, and appears full of serene human truth. He was also a religious painter. However, let us listen respectfully to Ivanov, the subjective critic and objective idealist who expressed his credo and formula clearly and forcefully:

> Intimate art is the art most important from the point of view of artistic *techné*. It is primarily "art for art's sake." It singles out the artist and cultivates the virtuoso. It makes demands of refinement and taste. Insights and discoveries of a purely esthetic order are accomplished in its closed circle. In it a painter is for the first time only a painter—like Velázquez; a musician is only a musician—like Mozart. It is centripetal, passive with relation to the general goals of the cultural-historical trend; finally, it is analytic in method, in contrast to high art, which is in essence synthetic. To the extent that one can think in static types of abstraction, intimate art (as, for example, the aristocratic art of the eighteenth century) can achieve that unity of style which constitutes a primary characteristic of high art, and affect indefinitely wide circles with it; only thus do we have the right to speak of the style of the eighteenth century at all.

> Art of the cloister, on the other hand, is centrifugal in its deepest strivings, active, and again, synthetic. If intimate art draws around itself a wizard's circle, art of the cloister desires to seize the magic wand. Its reticence is the forced reticence of self-defense and concentration; the creative monad of new fermentation defends itself with impenetrable armor, as if to draw into its own

shell, and thus accumulate in itself its own explosive energy. It is the catacomb creativity of "the hermits of the spirit."

Intimate art is art of pure unalloyed contemplation; art of the cloister is art of metaphysical desire. Intimate art contemplates the outer and private, art of the cloister, the inner and general. The first is celebration of personality and its rule; in the second, as in universal art, the suprapersonal triumphs again.[7]

Ivanov was not interested in Somov alone, of course, but perhaps the only other artists about whom he wrote with such intimacy and fondness were Nicolas Poussin and Claude Lorrain, the subjects of the poem "Two Artists" (*Dva khudozhnika*) in the collection *Pilot Stars* (*Kormchie zvezdy*, 1903).[8] Is there not a certain superficial similarity between these artists—and especially between the work of Lorrain, the prince of landscape painters, the communicator of a sense of enchantment and repose—and some of the diaphanous Arcadian pictures by Somov? Above the title "Two Artists," Ivanov put another, Greek title "Epimetron," which may puzzle us. Was he striving for esthetic distance from this "unassuming" idyllic world of French artists? Or does "Epimetron" mean "Beyond measure," or simply "Enclosure" or "Conclusion," in a positive sense? The question is important since all artists mentioned in Ivanov's poems, except these two and Somov, seem to have dealt with questions of the cognition or mystery of being.[9]

Only seven specific paintings and one sculpture are subjects of individual poems, poems which are translations of Ivanov's esthetic and philosophic experience. These poems are: "La stanza della disputa" [*SS*, I, 621] on Raphael's painting of the same name, "The Last Supper of Leonardo" (*Vecherja Leonardo, SS*, I, 615), "Botticelli's Magnificat" [*SS*, I, 616], "Hermit of the Spirit: to a Picture by Redon" (*Pustynnik dukha: k kartine O. Redona, SS*, I, 783), and "Il Gigante" [*SS*, I, 615], whose epithet is taken from the popular name for Michelangelo's *David*. One of his finest poems, written in the elegiac distich, a metrical scheme in which Ivanov the poet as well as Ivanov the translator has, in my opinion, no equal in Russian poetry, is entitled "Narcissus: Pompeian Bronze" (*Nartsis: Pompeis-*

kaja bronza, SS, I, 744). Finally, there is a celebration of one of the temples of Paestum, "Temple of Paestum" (*Pestumskij khram, SS,* I, 583). Actually, all of Ivanov's poetry is laudation, since he is essentially a hymnodist. From the very first poem after the dedicatory poem in his first collection *Pilot Stars* to the end of *Evening Light* (*Svet vechernij*), his last collection, the poet was a praiser, a commender, a solemnizer. In that first poem, "Beauty" (*Krasota*), the memorable opening lines demonstrate Ivanov the writer as the possessor of the "third eye," the visionary eye of an artist as well as of a musician:

> Divine distances, I see you—
> the ever bluer crystal of the hills of Umbria, . . .

> Vizhu vas, bozhestvennye dali,
> Umbriskikh gor sinejushchij kristall, . . .[10]

In this poem he proclaims that his countenance is a meek, gentle ray of sacramental "Yes," "Yes" being written with a capital letter (. . . krotkij luch tainstvennogo Da.) In Ivanov's case it must be a sacramental and not simply a "hidden" *Yes.* Modernistic poetry, that of the Eliot era, is poetry of the wastelands, poetry in which either for sincere or snobbish reasons not "Yes" but "No" (again with a capital letter), the great "Nothingness," is elaborately eulogized, acclaimed, and extolled. In all his poems, poems about art and life or even about death, Ivanov remains a metaphysical optimist. I cannot at this moment think of a modern poet-philosopher who could stand in deeply-felt cheerfulness and reliance as Ivanov's companion, except the modern master Jorge Guillén, that permanent poet of the Spanish tongue.

There are many reminiscences of art and artists in Ivanov's poetry and prose. We meet, among others, the Russian classicist painter Alexander Ivanov and the Symbolist Mikhail Vrubel. We encounter Phidias, Memling, and among the Italians Piranesi, Bernini, Taddeo Landini, Luca Signorelli, Titian, and Giorgione. Giorgione's *The Tempest,* the subject of the second poem of the cycle "At an Exhibition of Paintings of the Old Masters" (*Na vystavke kartin starinnykh masterov*) in Ivanov's *Evening Light* [*SS,* III, 642] was,

according to Dmitry Ivanov, one of the poet's most beloved paintings. It is not surprising that Giorgione, the master of grace and
sensuality, would inspire Ivanov; it is, however, unexpected that
Ivanov would love a work which has no precise religious or mythological subject. But then it seems that the Ivanov of the late years
was a different poet-critic, one who was able to enjoy fully Giorgione
the pure artist and innovator for whom *The Tempest, Sleeping Venus,*
and *Three Philosophers* were simply pretexts for indulging the painterly
imagination. Giorgione's lack of, or indifference to, subject matter
was, of course, in great contrast to the earlier, literary traditions of
Italian painting.

In one of his prose pieces Ivanov even mentioned Picasso, in
whom (as in Pirandello) he saw an analytical dissector *forma formans—forma zizhdushchaja,* the forming or building form, or form
as the creator [*SS,* III, 678–89]. There are poems by Ivanov to artists
either unknown to us or imaginary, pieces like "Artist" (*Khudozhnik,
SS,* II, 380) and "Le nu dans l'art" [*SS,* I, 631].

Finally there are the well-composed, although somewhat heavy,
translations from Baudelaire (heavy because the Russian tongue lacks
the feathered lightness of the French language). In his rendering of
Baudelaire's famous poem "Les phares" (*Majaki,* Beacons), Ivanov
skillfully created epigrammatic Russian variants of the French poet's
characterizations of Rubens, Rembrandt, Michelangelo, Puget, Watteau, Goya, and Delacroix. Ivanov's translation of "Les phares" is
one of the finest examples of this kind of sovereign, ingenious, visionary rendering. Let us quote first the French original of the poem's
second stanza, then the musical, almost scientifically exact German
version by Stefan George, and finally the rich, space-creating lines
of Vyacheslav Ivanov.

> Léonard de Vinci, miroir profond et sombre
> Où des anges charmants, avec un doux souris
> Tout chargé de mystère, apparaissent à l'ombre
> Des glaciers et des pins qui ferment leur pays;[11]

> Leonardo da Vinci ein spiegel tief und dunkel
> Wo reizende engel mit ihrem süss-lächelnden mund

Und voll von geheimnis erscheinen im abendgefunkel
Der gletscher und fichten des heimatlands hintergrund.[12]

O Vinchi,—zerkalo, v ch'em omute bezdonnom
Mertsajut angely, ulybchivo-nezhny,
Luchom bezglasnykh tajn, v zatvore, ograzhdennom
Zubtsami gornykh l'dov i sumrachnoj sosny!   [SS, II, 344]

In addition to Baudelaire, Ivanov presents a version of Michel-angelo's poem "Non ha l'ottimo artista . . . ," a sonnet dealing with the art of sculpting. Again, Italian is lighter than the rigorous Russian; once more Ivanov enters with absolute sympathy into the spirit of Michelangelo's literary work, but again he secures for him-self the freedom of interpretation and enlargement of poetic sub-stance.

Ivanov's artistic imagination is manifested not only in poems dealing with fine arts, but is also present either as visual or meta-phorical signification in many other poems and essays. He recognizes the intimate tie between image and expression. Like Goethe, for example, Ivanov is concerned with his own broad observations, con-victions, and visions, but his belief is partly also Winckelmann's belief that the standards of antiquity and the Renaissance should govern the creation of art in the twentieth century. Winckelmann's rationalism, however, is not reflected in Ivanov's writings about art. Ivanov simply was not interested in esthetic generalizations, yet how-ever image-possessed a Dionysian artist-thinker he appears to our superficial eyes, we must not forget that in his poems he was a master of *closed* form, of "significant form," as Clive Bell denoted it, speaking of Giotto and Cézanne.[13] His poetry is classical, Apol-lonian in structure, although not always in content. Ivanov's poetic art is essentially humanistic, orderly, well-proportioned, and sym-metrical, with lucidly defined verse schemes and sensitive refine-ments of rhythm. As a classicist, Ivanov made some exceptionally strong formalist statements. At the end of his poem "Le nu dans l'art," mentioned above, Ivanov demands that the artist's talent ap-proach the eternal Forms. I would here refer especially to the poet-philosopher-critic's categorical maxim from his 1913 essay "On the

Frontiers of Art" (*O granitsakh iskusstva*): "The artist's concern lies not in the transmission of new revelations but in the revelation of new forms" (*Delo khudozhnika—ne v soobshchenii novykh otkrovenij, no v otkrovenii novykh form* [*SS*, II, 641]). One of his finest poems dealing with the esthetic question of form and content, "Entelechy" (which may be translated as "quest for fulfillment" or "towards the finality of essence and perfection"), asks how it would be possible to unite eternity and beauty:

Entelechy

From my brimming vessel make me not, O Muse, pour forth
  libation!
Thought in its abundance fills every edge of measured
  Form.
Beauty is at one with Measure; but Thought strives toward
  Eternity:
  You, though, demand I fit Eternity in Beauty's bounds!

Vlagu ne daj mne prolit' chrez kraj preispolnennyj, Muza!
  Polnit obil'naja Mysl' Formy razmerennoj gran'.
S Meroj druzhna Krasota; no Mysl' presleduet Vechnost':
  Ty zhe vmestit' mne velish' Vechnost' v predel Krasoty![14]

Wider considerations of problems in art emerged as Ivanov intimately associated himself with contemporary artists, writing contemplative longer essays on them. Here, meditating on a work of Bakst or on the whole work of Čiurlionis, his writing moved to a higher literary and philosophical plane and produced significant historical-philosophical, and, in part, esthetic criticism. Through identification with the artist, especially with Čiurlionis, Ivanov became his champion and interpreter. In Čiurlionis's case it is Ivanov's philosophy of substantial things that stands as a *via media* between a philosophy of cosmic feeling and a philosophy of mind.

A faithful Hellenophile, Ivanov could well agree with H. D. (Hilda Doolittle) who in her prosework entitled *Palimpsest* declared: "Roman laurel—there was no such thing—laurel was always Greek."[15] Ivanov loved the city of Rome; in 1926 he became a

Roman Catholic, but from his youth to the very end of his life Greek culture was the only great culture worth affectionate admiration, study, and continuous meditation;[16] and when the artist Lev Bakst exhibited his large canvas "Terror Antiquus," painted on an imaginary subject of Greek antiquity, in the St. Petersburg Salon of 1908, it was probably difficult for Ivanov not to react to it. Bakst is best known as a theatrical designer, especially during his Diaghilev period. His imaginative sets and costume designs with their effective blending of colors were delightfully sophisticated and extremely artful. He was a sensual master-servant of the light muse. In "Terror Antiquus," however, he decided to leave the world of levity and gaiety and produce a work of earnestness and gravity, even more, to attempt to create Symbolist art. The painting presents a bird's-eye view of a seascape panorama and a terrifying deluge, illuminated by flashes of lightning. The raging waters are swallowing ships, fortresses, temples, people. High above this spectacle is elevated an archaic sculpture of the goddess Aphrodite, painted after an Athenian koré in the Acropolis museum. Beautiful in a masculine way, cool-headed, imperturbably self-possessed, with a frozen smile, she holds in her hand, pressed against her breast, a blue bird, perhaps a dove since the dove was sacred to Aphrodite. (We may recall the dove used for the lustration of the temple of Pandemus, mentioned in the *Inscriptiones Graecae*.)

The artist gave no explanation of this philosophical painting, and critics have tried to explain its message in many ways. One of the most popular explanations, given by many critics, was that the painting represented the destruction of Atlantis; another was that the inert, adamantine Aphrodite, who is disregarding the elemental rage of waters behind her, is the personification of art itself, standing above time and space, possibly in the sense of Théophile Gautier's famous lines:

> Everything passes.—Only strong art
> survives in eternity . . .

> Tout passe.—L'art robuste
> seul a l'éternité . . .[17]

Ivanov would not have been satisfied with such a simple interpretation. Also, for him this Bakst painting was the perfect means to force on the work and on the reader a vehement demonstration of his own suppositions and convictions. What happens is that by the end of his fascinating essay, Ivanov has created his own painting, a different "Terror Antiquus."

Ivanov begins his article "Ancient Terror" by surveying the wide panorama of Greek spiritual reality—philosophical, psychological, and mythological. One of Ivanov's principal motifs throughout his life was the reality of memory, and here again he sang praises to its creative power. In general, he saw in the painting three immanent ideas: the terror of cosmic catastrophe, faith as *terror fati,* and the immortality (as well as the socio-psychic *terribilità*) of woman, the destroyer. Ivanov was little concerned with the esthetic qualities or deficiencies of Bakst's work. Because of its symmetry (notwithstanding a slight shift of compositional axis) and of its clearly defined classicizing tendencies, he characterized the painting simply as Apollonian. One may regret that he did not criticize it as overly premeditated and rhetorical, made according to rule, too susceptible to artificial pathos, and thus lacking the immediacy and lyrical manifestation necessary to becoming a living work of art. Bakst's pretense was, of course, to create a great painting full of *dignitas* and *auctoritas,* but he failed because he adopted a rationalist attitude and because the content of the painting became stronger than the form. The demonstrative title, too, adds to the failure; viewers of the picture are not terrified by it, but, rather, are disappointed by its lifelessness. He himself understood his labor to have been in vain. In a letter written to his wife in the summer of 1908, Bakst confesses: "I did not wish to achieve what has happened to the picture. Perhaps next time I will be able to express fully what I have striven for." But as has been already said, these problems did not prevent Ivanov from using "Terror Antiquus" for his self-contemplative thoughts. Towards the end of the essay he came to the following conclusion:

We may gauge in what grandiose and monstrous forms the

dominion of women and the mother goddess had become established by the energy of the male reaction against women's despotism and their extermination of men, energy still vivid in the memory of the *Oresteia*'s author. As Aeschylus portrays it, the essence of Orestes' spiritual struggle is summed up in the choice between mother and father. Sons took the side of their murdered fathers and unsheathed their swords against their mothers; the new priest, affirming the patriarchal beginnings and the cult of ancestor-heroes, glorified them for this. This was the reaction of structure and order against the orgiastic, of the solar religion against the lunar. The sun, the oak, and the snake were the movement's symbols. A Priest of the Sun, Orpheus, fell, sacrificed by women, and, torn to pieces, was likened by them to Dionysus. Druids raised the golden bough of mistletoe, a plant sacred to the Sun and a climber on oak branches.[18]

At the very end of his speculative venture, and again without direct relation to the painting, Ivanov rather unconvincingly assures the reader that only in Christianity does the conflict between the masculine and feminine principles disappear.

Five years after the appearance of "Ancient Terror," Ivanov published in *Apollon* his essay "Čiurlionis and the Problem of Synthesis of the Arts" (by "the arts" he meant painting and music). This essay marks the climax of Ivanov's creative imagination as an art viewer; it is both a masterpiece in the philosophy and criticism of art and a masterpiece of elevated prose style or perhaps poetry—because of its rhythmical tension and nobility.[19]

This magnificent essay is constructed on a balance between the general and the specific, the latter serving as illustration to the former. It has the freshness and spontaneity that the conjunction of Ivanov and Čiurlionis would lead one to expect. Ivanov felt a definite affinity with Čiurlionis, an artist also concerned with spirituality and with art as revelation. Since 1914 when the article was published, many books, articles, and studies on Čiurlionis have appeared in diverse languages. Among the best are those written by such remarkable Lithuanian critics as Vytautas Bičiūnas, Mykalojus Vo-

robjovas, and Vytautas Landsbergis. Ivanov's essay nonetheless occupies an honored place in Čiurlionis criticism. His thoughts on
Čiurlionis combine remarkable breadth of vision with the ardor of
the mature thinker. In the first paragraph, which reads like a terse
formula, Ivanov attempts a description and definition of Čiurlionis's
art. The definition is still valid because the critic understood the
kind of abstraction and abstractionism Čiurlionis was seeking, a
transcendental unity of large and small pure forms.

> The visionary art of Čiurlionis approaches clairvoyance. His
> spirituality is most winning and convincing when the artist en-
> gages himself in making painting supernatural, that is, when he
> yields to his gift of double-vision. Thanks to this double-vision,
> the forms through which he expresses the real world approach a
> simplicity of design that becomes translucent. Reduced to its basic
> qualities this world retains only the geometric and rhythmic prin-
> ciples of its essence. Space itself is nearly conquered by the trans-
> parency of forms which do not exclude but rather absorb the
> neighboring forms. This geometrical transparency seems to be an
> attempt to approach the possibilities of visual signalization of such
> a nature that the three dimensions we have at our disposal become
> insufficient. . . .[20]

Ivanov is nonetheless critical of Čiurlionis's idea of attempting
to unite painting with music and space with time. The problem is
an old one. Philosophers and mathematicians have long looked for a
unified notion of space-time, for the spatio-temporal structure of the
universe, and for a concept of time as the fourth dimension. In a
naive manner, modern artists like Delacroix, Redon, and Whistler
spoke about a possible union of painting with music. The difference
between them and Čiurlionis was that the Lithuanian painter was
an educated musician who applied the principles of musical composition to his paintings as major structural ideas. Rhythm and
meter exist in music on different levels simultaneously, and to suggest the succession of these levels, Čiurlionis sometimes used four
different perspectives in one single painting, bringing about tension
and the implication of *movement*.[21] The musicologist Vytautas Lands-

bergis has dealt seriously with these problems in his book *Sonnet of the Spring* (*Pavasario sonata*) published in 1965.[22] Ivanov was unaware of Čiurlionis's musicological conceptions, since at that time nobody had analyzed Čiurlionis's art with the help of musical structure, musical texture, or melodic, rhythmic, harmonic, and tonal relationships. Nonetheless, he states that Čiurlionis's method of reworking in painting the elements of visual contemplation according to principles taken from music was indeed a new method. Ivanov writes:

> Music and painting are not only opposite to each other but are also incompatible. Čiurlionis avoided the danger of poorly combining and depriving these two branches of art of their characteristics but he did face the aesthetic antinomy. He had to contemplate time and space as an inseparable unity, since antinomies are the gates to knowledge—the artist becomes the seer. In art he again limits himself to suggesting such a contemplation—he forces us to find ourselves in space which absorbs time and motion—in space which is a pure stratum of vibrating forms.[23]

Ivanov argues, mistakenly, that Čiurlionis's experiment with the synthesis of painting and music was not adequately thought out, that it was not based on a theoretical search, and for that reason is only metaphysically convincing, developing not *in artibus* but *inter artes*. Čiurlionis's art is a miracle, however, and in such art, naiveté can be united with analytical knowledge, and originality as a form of naiveté can be combined with technical perfection. What Čiurlionis contributed to the art of painting was an unearthly, ethereal, half-mystical, religious conception of elegance and grace, a kind of beauty which Edgar Allan Poe called "supernal beauty," and, touched by the same kind of beauty, Ivanov—who termed Čiurlionis a genius-inspired artist[24]—was Čiurlionis's perfect philosophical interpreter, one endowed with deep critical understanding. In this essay his reasoning powers are applied to logical perfection, allied with deep imaginative intuition. Ivanov saw Čiurlionis's work as a hymn-like affirmation of being, and this, too, was Ivanov's own poetic and human attitude. Čiurlionis's and Ivanov's natures were

so contemplative, and, in a way, so centered upon reflection, that
they perhaps never gave full utterance to their own individuality.
This was unquestionably true of Čiurlionis. The cumulative richness
and full-sounding depth of Ivanov's language harmonizes intimately
with the sonority and monumentality of Čiurlionis's paintings. Čiurlionis achieved this monumentality, this grandeur of conception and
space, even in the smallest of his compositions, as did Ivanov even
in the shortest of his poems.

In the presence of Čiurlionis's paintings, Ivanov follows a scale
of progressive appreciation and empathy, until he reaches the extreme
point of abstract as well as sensuous philosophic certainty. He says
that "the synthesis of the arts could exist only in a liturgical sense,"
and continues:

> What remains is to reach the final conclusion. The attempt to
> synthesize the different branches of art that we observe in the work
> of Čiurlionis derives from the attempt to transform the various
> arts into useful means for achieving goals outside the limits of
> these same arts. During this process the specific nature of each of
> the arts is violated and the artist's relationship with them loses
> its integrity and, therefore, these efforts cannot be considered as
> legitimate.[25]

Yet only a year after Čiurlionis's death, in the foreword to the
first Futurist exhibition in Paris, the so-called *linea-forza,* or line-
force, was proclaimed as the time element of space.[26] Eight years
later, in 1920, Naum Gabo (an admirer of Čiurlionis) and Gabo's
brother Antonin Pevsner presented the following new concepts of
form:

> In order to interpret reality, art must be based upon two
> fundamental elements: space *and* time. Volume is not the only
> concept of space. Kinetic and dynamic elements must be used to
> express the true nature of time.

Since then, in countless attempts, the two apparently contradictory
states—the dream of movement (music, in Čiurlionis's sense) and
extensional reality (space)—have merged, according to modernist

critics, into a reality of time and space, though some conventional critics still may not agree with this belief or may dislike, for example, even the idea of mobile sculpture.

But none of this can change the philosophical, critical, and literary value of Ivanov's Čiurlionis essay. This interpretative analysis by Ivanov, the experimental traditionalist, is conclusive in its purity of logic and vision because there is in it a spiritual craving in the mood of Čiurlionis, an ideal in Ivanov himself, that found fulfillment here. This massive, intellectually powerful, lyrically melodious essay actually creates a panorama worthy of Čiurlionis's cosmogenic vistas. Ivanov not only established new perspectives for the understanding of Čiurlionis's philosophy of art, but also elevated it to lofty significance. With Čiurlionis in mind, Ivanov recalls Goethe's words: "Everyone would like to disappear individually in order to find himself in infinity."[27] This is exactly what happened to Ivanov the critic. Is not this mythical and mystical union with the artist the best and the highest that a critic could ever achieve?

Notes

1. Vladimir Markov, ed., *Modern Russian Poetry* (London, 1966), p. lviii.

2. *SS*, III, 62. Passage translated by Paula Radzynski and Brian Carter.

3. Andrej Belyj, *Poezija slova* (Petrograd, 1922), pp. 78, 91.

4. *SS*, II, 325–26. Translated by Lowry Nelson, Jr.

5. Olga Deschartes, "Ivanov, Vyacheslav Ivanovich," in *Encyclopedia of World Literature in the 20th Century*, 2 vols. (New York, 1969).

6. Homer, *Iliad* 5: 856.

7. *SS*, I, 729. Translated by Paula Radzynski and Brian Carter.

8. *SS*, I, 632–33.

9. The recent Soviet edition of Ivanov—*Stikhotvorenija i poemy*, ed. R. E. Pomirchij (Leningrad, 1976)—errs when it removes this ambiguity by making this simply the last poem in a cycle.

10. *SS*, I, 517. Translated by H. W. Tjalsma.

11. Charles Baudelaire, *Oeuvres complètes* (Paris, 1961), p. 13.

12. Stefan George, *Werke*, II (Munich, 1958), 241.

13. Clive Bell, *Art* (London, 1928), pp. 8 ff.

14. *SS*, I, 640. Translated by Lowry Nelson, Jr.

15. H. D., *Palimpsest* (Carbondale, Ill., 1968), p. 38.

16. See my essay "Viacheslav Ivanov and his *Vespertine Light:* Notes from my Critical Diary of 1966," *Russian Literature Triquarterly*, 4 (1972), 285–87.

17. *Oxford Book of French Verse*, ed. St. John Lucas (Oxford, 1923), p. 421.

18. *SS*, III, 105. Translated by Paula Radzynski and Brian Carter.

19. *SS*, III, 147–70. Reprinted in the book of essays *Borozdy i mezhi*, introd. J. D. West (Letchworth, 1971), it was unfortunately spoiled by the addition of a publicistic post-scriptum which destroyed the article's perfect composition.

20. *SS*, III, 149. Translated by Tatiana Fedorow. For her translation of the complete essay, see: *Lituanus* 7, no. 2 (June 1961), 45–57.

21. For further commentary on this question, see my study, *Mikalojus Konstantinas Čiurlionis: Lithuanian Missionary Painter* (Chicago, 1984).

22. Vytautas Landsbergis, *Pavasario sonata* (Vilnius, 1965). There is also a reworked variant in Russian: *Sonata vesny* (Vilnius, 1969).

23. *SS*, III, 152–53. Translated by Tatiana Fedorow. Translation from *Lituanus* 7, no. 2 (June 1961), 47.

24. *SS*, III, 160. Also *Lituanus* 7, no. 2, p. 52.

25. *SS*, III, 160. Also *Lituanus* 7, no. 2, p. 56.

26. Umberto Boccioni, Carlo Carrà, Luigi Russolo, Giacomo Balla, and Gino Severini, "The Exhibitors to the Public: 1912," in *Futurist Manifestos*, ed. and introd. Umbro Apollonio (New York, 1973), p. 18.

27. *SS*, III, 158. Also *Lituanus* 7, no. 2, p. 52.

CLASSICAL SCHOLAR
AND
PHILOSOPHER

Vyacheslav Ivanov and Classical Antiquity
Vasily Rudich

Classical antiquity played a central role in the creative and artistic concerns of Vyacheslav Ivanov. Arguably one of the most prominent authorities in classics in the Russian Silver Age, he was regarded by many, with a mixture of bewilderment and admiration, as the Hellenic spirit incarnate. A voluminous study would be needed to adumbrate all the subtlety and sophistication of his attitudes toward the classical heritage. His thought, frequently based on uncanny insights, is replete with antinomy and paradox, of which he was well aware. "I am not an architect of systems," he rightly asserts in *A Correspondence from Two Corners* (*Perepiska iz dvukh uglov,* 1921 [*SS,* III, 386].

We cannot expect here to explore all of Ivanov's multifaceted ideas on antiquity; least of all to derive a consistent doctrine from his many views. We shall seek rather to consider the effect that immersion in classical studies had on his spiritual development and to discuss certain characteristics of his thought that may clarify the nature of his "elective affinities" with the classical world.

One initial fact of great significance cannot be overlooked: Ivanov was a man of extraordinary learning, indeed one of the most learned people in the history of Russian culture. His professional training was formidable. Having started his scholarly work as a Roman historian, he joined Theodor Mommsen's famous seminar at the University of Berlin in 1886. The great teacher was pleased with the young and promising foreigner. Ivanov recollects in his poetic diary:

That happy day sarcastic Mommsen
Praised me with a smile.

V tot den' schastlivyj Mommzen edkij
Menja s ulybkoj pokhvalil.   [SS, II, 17]

Ivanov had already learned Greek and Latin in his school years; he developed his knowledge to the point of perfection. There hardly can be any doubt that he was able even to think in both classical languages as naturally as in his native Russian. His own poetry in Greek and Latin, found in *Cor Ardens* and *Tender Mystery,* is ingenious and accomplished.

Ivanov's Latin dissertation *On the Tax-Farming Companies of the Roman People* (*De societatibus vectigalium publicorum populi Romani*), completed in 1895 and eventually published fifteen years later, was an effort to elucidate the activities of public tax-farmers throughout Roman republican and imperial history. It was undertaken in accordance with Mommsen's methodology and in the spirit of his *Römisches Staatsrecht*. All the more remarkable is the fact that Ivanov's conclusions ran counter to Mommsen's own theory. The young Russian scholar apparently found flaws in his teacher's concepts. Mommsen firmly believed that the Romans possessed an elaborate public as well as criminal code. Ivanov's investigation, however, did not turn up any system of deliberately designed institutions; rather it revealed a series of *ad hoc* arrangements, contradictory and confusing.

Modern scholarship recognizes that the great German historian was wrong: involuntarily he projected into the distant past the historical experience of nineteenth-century Europe. Ivanov's skepticism was well-founded. In his later studies of Greek religion he would repudiate the positivistic approach with its pretense of objectivity and impartiality: ancient people had a different logic and mentality from ours, and to recreate them according to our own image and likeness means to distort historical truth, though it does not mean that one should abandon the search for universals. But empathy is to be substituted for impartiality as a psychological starting point in a scholarly procedure.

Ivanov's thesis was lavishly praised by Otto Hirschfeld. To Mommsen's credit, the disagreement did not prevent the master from acknowledging great merits in the work of the young challenger. As Mommsen put it, the dissertation was far above the usual level and was written "diligenter et subtiliter" [SS, II, 20]. Hirschfeld's support and Mommsen's approval opened up before the young classicist the prospect of a brilliant academic career in Germany. But the outcome was unexpected: the young Ivanov chose not to grasp the opportunity. Several reasons for this decision suggest themselves. Throughout his life Ivanov displayed scant concern either for personal fame or public recognition. In his late years he wrote in a poem:

Do not pursue the shadow of fame:
She is after you, not you after her

Za ten'ju slavy ne gonis',
Ten' za toboj, ne ty za nej   [SS, III, 599]

He neglected to publish his dissertation when it was finished; however, it is probable that, still in manuscript form, it gave impetus to the early work of Mikhail Rostovtzeff, Ivanov's friend and colleague.

Rostovtzeff's book on Roman publicans, which appeared in 1899, was translated into German;[1] it constituted his first step toward celebrity. As for Ivanov's Latin dissertation, its scholarly value was acknowledged by its reprint in Italy in 1971. However, there was a deeper cause than mere indifference to career that motivated Ivanov to turn down the temptation offered by Hirschfeld and Mommsen. While doing research in the British Museum on the historical roots of Roman belief in the universal mission of Rome, he grew more and more disenchanted with Roman history, having fallen in love instead with "the fiancée of his heart," Greek philology. After a year of studying Sanskrit under de Saussure, he arrived in Paris and delivered in 1903 a series of lectures on the religion of Dionysus at the École Superieure des Sciences Sociales. These lectures enjoyed great success.

In the eyes of his peers Ivanov's achievements were remarkable. No one doubted at the time that he was indeed the leading specialist on Dionysian worship. Thaddeusz Zielinski, himself a formidable authority in classics, commended Ivanov the scholar in 1916 as a researcher of high merit, meticulous and diligent. In his 1933 Italian essay, published in a special volume of *Il Convegno* dedicated to Ivanov, Zielinski comments upon Ivanov's unique combination of poetic and scholarly genius. His conclusion is: "finally one is left only with amazement"—"*non rimane altro che meravigliarsi.*" An ardent believer in a Slavic Renaissance, Zielinski saw Ivanov as its initiator and central figure—"persona provvidenziale."[3] Zielinski's intuition was not mistaken: as a creative temperament, Ivanov undoubtedly harks back to the Renaissance archetype with its intrinsic blend of commitments to past, present and future. He always felt at home in the select company of Poliziano and Petrarch, Winckelmann and Goethe.

We may perhaps discern yet another reason for Ivanov's disinclination to pursue the study of Roman history. For all his tremendous knowledge of things Roman, he could in no way identify himself with the Roman spirit. In contrast to many Russian thinkers, he was indifferent to the imperial ideal, so crucial in Roman experience. If he had any profound concerns related to Roman culture, they were eschatological; hence his interest in Virgil and, indeed, in the emergence of Christianity.

The picture is quite different when we turn to Ivanov's attitude to ancient Greece. He always agreed with Goethe's contention that there is a self-developing form impressed on all things (geprägte Form, die lebend sich entwickelt). In this sense we might say that there was an impressed form in Ivanov's own psyche, and that that form was Hellenic. In certain periods of his life he seems to have felt an inner kinship with the Goethe of the Weimar Classicism, the Goethe of serene vision and infinite refinement. In any case, he was fond of quoting another saying of Goethe: "Everyone can be a Hellene in his own way, but everyone ought to be a Hellene." Being a Hellene, then, is a prerequisite in a classicist for genuine comprehension of his subject.

Finally, Ivanov's alienation from purely historical research might be attributed to a particular quality of his thinking, one related to religious and poetical aspects of his world view. His thinking was ultimately metahistorical. In this framework time is a very relative value. The cultural process or phenomenon is perceived not in terms of creation and destruction, but in terms of memory and oblivion. Historical development is an accumulation of spirituality that must be dealt with *sub specie aeternitatis*. Hence the inevitable shift in Ivanov's commitments from the field of conventional history into *Kulturphilosophie,* and especially the psychology of religion—from now on his life-long scholarly passion.

Ivanov's scholarship on the orgiastic cults is highly original, though the Dionysian problem itself obviously was suggested by his brief though profound encounter with Nietzsche. Yet we can hardly speak of Nietzsche's scholarly influence upon Ivanov. Though a "Philolog" by education, Nietzsche had renounced everything in his intellectual rebellion, including analysis of texts and other specialized philological techniques. Ivanov, to the contrary, was becoming exceedingly professional in his treatment of his subject.

In regard to philosophical influence, Ivanov himself formulated the difference between Nietzsche's attitude and his own in "Nietzsche and Dionysus," his earliest piece on the theme (1904). Nietzsche saw Dionysus as a phenomenon of a primarily psychological and esthetic character, an impersonal element, spontaneous and chaotic. For Ivanov its significance is psychological and religious, and Dionysus himself, first and foremost, is the suffering deity. Ivanov's distinguished scholarly predecessors were Sir James Frazer and Erwin Rohde, though an intellectual impetus to his work can be traced back to the science of mythology as postulated by Karl Otfried Müller and, above all, to the mythopoetic philosophy of Schelling. Frazer and Rohde, however, represented two almost opposite points of departure, and thus crucially influenced increasingly divergent developments in modern scholarship. On the one hand, Frazer and his followers gave birth to the British ritualist school, whose positivistic beliefs and claims of objectivity did not much differ from the cool rationalization of French sociologists as dissimilar as Durkheim and Lévy-Bruhl. Modern structuralism is in this sense their legitimate successor. On the other hand, recognition of religion as reality, both psychological and metaphysical, led to interpretations based on an attempt at spiritual empathy, on an effort to appropriate an ancient or alien religious experience. Walter Friedrich Otto found in Dionysus his personal god, whom he actually worshipped in accordance with Greek prescription. Soon the Jungian branch of psychoanalysis provided a convenient frame of reference that has been used successfully by professional classicists, notably Karl Kerenyi. A considerable degree of Jungian influence has exerted itself upon Mircea Eliade, arguably the most prominent contemporary historian of religion. Long before Jung, however, Ivanov had taken psychological empathy as a prerequisite for his scholarly stand. Though never going to such extremes as Otto, he believed nevertheless that he had experienced, at least once, a true Dionysian ecstasy. This contention is supported by his many scholarly and poetical insights. But his passionate commitment to making the Greek religious experience the inner reality of his consciousness, to living it through, "durchleben," as the Germans would say, never violated even inconsequential rules of a strict scholarly procedure.

As an admiring disciple of Ulrich Wilamowitz-Möllendorf, though at times also his sober critic, Ivanov was an accomplished philologist, whose method is essentially philological, based on the close study of texts. Archaeological or anthropological evidence is rarely used, owing to the as yet rudimentary development of these disciplines. Ivanov's *Wissenschaftlichkeit,* that refined accuracy the Greeks called *akribeia,* is supplemented by his ability to perceive the essence of the cultural process in every tiny detail. Finally, he had a genius for metaphysical interpretation, never arbitrary but carefully meditated and verified upon the material at hand.

Ivanov's *The Hellenic Religion of the Suffering God,* written in 1903–1905, but never published in full because of a series of accidents, is an insightful and provocative work. A brief glance at several of its many propositions may be needed to give an idea of how profound and pioneering his views were.

Ecstasy, according to Ivanov, is the most ancient phenomenon of religious experience, of the transcendence of the human self. Thus the god is preceded by the cult, the cult by the victim, the victim by ecstasy. In this sense Dionysus is the means, not the substance. God, priest, and victim are one and the same, a notion corroborated by modern anthropology. Both constructive and destructive aspects may be discerned in Dionysianism. The constructive aspect is *orthōs manēnai,* righteous revelry, aimed at experiencing communion with the deity.

Ivanov's second book, *Dionysus and Predionysianism,* published in 1923 in the Caucasian city of Baku and now a bibliographical rarity, is much more specific. It is a masterpiece of sophisticated scientific investigation, replete with brilliant conjectures, some of them later confirmed by archeology. Ivanov illustrates in detail an argument of the preceding book and traces the Dionysian myth and Dionysian features in multiple disguise throughout the great variety of legendary motifs. In the most complex problem of the origin of the Dionysian worship he does not fail to notice the weakness of Rohde's "Thracian theory" (then universally accepted). He questions its validity, finds an Hellenic imprint on the most ancient elements of the Dionysian rites, and comes to the conclusion that "its adoption in the absolute sense of the word should be denied."[4] This is precisely the view of present-day scholarship. But we should not forget that in the West the idea of an essentially Greek origin of Dionysiasm was offered for the first time (and in passing) by Charles Picard in 1930, seven years after Ivanov's monograph.

Ivanov's thesis about the cults of the "unnamed Dionysus" which go back "to the epoch of the worship of the empty thrones or altars of the deity invisibly present"[5] is proved, with few variations, by Kerenyi on the basis of archaeological material from Crete. Ivanov's intuition was also correct in relegating the primordial Dionysiasm to the pre-Dorian period. Now even the name of Dionysus has been discovered in the process of the decoding of Linear B, though it is still not clear whether it refers to that particular deity. Much more convincing than Martin Nilsson's "Thracian-Phrygian syncretism" is Ivanov's differentiating between "continental" and "insular" cults of Dionysus, which coexisted in "mutual *syzygeia.*" This demarcation is very close to Kerenyi's theory of the simultaneous movement of Dionysus from the north and from the south. In our view, Ivanov proved beyond doubt Apollo's original existence in Delphi in his Dionysiac and chthonic capacity. This notion runs contrary to Nilsson's much later argument, which persists in postulating Apollo as the reformer of orgiastic religion. Ivanov's most important and meticulously elaborated argument was never to our knowledge developed by Western scholars. It is his discussion of the cults of the "otherwise named" Dionysus, that is of the pre-Dionysian phenomena that later acquired many and different forms. It is clear that in this respect he was ahead even of the most recent scholarship. Many of these results are due to Ivanov's uncanny scholarly intuition: his predictions of at least two sensational archaeological discoveries are recorded. Combined with his proficient research it produced a creative balance suited ideally to his interests and his task.

The range and the quality of Ivanov's achievements in the history of religion and in the study of religious psychology are astonishing. Through an unfortunate series of accidents his work was never published in any Western European language and thus remained inaccessible to most of his colleagues. There can be hardly any doubt that otherwise he would have acquired an international reputation matching that of Kerenyi or Eliade.

Ivanov's attitude toward antiquity as toward the world of his own habitation is poignantly reflected in his poetry. He was able to discover his own ego not only in a Dionysian bacchant or in the hierophant at Eleusis, but also in a symposiarch and a ploughman, a shepherd and a charioteer, a Homeric warrior or a Pythagorean philosopher. And above all, he was the *vates,* the poet possessed by the sacred madness, the favorite of Apollo and the Muses, the new Arion, Musaeus, and Orpheus. His beloved wife, Lydia Zinovieva-Annibal, was easily transformed into Diotima, the wise priestess and the counselor to Socrates, and he would recognize the Lateran Sophocles in the imposing personality of his friend Zielinski.

Like Socrates, Ivanov was a virtuoso in the art of maieutics, the midwifery of thought, being in every respect "maestro di color che sanno." And he knew well, with Plato, that the Spirit is to be born out of beauty. A teacher of great charismatic power, he exercised a true Hellenic paideia upon his students in Baku and Pavia, many of whom believed that their years under Ivanov's guidance were not only the years of their cultural initiation but also of crucial existential experience.

Vyacheslav Ivanov's perception of the classical heritage had yet another facet that relates to his life-long views on the essence of culture. Introducing the Platonic notion of *anamnesis,* Ivanov defines culture as "the cult of memory." Its ultimate goal is the recognition of primordial recollection—that of the unity of Man and God. Its destructive opposite is oblivion. Culture therefore is not a petrified thesaurus, an object of abstract academic interest. It is an ever-living treasury of sacred values embodied in our hearts and immanent in the being of mankind. Thus it requires a most fervent commitment from the student of the humanities. The classical heritage is not merely part and parcel of this treasury. "There is no culture in Europe," Ivanov contends, "except it be a Hellenic one" [*SS,* III, 69 ff.]. Everything untouched by the Hellenic element remains barbarian and functions independently as the principle of chaos. This coexistence underlies the dynamics of intellectual and spiritual movements. "The classical antiquity that rises every morning virgin and young anew, like the celestial spouse of supreme Jove," Ivanov writes, "continues to ennoble, refine, and stimulate the mind of posterity, but only insofar as our soul, as Livy puts it, *'fit antiquior'*" [*SS,* III, 436]. This appeal to shape our souls *antiquior* is the crux of the matter. No step up is possible without a step down. "The higher the foliage the deeper the roots," Ivanov remarks elsewhere [*SS,* III, 392]. This immense Hellenic spiritual *oikoumene*—from pre-Homeric presentiments to Alexandrian sophistication—was familiar to him in all particulars as a native and beloved abode. It was both means and substance of his poetic and scholarly meditations.

The first poem of his first collection *Pilot Stars* (1903) begins with a classical image:

Last evening Titans soared in darkness

Vchera vo mgle neslis' Titany   [*SS,* I, 515]

The feeling of immediacy is here remarkable, as if the Titans' flight happened just recently, yesterday or last night. Likewise in his last masterpiece, the posthumous collection entitled *Evening Light* (published in 1962), the final poem pointedly sets a classical ending— an invocation of the Muse. His Muse advises the poet to pay homage to Pallas Athene, who summons him now:

> What the Virgin is dreaming of,
> Who bows her head upon the spear
> We should surmise . . .

> O chem zadumalasja Deva,
> Glavoj sklonivshis' na kop'e,
> Pojdem gadat' . . .   [*SS*, III, 644]

Here his gaze leaps ahead into the immediate future, steady and hopeful. By juxtaposing these lines one realizes to what extent the classical imagery, reacting backward and forward in time, remains one with his artistic work from beginning to end.

The excellence of his translations from Greek into Russian can be only briefly mentioned here. He published Russian versions of the poems of Pindar and Bacchylides, Alcaeus and Sappho, and almost completed a translation of the whole corpus of Aeschylus, which is still in manuscript. Ivanov displayed perfect mastery over ancient metrics. In his own original verse he reproduced the variety of Greek meter so that in Russian it sounds natural and fluent—from the hexameter and elegiac distich to the difficult Sapphic and Asclepiadic lines. His achievements in this respect may be equaled only by what Friedrich Hölderlin had done in German.

Ivanov wrote voluminously on the theory of drama. Here we can barely touch upon his ideas. He argued at length for the importance of the choric principle, the only means, in his view, of transforming theater into sacred and communal action. Relating the choric principle to the concept of "sobornost'," he was dreaming of a future Russia where sacred and artistic rites would be performed by thousands of orchestras. Along the same lines he experimented with his own two tragedies, *Tantalus* (1905) and *Prometheus* (1919), which treat one of the most ancient classical motifs, that of *hubris*. The classical plots are elaborated in a very unusual way by exploiting obscure and apocryphal legends in order to reflect in them as many facets as possible of the modern predicament. At the same time both tragedies are mythopoetic compositions that attempt to recreate Greek tragedy in its original sense. Probably the most fascinating aspect of Ivanov's attitudes is his perception of classical antiquity as a universal, never-ending and metaphysical value.

If one may discern in the spontaneous inner movements of any creative personality the tangible coloration of some philosophical strain, in Ivanov's case this coloration would decidedly be Platonic. The Platonizing element in his frame of mind was in harmony both with the fact that he was a poet and at the same time the prophet and theoretician of the Russian Symbolist school. Symbolism, articulated in philosophical language, naturally tends toward Platonism.

We would contend that Ivanov's sympathy lies primarily with Plato himself, rather than with the neo-Platonism of the various sects related to Gnosticism. This does not include, however, patristics, which absorbed many neo-Platonic views, nor the Platonic revival of the Renaissance. The symbol, after all, is a representation of the transcendental, and Ivanov accepts "Plato's dialectical description of Eros" as the definition of Symbolism [*SS,* II, 606]. Plato is also consistently invoked for final arbitration on different esthetic issues.

In this way the classical heritage acquires for Ivanov the status of a metaphysical existence in the Platonic sense. It represents the ideal spiritual experience of the Hellenes. "The pagan genius," he remarks, "had projected all its best into the transcendent image" [*SS,* III, 403]. And in this capacity "the best" continues to dwell, beyond time and space, in the "sphere of *Werden,* or coming-to-be," as eternal, immutable and universal. He beautifully echoes Platonic imagery in his essay "Ancient Terror" (1909): "A profound and golden silence embraces the soul, surrendered to self-negation, and in the distant distances images rise before it, preserved in the recollection of the World Soul. For truly, not one iota in the scroll of her memory is transient, and everything that has passed is happening eternally, and this very day Cleopatra is steering the gilded stern of her galley to flee the watery field of the Actean battle . . ." [SS, III, 100]. It is no wonder, then, that he maintains that the Hellenic soul is immortal [SS, III, 377]. Viewed more pragmatically, this outlook implies that the classical heritage serves as an existential context in which moral, psychological or esthetic challenges can be interpreted and acted upon. We have already stated that Ivanov's poetry is dense with classical imagery. His melopoeia *Man* (written in 1916 and published in 1939) had chosen the mysterious Delphic inscription *ei*—thou art—as the starting point for a complex philosophical argument on the ultimate creed of mankind whose purpose is achieved when the Man acknowledges the God as his Father and Creator saying to him: "Thou art, and this is why I am."

On almost every page of his essays, whether on the dignity of women or on the Russian Revolution, his views might be conveyed in concepts drawn directly from the classical past. It is not only an inexhaustible source of reference, it is the means of cognition of problems of both immediate and ultimate significance. This latter procedure connects lower and higher levels of our existence and that of the cosmos, and it exemplifies Ivanov's famous formula *a realibus ad realiora*: from this reality to the greater one. This impetus finds its ultimate realization in myth and mythopoeia. Ivanov was interested in the great diversity of myths, not necessarily relevant only to the metamorphosis of Dionysus. He interprets the Hellenic myths, often obscure ones, on a universal scale, and this is a natural consequence of his doctrine concerning the nature of the symbol. The myth, contained in the symbol and growing out of it, becomes an objective truth of our being, or, in Ivanov's own words, "the purest form of representational poetry" [SS, II, 554]. And again he quotes Plato: if a poet wishes to be the Poet he has to create myths [SS, I, 713].

Ivanov's personal created myth—the startling child of his declining years—*The Tale of Svetomir the Prince*, fuses and transfigures many ancient motifs into a unique and unexpected whole, again relegated beyond time and space. Philoctetes and Alexander the

Great coexist with the Knights of the Round Table, the imagined Russian dynasts and the apocryphal Prester John. As far as the past and the future are concerned, Ivanov believed that the mythical chronicle of the world comes closer to truth than the actual history we know.

We have already suggested that Ivanov's various meditations on classical culture, his perceptions and intuitions, are intimately interrelated. The result is an organic and harmonious vision which makes no significant distinction among the endeavors of a philosopher, a scholar, or a poet. Poetry, philosophy, scholarship are only manifestations of a spiritual integrity given impetus by deep religious belief.

Vyacheslav Ivanov was a devoted Christian. With Euripides, he might acknowledge the multiplicity of the divine forms: πολλαὶ μορφαὶ τῶν δαιμονίοω [SS, III, 117]. But he knew that polytheism is only the earliest stage of the recognition of God as manifold unity. For Ivanov the Christian religious thinker, the philosophy of history is naturally Christocentric. It is the realization of God's design for Man's salvation. If this is so, every great culture is an aspect of the incarnation of the Word. Classical antiquity is seen as the crucial stage in this gradual involvement of humankind in the process of comprehending God: the pagan truth "is purged and baptized in Eucharistic Jordan" (V novozavetnom Iordane ochishchena i kreshchena [SS, III, 632]).

The human soul was being prepared for the coming of Christ. But if the pagans were not given the Messianic Revelation it does not mean that they were dwelling in absolute darkness. Their "daybreak dreams" (rassvetnye sny) were the Heraclitean Logos, the Eleusinian mysteries, the Orphic hymns. In that and only that sense is Dionysus, with his passions, righteous revelry and palingenesis, called "an ally of the Galilean fishermen." Ivanov's view of paganism is very close to that of the ante-Nicaean apologists, such as Clement of Alexandria and, especially, St. Justin the Martyr, whom he quotes with sympathy and pride: "beautiful things to be found anywhere are Christian and ours"—ὅσα παρὰ πᾶσι καλῶς εἴρεται ἡμῶν, χριστιανῶν 'εστίν [SS, III, 443].

In his Italian letter to Alessandro Pellegrini (1934) Ivanov med-
itates upon the character of true humanism, a humanism rooted in
faith in God. And he emphasizes both its Christian and its Platonic
nature. He reminds us that St. Basil the Great and St. Augustine
were Platonists, just as a thousand years later the Platonic humanists
of the Renaissance were Christians. And once again Ivanov formulates in triumphant Greek the principal thesis of his religious humanism, which projects the unification of Man with God: Man is a
unity. Humanism is thus transformed into monanthropism—μόνος
'ο ἄνθροπος [*SS*, III, 380].

Occasionally, inner conflicts could emerge between his ideas of
Christian devotion and what he might take to be excessive passions
and pagan temptations. There is a beautiful poem "The Palinode"
in his *Evening Light,* in which he asks in bewilderment:

> Have I, in fact, O Hellas, stopped loving you?

> Uzheli ja tebja, Ellada, razljubil?

And then follows:

> I fled, and in the foothills of Egyptian Thebes
> I eat the food of silence, locusts and wild honey . . .

> I ja bezhal, i em v predgor'jakh Fivaidy
> Molchan'ja dikij med i zhestkie akridy . . .
>
> [*SS*, III, 553]

However, these discords were never profound or serious. Probably
the poet himself treated them not without humor and, following his
favorite concept, as if they were love quarrels between *animus* and
anima, happily reconcilable the next moment.

Ivanov's very last poem, a somber sonnet completed a few days
before he died, describes Heracles on his funeral pyre and ends with
the line:

> Death cleaved with her relentless hatchet

> Rassekla Smert' sekiroj besposhchadnoj   [*SS*, III, 575]

Aleksis Rannit, who visited Vyacheslav Ivanov not long before that
line was written, recalls that, speaking of the future, the poet confessed with a smile that he would be deeply unhappy if in any world
to come he could not read, speak, and write Greek.[6]

Notes

1. M. Rostovtsev, *Geschichte des Staatspacht in der römischen Kaiserzeit bis
Diokletian* (Leipzig, 1902).
2. Th. Zielinski, "Vjacheslav Ivanov," in *Russkaja literatura XX veka,*
ed. S. Vengerov, vol. VIII (Moscow, 1917), p. 113.
3. Th. Zielinski, "Introduzione all'opera di Venceslao Ivanov," *Il Convegno,* nos. 8–12, (1933), p. 243.
4. V. Ivanov, *Dionis i pradionisijstvo* (Baku, 1923), p. 273.
5. Ibid., p. 279.
6. A. Rannit, "Vyacheslav Ivanov and his *Vespertine Light,"* *Russian
Literature Triquarterly,* vol. 3 (1973), 287.

The Myth of the Suffering God and the Birth of Greek Tragedy in Ivanov's Dramatic Theory

Fausto Malcovati

Ivanov's passionate essay *The Hellenic Religion of the Suffering God* (El-linskaja religija stradajushchego boga, 1904) provides us with an example of his life-long interest in the ancient Greek spirit, which he felt should serve as a source of inspiration and as a model for the contemporary world. The study of the cult of Dionysus, the suffering god, assumed a central role in Ivanov's esthetic research. His writings on Homer, Pindar, Alcaeus, and Sappho represent an important philological and critical contribution, but the Dionysus essay serves as the foundation for an entire cultural concept. Published in 1904, it is Ivanov's first treatise expressing his hope for a great spiritual renaissance in our century.

Ivanov sees the Dionysus cult as the first seed of the concept of religion in man, the primordial ecstatic experience from which religion later evolved. He writes: "Man is to be distinguished from the other animals because unlike them he is an *animal religiosum* (a state of being that precedes that of the *animal politicum,* πολιτικὸν ζῷον). The germ of religiosity can be detected in the first ecstatic experience of Man. Man is first and foremost an *animal ecstaticum.*"

Ecstasy, which forms the very core of the Dionysian religion, is therefore the alpha and omega of the human religious condition. But what is the meaning and origin of this ecstasy in the Greek world? Ivanov observes that the ancient Greeks were unique in their capacity to look the horrors of death in the face without resorting to the consolation of negating human mortality as the Hindus did, or denying the immortality of the Gods as the pre-Roman Italic people did. Ecstasy, therefore, becomes the only means of accepting the inevitability of death, the only means of tolerating human suffering, the only force capable of relieving the desperate pessimism of man confronted with the disintegration of his own self. Dionysian ecstasy provides the certainty of mystical unity with the figure of the suffering god, at once the priest and the victim. In Dionysian ecstasy the duality of being, in which life and death coexist as two opposing aspects of the universal mystery, is revealed. It implies two spiritual ways, the ascending way (*put' vverkh*) with Dionysus as Helios, and the descending way (*put' vniz*), with Dionysus as Hades.

The Dionysus cult was, in fact, initially a state of mind (*nekotoroe kak*) without any specific content (*opredelennoe chto*). That is why the Dionysian myth had first and foremost an etiological significance, and, like all myths, provided an explanation for an already existing phenomenon. Ecstasy did not, therefore, derive from an image (*predstavlenie*) of the god, but rather the god was the incarnation of an undirected collective ecstasy (*bezpredmetnoe isstuplenie*). In the Dionysian religion, the myth of the suffering god, although very ancient in origin, is still more recent than the god's image, and his image is more recent than the idea of his sanctified and sanctifying suffering (*svjashchennoe i osvjashchajushchee stradanie*). The god is more ancient than his own history, the victim is more ancient than the god, and the ecstatic collectivity is the oldest of all. The victim, the god, and the myth of the god do share, however, one common element which has remained constant from the beginning: the sanctification of sacrifice and of death as a sacrifice, which constitutes the religious embryo of what many centuries later became Greek tragedy.

Primordial Dionysian ecstasy was intimately bound up with cannibalistic rites, which recalled the biblical temptation by the serpent: "Eat, for your eyes will be opened and you will be like gods." In other words: eat god to become god. The cannibalistic aspect gradually disappeared over the centuries with the substitution of symbolic animal victims, but the first participants in the Dionysian mysteries were not acquainted with the use of symbols. For them it was Dionysus himself who was the victim, who was torn apart and devoured by the participants who thereby became like their god. Here we have the center of the Dionysian religion at its inception, that is to say the identity of the victim with the god. This is why, in later hypostases of Dionysus, there coexists the double nature of the god as goat and as shepherd, the god as devoured and as devourer. The early participants in the rites, thanks to their identification with the venerated and devoured god, had no need of priests. Every member of the group was consecrated during the performance of the choral chants; and when the group achieved the ecstasy of possession by the god, they also became the god.

In the Dionysian cult, the laceration of the god was related to the chaotic ancestral conflict between the masculine and feminine principles. In fact, in addition to ritual death, the sexual act constitutes the other fundamental experience of Dionysian ecstasy. The Dionysus cult is the cult of death which gives birth to life. Dionysus is the god of the cradle and the god of the tomb. Death is the opposite of the sexual act: the seed must die in order to give life to the new plant. In the struggle between the sexes, the Dionysus cult represents the victory of the feminine principle: the rites of the cult are pervaded with female fury. Mothers kill their sons and wives tear their husbands apart. The Titans, who rend Dionysus, are indeed images of old Mother Earth exacting revenge on her Olympian consort. Dionysus can therefore be said to be a women's god. He was cradled by women. He was nourished by women. He was even dressed as a woman during his adolescence. He was loved by women who were possessed by his demoniacal frenzy, by his ecstatic and tormented madness. At last, he was torn apart and devoured by women.

In contrast to Apollo, the god of unity, of monad, of harmony and equilibrium, Dionysus is the god of multiplicity, of the breaking up of primordial unity, of *dyad,* which was a term employed by the Pythagoreans. Dyad, the concept on which Ivanov's essay "The Substance of Tragedy" (*O sushchestve tragedii,* 1916) is based, presupposes an original primordial unity which harbors within itself an intrinsic conflict. The use of the word "conflict," however, does not imply the struggle of hostile forces alien to one another. It is not the conflict of pre-existent elements, rather it derives from an absolute unity in which antipodal energies slowly manifest themselves and move toward a final irrevocable breaking point. According to Ivanov, the dyadic principle is at the basis of the inner life of the hero, at the basis of the art of tragedy, "which is the most human of the arts." The psychological structure of man is not as simple and unilateral as that of the animal or, for that matter, of the angel; the psychological structure of man is characterized by the inner dialectic, the tragic feeling of limitation, the necessity of choosing good or evil in the eternal conflict between himself and the world around him. The art of tragedy must make manifest this inner dialectic. The art of tragedy must show the thesis and antithesis of man's inner world in its concrete development, what Hegel termed "das Werden." This development proceeds in a state of continual tension until it reaches the point of explosion, the point at which the dark abyss that divides the two poles of man's spiritual life, being and its negation, non-being, is revealed. This explosion cannot be hindered by the introduction into the conflict of a third element, from within or without, to form a conciliatory triad. The antipodal forces of the dyad are inseparable and completely independent of external factors. Therefore, the explosion always signifies death. Ivanov provides us with a clarifying example. If Hamlet were merely a weak person in conflict with a world of strong and violent men, Shakespeare's tragedy would not exhibit such depth and, in fact, would not even exist as a tragedy. It is the profound enigma of the inner chaos of his soul that drives him to the destruction of his personality.

Although women played an ever diminishing role in the historical development of the Dionysian cult, they remained a central factor in tragedy, functioning either as protagonists or as chorus. The female loves and kills. Here we have the two principles of Dionysian ecstasy clearly united, sex and death. In the double instinct of possession and annihilation, the female becomes completed and achieves the authentic integration of her feminine being. One need only think of the female characters in Aeschylus: Clytaemnestra, Cassandra, Antigone, and Niobe, the heroine of his lost play. In his play *The Suppliants,* which is perhaps the oldest tragedy extant, the chorus is a female chorus, the Danaïds. As Dionysian ritual ecstasy

progressively weakened, tragedy also underwent a profound metamorphosis, and the masculine principle became more and more important. The dyadic principle gradually gave way to more
externalized conflicts between persons bound to each other by family
ties, characters like Orestes or Medea, caught up in parent-child
conflicts, Eteocles and Polynices, or Ismene and Antigone in their
sibling rivalries, or Hercules and Deianeira, in their husband-and-
wife struggle. The clearest example of the proliferation of what we
might term the exteriorized dyad occurs in Aeschylus's *Seven against
Thebes*. Two brothers fight and kill each other, and their sisters
violently confront each other in the presence of their dead siblings.

We spoke before of the Apollonian principle. The introduction
and mixture of this principle into Dionysian rites made possible the
development of tragedy as an art form. It is hardly necessary here to
repeat Nietzsche's theory of the relationship between the Apollonian
and the Dionysian principles in the *Birth of Tragedy*. Ivanov emphasizes the religious element, which in Nietzsche's discussion assumes
minor importance. The affirmation of the Apollonian element
brought with it a sense of form and harmony, but also the gradual
extinction of the pathetic element, the paralysis of Dionysian inner
energy, the demagnetization of the tragic nucleus, and, especially,
the final disappearance of catharsis. Why did all this happen? It
happened because of the developing *principium individuationis,* the
ever increasing differentiation between the components of tragedy
and their functions. The dithyramb, no longer an expression of the
group in chorus, became a particular kind of lyric poetry. The passion and suffering of the hero assumed an autonomous role in the
tragic action and drew upon itself the exclusive attention of the
public. The group, which once acted as a chorus during the Dionysian rites, was limited to the role of spectator, and was reduced
from its original double function, actively theurgic and passively
sacrificial, to a single function. As Aristotle says, they became the
uninvolved observer (παθή/πάσχειν, to experience passively).

There were also changes, in the logistical sense, through the
centuries. The action no longer took place in the orchestra, but was
transferred to the proscenium. The proscenium was increasingly

above and more isolated from the public, of whom the action was no longer the expression. The stage, separated in this manner from the public, became the magic place that divided the actor, who only acted, from the spectator, who only observed the action.

The real crisis of tragedy, however, was manifested in the changed role of the chorus.. Once bearer of the conflict between the god and the group, it became a simple organ of accompaniment to the central action, commenting on it. It became extraneous to the tribulations of the hero; it became more and more superfluous and then disappeared completely. Its disappearance signified the definitive twilight of the ecumenical principle in the theater. Religion was no longer a factor in the theater, and with the last remnants of religion, catharsis was eliminated once and for all. The drama was transformed into a sort of mathematical demonstration of a theorem, and the stage into a kind of arena where gladiators of passion performed their struggle. Theater of this kind became progressively less and less necessary to the public, and the dissatisfaction of Ivanov's contemporaries with the two most widespread forms of theater of the time, the realistic (Chekhov) and the illusionistic (Maeterlinck), gave eloquent testimony to the fact. As Ivanov often said in other writings, "we are living in a 'critical epoch,' an epoch of cultural differentiation, of sterile individualism, of the lack of circulation of vital energy." He also, however, thought he saw the first signs of the end of this period and the beginning of the new "organic epoch" of the reintegration of cultural energies, of tendencies toward a spiritual synthesis. The art of the new age would be syncretic (*sobornoe*) and universal. The most direct manifestation of the new tendencies would be the choral drama, the dynamic expression of the new community, in which every participant would become an active molecule in a collective ritual. There would be no more theater in the sense of spectacle (*sozertsanie*), no more *circenses*. No more contemplation, but syncretic creation. "Zu schaffen, nicht zu schauen."

The spectators would once more take up their previous role as participants (*dejateli*), as they did at the inception of the Dionysian religion, and would unite into a common body, the chorus reborn. *This* would be the real sign of the new epoch. The chorus would function again in a reduced form, integrated into the action, as it does in Aeschylus, and in a wider, unlimited form, as a real symbol of the group. It would enter into the action at moments of greatest pathos and demonstrate the complete liberation of Dionysian energy. The Schiller chorus, in the last movement of Beethoven's Ninth Symphony, was the example most often used by Ivanov.

The chorus would be necessary to the public and be completely understood by the public. It would reconquer the stage, breaking down the barriers between stage and auditorium, which is what avant-garde directors attempted at the beginning of the century in some of their famous productions. Meyerhold's staging of *Balaganchik* at Komissarzhevskaya's theater, and Vakhtangov's staging of *Turandot* come to mind. Ivanov proposed as new forms for the theater the heroic tragedy based on the ancient models and also the medieval mystery plays. These forms would revivify the dyadic principle, re-open the abyss of the human soul when faced by the anguishing dichotomy between life and death, and reconstitute a new ecumenical religion of the suffering god.

In a short article written in 1920, Ivanov once more underscored his idea of the impossibility of this rebirth without the employment of the choral principle. The new organic epoch would arise when the spectator ceased to be identified exclusively with the hero and his destiny, but would become immersed in the group. With his newly found universal consciousness, he would follow the course of the hero as an immanent act in its transcendent significance. The hero would be once more the victim immolated in the name of the group, and *for* the group that gave expression to him.

Vyacheslav Ivanov and Nietzsche
Heinrich Stammler

Gottfried Benn, the German expressionist and post-expressionist poet, remarked in an essay entitled "Nietzsche after Fifty Years":

> First, I asked myself what of Nietzsche's work seems to be antiquated today, limited, as it were. And there I should like to say . . . [that] his glorification of all things Greek appears remote nowadays. Statements such as "The Greek—the man who has gone the farthest way ahead," or "The Greek people, the only people of genius in the entire history of the world," or "The Hellenic world—the only possible, the deepest fulfillment of life," or "The Greeks have certainly never been overrated," or "Only the resuscitation of true Hellenism will bring back true culture"—this, his existential attachment to the Greeks does not live within us any more. [1]

But it was just this profound involvement with the ancient Greek religion, mythos, and thought which led to the fated encounter of two kindred minds, two souls, if you will—Vyacheslav Ivanov and Friedrich Nietzsche. During his Berlin years, as a student of the famous historian Mommsen and other renowned classical scholars, Ivanov for the first time began to immerse himself in the works of Goethe, but also in Khomyakov and Vladimir Solovyov, and last but not least, in Nietzsche, whose shocking and provocative books had begun to excite literary and intellectual circles shortly after the philosopher's mental collapse in 1889. And when Ivanov moved in 1891 to Paris in order to round out his studies of classical philology and history he also took with him a volume of Nietzsche's writings, especially the essay with the suggestive title *The Birth of*

Tragedy from the Spirit of Music. From this time on he was to find
himself under the spell of the thought and visions of this man who
had said about himself: "I am a fatality," of the prophet of Dionysus
resurrected. Even in later years when it seemed he had emancipated
himself from the tremendous impression that the magic of
Nietzsche's words had made upon him, when it seemed that he had
parted ways with him, he returned, indeed critically and with reservations, but again and again, to the idol of his youth. His was,
of course, not a case of mere borrowing, but as James West has
pointed out, an initial inspiration and a great stimulation for the
further development of his own thoughts and insights.[2] And he never
ceased to acknowledge his debt to the author of the *Birth of Tragedy.*
What he immediately understood after reading this celebrated as
well as controversial essay was that Nietzsche with his juxtaposition
of the two elements, the Dionysian and the Apollonian, had discovered or rediscovered the two motive principles of creative action as
well as poetic intuition. He conceived of Nietzsche's demonstration
of this duality, organically combined, however, in the great work of
art, not in terms of some philosophical or esthetic doctrine, but
grasped it as a new way of viewing the world, a new method of
perceiving individual as well as universal life, of intimately communicating with the essence of things, a new revelation of the forces
of the inner life.[3] Not that a mere literary and scholarly "influence"
had been assimilated—what had occurred was a true "parousia,"
the immediate awareness of an explosive, overwhelming, terrifying
and at the same time infinitely blissful, liberating presence, the
presence of Dionysus. That is why Ivanov himself could say about
this encounter that in those years Nietzsche became in an ever more
powerful way the ruler of his thoughts. And it may seem a paradox,
but a paradox fraught with meaning, that the blasphemous foe of
Christianity was to lead him onto the path to Christ, because it was
from Nietzsche's words, from the passion of his life, that the great
imperative "Transcende te ipsum," so emphatically pronounced by
St. Augustine, came to him. Nietzsche had appealed to man to
transcend himself in order to raise himself up to a new unprecedented
level of fulfilled existence, that of the superman—"man is something

that must overcome"—while Ivanov gave this exhortation another
meaning, pursuing the process of overcoming and transcending in
search of perfection by looking up to the image of Christ, the suffering God whom he came to feel prefigured in the suffering god of
the ancients. But in parting ways with Nietzsche he remained grateful to him to the end and cherished what had united them: the
revelatory power of the only religious and esthetic spirit of classical
antiquity. The more so as Ivanov, according to an observant remark
of Georgy Adamovich, not only was a man of learning but possessed
the wonderful, exquisitely rare gift of penetrating and identifying
with epochs close to his mind and heart, and especially the world
of ancient Hellas.[4]

It must be noted in this context that the moment for this
encounter, the *kairos,* was exceptionally propitious. It was the time
when Nietzsche's thought began to find a manifold echo in Russia
also. Boborykin had brought with him from a trip abroad works
such as *Morgenröte, Jenseits von Gut und Böse* and *Also sprach Zarathustra,* and soon, in 1892, there appeared in the respectable academic journal *Problems in Philosophy and Psychology (Voprosy filosofii i
psikhologii)* Preobrazhensky's trail-blazing article "Friedrich Nietzsche. A Critique of the Ethics of Altruism" (*Fridrikh Nitsshe. Kritika
morali al'truizma*). It contained a number of skillfully arranged quotations, thus offering the possibility of referring to the words and
dicta of the philosopher without having to read his works in the
original. But soon translations began to appear also. Nietzsche was
in the air. He had an enormous impact on many of the representatives
of what we now call the Silver Age of Russian literature and thought.
But it appears to me that among the protagonists of this movement
only two really understood him, taking from him what they could
use and creatively adapt, rejecting what did not fit in their intellectual and artistic orbit: namely, each in his own way, each one very
different from the other, Vyacheslav Ivanov and Vasily Rozanov. It
was Rozanov who in his book *Among Artists (Sredi khudozhnikov)* said:
"And what about Nietzsche? We quoted from his *Zarathustra* as if
this were a book containing our favorite poetry, a much longed-for
fairy tale banishing sleep. Even Pushkin never enjoyed such a time

of enthusiasm for his verse as was the case with Nietzsche during his 'golden days.'"

What made Nietzsche's discovery of the Dionysian and the Apollonian so convincing for Ivanov was the fact that what he found here was not merely a clever esthetic device for the analysis of the creative process, but the encounter with a spiritual reality. For it became clear to him that Nietzsche's entire life was a profound mystical experience in broad, occasionally sublime, outlines, ending tragically in an abrupt collapse. Even Zarathustra was but a mask of Dionysus, whom Nietzsche loved. And you cannot love unless you say to the Beloved: Thou art! Even in later years when he already had greatly modified his views on Nietzsche, had emancipated himself, as it were, from the philosopher's paramount influence, he once again affirmed what he owed him in the article "The Essence of Classical Tragedy" (O sushchestve tragedii, 1916), declaring:

> Nietzsche did not err when he introduced his book on the birth of tragedy with the promise that our esthetics would significantly be enriched if we were henceforth to distinguish in every work of art two principles opposed one to the other in polarity and yet complementing each other in interaction. He suggested that these principles be named after two Hellenic deities, Dionysus and Apollo, which would give precise expression to this esthetic polarity. . . . This pronouncement can rightly be called a unique discovery. . . . Furthermore, it soon became evident that what we have here is the criterion of all true knowledge: independence from the context in which it originally was conceived, and freedom from the person of its discoverer. Indeed, we can describe, substantiate and evaluate these two principles in ways unlike those of Nietzsche, and to some extent we even must do this. However, we cannot and must not overlook or forget these principles, we cannot deny their validity. For what Nietzsche discovered here was the structural formula for the very character of the work of art—an incontrovertible formula despite all objections to Nietzsche's overall vision of the Hellenic soul. . . . His ideas concerning the pessimistic premises of the cult of Dionysus which is said to have

been devoid of all consolation and hope for immortality, the allegedly Greek view of life as a mere esthetic phenomenon, can all be considered as open to refutation. His esthetic axiom, however, can by no means be shaken by all these critical arguments—the axiom, namely, of the dyadic, Apollonian-Dionysian nature of the arts, especially of lyrical and epic poetry, drama, dance, and music.[5]

At this juncture it would be appropriate to say a few words about how Ivanov developed Nietzsche's vision of Dionysus in his own creative manner, how he arrived at the idea of the prefiguration of the crucified God by the suffering gods and demigods of antiquity, Dionysus, Orpheus, Pentheus, and others, how he deepened and intensified his views by insights gained from the psychology of C. G. Jung—thoughts and reflections which all led him far beyond the originally Nietzschean impetus. Since, however, these topics are treated by others in this volume I shall limit myself to a few remarks about how Ivanov overcame his infatuation with Nietzsche without, however, forgetting how much he was indebted to him. Nietzsche had interpreted the Greek world view in terms of despair which through beauty tends to reconcile itself with life. But Ivanov did not want to persist in somber desperation, seeking consolation and redemption in the Apollonian appearance of the Beautiful. He would not evaluate beauty in merely phenomenal terms as appearance, for he saw in it a constitutive element of a higher reality, a theophany.

Fedor Stepun pointed out that all of Ivanov's philosophic and esthetic reflections are determined, on the one hand, by Christianity and by Hellenic wisdom on the other.[6] This intense and creative closeness of Ivanov to the wellsprings of classical civilization—a phenomenon absolutely unique in the annals of Russian culture—reveals him as a spiritual kinsman of Goethe, Hölderlin, the Swinburne of *Atalanta in Calydon,* and Nietzsche. Sergey Makovsky, on the other hand, stated that around the turn of the century Ivanov was not yet a Christian. We also hear that in some symbolist circles people were inclined to take offense at what they considered his "neopaganism." Now this suspicion or reproach was certainly directed

to the wrong address. What the cultural historian Egon Friedell says
about Nietzsche applies with equal force to his disciple: "This had
been the chief problem of his life: Dionysus or the Crucified! It was
an abysmal misunderstanding to see neo-paganism in this. It was
absolutely un-pagan even to posit the alternative between the Cross
and Hellas. For the true pagan is no antichrist, he does not see
Christ at all."[7] Moreover, by grasping the essence of "Dionysianism"
not only esthetically and vitalistically, as Nietzsche had done—or so
it seemed to Ivanov—but religiously and metaphysically; he was
about to take the decisive step in the direction of widening and
deepening the Nietzschean vision, and also of overcoming it. For
just in those years around 1900 Ivanov was gradually coming to the
conviction that not only the Hebrew but also the Hellenic religion
(the religion of the sacrificial, tortured and suffering god) is the
precursor of Christianity—the Old Testament of the pagans: "And
Bacchus's sowing for the Supper of Christ" (*I Vakkha sev dlya vecheri
Christa*). It became clear to him that a profound difference prevailed
between the mythic conception of Dionysus as revealed by Nietzsche
and his own vision of Dionysus as the suffering god. Again, Ivanov
through his entire life remained grateful to the author of the *Birth
of Tragedy*. Nonetheless he more and more felt the necessity of coming
to grips with Nietzsche not only in agreement and assertion but also
in critique and denial. For even if we concede that in his youth he
was not entirely free from touches of neo-pagan, vitalistic, Dionysiac
pantheism, he never accepted that God was dead. He also firmly
maintained that the Greeks believed in Dionysus not only in terms
of some primordial life force, but in truly religious terms. So Ivanov
came to see Nietzsche's, the atheist's, greatest error in not wanting
to admit that for the Greek people Dionysus was indeed a god. He
reproached the philosopher with having overlooked in the course of
his classical studies that the mythos of Dionysus and his cult is part
and parcel of the history of religion. According to Ivanov, Nietzsche
was interested only in the esthetic and socio-historical consequences
of this cult. He was too much dazzled by the purely esthetic aspects
of the Dionysus religion, a phenomenon that he considered above all
psychological and artistic. And so he fatefully neglected the religious

and metaphysical values of the veneration of Dionysus. Nietzsche, it is true, had an eye for the suffering soul of Dionysiac man, but the tortured face of the suffering god he did not perceive. Nietzsche led Dionysus back into the world. This was his great message, and he pronounced it with authentic prophetic frenzy. But he revealed only one aspect of the resuscitated god; the truly divine features of this deity remained hidden from him.

Another ingredient of the Dionysiac ecstasy which Nietzsche, in Ivanov's opinion, did not sufficiently take into consideration was the loss of the sense of time. For the Dionysian state of mind is characterized by a transition into a realm where time no longer matters, by an immersion in timelessness. Nietzsche, however, had fixed his gaze upon the future, preoccupied with the dizzying possibilities that a future along Nietzschean lines might bring. So he altogether remained in what Ivanov called "the prison of time" (*temnitsa vremyon*).[8]

And there is yet another characteristic trait in Nietzsche's entire attitude of mind which Ivanov did not share. Although Sergey Averintsev has declared that the heavy brew of Nietzschean thought of which Ivanov began to partake in the early nineties turned his head, he nonetheless emphasized that the poet was not inclined to follow his master on the path of radical individualism or, as Georg Brandes called it, "aristocratic radicalism." He read Nietzsche, as Averintsev observes, with the eyes of the Russian intellectual, the *intelligent* for whom thinking in social terms and categories had become something like second nature.[9]

This explains his interest in Schiller and Richard Wagner. For in the poet of the "Hymn to Joy" and the creator of music drama he saw the restorers of true Dionysian dithyrambic poetry and the choric principle. The place of the chorus, the voice of the people, which establishes a true communion between the dramatized mythos on the stage and the spectators united in awe and deep emotion, was taken in Wagner's music drama by the orchestra: "The assembled crowd becomes mystically one with the elemental voice of the symphonic music; and inasmuch as we enter the inner sanctuary of Wagner . . . we become, as it were, the ideal molecules of the orgiastic

life of the orchestra." What he admired in Schiller's poetry as well
as his tragedies and dramas is what he called the democratic spirit
permeating them. In this, nothing was further from his mind than
purely political tendentiousness. Something else was important to
him: the pathos of a true communal art embodied in Schiller's poems
as well as his plays. "Everywhere Schiller is in the crowd and with
the crowd; everywhere he is its herald, its voice. His entire poetry
is a constant intercourse of the poet with his people, whether he
appears in priestly or in tragic garb, crowned with the wreath or
under the mask. From this resulted also the deeply felt need to
resurrect the chorus of the classical theater, a need which found its
expression in the design for *The Bride of Messina*." And even though
Schiller as well as Wagner left much to be desired in the execution
of their concept of a Dionysian and demotic poetry and drama,
Ivanov yet believed he could discern here the first hopeful steps on
the way to a new mythical, religious, communal art which would
help mankind to emerge refreshed and rejuvenated from the modern
"crisis of individualism."[10]

The moment has come to recall another author who lent a
helping hand to Ivanov in his search for a new elucidation of the
true meaning of Hellenic mythology and its symbolic, ontological,
and metaphysical significance. This was Johann Jakob Bachofen, the
Swiss scholar to whom we owe the discovery, the first full-blown
description and presentation of the primeval matriarchate and its
traces and reflections in the legends, sagas, and *mythoi* of the ancient
Mediterranean world. It is a strange coincidence that around the year
1870 there should have lived and worked together in Basel three
outstanding thinkers and scholars: Jacob Burckhardt, Johann Jakob
Bachofen, and Friedrich Nietzsche. Burckhardt, whose friendship
Nietzsche vainly sought, can for the moment be left out of consideration. And Bachofen, a man shy and retiring in his habits, does
not seem to have made a lasting impression on Nietzsche. But his
works, which immediately became the object of heated controversy
for historians, folklorists, anthropologists, and classical scholars,
could not for long remain hidden under a bushel. Ivanov must have
made himself familiar with Bachofen's writings soon after the turn

of the century. Reading, for example, his thoughtful essay of 1908 entitled "The Dignity of Woman" (*O dostoinstve zhenshchiny*), one feels at every step reminded of Bachofen, although his name is not mentioned. Woman as the unconscious keeper of some trans-personal mystery of nature, womanhood as close to the soul of Mother Earth, dark and prophetic—these and other epithets pointing to the special cosmic role of woman in the great scheme of things could just as well have been pronounced by Bachofen:

> Preserving by means of the mystery of her sex a constant access to the realm of subconscious life, woman is almost universally regarded as gifted above all with those faculties of the soul which are rooted in the subconscious, the powers of instinct and clairvoyance. So down to our own day her sex has preserved in woman, even though weakened now and to lesser degree than in times of old, some special psychic energies—a greater intensity of cosmic feeling, a greater faithfulness to the earth and sensitivity to its truth. . . . So it is not surprising that the farther we go back into antiquity, the more majestic appears before us the image of woman as the soothsayer, the knower of original, primordial mysteries of being . . . the wisdom-filled servant and confidante of two goddesses, the dark Earth and the bright Moon, obedient to their voices within herself, the priestess and enchantress, the first teacher of incantations and prophecies, of verse and divine enthusiasm . . . [*SS*, III, 40].

And when Ivanov went on to say that the evolution of woman describes a curve descending from the prehistoric apogee of her power which was the matriarchate, down to the stage of her enslavement by man as represented by the solar energies of an Apollo victorious over the nocturnal lunar world of woman, he reproduces in his own inimitably eloquent fashion the design of human development as outlined by Bachofen. Only one year after the publication of his article on the dignity of woman there appeared his grandiose essay entitled "Ancient Terror" (1909), and here he did not hesitate to acknowledge what he owed to Bachofen. He expressly stated:

Recent attempts to deny the existence of an original matriarchal order are of significance only inasmuch as they supply corrective arguments. It is indeed impossible to assert that there existed during a definite period of antiquity a general and widely spread matriarchy: the latter occurs only sporadically. Bachofen's *immortal works,* however, have enriched classical research not only with an hypothesis, but with a well-founded discovery. . . . However that may be, the manslaying cults of Artemis with their amazonic communities and the ritual chastisement of youths, the cult of Dionysus with his maenads, as well as manifold traces of sacrifices of men in other cults of female deities reach far back into the epoch of matriarchy and the great struggle between the sexes.[11]

In his essay on Ivanov's poetry Averintsev points to the psychological role the encounter with Nietzsche played in the process through which the Russian adept of Nietzschean wisdom was becoming what he was destined to be. The tremendous emotional shakeup provoked by the passionate effusions of the philosopher caused a considerable quickening of his spiritual and intellectual pulses. It set the poet free from a certain mental shyness and psychological constraint. It compelled him no longer to hide himself from his calling behind the shield of purely academic concerns. The study of Bachofen was emotionally reinforced by the fateful meeting with Lydia Zinovieva-Annibal, his second wife, in erotic and spiritual communion with whom he became aware of yet another aspect of the Dionysian world, the prominent position of woman in the cult of the life-giving, sacrificial and suffering god. Not in vain do maenads and bacchantes, overcome by wild enthusiasm and divine madness, adorn and enliven the stateliness of his verse in the volumes *Pilot Stars (Kormchie zvezdy,* 1903) and *Cor Ardens* (1911). The poem entitled "The Maenad," introducing *Cor Ardens,* erects a monument to this woman who with her undaunted as well as indomitable soul, her corybantic inspiration, her untamed charm and her unquenchable thirst for ever-renewed revelations of the life-enhancing Dionysian spirit became for him the incarnation of the cosmic-erotic nature of woman. Thus the study of Bachofen and the finding of Lydia Zinovieva enriched intellectually as well as emotionally and existentially his conception of the Dionysian image of the world. The elation he may have felt at this new fateful encounter with Dionysus, now closely linked to Eros, may evoke reminiscences of Euripides' *Bacchae,* in which the messenger pleads with King Pentheus to admit Dionysus to the city of Thebes:

> Therefore, I counsel thee,
> O King, receive this Spirit whoe'er he be
> To Thebes in glory. Greatness manifold
> Is all about him—and the tale is told
> That this is he who first to man did give
> The grief-assuaging vine.—O let him live
> For if he die, then Love herself is slain:
> And nothing joyous in the world again. [12]

One could say that Ivanov had found his Ariadne, the symbol of womanhood lovingly devoted to Dionysus, the leader of the chorus of all the maenads, dithyrambic dancers, thyiades and bacchantes who played the most important role in the cult of the vintner-god. According to classical mythology, Ariadne is an Aphrodite in human form, and also the image of beauty which, touched by the lover, bestows immortality on life. And yet she has to tread on the path of her own calvary whose inevitable stages are grief and death. And as Walter F. Otto says in his beautiful book *Dionysus: Myth and Cult,* it is an inalienable mark of the Dionysian essence that in the life of those close to the god, life and death, mortality and eternity are blended in a wondrous fashion. For the god himself is, after all, the son of a mortal mother. In the same way as he has to suffer grief and death, so also the women to whom he is tied by the most intimate awe and affection can enter the ultimate realm of his glory only by passing through the deepest woe and suffering. [13] Thus, through the study of Bachofen on the one hand, through profound personal experience on the other, Ivanov discovered one more dimension of the Dionysian world somewhat neglected by Nietzsche: namely, that this world is above all a world of woman. Women awaken and cherish Dionysus, women accompany him wherever he

goes. Women wait for him, and they are the first who will be
overcome by his sacred madness. For this reason, the erotic element
as such remains peripheral. Much more significant than the sexual
union in this cult is childbearing and nurturing. The Dionysian
world is the world of life springing forth and blossoming in all its
glory. But it borders directly upon grief, sorrow, and death. It is
constructive and yet bears the seeds of destruction within itself. In
this sense it is a primeval phenomenon of life. To this world of
woman the world of Apollo as the decidedly masculine element is
opposed. What prevails here is no longer the profound mystery of
the blood and the chthonic powers, but the clarity and wide scope
of mind and spirit. The Apollonian world, however, cannot exist
without the other, the Dionysian. Therefore it has never refused
recognition to it. If one has in mind Ivanov's later elaborations of
Dionysianism in terms of the prefiguration of Christianity, should
one not pause here to remember the women surrounding Christ,
lovingly taking care of him, opening their minds and hearts to his
words, visiting his grave, witnessing his resurrection, experiencing
the profoundest grief and sorrow, the most sublime joy?

A few critical remarks may be appropriate here. It is evident
that in the nineties of the last century Ivanov was confronted with
a course of events which led to far-reaching changes in his life and
work. He declined flattering offers to join renowned academic institutions. And after a prolonged spell of *Wanderjahre* he decided to
spend his life not in the service of organized scholarship, but in the
free pursuit of his calling as a poet and writer. Through all these
formative years he passed under the tremendous shadow of Nietzsche.
But a moment arrived when he was saturated with Nietzsche's
thought. He had received from the philosopher everything from
which he could profit in the further course of his artistic, intellectual
and spiritual development. It was time to assert his own self over
against the sonorous voice that threatened to overwhelm his own
song. Once again, in order to become what he felt he was destined
to be, he had to detach himself from Nietzsche the teacher, while
continuing to respect him as the discoverer of a great truth. In the
process of emancipation it becomes necessary to subject the positions
of the master to critical analysis based on one's own insight and
knowledge.

But along this path lurk the dangers of misunderstanding. For every philosopher presents special problems of interpretation, and with Nietzsche these problems are especially crucial. In *Beyond Good and Evil* Nietzsche said: "It has generally become clear to me what every great philosophy up till now has consisted of—namely, the confession of its originator and a species of involuntary and unconscious autobiography." And this applies, of course, with redoubled impact to his own thought. The very richness of Nietzsche's reflections and expression becomes a trap for the incautious or imaginative mind. Perhaps the greatest temptation for the interpreter or critic of Nietzsche is to attempt to "systematize" his thought into a consistent whole. Any such attempt necessarily results in exaggeration or distortion, for there is a fluidity in Nietzsche's thought which does not lend itself to strict categorization. This is not to deny that there are certain organic patterns in his philosophizing. These patterns, however, become visible only upon careful critical comparison of pertinent passages drawn from the entire corpus of Nietzsche's works. Or, as Karl Jaspers said, "the whole is not a concept or a system; it is the passion of the quest for being, together with its constant overcoming through relentless criticism, as it rises to the level of genuine truth."[14]

Ivanov preferred only two crucial points which, when criticizing Nietzsche's thought, may be taken into consideration here: Nietzsche's atheism, and his great postulate and preachment of the "Super-Man" (*der Übermensch*). For Nietzsche the assertion that God is dead was not a war-cry of defiance but a personal as well as universal tragedy. He understood the true essence and core of Christianity very well. So at the time he was writing the *Antichrist,* perhaps the most vitriolic of his many declarations of war against Christ and Christianity, he quite dispassionately summed up in *The Twilight of the Idols* what is at the center of Christian doctrine and practice:

> Christianity is a view of things consistently thought out and complete. If we break out of it a fundamental idea, the belief in God, we thereby break the whole into pieces: we have no longer anything determinate in our grasp. Christianity presupposes that man does not know, cannot know what is good for him and what is evil; he

believes in God who alone knows. Christian morality is a command, its origin is transcendent, it is beyond all criticism; it solely has truth, if God is truth—it stands or falls with the belief in God.

After the destruction of the Socratic ideal of right reason and after the axiom that God is dead, all doors stood open for the powerful influx of nihilism and the frightening consciousness of total meaninglessness. Here Nietzsche comes very close to Dostoevsky's famous dictum that if there is no God and no immortality everything is permitted. Or, as Erich Heller has said, with God's "being dead" man cannot find any lasting spiritual satisfaction in the pure contemplation of a creation deserted by its creator. [15] If nature and history have lost their meaning, they must be abolished. If the fallen creature has ceased to be redeemable, good and evil have to be transcended by the Super-Man. The Super-Man appears when man has no more meaning. He is the man who endures to live a triumphantly creative life in a world without sense or meaning. That is the ultimate intent of Nietzsche's insistence on the "will to power." For, in Erich Heller's words, "the Super-Man is the creature strong enough to live forever a cursed existence, even to derive from it Dionysian raptures of tragic acceptance." [16] That Nietzsche clothed his visions about the future Super-Man occasionally in biological, Darwinian terms was only the tribute he paid to the scientific jargon of his time. The tragedy was that the soul-rending spiritual and moral torment of Nietzsche's entire life was the result of his inability to believe in God. Out of the totally different structure of his own mind and spirit Ivanov caught only some rare glimpses of this tragedy. But it must be stressed in this context that Ivanov set a great example to his contemporaries as well as to posterity by not giving in to the pervasive temptation of nihilistic indifference, moral flabbiness, and gloom, to which his discussions with Mikhail Gershenzon and his letters to Charles Du Bos and Alessandro Pellegrini bear eloquent testimony.

One last reservation. Did Ivanov perhaps take the content of some of Nietzsche's most alarming, startling and sacrilegious utterances too seriously? Had Nietzsche not himself fallen prey to the nihilism he so penetratingly discerned, diagnosed and described as the chief signature of our entire age? When he said, "Everything that can be thought out must be a fiction," he also reduced everything he himself had thought to an absurdity. All contents, substances and systems had lost their meaning for him. What remained was the urge to express himself, to formulate dazzlingly, to blind with the splendor of his words, to sparkle and to shine in ever more daring effulgence. Or, as Gottfried Benn said, his way was the way from content to pure verbal gesture, the extinction of substance in favor of expression.[17] At the end of one of his Dionysus dithyrambs he exclaimed:

> O that I be banished
> from all truth!
> Mere jester! Mere poet!

Had this been revealed to Ivanov he would probably not have failed to give assent to Stefan George's beautiful brief poem dedicated to Nietzsche:

> And when this stern and tortured voice
> Resounds deep in the night and over the bright sea
> Like a hymn of praise, they say, regretfully:
> She should have sung, not preached, this new soul . . .

> Und wenn die strenge und gequälte stimme
> Dann wie ein loblied tönt in blaue nacht
> Und helle flut—so klagt: sie hätte singen
> Nicht reden sollen diese neue seele . . .

Notes

1. Gottfried Benn, *Gesammelte Werke, 4: Reden und Vorträge* (Wiesbaden, 1968). See the address entitled "Nietzsche—nach fünfzig Jahren," p. 1049.

2. James West, *Russian Symbolism* (London, 1970), p. 81.

3. See the fundamental biographical introduction by Olga Deschartes in *SS*, I, 30 and 35. Other recent books offering interesting and revealing glimpses of Ivanov's life and personality are Bernhard Schultze, *Russische Denker* (Vienna, 1950), pp. 423 ff., Evgenija Gertsyk, *Vospominanija* (Paris, 1973),

pp. 37 ff., and Carin Tschöpl, *Viačeslav Ivanov: Dichtung und Dichtungstheorie* (Munich, 1968).

   4. Georgij Adamovich, *Odinochestvo i svoboda* (New York, 1955), p. 255.

   5. Vyacheslav Ivanov, *Borozdy i mezhi* (St. Petersburg, 1916; reprint 1971). See the essay "O sushchestve tragedii," pp. 235 ff. Cf. the excellent German version prepared by J. Schor in the volume *Wjatscheslaw Iwanow, Das alte Wahre: Essays* (Berlin-Frankfurt, 1950).

   6. Fedor Stepun, *Vstrechi* (Munich, 1962). See the article about Vyacheslav Ivanov, p. 144. See also Stepun's profound and penetrating presentation and interpretation of Ivanov's thought world in the standard work *Mystische Weltschau: Fünf Gestalten des russischen Symbolismus* (Munich, 1964).

   7. Egon Friedell, *Kulturgeschichte der Neuzeit* (Munich, n.d.), pp. 1408 ff.

   8. Vyacheslav Ivanov, *Po zvezdam* (St. Petersburg, 1909); see the essays "Nitsshe i Dionis" and "O Dionise i kul'ture."

   9. S. S. Averintsev, "Poezija Vjacheslava Ivanova," in *Voprosy literatury,* 8 (Moscow, 1975), 152.

   10. See Ivanov's essays about Schiller and Richard Wagner in the volume *Po zvezdam.*

   11. "Ancient Terror," originally published in 1909 in *Po zvezdam.* Here quoted according to the faithful German translation prepared for the journal *Corona* (vol. V, 1934/35) by Nikolai von Bubnoff, and reprinted in the volume *Das alte Wahre,* mentioned above, pp. 63 ff. *Corona* was a high-level literary magazine to which Vyacheslav Ivanov was a frequent contributor in the 1920s and 30s.

   12. Euripides, *Bacchae.* Here quoted according to the translation of Gilbert Murray in *The Athenian Drama, vol. III, Euripides* (London, 1906), pp. 769–74.

   13. Walter F. Otto, *Dionysos: Mythus und Kultus* (Frankfurt, 1960), pp. 55, 115, and 167.

   14. This passage is an almost verbatim quotation from the book by Richard Lowell Howey, entitled *Heidegger and Jaspers on Nietzsche* (The Hague, 1973), pp. 1 and 11.

   15. Erich Heller, *The Disinherited Mind: Essays in Modern German Literature and Thought* (New York, 1957), p. 87.

   16. Erich Heller, *The Disinherited Mind.* See the essay "The World of Franz Kafka," p. 207.

   17. Benn, *Gesammelte Werke,* p. 1053.

Ivanov's Theory of Knowledge: Kant and Neo-Kantianism

James West

Even the most casual reader of Ivanov's essays will take note of a number of passages in which Ivanov remonstrates with Immanuel Kant or the German Neo-Kantian philosophers. The reader who is at all acquainted with German philosophical writing from Kant to Ivanov's day will find that the presence of Kant makes itself felt even between the remonstrations, and indeed is a constant part of the background to Ivanov's theoretical discussions of art. It is not just that Ivanov's esthetic embodies a theory of knowledge, and one which explicitly counters what he sees as the baleful after-effects of Kantian cognitive philosophy on the very self-perception of humankind in the Western world; Ivanov is himself a post-Kantian thinker whose philosophy incorporates directly or indirectly more of the heritage of Kant than is immediately apparent; many of his ideas, while unquestionably a part of his own coherent philosophical scheme, display a tantalizing proximity to those of the sage of Königsberg, once the reader is accustomed to the idiosyncratic language of both philosophers. I have previously compared Ivanov's philosophy of art in some detail to that of the late Neo-Kantian Ernst Cassirer, concluding that the difference between them is slight and rests mainly on Ivanov's faith in the life-transforming powers of poetry that for Cassirer remained in the long run metaphorical.[1] I have also made much of passages from Ivanov's essays that can be construed as an ultimate disavowal of Kant by Ivanov and a disassociation of himself from the contemporary Neo-Kantians.[2]

I have erred in not giving to the complicated relationship be-

tween Ivanov's esthetic and Kant's the attention it deserves, and this
paper is a modest attempt to make amends. There is an obvious sense in which Ivanov's esthetic must have
some affinity with Kant's. It was Kant who raised esthetics from
the category of subjects of which a comprehensive philosophy must
give some account, and made it into one of the cornerstones of all
philosophical inquiry.[3] More than this, the grounds on which Kant
assigned to esthetics its fundamental role—or to put it another way,
the rationale for the *Kritik der Urteilskraft* in his system as a whole—
provide a vital background to the exploration of subsequent esthetic
theories in their relationship to Kant. Having established *a priori*
principles for the faculty of cognition in the *Kritik der reinen Vernunft,*
and for the faculty of desire in the *Kritik der praktischen Vernunft,*
and having in his earlier writings on esthetics openly doubted the
possibility of finding such principles for judgments of taste or feelings of pleasure or displeasure, Kant came by 1787 (when the second
edition of the first *Kritik* was published) to think that with some
modification of the same principles, taste and judgment could be
subsumed into the critical system. When it was published in 1790,
the third *Kritik* was more than a simple extension of Kant's system.
Its place in the overall scheme rests rather on its goal of establishing
a necessary connection between the faculties of knowledge and desire,
or between "understanding" (*Verstand*) and "reason" (*Vernunft*) in the
strictly Kantian sense of these terms. The esthetic component was
to provide nothing less than "a link binding the two parts of the
Philosophy into a whole."[4] Even more significant for our purposes
is the division of the *Kritik der Urteilskraft* into two parts, the second
(the *Kritik der teleologischen Urteilskraft*) dealing with human judgment
of the purposiveness of nature. For Kant, esthetic pleasure derives
essentially from our capacity to place the object of esthetic contemplation in an ordered scheme of nature, to understand its interrelat-
edness with other phenomena and so achieve a sense of harmony
between a teleologically conceived natural world and our own cognitive faculties. I have taken a few liberties here in summarizing
Kant's objectives in the third *Kritik* in not strictly Kantian language,
but have done so in order to provoke some fairly obvious associations

with the main postulates of Ivanov's esthetic, and so suggest that Ivanov sets out to answer, with few exceptions, the Kantian questions. In other words, his relationship to Kant requires elucidation not so much at the level of agreement or disagreement with specific conclusions or pronouncements, as at the level of the fundamental group of interrelated questions posed by either philosopher, and the *kind* and comprehensiveness of the answers sought to them.

Assuming a familiarity with the basic points of Ivanov's philosophy of art, I will begin with an examination of a number of characteristic statements by him about the interconnectedness of art and cognition as a general proposition, about the legacy of Kant in particular, and occasionally about both.

The collection of extended aphorisms, *Sporady,* included in Ivanov's 1909 collection of essays, *By the Stars* (*Po zvezdam,* 1909) contains a number of concise statements on the cognitive aspect of art. The following is a fairly generally valid summary of Ivanov's position on this question:

> Poetry is complete knowledge of man and knowledge of the world through human cognition.
>
> Lyrical poetry, above all, is the mastery of rhythm and number, as the motive and the architectonic principles of the inner life of man, and through mastery of them in the spirit, assimilation to their universal mystery.
>
> It is the task and goal of lyric poetry to be a constructive force, heralding and commanding order. Its supreme law is harmony; it must resolve every discord into an accord.
>
> Epic and drama are concerned with events in the flow of time and the resolution of conflicting wills. For lyric poetry there is one event only—the harmony of the moment, sounding from the strings of the cosmic lyre. [5]

What is most familiar here is, of course, the primacy accorded to poetry, and the suggestion that a certain kind of self-knowledge is a prior key to knowledge of the world outside the self, as well as the declaration that poetry does not merely extol order and harmony, but helps in some positive way to bring them about. We might also note in passing the hierarchical distinction between forms of verbal art that deal in the human time-span, and poetry which is, as it were, exempt from temporal order.

For Ivanov, as for Vladimir Solovyov, the ordering principle which poetry helps to realize is the will of God, destined to restore matter, through universal art, into its ideal form. The special knowledge of the divine order that is attained by the artist brings about a fusion of the individual will with the divine will and makes the artist a part of this process. A few words from another of the *Sporady* sum it up:

> God is an artist; His judgment, I rather think, will be the judgment of an artist, His judging gaze will be that of a master disappointed in his expectations of a lazy or untalented pupil.[6]

In the context of this view of the cognitive function of art, Ivanov repeatedly introduced three further interconnected questions: the isolation of the individual in the modern world, the fragility (but also the importance) of human communication in the necessarily restricted language of verbal discourse, and the problem of freedom and human volition. The thread uniting all these preoccupations is the polarity between absolute and relative, the certainty or otherwise of success in the quest for absolute knowledge of at least one's own existence and that of the divine ordering principle of the universe. The resulting tension in human existence is summed up in *A Correspondence from Two Corners* (*Perepiska iz dvukh uglov*, 1921) in a way that explicitly brings Kant into the argument:

> . . . on the fact of our belief in the absolute, which is something other than culture, depends our inner freedom—and this is life itself—or our inward bondage to a culture that has long been godless in principle, for it has confined man (as Kant proclaimed once and for all) within himself.[7]

In the 1916 collection of essays, *Furrows and Boundaries* (*Borozdy i mezhi*), Ivanov elaborated this fundamental reproach directed at modern Western society. The essay "Lev Tolstoy and Culture" (*Lev Tolstoy i kul'tura*) compares Tolstoy to Socrates (both sought moral bearings in a society spiritually crippled by relativism in philosophy) and provides more interesting material for our eventual comparison of Ivanov with Kant. In both Socrates' Greece and Tolstoy's Europe, Ivanov writes,

> It was necessary to rebel against instinct and save knowledge for living at the expense of knowledge of the essence of things. If there was not a more real god to be found outside the natural creative instinct of life . . . then the divinity had to be sought in the normative value of rational consciousness, the capacity for logic had to be deified, and objective moral criteria had to be derived from human self-determination. Morality had to be used to exorcise the chaos of an existence deserted by the gods. It was hunger for real knowledge that made men moralists.[8]

This veiled indictment of the consequences of post-Kantian relativism is echoed in the essay "The Religious Work of Vladimir Solovyov" ("Religioznoe delo Vladimira Solov'eva," 1910) in which "the Neo-Kantians" are blamed for the chaos of philosophy of knowledge in our day, and the point is made even more forcefully that "it is impossible to live in accordance with such a theory of knowledge."[9] In the earlier *Sporady* Ivanov had already likened Kant to Socrates, again in the context of the moral philosophy that results from a relativistic theory of knowledge:

> Kant retraces Socrates' steps, juxtaposing moral philosophy to the cognition of objects, and is as misled in this matter as was Socrates by the conviction that virtue springs from knowledge and that goodness is wisdom.[10]

It is not altogether clear what Ivanov would have us conclude from this; the rest of the rather long "aphorism," one of several under the heading "On Daring Love" (*O ljubvi derzajushchej*), extols in directly Nietzschean terms the capacity of the human will, all too seldom exercised, to assert with compelling immediacy its independent existence and freedom from the limitation of human cognition. However, the most interesting part of this "aphorism" is a suggestion that Kant offered, or attempted, his own solution to this dilemma, but failed in exactly the way in which Christ failed for Dostoevsky's inquisitor:

> Kant's attempt to free "practical reason" from the fetters of theoretical cognition has to this day borne little fruit. From the very beginning, the vast majority of minds could not follow him, for they, creatures of the day, longed to avoid the fatal parting of the ways, and to save their clear, day-time knowledge in order to build on its achievements. It happened this way, perhaps, because Kant himself bases his practical reason after all on pure reason, and does not take as the exclusive source of practical philosophy the axiom of immediate consciousness: *sum, ergo volo*. [11]

We shall return in due course to the suggestion implied here that the primacy of the *a priori* principles of the first *Kritik* is the Achilles' heel of Kant's system, but should note at this stage the repeated emphasis on the practical philosophical needs of the human, who craves—and for Ivanov is unquestionably owed—guidance toward higher ends than are intelligible in the language of this world.

The essay "On the Trouble of the World" (*O neprijatii mira*) in the same collection allows us to follow this thread a little further. Here Ivanov describes "Mystical Anarchism" (a movement within Russian Symbolism associated primarily with Georgy Chulkov, and subscribed to by Ivanov strictly on his own terms[12]) as "an attempt to set against *cognition,* which seeks awareness of what exists in the category of necessity, *practical reason,* directed toward the realization of what is morally necessary in the category of freedom. . . ."[13] Ivanov is at this point supporting the idea of Mystical Anarchism, which he treats as an attempt to realize in practice the Solovyovian ideal of *sobornost'*—"the supra-individual assertion of the ultimate freedom." What is most striking here is not only the explicit espousal of practical reason as if it were a cause, but its equally explicit dissociation from cognition; since Ivanov's language is here overtly Kantian, we are probably justified in assuming that he is declaring the primacy of Kantian "understanding" over Kantian "reason" and proposing by implication a correction to Kant's system—a correction, moreover, that is in the ordering rather than the "categories" of that system.

It is worth observing in passing that Ivanov often made conscious use of a certain amount of Kantian terminology. Even in rather later essays such as "On the Boundaries of Art" (*O granitsakh iskusstva*, 1913) in which Ivanov's own richly metaphorical language for the discussion of the principles of mythopoeic art is quite fully developed, he employs words such as "synthetic" and "transcendental" in a sense that is close to Kant's, and also uses what appear to be calques on key terms from Kant's vocabulary; an example is the word translated as "super-sensible" (following the usual practice in English discussions of Kant) in the Ivanov passage cited below—Ivanov's "sverkhchuvstvennyj" in this context invites equation with Kant's "übersinnlich."

"On the Boundaries of Art" is well known as the essay in which Ivanov developed most fully what might be termed his psychology of creativity, his account of the artist's "ascent" to intuitive awareness of *realiora,* of both the ideal forms of things and their place in the divine scheme, and his agonizing "descent" to the everyday world to fulfill his painful obligation to express in the language of *realia* what he has learned. A short passage will serve both to exemplify this idea and provide a final illustration of Ivanov's categorical allegiance to the phenomenal world:

> Thus for the descending artist the highest law is reverence for the lower order of things and obedience to the will of this world, to which he offers the instrument of betrothal with the highest order, and not a scroll inscribed with super-sensible truths. . . . And that knowledge which is to be gleaned from works of genuinely descending art is knowledge of the true will of the world. . . . In this the most important thing is the true determination of relationships, correspondences and congruences between the higher and the lower . . . between what is generally acknowledged as fundamental and essential and what seems only fortuitous—and such a correct determination and accurate choice of observed features of reality for depiction is what we find in works of true art,

because their creators have derived from their penetration into the
sphere of higher reality a true synthetic understanding of the reality they depict.[14]

It should be apparent by now that even in the most original
and characteristic formulations of Ivanov's esthetic there is just below
the surface a dialogue with Kant that is distinct from his open
objections to the pernicious effects of a climate of relativism in
European thought, which he ascribed sometimes to Kant but more
often to unspecified post-Kantians and Neo-Kantians. This is not
an explicit rebuttal of any particular Kantian proposition so much
as a deliberate use of transformed elements of Kant's philosophy that
amounts to a tacit reproach that Kant had ultimately missed the
key that would after all make of his system a liveable philosophy
rather than a mere construct of the human mind, however ingenious.

Let us look at the situation again, from Kant's point of view.

We can indeed find in Kant, particularly in the *Kritik der
Urteilskraft,* many of the preoccupations that run through Ivanov's
philosophy. Kant's faculty of judgment, even as formulated in the
Kritik der reinen Vernunft, is the synthesizing faculty that enables us
to make sense of individual phenomena by placing them in an ordered relationship to a universal, i.e., to a concept. Judgment brings
to what Kant calls "the manifold of intuition" a form of ordering
that is essential if human beings are to communicate with one another. In the *Kritik der Urteilskraft* he goes further and provides an
argument for the possibility of a universally communicable mental
state, which links the understanding and the imagination with the
faculty of reason and esthetic perception with cognitive perception.
Kant accords to the artist a special role in this human activity that
is in its main points identical to that of Ivanov's artist. Kant's artist
possesses qualities that set him aside from his fellows as a "genius."
Ivanov follows him in using the word "genius" to distinguish the
true artist, and in the first section of *Sporady* (entitled "On Genius"
[*O genii*]), he makes, with explicit reference to Kant and Schopenhauer, the same distinction as Kant makes between the products of
mere artistic talent which "only multiply our knowledge of what has

already realized itself historically and therefore ceased to exist," and the creations of genius which are "something other than, and greater than, reality."[16] Kant even singled out poetry as the art which plays the greatest role in the task of communicating the super-sensible (*das Übersinnliche*) in terms of man's sensible perceptions.[17] Into his discussion of the artist's role Kant injects the conclusions of his consideration of the purposiveness of nature, making his genius, as Ivanov's later, the agent of a force beyond himself. But for Kant the force is nature, and in a sense the circle of his esthetic is closed when he insists that the talent of the genius for attaining an ordered understanding of the natural world is itself a phenomenon within the sphere of nature,[18] and results only in the illusion of a higher reality. For in Kant's view, the harmony of the artist's ordered perception, though in an objective sense communicable, remains ultimately in the mind of the subject; in Kant's terminology, the faculty of judgment is reflective, and esthetic judgment cannot lead to knowledge, in the strict sense, of the objects of such judgment. Ivanov's wry characterization of the sterility of a world dominated by relativist thought springs sharply to mind when one reads any of the several statements of this limitation in the *Kritik der Urteilskraft;* for example:

> Reflective judgment, which has the task of ascending from the particular to the general in nature, needs a principle which it cannot derive from experience, since it must be the basis for the unity of all empirical principles under higher, but still empirical, principles. Reflective judgment can derive such a transcendental principle only from within itself, and not from elsewhere (since it would then become determinative judgment), nor can it prescribe such a principle for nature. . . .[19]

The assimilation of the faculty of esthetic judgment into the critical system is in the last resort by analogy. The esthetic faculties are for a number of technical reasons able to operate as if their goal was knowledge, and for Kant the esthetic pleasure consists in the conscious attainment of this state that is one degree short of knowledge; the appreciation of the purposiveness of art in the natural order of

things remains vicarious: "Consciousness of the merely formal purposiveness in the exercise of the subject's cognitive powers . . . is
the esthetic pleasure itself. . . ."[20] Modern commentators find this
aspect of the *Kritik der Urteilskraft* unsatisfactory since it rests on a
somewhat unclear theoretical distinction between "transcendental"
and "empirical" faculties that operate in parallel.[21] Ivanov comes
close to voicing the same objection in the passage of *Sporady* cited
earlier, when he disavows Kant's restriction on what is attainable by
the genius, and nothing suggests more clearly than this passage the
nature of his underlying relationship to Kant, for he makes his point
not by contradicting Kant but by following a basically Kantian assertion to a conclusion that Kant could not allow himself:

> Kant and Schopenhauer distinguish the empirical from the
> transcendentally knowable. The relationship between them must
> correspond to the relationship of our empirical world to the po-
> tential world. The latter coexists with the former but is wider in
> its scope. The "genial" is like the seed that it produces. This is
> why historical reality will never express its age more completely
> or more accurately than the genial creations of the spirit that arise
> in the given age, precisely because they express something other
> than, and more than, reality.[23]

In the context of the "aphorisms" that make up *Sporady* this ma-
neuver may look like unsupported assertion, but in Ivanov's work as
a whole this is very far from the case. What enables Ivanov to assert
the reality—or hyper-reality—of the artist's intuitions of both the
order and the purpose of the universe is the religious faith, simultaneously Christian and Hellenic, the dual legacy of Solovyov and
Nietzsche which he developed so rewardingly into an ecstatic positive
philosophy of being. The most relevant statement of this philosophy
of being is the essay "Thou Art" (*Ty esi,* 1907), which Ivanov begins
with an indirect but unmistakeable challenge to Kant:

> Metaphysics (let us take as just one example the theory of the
> empirical and the transcendental) and moral philosophy, gnoseol-
> ogy and psychology, the "reflection" of our forefathers and the

phenomena of intellectual and spiritual life that occurred toward the end of the last century in the form of esthetic illusionism, impressionism and, finally, symbolism as a specific sect and school of art, have deprived us not only of the old *cogito, ergo sum,* but even of its separate elements, *cogito* and *sum* (we would find it easier to comprehend *fio, ergo non sum*).

In recent times some unseen plough has furrowed the soul of contemporary man—not in the sense of the diseased condition of his inner forces, but in the sense of the disintegration of that solid, impenetrable, indivisible lump of living energy which in a heroic age of immediate individualism could call itself "I" and "the complete individual." This ploughed field of individual self-awareness is the first condition for the rise of new shoots of religious creativity and perception of the world.[24]

Ivanov proceeds to expound, more clearly perhaps than anywhere else, the essence of his theory of knowledge, founded in the synthesis of re-mythologized Christian religion and mythopoeic religious art that is the characteristic of his life's work. For the present purposes, "Thou Art" provides the most intriguing suggestion as to where Ivanov stood in relation not only to Kant, but to the post-Kantian idealists to whom he would appear to owe a great deal, and to many of his fellow Symbolists in Russia.

Kant was not, of course, a godless man, and Ivanov probably did not mean to suggest this in the obvious sense when he made the observation cited above that the formal strictures of Kant's philosophy had reaffirmed in its godlessness a godless culture. It should not be forgotten that Kant had a particular and rather circumscribing mission behind his monumental life's work: not necessarily to demolish any one of the prevailing metaphysical theories of his day or to undermine metaphysics as such, but to establish the rigorous critical foundation for metaphysics in general that was so conspicuously lacking in the various philosophies in question. This emphasis prescribed certain limits for Kant's treatment of metaphysics in his system, but these limits by no means imply that he would have closed the door on further metaphysical speculation. Indeed, it has

324   JAMES WEST

been noted that there is a paradoxical continuity between Kant and
the German idealist philosophers of the nineteenth century, who in
reasserting in various ways the knowability of ideal forms were extending Kant rather than reverting to pre-Kantian dogmatic metaphysics. In particular, the characteristically idealist notion of
philosophy and art as the forms of self-knowledge of the Absolute
easily betrays its Kantian lineage.[25] But perhaps the most telling
effect of Kant on subsequent German idealist philosophy, where we
are concerned, is the caution he seems to have inspired in the ad-
mission of the question of faith into philosophical inquiry. Indeed,
in the view of at least one intellectual historian,

> . . . we find a marked tendency to substitute metaphysics for faith
> and to rationalize the revealed mysteries of Christianity, bringing
> them within the scope of the speculative reason. To use a modern
> term, we find a tendency to demythologize Christian dogmas,
> turning them in the process into a speculative philosophy.[26]

The direction that German idealist philosophy took after Kant was
a product of the vulgarization of Kant in a number of ways which
constitute the very ills that Ivanov decried at the beginning of our
own century. His fundamental reproach that Kant could not take
the final step back into the world of human psychological and spiritual necessities still stands, provided we acknowledge that Kant had
a more circumscribed goal, that despite the comprehensiveness of
his critical system he did not even seek the key that Ivanov sought,
and that Ivanov in some crucial instances did not so much repudiate
Kant as extend his system. It is the post-Kantians, despite Ivanov's
obvious partial debt to at least some of them, who are the real target
of his pained reproaches; himself a post-Kantian, Ivanov differs from
them in being able to use or take issue with Kant without vulgar-
izing him, as Ivanov in his turn was vulgarized by some of his
symbolist contemporaries in Russia.

Notes

1. James West, *Russian Symbolism* (London, 1970), pp. 93–106.

2. Ibid., p. 59.

3. See for example D. W. Crawford, *Kant's Aesthetic Theory* (Madison, 1974), p. 4, and J. Margolis, *Philosophy Looks at the Arts* (New York, 1962), which Crawford quotes.

4. Title of the third section of Kant's introduction to the *Kritik der Urteilskraft* (hereafter KU), p. 29 in the Reclam (Stuttgart, 1963) text, to which all subsequent page numbers will refer.

5. Vyacheslav Ivanov, *Po zvezdam* (St. Petersburg, 1906; hereafter PZ), p. 350.

6. PZ, p. 344.

7. M. O. Gershenzon and V. Ivanov, *Perepiska iz dvukh uglov* (Moscow-Berlin, 1921), p. 23.

8. V. Ivanov, "Lev Tolstoy i kul'tura," in *Borozdy i mezhi* (Moscow, 1916; hereafter BM), p. 85.

9. BM, pp. 109–110.

10. PZ, p. 375.

11. PZ, p. 374.

12. It would be a mistake to identify Ivanov too closely with Mystical Anarchism, even though the article in question served as the introduction to the volume published by Chulkov to inaugurate the movement. Ivanov felt obliged on several occasions to write to the editors of periodicals stating his limited involvement with the movement, strictly on his own terms.

13. PZ, p. 120.

14. BM, p. 216.

15. KU, Einleitung VII and Section 9, pp. 48–53 and 89–93.

16. PZ, p. 339.

17. KU, Section 49, pp. 245–54.

18. KU, Section 46, p. 235.

19. KU, Einleitung IV, pp. 34–35.

20. KU, Section 12, p. 98.

21. Crawford, *Kant's Aesthetic Theory,* pp. 88–89.

22. PZ, p. 339.

23. PZ, p. 339.

24. PZ, p. 426.

25. See Frederick Copleston, *A History of Philosophy,* Vol. 7, Part I (New York, 1965), pp. 15 ff., for a succinct discussion of this.

26. Ibid., p. 28.

Vyacheslav Ivanov's Esthetic Thought: Context and Antecedents

Victor Terras

In no other Symbolist are the antinomies of Russian Symbolism as poignant as in Ivanov. Symbolism meant a return of Russian literature to the intellectual concerns of the West. Nobody shared these concerns more strongly than Ivanov. Yet his Russianness was also stronger than that of any of his confrères.[1] Symbolism was more "learned" than any other literary movement in Russia. Ivanov was the most learned of the Symbolists. Yet Symbolism was also actively involved in Russian public life. Nothing was farther from Ivanov's thought than *l'art pour l'art* or literary escapism.

Russian Symbolism had some Alexandrian traits. Nowhere are they stronger than in Ivanov. Yet it was also Ivanov who most passionately believed in a literature for and of the people and in literature's role in creating a new integrated society.

Ivanov, who always condemned decadence, French or Russian,[2] was not quite free of some decadent traits of his own. Russian Symbolism was a modernist movement, yet it was also a return to Hellenism.[3] Ivanov was fully abreast of the most recent developments in modern thought and in modern art, yet he gravitated toward a Neoplatonic world-view.

I

The focal quality of Ivanov's philosophy of art is a basic idealist monism, dialectically realized. Ivanov perceives all art forms as a continuum, polarized in a dynamic and a static pole (music and architecture being the extreme forms). In this he follows the German idealist tradition of Schelling and Hegel, which also prevails in the entire Belinskian tradition of Russian criticism.

Ivanov's esthetic is "organic" in every sense of that term. To him, "it is obvious that a symbolist-artisan is unthinkable, likewise a symbolist-esthete."[4] Russian Symbolists in general join Ivanov in this attitude, though some formalist and hedonist opinions may be found among the "decadents." Art, like religion, is to Ivanov a necessary function of life; it is an organic part of the human and of the national spirit. The work of art is a living function of its creator's spirit, and hence an integral whole. In Ivanov, these familiar positions of organicist esthetics assume a strong Schellingian (= Neoplatonic) coloration. The Plotinian *endon eidos* (Ivanov uses the term *forma formans* = *forma ante rem,* where *forma formata* is the finished work) is accepted not only as a metaphysical, but also as a psychological reality. Symbolist esthetics overlaps with the formalism of Futurist esthetics on this score. When Ivanov revives Plotinus's notion that the sculpture is already given in a block of marble and is merely freed from it by the artist,[5] he endorses the Futurists' position that the artist's point of departure should be his material, rather than anything extraneous to it.

Ivanov also emphasizes other peculiarly Neoplatonic traits of organic esthetics: the belief in poetry as a source of intuitive knowledge and the notion that the poet is a bearer of the "inner word, an organ of the World Soul."[6] While the organicist tradition, from Belinsky to Socialist Realism, credits the poet with cognitive powers, it generally does not elevate him to the rank of a mystic seer, as Ivanov certainly does. In this respect, Ivanov is entirely with Novalis, to whom he is linked by many bonds.[7]

It is in the organic tradition, though clearest in its German romantic version, that art be defined as inherently symbolic, revealing of a higher reality. Ivanov's *realiora* is the pivot of his monistic esthetics. His emphasis on the mythopoeic function of art likewise takes us directly to German romanticism, and to Schelling in particular.[8]

Ivanov's thought patterns are those of the dialectics of German idealism, rather than those of modern social science. The creative process as well as the interaction between art and society, and thus the progress of history, are seen in terms of a sublation of phenomena into their opposites.[9] A significant detail is Ivanov's understanding of creation as a dialectic fusion of freedom and necessity, one of the key features of Schellingian esthetics.[10] Other aspects of Ivanov's dialectics are likewise familiar from the tradition of organic esthetics. The identity of "content" and "form" is one of these.[11] The dialectics of the individual and the universal is another. Somewhat surprisingly, in the context of Russian modernism,[12] Ivanov's emphasis is decidedly upon combating the *principium individuationis* in its various forms (Titanism, solipsism, man-godhood, subjectivism) and restoring the principle of a universal community (*vselenskaja obshchina*) whose artistic expression is choral action (*khorovoe dejstvo*). The conflict of subjective (individual) and objective (communal) truth has Ivanov on the side of the latter. Here as elsewhere we find him on the side of objective idealism (Schelling, Hegel, Solovyov), rather than with the subjective idealism of Kant.[13] Ivanov's downgrading of the individual (or psychological) "I" is not at the expense of any specific collective body (nation, class, etc.), but of a timeless and superpersonal "I," much as in Schelling and Hegel. Ivanov's conception of any temporal identity as a succession of "doubles" of a higher Self has a correspondence in Plotinus's procession of hypostases.[14]

In human experience pure white light is an unrealized ideal. Yet a fascination with the colors of the spectrum without a striving for such purity is dangerous, Ivanov feels.[15] This metaphor was also a favorite of Apollon Grigoriev's and of the German romantics.

Yet another dialectic important for Ivanov is that of the Word and the Ineffable, which Ivanov recognizes as the subject of Tyutchev's "Silentium!" Unlike Tyutchev, Ivanov has confidence in the power of the word. He believes in that "peculiar intuition and energy of the word, sensed immediately by the poet as a secret code of the ineffable, which gathers into its sounds many an echo of native subterraneous springs and serves . . . both as letter of external and hieroglyph of inner experience."[16] Interestingly, this conception, while clearly Neoplatonic, is not very far removed from certain ideas of Ivanov's Futurist contemporaries (*zaum'*, *samovitoe slovo*, and such).

The conception of the work of art as a synthesis of the ideal and the real, familiar from German idealist esthetics, appears in Ivanov as well. While he rejects any excesses of *mimesis* ("naturalism," for example), he is even more intent upon asserting the need for realism in art. In fact, he uses the term "idealist art" in a somewhat pejorative meaning. [17] He perceives "idealist symbolism" as a sort of "illusionism," where symbols are a means of infecting an audience with a certain subjective experience, while "realist" symbols are catalysts of objective truth. Here Ivanov means "realism" and "realist" in the ordinary sense of these words, i.e., in terms of the mimetic principle and without any mystic implications of a "higher" reality. [18] Ivanov's main apprehension relates to the artist who, in his pursuit of the ideal, will succumb to the temptation of subjective creation—a thought we know well from Solovyov and Blok. [19]

Ivanov's conception of realism is independent of historical labels. In a magnificent passage of "Two Elements in Contemporary Symbolism" (*Dve stikhii v sovremennom simvolizme*, 1908), he identifies Shakespeare and the "romantics" Hoffmann and Balzac as "realists," while defining classicism as "idealist." [20]

The most peculiarly Ivanovian esthetic category is that of the Dionysian/Apollonian, which he applies to the creative process, to the typology of art, and to historical analysis. [21] It is here that Ivanov's debt to Nietzsche is greatest. While the anthropological universality of the Dionysian principle had been clearly stated as early as in Schelling's *Mythology*, its esthetic meaning is specifically Nietzschean. The specific esthetic qualities which Ivanov associates with the Dionysian/Apollonian are also taken from Nietzsche, whose thoughts Ivanov uses creatively, however. Such are the Dionysian dyad as against the Apollonian monad, the female versus the male principle, hunger versus plenitude, and, first and foremost, ascent versus descent.

II

Ivanov's ontology as well as his esthetics is dynamic. Art is conceived as a form of energy, and so is the Word. [22] Ontological

distinctions are seen in terms of a hierarchy which is essentially one
of power or intensity. In this, as in so many things, Ivanov follows
Schelling. His distinction of Being versus Existence is likewise found
in Schelling. Nonbeing is perceived as existentially concrete: it can
be artistically expressed.[23] Ivanov's hierarchy of Being has several
stations, as does that of the Word.[24] Art has various levels below the
highest, the theurgic. Thus, so-called "pure art" creates idols which
are alive but are not themselves life-creating. Their magic is inferior
to the mystic visions of the highest art.[25] Contemporary Symbolism
on its highest level is seen as a return to the Orphic visions of
primitive humanity.[26] Certainly the cosmic quality which one so
often finds in Ivanov's poetry is also an element of his philosophy of
art.

    Ivanov considered himself a Christian poet and a Christian
thinker. His attempts to wed Christianity to Dionysianism are not
unprecedented. Even Schelling had seen the myth of a suffering,
slain, and resurrected god as a human universal and Ivanov was of
course familiar with Erwin Rohde's treatment of this idea.

    As characteristic of Ivanov's esthetics as the Dionysian/Apol-
lonian dichotomy itself are its various manifestations. Dionysus is
the god of descent, Apollo the god of ascent. Apollo stands for the
monad, Dionysus for the dyad. Dionysus is also related to the feminine, and Apollo to the male, principle.[27] (Occasionally, Ivanov will
deviate from this scheme and replace it by a triadic scheme, where
Apollo, the male principle, still stands for ascent, but Aphrodite,
the female principle, becomes descent, while chaos is the sphere of
an androgynous Dionysus.)[28] Ivanov's sympathy is with descent
rather than ascent, with the dyad rather than the monad, and with
the feminine rather than the male. The titanism of Prometheus, seen
by Ivanov as a victory of the male principle, is ultimately sterile,
while the eternal-feminine (as manifest in Dostoevsky's *khromo-
nozhka,* for example) is joyously embraced.[29]

    While the ontological distinction of a male/female principle is
a common one, particularly in Romantic philosophy, the distinction
of "hunger" and "plenitude" as complementary impulses of artistic
creativity, closely related to ascent/descent, comes from Nietzsche.[30]

In fact, Ivanov also uses Nietzsche's principal example of plenitude, that of the Sun, whose tragedy is that it can only give and never take.[31] It may not be superfluous to observe that a metaphysical preoccupation with the Sun as a negative symbol is characteristic of Russian Futurism. Ivanov's occasional observations on this esthetic category are interesting and valuable, such as when he defines *Macbeth* as a tragedy of hunger, *King Lear* as a tragedy of plenitude.[32] His own tragedy, *Tantalus* (*Tantal*, 1904) is an allegory of man refusing the gifts of the gods and wanting to be a giver only. The pride of Tantalus is his undoing, but his glory too.[33] Ivanov extends this category to Christian symbolism: the hunger of the soul and the *kenosis* of Christ's godhead in His passion.

The ascent/descent category, clearly taken from Nietzsche[34] (though it is prominent in Platonic, Neoplatonic, and Christian thought), permeates every level of Ivanov's creativity. Every aspect of his thought is organized on a vertical axis. Ivanov's ontology, anthropology, ethic, esthetics, and even his history are dominated by this model. Vertical imagery plays a dominant role in Ivanov's poetry.[35] The action of his tragedies *Prometheus* and *Tantalus* is arranged on a vertical.[36] Ivanov sees ascent/descent patterns in other genres as well. The sonnet, his very special favorite, is characterized by a scheme of ascent/descent.[37]

The primary form of the ascent/descent category is mythical. Ascent is quite literally "winged victory over earthly sluggishness,"[38] while descent is, also literally, a descent to the bowels of the earth or a return to the womb of Mother Earth.[39] Both of these mythical conceptions appear in Greek mythology, in Platonic, and in Neoplatonic myths.[40]

Ivanov readily applies the ascent/descent category to Christian thought. He recognizes ascent in human striving for a union with the Divine, in Jacob's ladder, in a human soul's renunciation of this world. He sees descent in God's second hypostasis, the Son, in Christ's *kenosis,* in Christian sacrifice and humility (which latter he perceives as a distinguishing trait of the Russian people).[41]

Ivanov's view of the creative process develops from his understanding of the religious basis of true art. Art is generated by a fusion of the ascent toward an epiphany of the ideal and the descent to its realization in a proper artistic form. The creation of a work of art is a sacrifice, since it represents a lofty spirit's descent to the real, through which the ideal is expressed. Artistic form always means descent.[42]

Ivanov's attention is with descent more than with ascent.[43] He suggests that in lyric poetry there exists a possibility to create by ascent only. It is here that the "poet" is sometimes more important than the "artist." In fact, lyric poetry is "art" to a lesser extent than other art forms, all of which require some descent. Ivanov is not very much in favor of poetry created through the élan of ascent only.[44]

Ivanov's conception of the creative process may be called psychoanalytic in that the events leading to the creation of a work of art are seen as stages in a mental process over which the creative subject has no conscious control. Ivanov's conception is remarkably close to that of Gaston Bachelard.[45]

In his article "On the Boundaries of Art" (*O granitsakh iskusstva*, 1913) Ivanov presents a diagram of the creative process as ascent toward an epiphany which takes the creator's spirit through several regions of Being, followed by a descent to "a point of Apollonian contemplation of the apogee of ascent," and further down to an incarnation of the vision gained through the earlier ascent. Here the lowest form of art takes the artist to "a point of 'subjectivist' mirroring" of his own consciousness. Realist art, such as Flaubert's, takes the artist somewhat higher, to "a point of transcendent contemplation of a reality to be overcome" (called a "desert"). Art of "high symbolism" is capable of traversing the "desert" and reaching "points of intuitive grasp of higher realities." Finally, some rare artists, such as Dante, reach the highest level of intuition.[46]

On its ascent as well as on its descent, the artist's soul experiences several stages of Dionysian excitation (*dionisijskoe volnenie*). The details of Ivanov's model of ascent/descent are Neoplatonic. In the late Hellenistic age, religious topography, mostly vertical, invaded every area of thought, as all things were ordered in a hierarchy of ascending/descending values. The topography of ascent/descent of the soul through diverse regions of a spiritual cosmos is linked to Hellenistic cosmology as it appears in Ptolemaic astronomy.[47] Ivanov's diagrams bear a striking resemblance to astronomical charts. It may also be remembered that the ascent of the soul through various regions of the heavens is also a part of Orthodox eschatology.

Ivanov documents his model of the creative process with references to various poets: Dante, Pushkin, Wagner, Goethe, Nietzsche, and others. He quotes lines from Pushkin's "Autumn" (*Osen'*, 1833) as marvellous descriptions of Dionysian excitation and Apollonian dream.[48] Nietzsche's *Birth of Tragedy*, but also Wagner's *Meistersinger*, are other sources of "Apollonian dreams" [*SS*, II, 632].

The general scheme of an "inner canon" in the artist's soul coinciding with the "inner canon" of the work of art and symbolic of the mystic essence of things is Neoplatonic. It corresponds to the Plotinian concept of artistic creation "from inside," an "inner form" which recreates the true essence of things. This Plotinian conception dominates German idealist esthetics.[49]

Ivanov applies the ascent/descent model to human affairs at large, and so to history. He is convinced that "not a single step on the ladder of spiritual ascent is possible without a step down the rungs that lead to its subterranean treasures: the higher the branches, the deeper the roots."[50] Thus, Dostoevsky "was the master builder of that subterranean labyrinth which was to give birth to the new spirituality of the universal, all-human Ego."[51]

Ivanov's philosophy of history is genetic, like Nietzsche's, rather than historical. He believes in a perennial alternation of "organic" and "critical" epochs, terms taken from Saint-Simon, and sees his own age as a "critical" epoch which has reached its apogee and is about to be replaced by a new "organic" period already inaugurated by Wagner, Nietzsche, Ibsen, and the great Russian novelists.[52] Ivanov's conception of an organic epoch implies a resurgence of religious art, which he expects to arise from "the elemental creative power of the barbarian soul of the people."[53] He sees the role of the Russian intelligentsia as unique in history: a ruling class voluntarily descending to poverty, simplicity, and self-destruction.[54] Ivanov is convinced that "a true talent cannot but express the ultimate depths of the consciousness of his age" and thus will "in such epochs surely serve the revolution even if he may appear to others, and even to himself, as its enemy."[55] This particular notion, Hegelian in origin, is found also in Plekhanov and in Lukács.

III

Ivanov's monism extends to his view of art and society. He wholeheartedly follows the Russian tradition of social organicism started by Belinsky: "For a true creator art and life are one."[56] The artist is, fundamentally, a craftsman (*remeslennik*) who fulfills the orders of his community.[57] He may do this in various ways. There are mystifiers, Dionysian artists who create riddles, mysteries, and masks (*oblachiteli*). There are also pluralists. Such were Aeschylus, Shakespeare, and Goethe. And there are demystifiers, those who reveal the patterns of life, who tear off masks. Such were Sophocles, Cervantes, and Tolstoy.[58]

Ivanov also distinguishes "grand art," an expression of the communal soul (*sobornaja dusha*) of a nation or of mankind, from "small art," an expression of social movements, trends, and such. There are two varieties of each. Grand art can be either pandemic (*vsenarodnoe*), such as Dante's or Homer's, or demotic such as the great European novels. "Small art" is either intimate, as in most lyric poetry, or monastic (*kelejnoe*), severing all connections with the people (and in so doing aspiring once more to be universal). These four types of art represent an ascending gradation of independence for the artist. Yet with each successive ascent the artist also gives away some of the plenitude of himself as an individual. In the first stage "the creator's 'I' is submerged in the Nirvana of the popular 'I,' " and in the last it becomes fused with a metaphysical or cosmic "I." We have here a dialectic relationship between the artist and the people.[59]

Ivanov sees the art of Russian *décadence* as "intimate art," but suggests that the period of "small art" is passing and that a period of grand national art is just around the corner.[60] He persistently calls for a new art that will revive the choral principle of Greek drama, making art a popular "happening," a religious celebration, and an outburst of communal emotion.[61] The theater of the future would become, through audience participation, a bearer of the "communal word" (*sobornoe slovo*), a creator of myths and an agent of theurgic art.[62] The new drama would be a syncretic art form, utilizing verbal drama, music, and the visual arts. Ivanov sees an evolution from Wagner's *Musikdrama,* through the fusion of verbal drama and music in Maeterlinck and Debussy's *Pelléas et Mélisande,* to what he conceives as verbal drama with musical support.[63] He sees this development as "a struggle for the democratic ideal of a synthetic Action."[64] In every possible way Ivanov battles for a return to a unified art and against the fragmentation of art into separate domains through elitism, insiderism, subjectivism, and formalism.

It is remarkable that Ivanov's theories were realized not so much by Symbolists as by Futurists and Proletcultists, in Kruchenykh-Matyushin-Malevich's *Victory over the Sun* and the mass happenings of the revolutionary period, which even Western visitors thought were fulfilling the prophecies of Wagner and Nietzsche in bringing about a rebirth of Greek drama.[65]

Ivanov tends to be critical of those aspects of modern art which are in conflict with his monistic philosophy of art. He deplores the "esthetic anarchism or eclecticism" of his age.[66] He sees much of modern music as "pure kineticism, movement without a goal" and "fragmentariness, atomism, and alogism."[67] He rejects abstractionism: ". . . some secret law of esthetics demands anthropomorphism in everything and punishes every deviation from it with the curse of amorphism, aridity, and monotony."[68] He also rejects French Symbolism (he must mean Mallarmé) on account of its making Symbolism into a game of riddles or patterns of connotative devices and declares that Russian Symbolism has nothing in common with it.[69] For the same reason Ivanov will have nothing to do with Russian *décadence* or Ego-Futurism: any art which abandons life, he says, also loses what it believes it possesses—art.[70]

Consistently with his monistic philosophy, Ivanov also rejects the psychologism so characteristic of much of contemporary literature, and drama in particular. With remarkable insight into Dostoevsky's art, he saw in that writer "a great psychologist who nevertheless opposes to psychological study a 'more real' penetration into the secret of human nature."[71] Ivanov wants dramatic characters to be symbols, not individuals. Subjective psychological details merely detract from the true meaning of art.[72] Interestingly, we meet a similar attitude in Left Art.

Ivanov always discussed the drama in terms of a living theater, even though his own plays have remained *Lesedramen*. He sees the theater as an inherently communal activity that resists the poet's efforts to convert it entirely into art.[73] The link of tragedy with the sacrifice and cathartic celebration of a suffering god, Ivanov believes, is still present in modern tragic art which, as ever before, signifies the external death and inner triumph of human self-assertion.[74] The heroic life and death of young Ilyusha in *The Brothers Karamazov* is a case in point.[75]

Ivanov perceives three basic components of the theater: the community, manifest in the choral principle of tragedy and in audience participation; the hero, who realizes the religious or national issues of his community; and the mimetic principle (Ivanov believes that true tragedy is possible only on the grounds of a realistic vision of the world).[76] Ivanov emphasizes the dialectic tension among these three elements, and thinks that any drama that leaves out one of these three elements fails to actualize the true nature of drama.

Ivanov links the dominance of the hero over the communal principle in Shakespearean drama, and modern drama at large, with the rise of bourgeois individualism. He perceives a new trend toward an expansion of the individual "I" in the direction of a cosmic boundlessness (*bespredel'nost'*) achieved through deepened personal suffering.[77]

Ivanov's conception of drama is basically Hegelian, as is borne out even by his use of Hegelian terms and explicit references to Hegel. He shares with Hegel the notion that the tragic is an attitude of the human spirit rather than a literary genre. (It is in this sense that Ivanov perceives Dostoevsky's novels, or even the *Iliad,* as tragic.) Like Hegel, Ivanov sees the content of tragedy as a dialectic of ideas which generates a logic of human consciousness.[78] External clashes (such as that between the forces of nature and the human spirit) are therefore unfit to serve as the subject of tragic art.[79] Ivanov's conception of the distinction between tragic and comic drama is also essentially Hegelian.[80] One does not find in Ivanov's theory of tragedy any tendency toward an existentialist metaphysics, such as in the young Lukács's "metaphysics of tragedy."

IV

Ivanov generally likes to give credit to his sources. Whenever he does not, it is due either to the more literary than scholarly nature of a given essay or to the fact that the reference in question would be obvious to his presumed reader. Such would be true, for example, of references to Plato, Goethe, Schopenhauer, and Nietzsche (and major Russian poets and writers, of course).

Ivanov's esthetic theory very largely coincides with that of German objective idealism (Schelling, Hegel) and the romantic poets associated with it, Novalis in particular. It stands to reason that Ivanov would consider Tyutchev "the true originator of our true symbolism."[81] The Platonic traits of Ivanov's esthetics are such as may be also found in German idealism and romanticism. Thus, Platonic *anamnesis,* the notion that mankind is seeking to remember something which it once knew, often alluded to by Ivanov,[82] is also found in Goethe and Novalis and in Schelling's philosophy of revelation. Ivanov's mysticism is well in accord with the transcendentalism of German idealism. Heaven and hell, to Ivanov, certainly reside within the human soul, and the World Soul reveals itself through the human soul. Ivanov's inner sky and inner sea are familiar images of mystic poetry and of romanticism.

The ascent/descent symbolism which dominates Ivanov's esthetics surely originated with Nietzsche. But it is found in Plato's *enanodos,* the disengagement of the soul from the day that is night, and the catabasis of Socrates to the Dendidia (both in the *Republic*),[83] and it dominates Neoplatonic thought. Ascent/descent symbolism is prominent in Goethe (here the descent to the Mothers in *Faust II* is surely a source of inspiration for Ivanov)[84] and in the romantics.

Goethe was Ivanov's favorite poet.[85] He often quotes Goethe's verses. Goethe's Neoplatonic organicism and vitalism appealed to-him. He is said to have often quoted Goethe's "Das Lebendige will ich preisen / Das nach Flammentod sich sehnet" and "Und solang du das nicht hast, / Dieses: Stirb und werde! / Bist du nur ein trüber Gast / Auf der dunklen Erde" ("Selige Sehnsucht," 1814). Goethe, of course, believed in anamnesis. Ivanov liked to quote his line, "Das Wahre war schon längst gefunden" ("Vermächtnis," 1829). One can recognize Goethe's preoccupation with archetypes in Iva-nov's chain of "doubles." Not infrequently, Ivanov will judge even Russian literature in Goethean terms. Stavrogin is the Russian Faust, and Marya Timofeevna is the Russian Gretchen, with all the symbolic implications.[86] When Ivanov finds fault with his *confrères,* the Russian symbolists who would be prophets rather than artists, he quotes Goethe's "In der Beschränkung zeigt sich erst der Mei-ster." Altogether, Ivanov does not conceal but, on the contrary, gratefully acknowledges his debt to Goethe. He will go so far as to entitle an essay of his "Manner, Person and Style" (*Manera, litso i stil'*, 1912), echoing Goethe's "Einfache Nachahmung, Manier, Stil" (1788). Ivanov's essay follows Goethe's in seeing "style" as the high-est form of creativity and a synthesis of objective and subjective art.

Ivanov refers to Hegel on occasion and is clearly conversant with his philosophy.[87] While direct references to Schelling seem to be absent in his writings, there are many traits that link Ivanov pre-cisely with that thinker, and especially with the late Schelling, author of philosophies of mythology and revelation. Ivanov's preoc-cupation with the universality of myth, with Christian myth, and with modern mythology is a trait which he shares with Schelling, whose belief in the cosmic or astral origin of all religion, and so of mythology, appears in Ivanov as well. Ivanov also shares Schelling's notion of a continuity between pre-Christian cults of a suffering, kenotic god (or son of god) and the Judaic-Christian myth.[88] Here, Ivanov stays with Schelling, refusing to join Nietzsche in using this position as a basis for an attack on Christianity. Altogether, Ivanov's religious symbolism in many ways parallels religious romanticism.

Ivanov's conception of ascent/descent includes a number of co-incidences with Schelling's *Philosophy of Mythology,* such as the identification of this principle with those of the male/female and the dyad/monad. The mythology of chaos (as the third principle, joining the other two), which appears in Ivanov's writings, is also discussed by Schelling.[89] I have found even more specific parallels. For example, Ivanov's magnificent sonnet which gives an allegorical meaning to the death of Heracles seems to echo Schelling's interpretation of that myth.[90]

Nietzsche must have been for Ivanov a catalyst for much Platonic, Neoplatonic, and romantic thought. Ivanov took for granted that his readers were aware of these connections. On occasion he will gratefully acknowledge his debt, for instance, by entitling an essay of his "On the Joyful Craft" (*O veselom remesle*),[91] echoing Nietzsche's *Die fröhliche Wissenschaft*. Of course Ivanov never accepts Nietzsche's estheticism: if Dionysian intoxication is merely an esthetic phenomenon, then mankind is only a band of actors and men are merely wearers of temporal masks, the fortuitous forms of human individuality. Ivanov, as a Christian mystic, transforms Nietzsche's vitalist-esthetic conception of "beyond good and evil" into a vision of the metaphysically holy.[92]

There are few references to French symbolism in Ivanov's writings. Baudelaire's "Correspondances" is quoted repeatedly, but little else. It must, however, be considered that Ivanov shared with some of the French symbolists, such as Maeterlinck, a whole complex of Neoplatonic traits, such as emancipation and hypostasis, ascent/descent, and elemental imagery.[93]

A circumstance to which relatively little attention has been paid so far is that many specific traits of Ivanov's esthetics also appear in Russian Futurist theory.

Notes

1. In his essay "Zavety simvolizma," Ivanov suggests that all that was truly valuable about Russian Symbolism grew from native Russian soil. See *SS*, II, 596.

2. See, e.g., "Dve stikhii v sovremennom simvolizme," *SS*, II, 551.

3. See, e.g., "Vagner i Dionisovo deistvo," *SS*, II, 84–85. To be sure, in his later years Ivanov to some extent renounced the Dionysian Hellenism of his youth. See, for example, his poem "Palinodija" (1927).

4. "Mysli o simvolizme" (1912), *SS*, II, 609. On the other hand, Ivanov also believes that an artist who claims that he works only for himself, or for Art, is insincere. In that sense, the artist *is* an artisan who needs an order (*zakaz*) from society. See "O veselom remesle," *Po zvezdam: Stat'i i aforizmy* (St. Petersburg, 1909), p. 222.

5. "Sledstviem iz vysheskazannogo javljaetsja, naprimer, esteticheski gluboko opravdannoe trebovanie, chtoby material khudozhestvennogo proizvedenija byl oshchutim i kak by veren sebe, kak by vyrazhal svoe soglasie na prinjatie pridavaemykh emu khudozhnikom form" ("O granitsakh iskusstva" [1913], *SS*, II, 634). Further in the same essay, Ivanov suggests that "there is more sanctity in marble or in the element of language and in every flesh of every art than in the human spirit which, in a work of art, vivifies the flesh that is visible to the eye or audible to the ear" (*SS*, II, 647).

6. "Zavety simvolizma" (1910), *SS*, II, 596.

7. Ivanov defines symbolism as "the world view of mystic realism or, to use Novalis' expression, 'magic idealism' " (*SS*, II, 599). Ivanov very much believes in the cognitive power of art: "Edva li ne bol'shinstvo ljudej nashego vremeni soglasno v tom, chto iskusstvo sluzhit poznaniju i chto rod poznanija, predstavljaemyj iskusstvom, v izvestnom smysle prevoskhodnee poznanija nauchnogo" ("O granitsakh iskusstva," *SS*, II, 641). This sounds very much like Schelling—or like Malevich or Kandinsky.

8. For a concise formulation of Ivanov's emanationist view of reality, see his essay "Sporady," *Po zvezdam*, p. 340, where "the mythical chronicle of the world and of man" is said to be "more truthful than history." It is for this reason, Ivanov adds, that Aristotle was right in suggesting that poetry was closer to philosophy than history. Obviously Ivanov interprets Aristotle's dictum in a Neoplatonic sense.

9. For example: "Zdes' svoboda perekhodit v neobkhodimost', proizvol delaetsja bezvol'nym, prorochestvennoe derznovenie obrashchaetsja v podchinenie prorocheskoe" ("Kop'e Afiny" [1904], *SS*, I, 731). Or: "Ideal vsekh stremlenij dvulik. Dukh volit soznat' sebja kak ob'ekt i kak sub'ekt" ("Novye maski" [1904], *SS*, II, 79). This is the language of German objective idealism. It prevails in most of Ivanov's writings.

10. "Titanizmu svojstvenno beskryloe soznanie prinuditel'nosti ovlade-vajushchej im voli, chuvstvo vnutrennego determinizma, kotoroe tak nepo-khozhe na radost' sovpadenija svobody s neobkhodimost'ju—etu

bozhestvennuju pechat' oblagodatstvovannoj dushi" ("O dejstvij i dejstve" [1919], *SS*, II, 159).

11. See, e.g., Vyacheslav Ivanov, *Freedom and the Tragic Life: A Study in Dostoevsky* (New York, 1971), p. 7.

12. Prometheanism was certainly a common trait of Russian modernism. Ivanov knows it well (see note 10 above)—and condemns it.

13. See James West, *Russian Symbolism: A Study of Vyacheslav Ivanov and the Russian Symbolist Aesthetic* (London, 1970), p. 59.

14. Cf. Émile Bréhier, *The Philosophy of Plotinus* (Chicago, 1971), p. 43. Statements such as the following definitely remind one of Plotinus: "Zhizn' vo vremeni—umiranie. Zhizn'—tsel' moikh dvojnikov, otritsajushchikh, umershchvljajushchikh odin drugogo" ("Kop'e Afiny," *SS*, I, 732). Cf. Armin Hetzer, *Vjačeslav Ivanovs Tragödie Tantal: Eine literarhistorische Interpretation* (Munich, 1972), pp. 111–12.

15. See, e.g., the poem "Iskushenie prozrachnosti" (*SS*, I, 756).

16. "Zavety simvolizma," *SS*, II, 598.

17. See West, p. 52. Ivanov's distinction between celebratory and transforming art has a parallel (or source) in *l'art admiratif/critique* of Fourierist esthetics.

18. Thus, Ivanov asserts that true tragedy, like true mysticism, is possible only on the soil of a deeply realistic view of the world (*Freedom and the Tragic Life*, p. 40).

19. See, e.g., "Dve stikhii v russkom simvolizme," *SS*, II, 541.

20. *SS*, II, 546.

21. For Dionysian and Apollonian stages in the creative process see "O granitsakh iskusstva," *SS*, II, 644–45. For Dionysian and Apollonian themes in lyric poetry see "Ekskurs: O liricheskoj teme" (1912), *SS*, II, 203–4. In a historical sense, Ivanov more or less identifies the Apollonian/Dionysian with the classical/romantic of Friedrich Schlegel and other romantic critics. See, e.g., "O veselom remesle," *Po zvezdam*, p. 233.

22. See, e.g., "Predchuvstvija i predvestija," *Po zvezdam*, pp. 199–200, and "Sporady," ibid., p. 339.

23. See, e.g., "O dejstvii i dejstve," *SS*, II, 159, and *Freedom and the Tragic Life*, pp. 38–39.

24. Cf. my remarks on ascent/descent, below.

25. See "O granitsakh iskusstva," *SS*, II, 647 (where Ivanov quotes Solovyov's "Kogda reztsu poslushnyj kamen' ") and *SS*, II, 649. For Ivanov's belief that "poetry is an immediate revelation of highest truth," see C. M. Bowra's introduction to *Svet vechernij* (Oxford, 1962), p. xv. To Ivanov, as to

the Neoplatonists of the Renaissance or to Schelling, "God is an artist, and His judgment, I believe, will be that of an artist" ("Sporady," *Po zvezdam,* p. 344).

26. "On byl iz tekh pevtsov (takov-zhe byl Novalis), / Chto vidjat v snakh sebja naslednikami lir, / Kotorym na zare vekov povinovalis' / Dukh, kamen', drevo, zver', voda, ogon', efir" ("Pamjati Skrjabina," 1915).

27. See, e.g., "O sushchestve tragedii" (1912), *SS,* II, 191.

28. See "Simvolika esteticheskikh nachal" (1905), *SS,* I, 829.

29. See "O sushchestve tragedii," *SS,* II, 198, and *Freedom and the Tragic Life,* p. 60.

30. Hetzer, p. 113, suggests Nietzsche's *Die fröhliche Wissenschaft* (1887) as Ivanov's source.

31. See Hetzer, p. 116.

32. See "Krizis individualizma" (1905), *SS,* I, 835.

33. See Hetzer, p. 197, and Olga Deschartes' introduction to *SS,* I, 83.

34. There are many examples in *Thus spake Zarathustra,* e.g., for ascent: "Erhebt eure Herzen, meine Brüder, hoch! höher! Und vergesst mir auch die Beine nicht!" ("Vom höheren Menschen"); for descent: "Wenn die Macht gnädig wird und herabkommt ins Sichtbare: Schönheit heisse ich solches Herabkommen" ("Von den Erhabenen").

35. See my article, "The Aesthetic Categories of *Ascent* and *Descent* in the Poetry of Vjačeslav Ivanov," *Russian Poetics* (preprint of paper read at a symposium held at U.C.L.A. in September, 1975). In his essay "Simvolika esteticheskikh nachal" (1905), Ivanov identifies a whole series of images which he associates with ascent/descent (*SS,* I, 823).

36. See "O dejstvii i dejstve," *SS,* II, 169. It may be noted that Georg Lukács, in his early (pre-Marxist) essay "Die Metaphysik der Tragödie" also introduces the ascent/descent category.

37. See "O granitsakh iskusstva," where Ivanov presents a sonnet from Dante's *Vita nuova* as an example of ascent/descent (*SS,* II, 629).

38. "Simvolika esteticheskikh nachal," *SS,* I, 827.

39. See Carin Tschöpl, *Vjačeslav Ivanov: Dichtung und Dichtungstheorie* (Munich, 1968), p. 126, and Olga Deschartes' introduction to *SS,* (I, 225–26.

40. Ivanov frequently points this out himself. See, e.g., "O granitsakh iskusstva," *SS,* II, 640, or "Drevnij uzhas," *Po zvezdam,* p. 394.

41. See "O russkoj idee," *Po zvezdam,* pp. 329–30.

42. See "O granitsakh iskusstva," *SS,* II, 635.

43. See Tschöpl, p. 172.

44. See "O granitsakh iskusstva," *SS*, II, 639.

45. The work most relevant to Ivanov is *L'Air et les songes* (Paris, 1943). For a concise description of Bachelard's ideas, see François Pire, *De l'imagination poétique dans l'oeuvre de Gaston Bachelard* (Paris, 1967). Nietzsche was for Bachelard the quintessential poet of ascent (Pire, p. 105).

46. See Hetzer, pp. 121–23.

47. See Bréhier, pp. 34–37.

48. "O granitsakh iskusstva," *SS*, II, 630.

49. See the chapter "Innere Form" (pp. 128–83) in Franz Koch, *Goethe und Plotin* (Leipzig, 1925). Plotinus's concept of creation "from inside" has a correspondent in Bachelard's "inherent imagination."

50. *Perepiska iz dvukh uglov* (Moscow-Berlin, 1922), p. 23

51. *Freedom and the Tragic Life*, p. 5.

52. "Predchuvstvija i predvestija," *SS*, II, 89.

53. "O veselom remesle," *Po zvezdam*, p. 245.

54. "O russkoj idee," *Po zvezdam*, pp. 319–21.

55. "O veselom remesle," *Po zvezdam*, p. 226.

56. "Manera, litso, stil' " (1912), *SS*, II, 617.

57. "O veselom remesle," *Po zvezdam*, p. 221.

58. "Sporady," *Po zvezdam*, pp. 345–46.

59. "Kop'e Afiny," *SS*, I, 730–31. See also Hetzer, p. 99.

60. "O veselom remesle," p. 242. See also Evelyn Bristol, "Idealism and Decadence in Russian Symbolist Poetry," *Slavic Review,* 39 (1980), 278.

61. See, e.g., "Poet i chern'," *Po zvezdam*, pp. 41–42, or "Estetika i ispovedanie" (1908), *SS*, II, 568.

62. See, e.g., "Novye maski," *SS*, II, 76, "Predchuvstvija i predvestija."

63. *SS*, II, 95, and "Dve stikhii v sovremennom simvolizme," *SS*, II, 559. "Predchuvstvija i predvestija," *SS*, II, 97.

64. "Vagner i Dionisovo dejstvo" (1905), *SS*, II, 85.

65. See Robert C. Williams, *Artists in Revolution: Portraits of the Russian Avantgarde, 1905–1925* (Bloomington and London, 1977), p. 5.

66. "Manera, litso i stil'," *SS*, II, 618.

67. *SS*, II, 619.

68. "Predchuvstvija i predvestija," *SS*, II, 98.

69. "Mysli o simvolizme" (1912), *SS*, II, 611, where Mallarmé is singled out as an exponent of this undesirable tendency.

70. "Manera, litso i stil'," *SS*, II, 619–20.

71. *Freedom and the Tragic Life*, p. 15.

72. See, e.g., "Manera, litso i stil'," *SS*, II, 621. Cf. Hetzer, p. 129.

73. "Esteticheskaja norma teatra" (1916), *SS*, II,213.

74. See Olga Deschartes' introduction, *SS*, I, 108. Hetzer (p. 102) suggests that the conception of Dionysian resurrection and catharsis implied in this is taken from Rohde.

75. *Freedom and the Tragic Life*, p. 14.

76. Ibid., p. 40. See also "Esteticheskaja norma teatra," *SS*, II, 213.

77. *SS*, II, 212–14. Ivanov's thinking here is decidedly Hegelian.

78. "O sushchestve tragedii" (1912), *SS*, II, 192. For an example of Hegelian terminology: "Ego [Prometeja] pervyj mjatezh, pervaja vina, est' vosstanie protiv sobstvennoj bytijstvennoj sushchnosti, kak bytija 'konkretnego' (v smysle, pridavaemom etomu slovu Gegelem)" ("O dejstvii i dejstve," *SS*, II, 161).

79. "O sushchestve tragedii," *SS*, II, 193.

80. Ivanov suggests that in high tragedy the people are a chorus, a single body with a single will and mind, while in comedy they are merely a crowd ("Esteticheskaja norma teatra," *SS*, II, 208).

81. "Zavety simvolizma," *SS*, II, 597.

82. See, e.g., "Poet i chern'," *SS*, I, 709; "Perepiska iz dvukh uglov," pp. 57, 58. Ivanov specifically acknowledges his solidarity with Plato and his *anamnesis*, see "Drevnij uzhas," *Po zvezdam*, p. 394.

83. See Miroslav John Hanak, *Maeterlinck's Symbolic Drama: A Leap into Transcendence* (Louvain, 1974), pp. 36, 45. The mythological basis of Plato's conceptions are identified by Rohde.

84. See, e.g., "Drevnij uzhas," *Po zvezdam*, p. 394. For a poetic echo, see the poem "Mat" in *Cor Ardens* (*SS*, II, 377).

85. Goethe's influence on Ivanov is both deep and manifold. I would like to point out only one detail to suggest its extent. The lead poem of *Kormchie zvezdy*, "Krasota" (dedicated to Vladimir Solovyov) is written in the exact meter of Goethe's "Die Braut von Korinth," whose basic theme and ethos it also shares. I am sure that more such instances may be found.

86. *Freedom and the Tragic Life*, p. 61.

87. This does not mean that he always follows Hegel's thought patterns to the letter. For example, Ivanov sees the epic as "objective," and lyric poetry as a synthesis of both, retaining the Hegelian dialectic structure, but adjusting its content ("Manera, litso i stil'," *SS*, II, 624).

88. F. W. J. Schelling, *Einleitung in die Philosophie der Mythologie* (Stuttgart and Augsburg, 1856), pp. 313ff.

89. Ibid., pp. 596ff.

90. Ibid., p. 345.
91. "O veselom remesle," *Po zvezdam,* pp. 220–46.
92. "Nitsshe i Dionis" (1904), *SS,* I, 721, 725.
93. See Hanak's above-mentioned work (note 84).

Ivanov's Humanism: *A Correspondence from Two Corners*

Robert Louis Jackson

There is a distinctively Russian drama in the opening line of Ivanov's first letter to Mikhail Osipovich Gershenzon in *A Correspondence from Two Corners* (*Perepiska iz dvukh uglov*, 1921).[1] "I know, my dear friend and neighbor in another corner of the room we share, that you have come to doubt personal immortality and a personal God." Part of the drama of this line comes from the juxtaposition of the eternal questions of God and immortality in all their amplitude or space, with the finite space of a room, indeed, a corner of a geometrical square. "And what will you tell me in reply from another corner of this same square?" Ivanov writes at the end of this first letter.

The image of a square bisected diagonally between two corners becomes a metaphor in *A Correspondence* for culture and the human condition. Is there a way out of the planimetric cultural geometry of the square? *That,* in essence, is the question that was posed by the poet Ivanov as he rested together with Gershenzon in a room in a sanatorium in Russia in the year nineteen hundred and twenty.

This was not the first time in Russian life or literature that the problem of the infinite was self-consciously posed within the limits of the finite. We may recall Dostoevsky's restaurant setting for the dialogue between Ivan and Alyosha in *The Brothers Karamazov.* The brothers Alyosha and Ivan are discussing eternal questions and sitting—Dostoevsky reminds us—behind a "partial screen." Real and metaphysical time, moreover, seem involved in Dostoevsky's play with spaces. "We've endless time before I leave," Ivan remarks. "A whole eternity, immortality." This setting, in turn, recalls the opening lines of Leopardi's "L'infinito," a favorite poem, we may note here, of Ivanov's.

It was always dear to me, this solitary hill, and this hedge which shuts off the gaze from so large a part of the uttermost horizon. But sitting, and looking out, in thought I fashion for myself endless spaces beyond, more than human silences, and deepest quiet.

Sempre caro mi fu quest'ermo colle,
e questa siepe, che da tanta parte
dell'ultimo orizzonte il guardo esclude.
Ma sedendo e mirando, interminati
spazi di là da quella, e sovrumani
silenzi, e profondissima quiete
io nel pensier mi fingo . . .

Sitting in their respective "corners" Ivanov and Gershenzon are doing what Leopardi and the brothers Alyosha and Ivan are engaged in behind their partial screens and hedges: "fashioning endless spaces beyond."

Ivanov's first sentence, indeed, his very first word (*znaju*—I know), breathes confidence and conviction and strikes the dominant and affirmative note in Ivanov's letters. Gershenzon's reply, indeed, the very first word of his letter, is equally dramatic and sounds the negative and skeptical note of his side of the correspondence as it pertains to the central questions of contemporary life and culture: "*Net.*" "No, Vyacheslav Ivanovich, I have not doubted personal immortality and, like you, I know the individual to be the repository of true reality." Gershenzon's decisive "no" seems not only to qualify his formal acceptance of personal immortality, but to anticipate his view of man as defined by the flat or horizontal dimension of human culture. "You and I, dear friend," Gershenzon continues, "are diagonal not only in this room but in spirit, too. I do not like to let my thoughts roam the metaphysical peaks, although I delight in watching you smoothly soar above them."

Gershenzon immediately introduces the leitmotif of his letters:

weariness not only with "other-worldly speculations"—which, he writes, "inevitably fall into systems"—but with "all these abstractions." He confesses that he is depressed and oppressed by "the whole intellectual heritage of man, all the discoveries, knowledge, values amassed and established through the centuries." Stifled as though by heavy clothes, he contemplates the "bliss" of "plunging into Lethe, washing off without trace the mind's memory of all religions and philosophical systems, of all science, art, poetry," and coming out "naked like the first man, naked, joyous and light." There he would "freely stretch out to the sky his bare arms, remembering nothing of the past except how heavy and stifling those clothes were." Gershenzon writes in a later letter:

> Culture is disintegrating from within—we can see this clearly; it hangs in tatters from our exhausted spirit. Whether this is how liberation will come about, or whether it will explode in a catastrophe, as it did twenty centuries ago, I do not know, and of course I myself shall never reach the promised land, but my feeling is like Mount Nebo, from which Moses saw it. And I am not alone in discerning it through the curtain of fog.

Confessing his dislike for the abstract, Gershenzon, paradoxically, will return again and again to his Mt. Nebo—to his abstract, idyllic and essentially passive dream. In contrast, Ivanov, while taking his point of departure from the absolute and the abstract, repeatedly plunges not into Lethe or forgetfulness but into the living stream of historical culture. For him, culture is a "hierarchy of reverences. And so many things and people in my surroundings fill me with reverence—from man and his tools and his great labor and his debased dignity down to the mineral—that I find it sweet to drown in that sea ('naufragar m'è dolce in questo mare')—to drown in God," he concludes, citing a line from Leopardi's poem, "L'infinito." For Ivanov, culture is at once finite and infinite.

"My dear friend," he writes in the opening of the fifth letter of *A Correspondence,* "we dwell in the same cultural environment as we do here in the same room, where each of us has his own corner, but there is only one wide window and one door." Gershenzon, he points out, cannot conceive of dwelling with a culture "without essentially fusing with it." Ivanov, however, insists that "while consciousness can be entirely immanent in culture it can also be only partly immanent and partly transcendent." "To the believer, his faith is by definition separate from culture, as nature is separate, or love. . . . And so? So it depends on our faith in the absolute, which transcends culture, whether we shall have inner freedom, that is, life itself—or grovel inwardly before culture, long essentially godless since it imprisons man within himself."

Gershenzon replies that Ivanov's corner "is also a corner limited by walls—there is no freedom in it." "Civilized man, contemporary man," he observes pessimistically, "is incapable of soaring toward the absolute; and if he does have faith, it shares the condition of all his other psychic states—it is tainted with reflection, distorted and powerless. I repeat what I wrote in my last letter: Our consciousness cannot transcend culture, except in rare, unusual cases." And once again, Gershenzon strikes one of the dominant notes of his letters: "What do I want? I want freedom of creation, and of quest, I want primordial freshness of spirit, to go where I want, along untrodden paths . . . first, because this would be pleasant, and second because we might find more on new paths. But no: mainly because it is boring here, as in our sanatorium. One yearns for meadows and forests." Gershenzon is overcome by skepticism, a feeling of nausea and an organic urge to seek out freedom in his idyllic beyond. "Like Rousseau I imagine some blissful state of complete freedom and unencumbered spirit, some heavenly insouciance (*bespechnost'*). I know too much, and this burden oppresses me." "I would gladly exchange all the knowledge and ideas I have gleaned from books . . . for the joy of discovering for myself, from my own experience, just one bit of basic knowledge of the simplest kind, but fresh as a summer morn."

Here in Gershenzon's Rousseauesque, Arcadian dream there is more than boredom, spleen and a surfeit of knowledge; there is also, as Ivanov rightly notes, "much despair." Ivanov goes on to observe of "my dear doctor Faust in a new incarnation" that Mephistopheles would by no means abandon all hope of success of drawing "the

overtired member of four faculties out of his zealously guarded 'corner' into the free world." But the "boundless freedom" (vol'naja volja)
Gershenzon would attain, Ivanov adds, would only turn out in the
end to be an "inescapable prison."

Freedom for Ivanov, as for Dostoevsky, is not to be found in
the bare opposite of containment, that is, in a notion of boundless
personal liberty or physical freedom. We are not surprised that Ivanov uses the word volja in this connection: a word that in Russian
literary use frequently has connotations of arbitrariness and self-will.
Ultimate freedom for Ivanov is not to be sought in the Faustian
"illusion of a free land and a liberated people," as he puts it, it is
not to be sought on the "horizontal" plane. Ivanov writes:

> Any number of planimetric designs and patterns can be drawn on
> a horizontal plane. The important fact is that the plane is hori-
> zontal. But I am no Mephistopheles and have no intention of
> enticing or luring you anywhere. In essence, what I am saying to
> you is that a vertical line can start any point, in any "corner" on
> the surface of any culture, young or decrepit. To me, however,
> culture itself, in its proper sense, is not at all a flat horizontal
> surface, not a plain of ruins or a field littered with bones. It holds,
> besides, something truly sacred: the memory, not only of earthly
> external visage of our fathers, but of the high initiations they
> achieved. A live, permanent memory that never dies in those who
> partake in these initiations.

With the word "memory" we are at the core of Ivanov's conception of culture and of the meaning of existence on earth. "Insofar
as it is 'forgotten,' the past, historical or primordial, is homologized
with death," Mircea Eliade has written in connection with the ancient Greek understanding of memory and forgetting. "The fountain
Lethe, 'forgetfulness,' is a necessary part of the realm of Death. The
dead are those who have lost their memories."[2] Gershenzon, in one
part of his divided nature ("I lead a strange, double life"), wishes
to plunge into the river of Lethe and wash himself clean of the past.
For Ivanov, as for Dostoevsky, loss of memory implies a static view
of the universe and, ultimately, moral and spiritual death. "Mem-

ory," Ivanov writes, "is the dynamic principle, while oblivion means weariness, interrupted motion, decay and a return to a state of relative stagnation. Let us, like Nietzsche, closely watch ourselves lest we harbor the poisons of decay, the infection of 'decadence.'" And Ivanov defines decadence as "the feeling of a refined organic bond with the material legacy of a past high culture, coupled with a painful pride in being the last in its line." "Decadence," he writes again, "is the numbness of memory no longer creative, no longer a living link with our fathers' initiation and a spur to our own initiative."

Ivanov, of course, is not accusing his close friend of stagnation, decadence or disregard for past culture. Gershenzon, as we know, was an indefatigable lover of culture and its art and artifacts, a scholar for whom memory of culture was all. Yet precisely that memory weighs upon him. And while in one part of his being he worships the past, in another he views it as a tomb. In the last analysis, his love of culture does contain an element of that decadence of which Ivanov writes. Respect for the forefathers of culture in him is not linked with a belief in their resurrection either in a spiritual or religious sense.

Gershenzon's ambivalent relation to culture is not a new one in Russian literature. Here we may recall another divided man, Ivan Karamazov, and his reaction to the great legacy of culture. Ivan is a man who also wants to live "in spite of logic" and who loves the "sticky little leaves of spring and the blue sky."

> I want to go to Europe, Alyosha. . . . I want to go only to the graveyard, but to a most, most precious graveyard, let me tell you! There lie the precious deceased. Every stone over them speaks of such burning life in the past, of such passionate faith in heroic achievement, in truth, in struggle and in science, and—I know beforehand—I shall fall on the earth and will kiss these stones and weep over them, all the while convinced in my heart that all this has long been a graveyard and nothing more.

Ivan, as Dostoevsky notes, "remembers everything." So, too, Gershenzon remembers everything. He worships the precious stones of culture, although in his heart he is convinced that they constitute nothing but a graveyard for our times. "O my friend, O swan of Apollo! Why were feelings so vivid, thought so fresh, words so meaningful then, in the fourteenth century, and why are our thoughts and feelings so dull, our language as if interspun with cobwebs?" But as Chateaubriand once remarked, and as Dostoevsky and Ivanov firmly believed, "We venerate the ashes of our ancestors because a voice tells us that not everything is extinguished in them" (Nous respectons les cendres de nos ancêtres, parce qu'une voix nous dit que tout n'est pas éteint en eux).[3] Not without reason does Alyosha call upon Ivan to "raise up your dead who have perhaps not died after all." "Culture is the cult of ancestors—and, of course, their resurrection."

Gershenzon in a striking way sums up for us the strengths and weaknesses of the nineteenth-century intellectual as he roamed much of Russian literature and life. If we assemble all that seems to define him in his letters: his self-proclaimed ambivalence, his anguish, his mistrust of reason, his disillusionment with a world whose lofty idealism has collapsed but whose materialism he cannot accept; his metaphysical boredom; his view of man—and himself—as poisoned with reflection, as distorted and impotent; his feeling of a surfeit of knowledge; and, finally, his yearnings for the idyll of primeval, so-called "natural" freedom; if we bring all these features together then the distinguished literary scholar of nineteenth-century Russian literature himself seems to emerge as a last and living example of these unhappy Russian Hamlets and Fausts, intellectuals, dreamers and superfluous men who inhabit Russian literature and about whom he wrote so keenly and well. Here is the "historic Russian sufferer," in the words of Dostoevsky, who sought refuge "in the bosom of nature from the confused and absurd life of our Russian educated society." This historic Russian type, this "wanderer in his native land," Dostoevsky maintained, early was embodied in Aleko, hero of Pushkin's narrative poem, "The Gypsies" (*Tsygany*, 1827):

Aleko, of course, still does not know how to express correctly his anguish: in him all this is somehow still abstract, he experiences only a yearning for nature, a complaint about fashionable society, universal strivings, a lament about a truth lost somewhere by somebody, which he can in no way find. Here there is something akin to Jean-Jacques Rousseau. In what this truth consists, where and how it could appear, and precisely when it was lost, he himself, of course, cannot say, but he suffers sincerely. A fantastic and impatient person, he thirsts for salvation. Truth, he as much as says, is somewhere beyond himself, perhaps somewhere in other lands. . . . In the final analysis he is an alien in his own land.[4]

Did Gershenzon, a brilliant critic of Russian literature and sensitive to all its moods, ultimately recognize himself, perhaps unconsciously, in the self-divided, superfluous hero? It is surely no accident that he echoes in an uncanny way another wanderer in Russian literature, the hero of Turgenev's story, "A Correspondence" (*Perepiska*, 1854), who mournfully writes in one of his letters: "Why have we been condemned only at rare moments to see the wished-for shore but can never stand on it with firm foot, never touch it— 'nor weep sweetly like the first Jew / on the border of the promised land'?"[5]

The boundaries of fiction and reality have always been blurred in Russian life and history. Gershenzon's anguish does indeed reflect the plight and pathos of the "historic Russian sufferer" as depicted in Russian literature. That anguish, of course, is also deeply personal.[6] Yet it also reflects the plight of Russia in 1920 and the constantly repeated drama in Russian history of failed hopes; it gives expression, finally, to a rightly perceived crisis of values, a crisis of humanism, that characterized European society after World War I.

Ivanov, too, was profoundly responsive to Russian literature and culture. But he was the opposite of Gershenzon in his religious humanism and in his constant emphasis upon the themes of memory and resurrection. In him, moreover, we recognize not so much a character from Russian literature as a maker of Russian literature. Reaching deeply into the recesses of Russian and European civilization, he sought to act upon the present and to lay the foundations for renewed cultural and spiritual life, for a new ecumenicity (*sobor-*

nost') that inevitably, he believed, belonged to the future. In this renewal the past cannot be neglected or scorned. Culture is built upon ruins and the respect for ruins. Nietzsche, Ivanov notes in *A Correspondence,* is "one of the great creators of ideals; from an iconoclast, he turns into an icon painter." And comparing Gershenzon's escapism unfavorably with Nietzsche's readiness at least to take on the burden of culture and man, Ivanov remarks prophetically:

> It is doubtful whether in today's cultural climate any personal initiation can take place without the "initiate's" . . . meeting [Nietzsche] as the "guardian of the threshold." Nietzsche has said: "Man is something that must be overcome"—whereby he declares once more that the way of personal emancipation is a way up to the heights and down into the depths, a vertical movement. . . . "Could be, could be," you hastily wave this aside, for your loins are girded and your feverish eyes scan the desert's horizon: "First of all, out of here, out of here, out of Egypt."

Ivanov, of course, was one of those "initiates" who encountered Nietzsche and who ultimately went on his own unique way. Yet rejecting much in Nietzsche he remained faithful to his central vision: "What is great in man," Nietzsche wrote, is "that he is a bridge and not an end . . . I love him who does not hold back one drop of spirit for himself, but wants to be entirely of the spirit of his virtue: thus he strides over the bridge as spirit."

One may, of course, respond with some reserve to Ivanov's remarks on the Russian revolution in 1920, his insistence that

> history is not proceeding under your sign, but stubbornly wants to remain *history.* Let us disregard what is random, unpredictable, irrational in the course of events, and look at the prevailing trends. The anarchic tendencies are not dominant; essentially, they seem to be correlates and shadows of the bourgeois social structure. The so-called conscious proletariat stands entirely on the ground of cultural continuity. The struggle is not for abolishing the values of the old culture, but rather . . . for the revival of everything in them that has objective and timeless significance. . . . I think

[it] will spoil much marble and durable bronze . . . but I think also that some unique, deep trace of the lion-claw [see "Of the Three Metamorphoses" in *Thus Spake Zarathustra*—ed.] will show forever on the memorials of our ancient Egypt.

More marble and bronze was to be destroyed in Russia than Ivanov or anybody else could anticipate in 1920. What is more, precisely the "random, unpredictable and irrational" were to become the hallmarks of the twentieth century. In the final analysis, however, Ivanov's cautious optimism with respect to the revolution (not unlike Blok's in "The Twelve") rested on a view of the revolution as an expression of spiritual forces that lay *beneath* consciousness and ideology.

> Perhaps (I really believe this) the proletariat fighting for the possession of the cultural values is honestly mistaken in thinking that it needs them for their own sake, when it needs them only as means toward other attainments. . . . The general direction of the road is known only to the spirit, and consciousness feels cheated after each step. . . . Whatever we may observe in the Revolution today tells us nothing of the long-range designs for which the spirit has called it forth.

Later, as the Stalinist darkness descended over Russia, Ivanov's views—at least on the nature of the proletarian cause itself—hardened. "The proletarian cause," he wrote in his *Lettre à Charles Du Bos* in 1930, "is either a pretext or a method; its real goal is to extinguish God, to tear Him out of human hearts. Let everybody take his stand on the side of one or the other of the warring cities!" Yet Ivanov's faith in culture, and in Russian culture in particular, had not diminished. As he wrote to a despondent Russian émigré in 1935:

> You mourn the 'destruction of Russian culture'; but it has not been destroyed; rather it has been called upon for new accomplishments, to make a new spiritual consciousness. Moreover, just as there is one Truth, and one Beauty, so culture in the fundamental and final meaning of the word—culture as the spiritual self-def-

inition and self-revelation of man—is an expression of universal unity and the task of universal unification. Thus Russian culture is only one of the types or one of the fringes of a unified culture. That which is immortal in art is immortal for all.

Whether contemplating culture in national or supranational terms, then, Ivanov resists corrosive skepticism and apocalyptic despair; everywhere his thought moves toward a notion of continuity and stability in culture.

Ivanov, we may note in conclusion, was translating Dante's *Purgatory* at the time he was "corresponding" with Gershenzon in the other corner. The mood of Dante's *Purgatory* surely pervades Ivanov's whole outlook in the *Correspondence*. At the conclusion of the seventh letter he addresses these words to Gershenzon's desire to free himself from reason and the heavy burden of a disintegrating culture:

> Let us have faith in the life of the spirit, in holiness, in revelations, in the unknown saints around us, among the numberless united throng of striving souls, and continue hopeful on our way, looking neither aside nor behind, measuring not the road, ignoring the voices of weariness and sloth that speak to us of "poisoned blood" and "tired bones." One can be a joyful traveler on earth without leaving one's home town, and become poor in spirit without quite forgetting one's learning. We have long since decided that reason is a tool and a servant of the will; it is useful, just as the baser organs of the body are. The theories that pervade it, as you say, can be given away as we give away the books we no longer need, unless we let them repose in peace on the shelves of our libraries at home; but the vital sap of these theories and religions, their spirit and logos, their revelatory power—let us quaff them in deep drafts, for the sake of Goethe's 'old truth,' and thus, carefree and curious like strangers, pass by the countless altars and idols of historical culture, some neglected, sacrificing in abandoned places if we come upon imperishable flowers that, unseen by man, have grown from an ancient tomb.

There is a particular pathos in the closing lines of the last letter of *A Correspondence*. Here Gershenzon speaks of his relation to European culture as that of "a stranger acclimatized in an alien land." He senses the beauty and freshness of the "promised world," but writes wistfully: "Where is my homeland? I shall never see it, I shall die in foreign parts." As for Ivanov, Gershenzon rightfully perceives that poet's relation to culture as different from his own:

> You, dear friend, live in your own country; your heart is here, where your home is, and your sky is above this land. Your spirit is not divided, and this wholeness enchants me, because—whatever its provenance—it is itself a flower of that land which is our future common home. And therefore I think that in our Father's mansion the same quarters are readied for you and me, even if here on earth we sit stubbornly each in his own corner and argue about culture.

Notes

1. Vjacheslav Ivanov and M. O. Gershenzon, *Perepiska iz dvukh uglov* (Petrograd, 1921). I have availed myself of the English translation of this work: Vyacheslav Ivanovich Ivanov, Mikhail Osipovich Gershenzon, "*A Corner-to-Corner Correspondence*," trans. Gertrude Vakar, in Marc Raeff, ed., *Russian Intellectual History: An Anthology* (New York, 1966), pp. 372–401.

2. Mircea Eliade, "Mythologies of Memory and Forgetting," *History of Religions* II, no. 2 (Winter, 1963), 333.

3. François-René de Chateaubriand, *Oeuvres complètes de M. le Vicomte de Chateaubriand* (Paris, 1926–28), XI, 290.

4. F. M. Dostoevskij, "Pushkin," in *Sobranie sochinenij* (Moscow, 1958), X, 443, 444.

5. "Ne plakat' sladostno, kak pervyj iudej / Na rubezhe strany obetovannoj?" Turgenev's hero paraphrases two lines from a poem of A. A. Fet, "When My Dreams beyond the Limits of Past Days" (*Kogda moi mechty za gran'ju proshlykh dnej*, 1845).

6. In this connection see O. Deschartes's discussion of Gershenzon in her preface to V. Ivanov, M. Gershenson, *Correspondance d'un coin à l'autre* (Lausanne, 1979), pp. 25–37.

Ivanov's Letter to Charles Du Bos: Confessionalism and Christian Unity

Cyril Fotiev

Charles Du Bos (1888–1939), the French essayist, philosopher and religious writer, started publishing *A Correspondence from Two Corners* (*Perepiska iz dvukh uglov,* 1921) in his journal *Vigile* in 1931. He asked Vyacheslav Ivanov to comment on *A Correspondence* which had come into being ten years earlier.[1] Ivanov's answer in French is dated October 15, 1930, during the period of his life spent in Pavia where he taught at the Collegio Borromeo. Ivanov's letter to Charles Du Bos appeared as a supplement in various foreign-language translations of *A Correspondence;* the French original is included in Ivanov's *Collected Works.*[2]

The decade that had elapsed between *A Correspondence* and the Charles Du Bos letter was one of great trials for Ivanov. The exchange of views on the fate of culture between Gershenzon and Ivanov concluded with the letter written by Ivanov on July 19, 1920. On August 8th of that year his wife Vera Konstantinovna died—three days after her thirtieth birthday. In 1919 Ivanov had wanted to take her abroad for medical treatment but he was not granted permission to leave the country. Two years later a similar request was at first withheld but finally granted to the ailing Alexander Blok after interminable intercessions on the part of relatives and friends, including Maxim Gorky. By that time, however, the poet was too weak to travel. He died August 8, 1921. In the autumn of 1919, Ivanov, accompanied by his son and daughter, moved south to Baku where they spent nearly four years. Ivanov taught at the local university and defended his doctoral dissertation there. He and his children left the country on August 28, 1924. "I have come to Rome to die," said Ivanov upon his reunion with the Eternal City. He was destined to spend almost a quarter of a century in emigration and, contrary to the popular opinion that creative natures cannot survive outside their native habitat, his talent was to experience a rich and ripe fruition.

Ivanov's letter to Charles Du Bos thematically exceeds the framework of the French writer's original request. It bears witness to Ivanov's faithfulness to his fundamental belief in culture as a set values, "a Jacob's ladder, a hierarchy of reverences"; it was that culture from which Gershenzon (a loyal follower of Leo Tolstoy and through him of Jean-Jacques Rousseau) wanted to detach himself spiritually. Furthermore, the "Letter" contains an appraisal of the spiritual state of the Western world and of Russian society, an appraisal that sheds light on Ivanov's decision to enter the Catholic Church not only as an act of personal faith but as the completion of the spiritual path of a Christian and a Russian European who is true to the tenets of the brotherhood of man.

As an ardent advocate of culture—the dominant theme of his correspondence with Gershenzon—Ivanov imparts to it a deeper and, to quote his own words, a "more rigorous" justification in the light of the personal experience of the past ten years. For Ivanov culture involves memory as more than preservation but as a living thing to which we must be grateful for the achievements of man's creativity, that same creativity which Gershenzon perceives as a once exquisite and now worn-out garment. In his letter to Charles Du Bos, Ivanov urges that a distinction be made between memory as the custodian of values and anamnesis as the creative recalling and contemplation of the past.

To illustrate the essential impotence of memory, Ivanov invokes Ernest Renan's prayer on the Acropolis: the weary son of a skeptical culture was able to conjure up only shadows of the past. Essentially, recollection is an attempt at halting the passage of time—a passionate but inevitably doomed look back at the fading light of the past. It is no coincidence that anamnesis is not only a philosophical but also a liturgical concept: that which "was" in a chronological sense continues to *be* as an integral part of the reality of our *esse;* that

reality is reactualized and continually sustains us for it is not subject
to the changes of time. "Non-created Wisdom," writes Ivanov in
his "Letter," "teaches humanity to transform the means of universal
separation—distance, time, inert matter—into means of unity and
harmony, thus implementing God's eternal design of a perfect creation," and he adds: "any major culture is but a manifold expression
of a religious idea which constitutes its core." The term "Non-
created Wisdom" readily reflects Vladimir Solovyov's teaching on
Sophia as a universal, divine fundamental principle. This principle
was taken up by Pavel Florensky and subsequently affirmed by Sergey
Bulgakov who attempted to formulate it as a finished philosophical
and theological system. Summing up his reflections on the nature
of culture, Ivanov with the utmost clarity rejects the idea of a culture
created in secular categories; to him, no culture exists without a
"religious nucleus."

Referring to his perception of revolutionary and Soviet Russia,
Ivanov touches only briefly upon his personal fears, ordeals and
losses, for to him they were not decisive in shaping his attitude
toward the events that affected his country after 1917. In discussing
his own life and that of his intimates he ascribes his fortitude in the
face of hardships and disaster to "an ability of long-standing to be
humble and, at the same time, to meditate on retribution." Like
many of his contemporaries—witnesses of the revolution—Ivanov
contends that in terms of history, violence is subject to a limitation
in time. The "relatively benighted condition of the empirical state,"
as he called it, came to an end after he had left Soviet Russia; he
was then in a position to visualize the situation (in Herzen's words)
"from another shore": his own vision became discerning and keen
as he gained geographical distance from the "fires that consumed
the sanctuaries of my ancestors." It was with a newly "synthetic
perception" and an "integral awareness" that he came to view the
events of which he had been an eyewitness. Post-October Russia
emerged as a country which exposed to the world the fatal split in
its personality, while pre-October Russia had merely forged it into
specific historical forms. Thus Ivanov's Russia had outgrown herself
and ceased to reflect her own destiny; the nature of the disaster was

determined by her national characteristics. Ivanov contends that Russia's moral impact is not to be sought in the radiance of her golden nineteenth century which nurtured him but in her revolutionary madness. Russia's universal humanitarian mission consists either in saving all people by her monstrous sacrifice or "implicating them in a universal godlessness, in a crucial war against the Lamb of God which, in the past, she had loved more than anything else in the world." Ivanov insists that no one has the right to stay away from that confrontation and struggle: the very development of the spiritual destiny of Man calls on each thinking and conscientious person "to stand up *for* or *against* the One who is the sole object of hatred of the apostles of hate." The so-called "cause of the proletariat," according to Ivanov, is merely an alibi or a method, at best, the true and ultimate goal being "to *drown* out God, to pluck Him out of Man's heart."

This image of a theomachist and profoundly sinful Russia—despite her greatness in the sufferings imposed on her—is pitted against the image of the West after the First World War as it appears to Ivanov after an absence of over ten years. At that time, in 1930, the retribution for fratricidal war which was coming to the West by way of dictatorial regimes which the anemic and impotent democracies were unable to oppose was only looming in the shadows.

In taking the West to task, Ivanov dealt harshly with the characteristics that had already been attacked by A. I. Herzen, Leon Bloy, Konstantin Leontiev and Nikolay Berdyaev. There is the sham optimism of the West, the tolerance that generates skepticism and the rejection of any kind of exacting dogmatic appraisal or thought, the pursuit of all types of exotica and, last but not least, an ineradicable faith in humanitarian progress that brings Western society closer to the East European pattern of a "collective homunculus." The criticism so familiar to us merely aims at Western cultural and axiological schemes.

The "Letter" contains no political appraisals and offers no positive solutions (on the whole, these are absent from Ivanov's writings). He speaks of the "spiritual parochialism of the bourgeois world" while contrasting that world with the revolutionary *frenzy* as a sort of strangely compatible "diabolic counterpoint." Such an "apolitical attitude" does not, of course, imply tolerance toward any type of totalitarian regime on the part of Ivanov. There is a persistent rumor that Ivanov held some government post in Baku under the Soviets. Berdyaev once dropped the totally irresponsible remark that Ivanov had allegedly "adjusted" to fascist Italy. Both of these allegations are not founded on any evidence either in his writings or his biography and have been refuted by Olga Deschartes in her introduction to the first volume of Ivanov's *Collected Works* in Russian.

Examining the tragedy of his country and his people and appraising the Western world, Ivanov concludes that the world's only salvation is the "Boat of the Fisherman" and only the great Western Church is the ultimate stronghold against general collapse, apathy, and barbarization. Ivanov contends that on his path of spiritual development he was providentially steered to that haven.

As to his religious awareness, it had taken a long time for his faith, instilled in him by his pious and profoundly Orthodox mother, to take root on the ruins of his pagan humanism. A decisive moment in Ivanov's spiritual growth was his contact with Vladimir Solovyov (1853–1900), whom he calls "a great and holy man."

We are not sure when Vyacheslav Ivanov met Vladimir Solovyov, but it may safely be assumed that their relations reached a height in the summer of 1900. Ivanov and his wife Lydia Dmitrievna met with Solovyov in St. Petersburg and proceeded directly to the Kievo-Pechersky monastery after that meeting. It was there, in the spiritual center of Orthodoxy, and not in Vilnius or Czestochowa, that they finally and consciously joined the Church, this decision being inspired by the meeting with Vladimir Solovyov. Ivanov was more prepared for it than his wife. She was more impassioned in her rejection of what to her were "*patent* Christians" and a "trite and *ignoble* Church." These sentiments almost fully coincide with Alexander Blok's position vis-à-vis the Church, one which he maintained until his death. Vyacheslav and Lydia Ivanov sent Solovyov a telegram from Kiev, unaware that he was on his deathbed in Uzkoe, the Trubetskoy estate near Moscow.

That pilgrimage to the Kievan monastery raises doubts about

the assumption that it was Solovyov who in his late years prompted Ivanov to join the Catholic Church. By the 1890s Solovyov had gone a long way from the ideas expressed in his books *The Russian Idea* (1888) and *Russia and the Universal Church* (1889), published in French in Paris. This is not the place to go into Solovyov's theories of a theocratic utopia which provides for an imperial, autocratic Russia in alliance with the Chair of St. Peter to save humanity from national wars and the temptations of socialism. Solovyov's *The Russian Idea* is more relevant in our context: he sums up his old argument with the Slavophiles, accusing them of substituting nationalism for universal consciousness. Nationalism, in Solovyov's terms, is a selfish attitude assumed by the people, and he is merciless in his criticism of Imperial Russia for its policy in Poland and its oppression of Jews and Old Believers. Solovyov traces the roots back to the Byzantine heritage as it was adopted by Russia. He writes in *The Russian Idea:* "It is not in the West but in Byzantium that the original sin of national isolation and caesarian-papal absolutism initially introduced death into the social Body of Christ."

But after the storms of Russia had subsided and his theocratic utopia had lost impetus, Solovyov's views mellowed greatly. No doubt the reason lies, in part, in the adverse reaction to his theocratic utopia on the part of the hierarchy of the Catholic Church. Upon receiving *The Russian Idea* from Solovyov's friend and admirer Bishop Strossmeyer of Djakovo, Pope Leo XIII commented: "A beautiful idea! But except for a miracle it is impossible" (Bella idea! Ma fuori d'un miracolo è cosa impossibile).

Solovyov wrote to V. V. Rozanov in 1892[3]: "I am equally far removed from both the Latin and the Byzantine narrow-mindedness. My own religion of the Holy Spirit is broader and, at the same time, richer than all other religions." Solovyov converted to Catholicism but on his deathbed confessed and received Holy Communion from Father Belyaev, an Orthodox priest, although he could have asked for Father Tolstoy, a Russian Catholic.

A predecessor of Ivanov on his path towards Rome was P. Ya. Chaadaev (1794–1856); to him the reunification of the Church was a corollary of the mystery of history; he went even farther than

Solovyov in his fierce condemnation of Russia's spiritual and confessional isolation and in the description of its fatal consequences. In his book on Chaadaev (1908) M. O. Gershenzon is not altogether mistaken in reproaching Chaadaev for a certain inconsistency in not converting to Catholicism. In full awareness did Ivanov embark upon his solitary path towards reunification with the Catholic Church. In writing about that decision Olga Deschartes says that Ivanov "knew that he would not be understood, yet he was serene." In the "Letter" to Charles Du Bos, Ivanov stresses that nothing could have shaken his decision, not even the feeling of brotherly solidarity with, and loyalty to, the suffering Mother Church; the hierarchy of the Eastern Church had for centuries been fostering in their flock profound suspicions of Rome. Ivanov sternly refers to that hierarchy as "inadequate shepherds, wheeler-dealers, enemies of theocratic unification." But Ivanov must have realized that no hierarchy could account for such deep-rooted distrust of Rome in the Eastern Christians, although he chose to pass over this issue in silence: it is not the fruit of indoctrination but the memory of multiple waves of a cruel march over the centuries against Eastern Christians by the state, the Church, and the military forces of the West.

Ivanov is right in his perception of the spiritual state of the Russian émigrés of the 1920s and early 1930s. By and large, as he points out in his "Letter," the Russian émigrés zealously cherished the familiar confessional forms that identified them with the idea of the fatherland, while at the same time they displayed a total indifference to the religious vision and the fate of the people whose hospitality they enjoyed. All émigré churches, built by political exiles and refugees in the poor neighborhoods of West European cities, seemed to carry an invisible slogan: "The only thing left to us of Russia is the Church." Even Russian exiles who were not really closely committed to the Church yearned for it or, rather, for the comforting beauty of its religious rites. Although this is true of most Russian exiles—who were refugees rather than political émigrés—the intellectual elite and the theologians took a different position. Surrounded as they were by distrust or, at best, by the indifference of the overwhelming majority of the Russian émigrés, people like Florovsky, Frank, Berdyaev, Bulgakov and dozens of others were not only deeply committed to the problems of Christian reunification, and keenly aware of the spiritual challenge which confronted the Russian diaspora, but they were also the advocates and inspirers of what has become known as the ecumenical movement. It is unfortunate that Ivanov does not mention them, even though during his years in Russia he was close to both Bulgakov and Berdyaev. The Russian theologians and philosophers in exile had raised the issue of Christian reunification as a vital problem of our time in the consciousness of the Orthodox churches on the Balkan Peninsula. These theologians wanted to see the Church reunited, but by a doctrinal consensus which had yet to be achieved. Ivanov's path was not theirs; his reproach to them for their adamant refusal to grasp the meaning of Christ's words about the rock of the Church, the sole, universal, and apostolic Church, was groundless. The alleged obstinate unwillingness to understand Christ's words (Mathew 16: 18–19) was, in fact, a commitment to a traditional interpretation more ancient than the centralist and monarchist idea of Russian primacy.

Ivanov knew that his entrance into the Catholic Church was his personal answer to the tragic division of the Christian world: even to him it was merely the "anticipation" of the one Church which would be universal:

> The holiness of another faith
> Makes the proud heart humble,
> The radiance of promise shines
> Over a unified and universal Church . . .   [SS, III, 592]

To Ivanov it was not a break with Orthodoxy, so close to his heart: he had, in his own mind, not crossed the line of demarcation that separated him from his own Church by merging with the sacredness of the Western Church, a merger which his friend and inspirer Vladimir Solovyov visualized in his late years as lying beyond the boundaries of history, as an eschatological event.

Notes

1. *The Correspondence from Two Corners* (*Perepiska iz dvukh uglov*) between Vyacheslav Ivanov and M. D. Gershenzon (1869–1925) dates back to June/ July 1920.
2. See *SS*, II, 418–32.
3. See *Letters*, vol. III, pp. 43–44.

Recurrent Motifs in Ivanov's Work
Dmitri Ivanov

One of my earliest recollections goes back to the 16th of November, 1917, to Moscow and to our apartment on the Boulevard Zubovsky. I was five at the time. My father was standing, perhaps he had just come into the room; I ran toward him and threw my arms around his knees. I looked up; he seemed so tall above me. I began solemnly to recite what had composed itself, I know not how, in my little head:

> Everything passed as in a distant dream . . .
>
> Vse proshlo dalekim snom . . .

My father, who always gave the closest and often the most respectful attention to what we had to say to him, was astonished. A few hours later (it was always at night that he wrote) he took the phrase I had communicated to him and wrote his poem "Vremja" (Time):

> Everything passed as in a distant dream;
> The shore of former days sank
> And melted like snow
> > In the boundless and the nocturnal . . .
>
> Or did our ships depart
> Silently into the distance,
> Trusting their free flight to the wind?
> > The shore began to float—
>
> Where, in the fog beyond the stern,
> Lulled in Ariadnean
> Slumber, widow-life
> > Is alive—

Where, beyond the hazy edges,
Seized by slumber,
Bygone life quietly awaits
    The bridegroom . . .

Have we not from our treacheries
Forged captivity,
What the mortal race
    Calls Time?

Time, like a wind, whirls us away,
Divisively divides us—
It will take into its maw its serpent tail
    And die.

Vse proshlo dalekim snom;
V bespredel'nom i nochnom
Utonul, izmlel, kak sneg,
    Prezhnij breg . . .

Ili nashi korabli
Tikhomolkom v dal' ushli,
Vverja vetru vol'nyj beg?
    Pòplyl breg,—

Gde,—v tumane, za kormoj,—
Ariadninoj dremoj
Usyplennaja, zhiva
    Zhizn'-vdova,—

Gde,—za mglistoju kajmoj,—
Obujannaja dremoj,
Zhizn' bylaja zhdet, tikha,
    Zhenikha . . .

Ne iz nashikh li izmen
My sebe skovali plen,
Tot, chto Vremenem zovet
    Smertnyj rod?

Vremja nas, kak veter, mchit,
Razluchaja razluchit,—
Khvost zmeinyj v past' vberet
I umret.   {SS, III, 544}

The images evoked are familiar already in the poems of *Pilot Stars*
(*Kormchie zvezdy*, 1903). Again, the boat, the river bank, the sea are
parts of the key images in *Svetomir,* the narrative on which Vyacheslav
Ivanov was still working on the day of his death. And behind these
images are the constant identifications: ocean-eternity; ocean-birth;
earth-death; earth-a bitter dream:

Ocean and Earth—as birth and death
And Earth—a bitter dream.

Okean i Tverd'—kak rozhden'e i smert';
I Zemlja—o, gor'kij son.   {SS, I, 597}

And finally, the call, the invitation, the order:

"Remember, remember," comes the call from the deaf
wave . . .

"Vspomni, vspomni," zvuchit za glukhoj volnoj . . .
                                            {SS, II, 306}

Memory is one of the major themes throughout Ivanov's work.
    The boat is the bond between sea and land, between eternity
and the kingdom of death. It is in the boat that the Bridegroom
will arrive, for whom the widow-Life waits. It is in the boat (in
Svetomir) that the Virgin Mary passes by. Time, redoubtable as the
wind, is the prison that shuts us in, separates us, whirls us away:
"Time, like a wind, whirls us away," writes Ivanov in 1917. And
it is like an echo of what he wrote in Athens in 1903:

Like a dead whirlwind, horses carry us far off,
Time whirls us away. [1]

Kak mertvyj vikhr' nesut nas glukho koni,
Nas vremja mchit . . .   {SS, I, 699}

The prison where Time detains us,[1] where the soul, deprived
of the unity to which it aspires, is condemned to its solitude: this
is the experience that the poet has himself lived, the experience
which is on the edge of the long narration of his life that is his
poetic work: "My life lies open in my songs. . . ."

As he emerged from adolescence the young man suffered a
profound sickness. The religious fervor of childhood gave way
"abruptly and without sorrow to a total atheism." At the same time
he felt called, like many of his companions, to the revolutionary
struggle. One problem troubled him, it is true: "terrorism as a
means of social revolution"—and after long and painful hesitation,
he opted against terrorism. Meanwhile, he remained a militant atheist. He gave lessons in atheism "by word and in writing" to one of
his most loved friends. But "my atheism cost me dear," Ivanov
recounts, "its consequence was a pessimism of spirit which weighed
on me for many years, a passionate desire for death which I sang in
my poems of that period and even a naïve attempt at suicide . . ."
[SS, II, 14]. The crisis led to an increasingly distressing state of
mind, a feeling of spiritual isolation of the individual trapped in
his closed universe, paralyzed by his inability to communicate, by
the illusory character of the world as it presented itself to him:

> Where am I? Where am I?
>   I am thirsting after myself
> I am in the depth
>   Of my mirrors.

> Gde ja? Gde ja?
>   Po sebe ja
> Vozalkal!
> Ja—na dne svoikh zerkal.   [SS, I, 741]

Such was his sense of the metaphysical solitude of man enclosed
within the insuperable limits of individuality, of his "cell" as Ivanov
used then to say. He was incapable of perceiving the reality of the
outside world and he doubted his own reality. Later, analyzing Dos-

toevsky's characters, he spoke of their "idealism with no way out" (*beziskhodnyj idealizm*).

The young man found himself in Rome when an event took place that provoked a salutary crisis and a radical change of spirit. This was his meeting in 1893 with Lydia Dmitrievna Zinovieva. Ivanov was to recall it in his *Autobiographical Letter.*

> This love took complete possession of me, went on to grow without ceasing and to deepen spiritually. . . . The one through the other, each of us has found himself, and more than just himself. I would say that we found God. Our meeting had been like a powerful storm in spring, Dionysiac, after which everything in me renewed itself, blossomed again, again grew young. The poet awoke in me for the first time and became conscious of himself, freely and strongly; not only in me but in her also. One can affirm without exaggeration that all our life together since then has been for both of us an almost unbroken period of inspiration, of tension, of spiritual ardor {*SS,* II, 20}.

The life of Lydia Dmitrievna ended abruptly in 1907. "What that meant for me," Ivanov writes, "he for whom my poetry is not made up of lifeless hieroglyphics understands; he knows why I live and what makes me live {*SS,* II, 21}.

Her presence made this world which, he thought, was illusory and spectral, suddenly real. The poet "mute and captive" until then was coming to know the word "thou" and thou was the first reality; more real, it seemed, than the uncertain reality of his captive ego. The same change was taking place with the "other."

"The one through the other, each of us has found himself." Later, Ivanov in his book on Dostoevsky was to analyze at length this mutation; this change in the spirit that the novelist used to call *proniknovenie* and which might be translated as "intuition" or "identification of oneself with the other."

> It is a transcension of the subject. In this state of mind we recognize the other *Ego* not as our object but as another subject. It is therefore not a mere peripheral extension of the bounds of in-

dividual consciousness but a complete inversion of its normal system of coordinates. . . . The transcension finds its expression in the unconditional acceptance by our full will and thought, of the other existence—in "Thou art." If this acceptance of the other is complete; if with and in this acceptance the whole substance of my own existence is rendered null and void (*exinanitio, kénosis*), then the other-existence ceases to be an alien *Thou;* instead, the *Thou* becomes another description of my *Ego*. "Thou art" then no longer means "Thou art recognized by me as existing" but "I experience thy existence as my own, and in thy existence I again find myself existing." *Es, ergo sum.* [2]

"The one through the other, each of us has found himself," Ivanov wrote, adding "and more than just himself; I would say that we found God." Through the experience of the reality of the other and of himself, man comes to postulate the existence of God.

Humanity is a multitude of beings and the reality of each is authenticated by the other. But just because each one is a real, independent universe, all these beings together postulate a still more real reality, a unifying principle which contains all *I* and all *Thou*. God alone "warrants the reality of my realism, the actuality of my acts and realizes for the first time what I vaguely feel as essential in me and outside of me" [*SS*, II, 21]. When man says: "Thou art, therefore I am" to each being, he says it, through them, to the Absolute Being.

The real meeting of two beings takes place only if the one and the other find God in their own selves. To be is to be together. The Absolute Being—God—is there as a "third party," as the contriver of unity:

You were the third, between the two,
    Hidden Spirit.

Tret'im ty stojal mez dvukh,
    Tajnyj dukh!   [*SS*, III, 211]

Saying *es—ergo sum* to each other and at the same time to God is the kernel of what Ivanov will later call *sobornost'*.

This finding of God again in oneself, at the same time as the rediscovery of the "other" and of the reality of the world, was the consequence of a profound mutation of the spirit—its outcome was abrupt and overwhelming—and to be sure, not at all the result of theoretical reasoning. Yet for a long time and at a different level, another mutation was brewing. A new teaching appeared: that of Friedrich Nietzsche. Under his influence Ivanov dedicated himself to the study of the history of religions and in particular the religion of Dionysus. In fact, from childhood his heart's desire had been to explore the Greek spirit, a desire long repressed on account of his long apprenticeship in Roman history under Mommsen and Hirschfeld (an apprenticeship culminating in his Latin thesis, recently reprinted).[3]

It was not a matter solely of scientific and abstract interest, though his philosophical and historical studies were very strict. An insistence within himself urged the young scholar on. The spiritual crisis persisted; the precepts of Zarathustra only aggravated it. He felt that he was freeing himself from the appeal of Nietzsche in the sphere of religious consciousness only by going more deeply into the message that came to him from Greece.

> The study of the Dionysiac cults actually estranged him from Nietzsche: Nietzsche, having discovered Dionysus, saw in him Christianity's antithesis. Ivanov, the admirer of Dostoevsky and Vladimir Solovyov's disciple, showed that the religion of Dionysus "was a stream that poured all its waters into the Christian ocean." He showed that the Dionysiac religion, as it is revealed in its true nature (and especially in the Orphic mysteries) is essentially a stepping-stone on the path of Christianity—"the Old Testament of the Gentiles."[4]

At the British Museum in London and then during a long sojourn in Athens, he collected material for what was to be, in 1903, his series of lectures in Paris and later his book, *The Hellenic Religion of the Suffering God*.[5] He retraced through the metamorphoses and the facets of the myth the various aspects of the passion, the death and the palingenesis of the god. He studied the orgiastic cults, the identification of the follower with the sacrificial victim and of the victim with the god himself. Through the Dionysiac ecstasy, the Ego rescued from the prison of the self reached a reality that transcended it, succeeded in "crossing the limits, in consummating the destruction and annulment of the individuality." It was the Orphic *kénosis,* the void, the death of oneself, the initial impulse of every authentic religious experience. But, as in the myth, the death of the god-victim opened the way to a new birth, the annihilation of Ego was a "creative" or "constructive" death—*zizhditeljnaja smert'*—and emerging into a life renewed. As in the Dionysiac myths that Ivanov explored, death and life, suffering and joy, are in his poems in constant dialectic, on intimate terms.

Thus the great upheavals of personal life were on a par with his exploration of the myth, an exploration that was at one and the same time exegesis, interpretation and verification through intimate experience in his innermost spirit.

> Always, and always in a different way, Ivanov conveys the same Dionysiac myth. Whether he sings of Spring or love, of Persephone or Orpheus, he invariably celebrates the oneness of suffering and exultation, of death and new birth [*SS*, I, 66].

Myth and symbol have fundamental significance in Ivanov's terminology. Let us confine ourselves now to recalling the brief definition that the author himself made: "myth is the instrument of imaginative knowledge of the supernatural realities; it is an objective truth about being. The true myth is never either invention or allegory; it is the hypostasis of a reality or energy." For Ivanov, as Olga Deschartes writes,

> a symbol is a sign or a signification. It does not stand for or express any single definite idea. Otherwise it would be merely a hieroglyph, and a combination of several symbols would be "graphic allegory," a communication in code which needs to be read with the help of a key. In different spheres of consciousness the same symbol has different meanings. Like a ray of light a symbol travels through all the levels of being and all the spheres of consciousness;

on each level it signifies different entities and in each sphere it fulfills a new function. The symbol, like a descending ray, appears at each point of intersection with each sphere of consciousness as a sign whose meaning is figuratively yet completely revealed by a corresponding myth. Thus, the snake has a symbolic relation both to the earth and to incarnation, to sex and to death, to sight and to knowledge, to temptation and to illumination. It represents different entities in different myths. Yet the whole body of snake-symbolism and every one of its different meanings are linked together by the great cosmogonic myth, in which each aspect of the snake-symbol has its place in a hierarchy of the planes of the divine all-pervading unity. A myth is the objective truth about entity; it is the key to the imaginative cognition of extrasensory entities. A true myth is far from being fiction or allegory; it is the hypostasis of a certain entity or "energy." In remote ages when myths were genuinely created, they answered the questions posed by experiential reason in that they represented *realia in rebus*. (Not all myths, however, are collective in origin; some derive from a mystical vision, and have become popularized.) By disclosing symbols, i.e. signs or another reality in the reality of surrounding objects, art makes our reality significant.[6]

The dialectic of I and Thou which is a constant motif in Ivanov's works appears not only in the relations between two beings. It exists as well within man himself. And here a new myth, that of Psyche, initiates Ivanov's research into the psychology of the religious experience. The name Psyche echoes throughout his poetry and is the starting point of two basic writings: *Ty esi,* of 1907, taken up again and elaborated in German in 1933 under the title *Anima.*[7]

Experiences of an ecstatic nature, Ivanov thinks, depend on the feminine element in us. They take place when Psyche, the Soul, tries to become free of the speculative and conscious Mind, always ready to keep it in tutelage. Psyche rejects the tyrannical power of the Mind; in her partner, who is nevertheless con-substantial with her, she does not recognize, or no longer recognizes, the divine Guest whom she has lost and for whom she seeks in vain [*SS,* III, 264 ff.].

Eighteen years after he wrote *Ty esi,* on reading in Rome *Parabole* in which Paul Claudel described, in terms astonishingly close to his, the conflict within our being between *Anima* and *Animus,* between Psyche in us and the spirit of knowledge and reasoning, Ivanov was very happy to find this chance meeting-point. It was the same when he read Carl Gustav Jung, in the same period, though Jung's approach was fundamentally different. Exploring the complex proceedings that go on in our ego, Ivanov takes up his position on the narrow line of demarcation between psychological analysis of religious phenomenon and the description of mystical experiences that this phenomenon implies. The dialectic between Psyche, *Anima,* the soul, and the Mind, *Animus,* is "the fundamental dogma of mystical psychology," as Ivanov was glad to read in Henri Bremond's *Prière et Poésie* when he was rewriting *Ty esi* in Rome.

This dialectic springs from the tragically dissociated state of our person. *Anima,* Ivanov says, knows that she must find again the supreme good that she has lost—something which is the best part of herself and is no longer herself, something divine. She feels lost, exhausted, captive; Ariadne abandoned, she waits for her Betrothed, the Friend who will come to set her free. She thinks she recognizes him in *Animus* but he betrays his mission, ignores the messages. Then, as "a wild Maenad," she rises up against him. *Cor Ardens* contains many poems evoking the Maenads and their tragic excesses.

Things are quite different in the reasoning and conscious part of our ego. *Animus* drives *Anima* violently out of his inner life although her participation is indispensable. Without her, he cannot reach the divine and transcendent Being in him. He is doomed therefore to an idealistic contemplation of himself in a world that seems to him to be constructed according to his own image. Or else he attempts, by a magical effort, to bring forth his double and thus obtain, through a kind of gnosis, knowledge of the transcendent world; knowledge that is illusory, however, without the presence of *Anima* who alone is capable of bringing about the change; the necessary transcension, so that the miracle may take place. And Ivanov refers to St. Paul saying in effect, What good is knowledge if I have not love?[8]

It is, in fact, a redeeming miracle which *Anima* awaits. It takes place through ecstasy. Then the soul plunges into the depths of its original self—its *samost'*, according to the expression used by Ivanov in Russian, its *Urselbst*, according to the term used in the German version of his text—these depths that constitute the third and most secret element of our selves. There, the soul—exhausted, helpless and venerating—discovers a reality against which man—were he the bearer of all human virtualities and realities—can no longer rise, and which he cannot claim for his ideal universe.

To transcend oneself, to cross the last frontiers of one's own immanence, means meeting God in the holy of holies of oneself, meeting the Absolute Being, essentially different from man though dwelling in him and united with him through an ineffable communication—God, the transcendent principle of Being. We find Him within our selves but He is not our self; He is the "Guest" who visits us, the Father, to whom we can only say: Thou art. Ivanov elaborates in *Anima* the Christian teaching on the life of the Holy Trinity in man's soul.

"How it is possible to reach knowledge of the absolute transcendence of God through an interior experience?" Ivanov asks himself. "Does not the latter, by definition, have its limits in the contents immanent within the human mind and does it not serve, therefore, only to know itself? That is what speculative reason (in the sense of Kant's theory of cognition) must ask itself. But we are exploring a field in which *Animus* is no longer all-powerful . . ." and Ivanov recalls the *noūs katharós* of the Neoplatonists.

The way in which the soul can know the transcendent is the experience of mystical death. This is not the delight of losing oneself in cosmic life, in the all animated by the divine breath. This loss of oneself can, it is true, interrupt the sense of our individual existence and of our will for a time but it does not deprive us of the feeling of the reality in which all things are plunged. It is different if we reach this region of the life of the soul in which everything that our phenomenological observation had been able to distinguish "disappears in the dark ocean of an all-powerful reality that suppresses all forms and washes away all the signs that the world has drawn on the quicksands of the soul" [*SS*, III, 284 ff.].

Is this new reality, one that completely wipes out preceding existence and can be compared only to death, still the same as the one intercepted by our phenomenological examination? Before it the soul feels incapable of continuing to exist; it sinks into a deep nothingness—in its death struggle it has to obey the order: "Die and become" (Goethe's *stirb und werde*). How else could it come about, the new birth to which it aspired so ardently and whose other name is resurrection? From antiquity on, in fact, mystical initiations were considered an anticipation of death.

A good part of Ivanov's book on Dostoevsky is dedicated to the metaphysical aspects of the writer's "novel-tragedies." Ivanov attributes the acute sense of the ontological destiny of his characters beyond their empirical vicissitudes to the psychical upheaval Dostoevsky experienced on the scaffold; an experience that reflects and recalls, in a way, this discovery of God in us, which he describes in *Anima*. Dostoevsky, Ivanov thinks, was initiated into "higher reality" on the scaffold:

> He underwent a sudden and decisive transformation of the soul—a beatified death, followed by the unexpected gift of divine mercy to his corporeal shell. The years of forced labor and exile were the swaddling bands tightly swathed about the new-born child, bringing about the extinction of his outer personality, of his stubborn self-consciousness that was needed to consummate his resurrection. At the place of execution, in those moments of preparation for death, he felt that his soul had overrun death and knew itself to be alive: indeed living more intensely than ever before, in a life already beyond the threshold of the grave. The personality was thus forcibly extricated from the conditions of his earlier existence and became, for the first time, conscious of its own true substance, revealed behind the receding vision of external things; behind the wrappings falling from the embodied spirit. Like a midwife, that hour seems to have brought forth from limbo the inner-Ego slumbering in the depths of the soul's being. . . . From then onwards all the spiritual doing and striving of Dostoevsky were sustained by the inspiration of the newly-created man within, for whom much that we regard as transcendent came to be in some way

immanent in his being—just as, conversely, some part of what is given to us directly was for him now removed to an exterior region.[9]

Here it is: the "constructive death," (*zizhditelnaja smert'*), the death-midwife, that brings forth new lives, which we find so often in Ivanov's poems.

By saying "Thou art" to God man chooses Being. But there may be—for man is free—the suicidal will to oppose this existential necessity that is faith in God. Then we have flight to non-Being—rebellion. The soul is called to make this fundamental choice even before the beginning of its empirical existence. It is this prior choice, this *Prolog im Himmel,* that underlies Dostoevsky's novels, according to Ivanov. It is this choice that foreshadows man's empirical decisions. In his novels Dostoevsky

> lays bare the most deeply hidden tragedy contained in the dualism of necessity and free will as components of human destiny. He leads us, so to speak, to the loom of life and shows us how the threads of both intersect and are enmeshed at every crossing of warp and woof. His metaphysical interpretation of events is implicit in his psycho-empirical interpretation. The main direction of the path that each individual takes is laid down for him by the inmost will—whether resting in God or opposing itself to God.[10]

The long poem *Man* (*Chelovek*) evokes this *Prolog im Himmel* and is the cosmic history of the world. It opens with this first "Thou art" said to God and also with the suicidal rejection. In the series of lyrics—of great freedom and perfection of form—the poet narrates the long dramatic confrontation between the creature and God. God would like to confirm the divine filiation that Adam is entitled to, provided Adam recognizes in God his father and says to Him: "Thou art."

It is impossible to summarize this complex work here (Pavel Florensky intended to write a commentary on it but the war and the Revolution put an end to that). The main theme of *Chelovek* is the one at the center of Ivanov's whole Weltanschauung, which he some-

times called "monanthropic." In it man assesses and assumes the
whole of history:

> There is only God and you: two of you.
> You alone have been made by the Creator.
> Everything heavenly, earthly
> Is you before the face of God.

> Est' lish' Bog—i ty: vas dvoe.
> Sozdan ty odin Tvortsom.
> Vse nebesnoe, zemnoe—
> Ty pred Bozhiem litsom.   [SS, III, 238]

But man said "No" to God. The descendants of Adam, divided
by hatred, suicide and fratricide, rise up against one another. Mother
Earth, sullied and offended, groans and calls in vain for Adam, the
liberator, whom she awaits since all creatures were conceived by God
and brought out of nothingness for him and since he, man, is responsible for them.

> Adam, Mother-Earth groans
>   For you, the liberator . . .
> But man does not remember
>   The sole aim of all things.

> Adame, Mat'-Zemlja stenaet,
>   Osvoboditel', po tebe.
> A chelovek ne vspominaet . . .
>   O tselogo edinoj tseli.   [SS, III, 233]

Yet, despite the division inflicted on them by the two principles of
separation, Time and Space, despite the hatred that set them against
one another on the two banks of one river, the enemies are actually
only doubles, for "one Adam lives in them."

> When will the enemies see
> From the two banks of one river
> That they hate each other
> As only doubles hate,
> That one Adam lives in them?

Kogda zh protivniki uvidjat
s dvukh beregov odnoj reki
Chto tak drug druga nenavidjat
Kak nenavidjat dvojniki;
Chto v nikh edinyj zhiv Adam?   [SS, III, 233]

The poet constantly feels this substantial unity in spite of the
countless individualities into which it has been broken. In a poem
written in 1919 during one of the most tragic periods of his life,
physically and psychically, Ivanov tells how he goes into a house
where an old woman who has died of hunger is being buried. In
this dead woman he recognizes himself. The priest who is censing
the corpse is again himself; and again he is the visitor who has
entered by chance and to whom a candle is handed. Pilate, showing
the Man to the crowd full of hatred, is again himself, as is the
fearful Galilean who watches the execution from a distance, and the
Roman, respectful of the gods, on duty near the cross.

An old woman who has starved to death,
I lie under the white shroud.
A priest, I cense the incense of the Spirit
Over the yellow mummy.

And a stranger who has happened by,
I hold a candle distractedly in my fingers;
I look perplexedly
At the bones under the withered skin . . .

To the joy of the brutish crowd
I lead out the Man
And with a white hand,
Pontius Pilate, I point to him.

And—a fearful Galilean—
I watch the execution from a distance.
And—a god-fearing Roman,
I superstitiously guard the cross.

Otgolodavshaja starukha
Pod belym savanom lezhu.
Svjashchennik fimiamom Dukha
Nad zheltoj mumiej kazhu.

I svechku, chuzhenin zakhozhij,
V perstakh rassejannykh derzhu;
Na kosti pod issokhshej kozhej
V nedoumenii gljazhu . . .

Tolpe na radost' ozvereloj
Ja Cheloveka vyvozhu
I na nego rukoju beloj,
Pilat Pontijskij ukazhu.

I—galilejanin puglivyj—
Za kaznju izdali slezhu.
I—rimljanin bogoljubivyj
Krest sueverno storozhu . . .   [SS, III, 233, 237]

The great collective task of humanity and the personal one of
every man is to reunite in the one Man who will recognize Himself
definitively as the Son of God, "and we know that Adam, when he
achieves his supreme goal, will remember himself, will live again
his whole life in his memory; he will remember himself in each of
his faces, going up through the reverse path of the times, up to the
threshold of Eden, and then he will remember his native Eden."
Then time will not exist any more.[11] But today this is only a fleeting
intuition. We are still living under the sign of the forgetfulness of
unity.

"Man, caught up in his fratricidal struggle, does not remember
the sole aim of all things." Man has forgotten. Time, Space, Matter
have become for him instruments of separation and the ransom of
non-Being which he has preferred to Being.

When we look behind us into the past, we see the night at the
end and we try vainly to distinguish shapes similar to remem-
brances. Then we experience the exhaustion of spirit that we call

forgetfulness. Non-Being is directly revealed to our conscience in forgetfulness.[12]

But man has a weapon against time and a remedy against forgetfulness: it is memory. Just as forgetfulness is non-Being, memory is the principle of Being. If God forgets us, we cease to exist. Memory is "the gauge of immortality," affirms the poet in "The Trees" [SS, III, 533].

Memory is the creative act by which God maintains in Him every image of the Creation, such as he conceived it and such as it must become. The gift of memory infused in us reveals the reality of the world . . . awakes in us the remembrance of the Soul of the world.[13]

Memory warrants the reality and the freedom of our personality. Memory realizes the true community (sobornost') of men because it roots it in absolute reality. Memory is the ecumenical energy (sobornaja energija). It establishes the union between living and dead. "Memory conditions our thinking, our knowledge, and the knowledge of our knowledge. Ivanov's gnoseology is an anamnesiology."[14] A Latin formula, whose words suddenly resounded in Ivanov's spirit, sums up this intuition: quod non est, debet esse; quod est, debet fieri; quod fit, erit.

The Creation that God calls into being is first in God's memory. In order to realize itself perfectly in God it must become and, during its existence, find again its image. In the divided world man is imprisoned in his individuality, but in him and around him "the permanent action of the infused memory" goes on. This action is the manifestation of the Word in time. It is a veiled manifestation that man becomes aware of by discovering the absolute reality behind the phenomena and learning their symbolic language: a realibus ad realiora [SS, II, 638 and 657]. In the history of humanity the ways of this internal revelation are different according to the different stages of mankind's spiritual evolution. Every great "spiritual event" illuminated by them announces and foreshadows the absolute revelation, the unique incarnation in history of God become Man, Christ.

In his letter to Charles Du Bos, Ivanov wrote:

> When talking about the great cycles of world history, what we usually call "general culture" . . . is, in my opinion, essentially based on the permanent action of the infused memory through which the Uncreated Wisdom leads humanity to transform the instruments of natural division—Space, Time, Matter—into instruments of union and harmony, to bring them back to their destination in conformity with the divine image of the perfect Creation. Every great culture, as an emanation of Memory, is the incarnation of a fundamental spiritual event; and the latter is an act and a particular aspect of the Word's revelation in history. That is why every great culture can only be a plural expression of a religious idea which is its basic element. The dissolution of religion is therefore an unmistakable symptom of the extinction of memory [SS, III, 428].

Quod fit, erit. The eschatological end of all becoming is in the recomposition of the initial unity. In no way does this mean that Ivanov—on a historical plane—believes in an optimistic evolutionism. Like man in his own self, culture always oscillates between memory and forgetfulness, between the will towards Being and the anguish of Nothing.

The action of memory and the quest for Nothing determine man's attitude towards culture. Culture, as man himself, is antinomian. It can be anamnesis, an ascension to the lost unity, to the absolute reality, a door always open to freedom. It can, on the other hand, enclose man in the circle of its phenomena. It then becomes "a system of subtle constrictions." Our belief in the absolute—which is culture no more—or our rejection of the absolute, depends on our inner freedom (that is to say our life) or on our inner enslavement to culture. [15]

We have dealt so far with problems of cognition, the epistemological meaning of "Thou art," in the sphere of relations between the ego and the external world, as well as within our ego. The tragic dissociation of the person led, as we have seen, either to the final wrench, the desire for non-Being, or to the discovery, in the depths of our being, of a principle that is at once transcendent and closely linked with us. But what is this transcendent principle? The exploration of Dionysian cults, the multiple variations of the religion of God the Victim and the suffering God, revealed to Ivanov the processes of religious experiences, ecstasy as a means of going beyond the limits of individuality. Study of the religion of Dionysus supplied a "how," a method, a mystical way but not a "what." Orgiastic cults initiated the faithful into the tragic sense of the world through a rupture, an initial fault. They showed them God the Victim whose sacrifice took place by a common will and encompassed the whole of creation. They celebrated the passion, the death, and the return of God, but these celebrations were only a rite; the palingenesis of God was only an appearance, starting over and over again. It could not be otherwise because the suffering God was only a symbol; he was not the concrete, real, unique and irreplaceable person that Christ would be.

"The religion of Dionysus," Ivanov wrote in *The Hellenic Religion of the Suffering God,* "was like ploughed land waiting to be fertilized by Christianity; it needed it as its final issue, the last word that it had not uttered." This last word was the Word become flesh, Christ.

Christ, a concrete person, unique and irreplaceable, was always present in Ivanov's soul. (The only time I remember seeing him with tears in his eyes was during a conversation about Christ). As a child he dedicated poems to Him; during his period of militant atheism he remained, nevertheless, deeply attracted to Him. When he emerged from his solipsist crisis, he found himself—spontaneously and naturally—a Christian.

Return to Christ meant return to the Church.[16] Christ is there where *sobornost'* is, i.e. where a real meeting of two beings takes place and where God attends as "a third party," as the contriver of unity. Church is the mystery of "universal love and of free union in Christ." Christ alone, in his human and divine reality, can accomplish, Ivanov believed, what our divided soul aspires to and what the whole Creation, for which man is responsible and whose spokes-

man he is, also aspires to. When the Son of Man dies His redeeming
death, the whole Earth—Mother Earth—is Golgotha; death, we are
again reminded, becomes birth and the grave leads to real life:

> The Tomb has become the womb of new births.
> "Not Earth is your mother, children, but Golgotha . . ."

> Lono rozhdenij stalo grob.
> "I ne Zemlja,—deti, vam mat'—Golgofa . . ." [SS, I, 556]

Christ is the Betrothed awaited by Psyche in us and by the whole
earth. Only Christ, the new Adam, brings about this reunification
of the whole of mankind, for "in each one the Word has become
flesh and dwells with everyone and resounds in a different way in
each one, but the word of each one finds an echo in all the others
and all are one free consent—for all are the same Word." Through
the peripeties of human life, *sobornost'* mystically continues its work
on earth. The eschatological aim is to transform all humanity into
the mystical Body of Christ, the Church. When this is accomplished,
Adam will be restored to his initial unity.

Then he will no longer remain in the "humiliation of the crea-
ture"; for having, through the mouth of Christ, said "Yes" to his
Father, he will again find his divine filiation definitively. The poem
Chelovek ends with this promise to Adam:

> Rest assured in your grateful heart:
> God does not want the man created
> By Him to remain for ever
> In the humiliation of the creature.

> Vedaj v serdtse blagodarnom:
> Bog ne khochet chtob navek
> Prebyval v smiren'e tvarnom
> Bogozdannyj chelovek.   [SS, III, 238]

Thus, not only will the re-establishment of unity take place one day
but what the Fathers of the Church call *theosis:* the divinization of
man, the assumption in God of His human nature. That is an
eschatological hope, but the transfiguring action of the mystical

Church is already proceeding. It is visible only to pure eyes, to those who are—as the Virgin confided to Seraphim of Sarov—"members of our family."

Where this meeting between God and creation takes place, Paradise blooms on earth. This secret Paradise around us—an idea familiar to Dostoevsky, a belief dear to the Russian people—is one of the great themes of Ivanov's last work, *The Tale of Prince Svetomir.* Another major motif appears then: Sophia, though Ivanov very rarely mentions it in his theoretical writings. "Sophia is there," he usually confined himself to saying, "where Logos touches the earth."[17]

Notes

1. On space and time in Ivanov see O. Deschartes, in V. Ivanov and M. Gerschenson, *Correspondance d'un coin à l'autre* (Lausanne, 1979), p. 165.

2. *Dostoevsky* (New York, 1971), p. 26.

3. *De societatibus vectigalium publicorum populi romani Petropoli, MDCCLXI.* Reprint L'Erma di Bretschneider (Rome, 1972).

4. O. Deschartes, "Vyacheslav Ivanov," *Oxford Slavonic Papers,* V (1954), 43.

5. The lectures were first published in *Novy put'* (1904) and *Voprosy zhizni* (1905). See SS, I, 59.

6. *Oxford Slavonic Papers,* V, 50. [SS, II, 537].

7. SS, III, 269. German translation in *Das alte Wahre* (Berlin and Frankfurt, n.d.), pp. 7–30.

8. I Corinthians 13:2.

9. *Dostoevsky,* p. 34 ff.

10. Ibid., p. 17.

11. "Terror Antiquus," SS, II, 92. German: *Das alte Wahre,* see note 7.

12. Ibid.

13. About the Soul of the world, see "Terror Antiquus," SS, III, 104.

14. O. Deschartes, "Être et mémoire selon Vyatcheslav Ivanov," *Oxford Slavonic Papers,* VII (1957), 94.

15. See *Correspondance,* Third letter, and *Lettera ad A. Pellegrini, SS,* III, 446. In French translation in *Correspondance,* p. 100.

16. Church in the mystical sense; with regard to the institutional Church, and particularly the official Orthodox Church, both Ivanov and Du

Bos expressed a great many reservations at that time. About the Catholic Church, see *Lettre à Charles Dus Bos,* in *SS,* II, 85 and 418. The way to Christ led Ivanov to the concrete reality of the Church, as Solovyov taught it in consonance with the whole Christian tradition. Ivanov felt a deep personal friendship and veneration for Solovyov, though he sometimes disagreed with his philosophical views. Solovyov, he wrote, "has been the true shaper of our religious search" (*SS,* III, 297).

After their last meeting with him, shortly before his death, Ivanov and Lydia Dmitrievna, his wife, went to Kiev where they confessed, after years, and received communion. This return to the sacramental life of the Church— particularly to the Eucharist—was a mystical necessity and a logical step on a long journey that began with Ivanov's reflection on the religion of the suf- fering God, the victim and the sacrifice. Quite naturally, this return to the Church—which was not a "conversion" but the result of long spiritual evo- lution—led to a pilgrimage to one of the great centers of Russian spirituality, Kiev. There, rooted in the Eastern Orthodox tradition, was Ivanov's (and Solovyov's) spiritual fatherland, and so it would remain for the rest of his life (though this did not prevent him from liking, and feeling at home in, the other "Latin" tradition).

For Ivanov, as for Solovyov, the Church is mystically and sacramentally *one;* but, on the plane of historical evolution and hierarchical structure, there is a tragic division, a split; in Ivanov's opinion, it initially had purely political origins: Byzantium's struggle with the West. In breaking the links with the Bishop of Rome, successor of Peter (the "foundation stone of the Church"), the Eastern hierarchy, Ivanov believed, lost its independence; the Church be- came "national" and fell more and more under the power of the State. The division had another, deeper spiritual consequence: it was a wound in the body of the one Church. For Ivanov this split had been a source of "increasing suffering" for many years; his duty, he felt, was to help restore the lost unity, at least through his own actions. Ivanov publicly joined the Roman Catholic Church on March 17, 1926 in the basilica of St. Peter; he then attended a mass celebrated in the Byzantine rite on the tomb of the apostle Peter. In so doing, he writes Charles Du Bos, "for the first time I felt myself to be Orthodox in the full sense of the word, the owner of a sacred treasure that had been mine from the day of my baptism, but the ownership of which up to this time had been clouded, over many years, by a feeling of a sort of dissatisfaction that became more and more agonizing with the consciousness that I was deprived of the other half of that treasure of holiness and paradise, that I was breathing like a consumptive, with only one lung. I experienced a great joy of peace, a freedom of movement that I had never known before; I felt the happiness of a communion with numerous saints whose help and tenderness I had involuntarily renounced. I had the gratifying feeling that I was doing my personal duty and, in my person, the duty of my people; I was certain that I was acting according to its will, which I then clearly saw as [indicating] a readiness for Union; I knew I had remained faithful to its supreme commandment: forget yourself and sacrifice to the universal cause of Ecumenicity."

17. Ivanov develops his ideas on Sophia in one of his last essays (1947): "Lermontov," in *Protagonisti della letteratura russa,* a cura di Ettore Lo Gatto (Bompani, 1958), p. 268. The Italian original and the Russian translation in *SS,* IV: "We would define the idea of Sophia," Ivanov writes, "analogically to what had been said on art, as *forma formans* of the universe in God's intellect."

REMINISCENCES

Reminiscences
Lydia Ivanova†

An old friend of the Ivanovs, Marusya (Maria Mikhailovna Zamyatina, 1866–1919) lived in Geneva with the children, Seryozha, Vera and Kostya (born from the first marriage of Lydia Dmitrievna Zinovieva-Annibal to Konstantin Schwarsalon); and Lydia Ivanova (Lydia Dmitrievna's daughter by her marriage to Vyacheslav Ivanov). The recollections here pick up at the moment the family was united in St. Petersburg in Vyacheslav Ivanov's flat called the "Tower."

Arrival in St. Petersburg

In the spring of 1907 our parents decided to give up our Geneva home and move the entire family to Petersburg. All our belongings were sent to Russia. Vera stayed behind with our friends the Ostrogas[1] in order to take her final examinations at the *lycée,* but Kostya and I, under the tutelage of Marusya, took a train and arrived in Petersburg on Easter day. My heart overflowed with happy patriotism. For the first time in my life I was in Russia. All the people around spoke Russian, even the cabbies. Rain and slush—what did it matter?—I was in my own country.

Mother met us affectionately, but I am afraid our arrival presented her with an unpleasant necessity: the Tower had to be enlarged and another three rooms added to the original four. This was done by breaking through the wall of the next-door flat, the windows of which looked onto Tverskaya Street. A household was established complete with children and a servant—an intrusion into her bohemian life, her freedom.

The first thing that Mother did, not more than an hour after our arrival, was to send Kostya and me, on our own, to Somov, Kuzmin and (I do not remember if at the same time) to Struve. It was unlikely we would lose our way since it was straight ahead from Tavricheskaya. We were told to introduce ourselves as Mother's children and to ask everybody to come to our place in the evening.

My memories of that day are rather dim, as if of a dream. No wonder, we had only just arrived after many days of traveling. I felt overwhelmed by patriotic emotions, excitement and natural shyness. I remember how Somov and Kuzmin arrived (separately, I believe). I liked Somov a lot; he was round, soft and gentle, like a cosy cat. Kuzmin riveted one's attention by his extraordinary eyes—enormous, dark, slanting downwards from the bridge of his nose.

Mother called us and we sat in her Eastern Orange Room on the floor on mattresses covered with soft material and cushions. In the evening the two of us and Marusya were moved into a big room with an attic window and grey wallpaper; it looked very gloomy. "It was the Voloshins who papered it in this way," said Mother. Later it was repapered in a lovely bright blue; yet I always remember that room with a certain dislike.

In the beginning of the summer of 1907 Mother sent Kostya and me to the Chulkovs for a few days' stay at their summer house in Finland. I believe she prefered introducing us gradually to her friends. Chulkov was one of them. He used to come to our place fairly often. He had the habit of tossing back his thick hair, pressing it down with all five fingers of his hand to keep it from falling onto his forehead, and exclaiming in an almost sing-song, declamatory voice: "The taiga! Vyacheslav, the taiga!" His talk about Siberia where he had been deported was most interesting and he adored the taiga. His wife, Nadezhda Grigoryevna, was a beautiful woman of a pronounced southern type, a woman of great spirituality and kindness.

We were happy at the Chulkovs. One day they took us in a boat along some narrow river. Leonid Andreyev was also with us. He was dark, bearded and good-looking. He wore a White Russian shirt. As soon as he was told that we were Vyacheslav Ivanov's children, Andreyev began talking about him at length and with great animosity.

Then, about two or three days after our arrival, Mother sent Kostya and me to make the acquaintance of our Uncle Sasha, Aunt Lisa and their six sons, our cousins. Uncle Sasha, Mother's brother, Alexander Dmitrievich Zinoviev, was at that time Governor of the St. Petersburg province (the town of St. Petersburg itself had its own Governor and was not under his jurisdiction). I remember his telling me when we met years later, "I am happy that there was not one single execution during my time." The Zinovievs lived in a magnificent detached house. On the ground floor there was a huge hall, a solemn-looking hall-porter and a wide, carpeted staircase to the floor above. We were taken into an enormous dining room. The table looked endless to me and it seemed as if a whole regiment of guardsmen was sitting at it; they all rose as one man and came forward to welcome and kiss us by brushing our faces with their fresh, smooth cheeks that smelled of lotion. There were, in fact, six of them; the younger ones were in the Corps of Pages, the older ones were Officers of the Guards. Uncle Sasha's elder son had been killed during the war with Japan. Aunt Lisa had always dreamt of having a daughter but continued giving birth to defenders of the fatherland. For a long time she dressed her younger son, Misha, as a girl and let his hair grow long. Kostya became very fond of the Zinovievs, saw them often and stayed with them; they treated him like another son. I met them less often and liked particularly Aunt Lisa.

Zagorye. Mother's Death

In the summer of 1907 Marusya's aunt, Elisaveta Afanasyevna, invited us all to her estate Zagorye in Mogilyov province. The estate itself was absolutely ruined and practically all the land was mortgaged, but Elisaveta Afanasyevna still lived with her large family in the manor house. The landscape there was amazingly beautiful: hills, fir forests, a copse of aspen trees looking like a temple with tall silvery columns, and a large pond.[2]

Apart from our hosts' house, there was a wing for our own use: for Marusya, Kostya, me and Vera, who arrived later; there was also a large newly built house that had not been lived in yet and which smelt of fresh wood and tar. This was for Mother and Vyacheslav; they slept and worked there, coming to our wing only for their meals.

As was customary, the outbuildings stood around the large courtyard: stables, cattle and poultry sheds, as well as the living quarters for the workmen of the house and for the German bailiff. As soon as Mother saw Zagorye and entered her new house she was overcome by the beauty of it all and suddenly burst into tears. Later that same autumn, on October 17, Mother died in this same house after a four-day illness. A violent epidemic of scarlet fever had broken out; Mother went around neighboring villages to look after the peasants and caught the infection.

I remember how Mother used to walk about Zagorye in her tunic. She felt proud of having lost a lot of weight by going on a diet of her own invention. She taught us how to distinguish the types of edible mushrooms, how to cook them, and how to flavor salads with garlic. While bathing, she taught me to swim both "like a dog" and "like a frog." There was a small boat on the pond and she enjoyed rowing.

I was the cause of a minor squabble between her and Vyacheslav. Mother was extremely fond of horses and was an excellent rider. At one stage of their travels in Palestine she and Vyacheslav had to make a lengthy desert crossing. They were riding in the company of their Arab guides. Vyacheslav's horse was temperamental and threw him. He fell heavily and injured his head against a rock; they found themselves in a very distressing situation in the midst of the desert and ever since, Vyacheslav retained a dislike and fear of riding. There were horses at Zagorye and I was longing to ride. In spite of Vyacheslav's fears, Mother decided to give me this pleasure and to train me gradually. For my first time on horseback an aged, 26-year-old water-carrier horse was saddled; I was placed on its back and told to ride. The water-carrier proceeded at a wise and measured pace straight along the road, past the manor house, the aspen copse and

farther on. My problem was how to make it turn back. I could not
pull the reins hard enough. Unfortunately I met Vyacheslav strolling
on his own towards me. I asked him, "Do take the horse by the
reins and turn it; it refuses to obey me." Vyacheslav overcame his
terror of horses and did as I requested. The water-carrier was pleased,
increased his speed and, without taking the slightest notice of me,
went galloping to the stables. Luckily I had enough sense to duck
before we went through the door. But Vyacheslav and Mother had
a violent argument and, as a result, my chances of riding at Zagorye
were gone.

In spite of all the pleasures and joys of this summer, my recollections of Mother seemed to fade and grow sad. Pilgrims passed
through Zagorye on foot on their way to Jerusalem. This inspired
in Mother the longing to go on a pilgrimage in the same way:
barefoot and alone.

At the end of the summer holiday Marusya took me and Kostya
back to town. Kostya went for a year to the private school of Gur-
evich, while I went to the New School of the Society of Teachers on
Preobrazhensky Street, as well as to the Borovka College of Music
to attend Sophie Enakieff's classes. Mother, Vyacheslav and Vera were
reluctant to leave Zagorye and remained there until late autumn.

Mother's death abruptly broke the whole course of our lives.
One period had gone, and another had begun. Although the life
surrounding me was varied and rich, it seemed as if all of us lived
and acted in a constricted, partly unreal atmosphere; as if a dark
cloud continually hung above us, the same cloud that had burst like
thunder on October 17 and refused to dissolve. It took years for it
to recede; this happened only at the end of our Petersburg period.

Some time after Mother's death, Aunt Lisa asked me to stay
with them for a month at Koporye, the Zinovievs' family estate. At
about three versts from the manor house and its unbelievably large
park, stood Koporye itself, the fortress famous in history for its
heroic resistance to the Swedes. The fortress was a ruin; around it
were the village and the church where the Zinovievs went to Sunday
service, always standing near the icon screen. An elegant horse-drawn
carriage took them there, driven by a coachman in splendid coach-

man's dress: a brightly-colored Russian silk shirt with a sleeveless, blue cloth jacket, a round cap with peacock feathers on his curly hair. When in town, the coachman's overcoat was lined with a thick layer of quilted padding and sitting on his box he looked like a roly-poly. Kostya and I called such coachmen "cushions"—"I drove on a cushion today"—"Really?"

At Koporye I was shown a 40-year-old horse, Caprice, that Mother used to ride in her youth, and a small, long-haired Siberian horse with its mane down to its knees; Sasha was riding it when he was killed in the war. Dunya, one of our former young girls,[3] came to see me from a nearby village. She had married a fisherman; she looked hungry and unhappy.

Aunt Lisa once told me that after Mother's death she had hoped to take her place as far as possible. However, this could never have been because we and the Zinovievs belonged to entirely different worlds.

The "Tower"

The house on Tavricheskaya 25[4] stood on the corner of Tver-skaya. It had a peculiar shape since its corner formed a tower; half of the tower consisted of outside walls with large windows, the other was part of the inside of the flats. The roof above the tower rose in a cupola; it was possible to enter it and to admire the marvelous view of the town, the Neva and the fortresses. I often went there, and even Vyacheslav made visits to it now and again. In the flats under ours, the tower contained large, round halls (in one of them there was a dancing school, in another a communal library); the hall in our flat was divided into three small rooms with a tiny dark entrance lobby. These rooms were a curious shape, like segments of a circle. Each had a huge window looking down upon the tops of the trees in the Tavrichesky Gardens. Father had the room in the middle.

Apart from the tower all the rest of the rooms had small, attic windows. Our flat was a modest one on the fifth floor. There was a lift up to the fourth floor. The large entrance hall on the ground floor and the staircase up to the fourth floor were covered with carpets. The hall-porter, Pavel, dressed in livery, reigned over the downstairs. He was middle-aged and had a well-groomed, gingery beard.

In 1904 General Kuropatkin, Commander-in-Chief of the Russian Army, took a flat in our house. Pavel liked bragging about such an important inhabitant and identified himself with him: "Yesterday [V. K.] Plehve [the Minister of the Interior] called, but we did not receive him." The telephone was next to Pavel's flat and to use it you had to walk down five floors (the lift took you upstairs only). An old, short fur cape hung in our entrance hall and was called "the communal cape," as both hosts and visitors put it around their shoulders when they had to go down to the telephone.

Crowds of people came to the "Tower." Visitors and friends not only came but occasionally remained—some of them for two or three days, others for longer. Some of our Moscow friends never bothered to give any warning beforehand but simply walked in with their luggage. The two flats joined together in Mother's day no longer sufficed, so a third was added by breaking a door through into it. This flat gave onto Tverskaya and had three small rooms and an entrance that led to a different staircase. (Kuzmin lived there during our last years in the "Tower.") A single servant was no longer able to cope. But Vyacheslav refused to have more than one servant, saying it would be too bourgeois. The tiled Dutch stoves were wood-burning; there were paraffin lamps to be attended to. Once, to my delight, I was allowed to tend them instead of practicing the piano. There were 26 of them, so it is easy to imagine what happened when they were neglected and one or more began to smoke.

Eight, nine or more people sat down to table at dinner. It went on and on, the samovar never stopped boiling until late at night. The diversity of those who sat at our table! Great writers, poets, painters, philosophers, actors, musicians, professors, students, beginners of every kind, people dabbling in the occult, people truly half-mad and others pretending to be so as to appear original; "decadents," exalted ladies. I recollect one of these ladies who called on Vyacheslav and insisted on his going to her house on an island so as to enable her to give birth to a superman. It was said that she made the rounds of famous men with the same request.

Conversation was animated and mostly unintelligible to me. Once I ran to the kitchen to talk to Matryosha and she remarked: "Isn't it odd? They are speaking Russian, aren't they? Yet one cannot understand a word they say!" It was snug in Matryosha's kitchen—the stove lit, something nice always cooking on it which could be tasted. Matryosha's cat, Flokin, sat in front of the range covered in coal dust; it loved to roll in coal and was not admitted to the Tower. Matryosha herself had given it the name Flokin because, she said, in the "most noble" family where she had been in service, a dog had been given that name. I think she must have Russianized the name "Flock." A similar transformation of a name took place later when Dima's[5] nurse announced Baltrušaitis as "Trushachkin."

Some of the conversations at table enthralled me. Such were, for example, Gumilyov's tales about Africa and his poems describing it:

Far, far on lake Chad
Wanders the exquisite giraffe . . .

Both Father and I listened spellbound. Father had many truly youthful strings in his heart and his vivid imagination helped him to experience what in real life lay beyond his capabilities. In his old age, lying in a deck chair in Switzerland, Father liked to look at the high mountains and imagine climbing them, with all that implied—difficulties, tiredness and delight. He took an active interest in our lives, down to the slightest detail and always shared it with us.

Visitors at the "Tower"

After Mother's death, the Wednesdays were given up, but a great many people continued to come in the evenings. On one such occasion I was introduced to Zinaida Gippius. She looked at me (through her lorgnette, I believe) and said in a slight drawl: "Tell me something interesting and frightening." But I am afraid I went numb and her request remained unanswered.

Another time Akhmatova stood on a rug with everybody around her; she was demonstrating her suppleness: bending backwards she was trying to pick up with her teeth a match placed vertically on a cardboard box that lay on the floor. I believe she managed to do it. She was tall, thin, dressed in something dark, long and clinging and she looked like some incredibly beautiful, snake-like, scaly creature.

Another glimpse—a rare visitor at our table. Everybody agreed that he was as beautiful as Apollo. Beautiful, yes, but what a heavy face! This was Blok. Another memory—a young student in a worn uniform, his hair brown, his nose very long. He kept silent, concentrating intensely on his thoughts with his nose down near his plate. He never lifted his head throughout the meal. This was Pavel Florensky.

Karatygin, the music critic, used to come to see Father and play the work of Debussy and Ravel for hours, introducing him to contemporary music. Father, who was musical to the highest degree, liked Ravel, but Debussy was alien to him. Beethoven was the composer he was linked with his whole life from his very youth, and my own impression is that the stuff of which Father's soul was woven contained many threads of Beethoven. Through the year following Mother's death he listened every evening to one or another of Beethoven's sonatas. They were played to him by one of his close friends, an excellent amateur pianist, Anna Mintslova.

Vyacheslav and I both enjoyed the evenings when Kuzmin demonstrated bit by bit, as he wrote them, the parts of a charming operetta he was composing. He himself wrote both the music and the words. The subject was borrowed from an Eastern fairy tale. The hero, in love with the Sultan's wife, was dressed as a bird and put into a cage that was brought into the harem. I remember some extracts from it.

Sultan's honor! Sultan's honor!
Who will dare to challenge it?

Who will dare to voice a doubt
That he'd ever be betrayed?

Andrey Bely was one of the Muscovites who used to walk
straight in with his suitcase. In the course of a conversation between
Bely and me it transpired that I liked to play with tin soldiers. Bely
was overjoyed and alleged that it was his favorite game too. There
was a half-empty room in the "Tower" where rings were suspended
for my gymnastics, where I played the violin, and in which stood a
long expandable table. This table became our kingdom. We mustered
whole armies of a variety of soldiers: infantry, artillery, cavalry. Make-
shift fortresses were erected, mine on one side of the table, his on
the opposite side. Battles were fought and enemy troops were attacked by firing dried peas from minute guns. Bely's eagerness for
the game lasted for a fairly long period. On several occasions he
brought new tin soldiers when he came to Petersburg.

At this time he was writing his novel *Petersburg*. He read the
new parts of it to Vyacheslav as soon as they were written. Vyacheslav
was enthusiastic about the novel. His affectionate nickname for Bely
was "Gogolek." Bely liked imitating the cinema (silent in those
days). He would jump toward a wall and move along it, gesticulating
and trembling spasmodically all the time. This was meant to be a
funny parody and to produce laughter, but with Bely's steely eyes
staring into the distance, I found it rather frightening.

Emil Medtner came from Moscow frequently. He was usually
full of complaints about his friend Bely, who was always blaming
Medtner for one thing or another. Bely, Medtner and Ellis lived in
Moscow. They were bound by a curious kind of friendship that alternated between tragic break-ups and pathetic reconciliations. At
one time Bely's charming wife, Asya Turgeneva, used to come also.
She was a painter and produced an unconvincing portrait of Vyacheslav.[6]

We saw a great deal of Sergey Gorodetsky who often stayed
with us. He was young, exceedingly tall and had an ugly face, but
it was always fun to be with him. Vera, Kostya and I (when Kostya
was home during the holidays) used to go with him, by special

permit, to the part of the Tavrichesky Gardens that was fenced off near the Duma. There was skating on the pond and very high, ice-covered toboggan runs. The toboggan flew down at breakneck speed. I remember sitting on Gorodetsky's back as he lay stretched out in all his endless length and steered. Gorodetsky was a wonderful caricaturist. Every week he produced a magazine dedicated to life at the Tower. He called it *Les puces de gamin*. I hope that it has been preserved in some archive in Russia; it was a talented production with good drawings of various people and of our family life.

The drawing *Le lever du roi* comes to my mind. In it, Father has woken up and rings the bell. The clock shows 2 p.m. Marusya wheels some kind of trolley at full speed along the corridor. There is a tray with Father's breakfast on the trolley, his mail, and all kinds of garments hanging on hooks. Another family picture: my return from school. I am shown from behind: two plaits and hands covered with ink spots; at one side of the staircase two pianos rush away from me in horror. A third picture: the steeple of the Fortress of Peter and Paul to which a balloon is fastened with the face of E. V. Anichkov on it—the caption: *Ballon captif*. Our portly friend Anichkov, a member of the Socialist Revolutionary party, had been imprisoned in the Fortress in solitary confinement.[7]

Country Life at the Anichkovs

The Anichkovs had lived in Paris for a very long time. Mrs. Anichkova wrote under the pseudonym of "Ivan Strannik." She was great friends with Anatole France, who was her literary guide and adviser. There were three children, the youngest, Tanya, my friend and contemporary. Vyacheslav had been asked to meet the elder two, Igor, 14 years old, and Vera, who was 16. He was much impressed by their intellect and maturity and told us they had had outstandingly clever philosophical discussions.

The Anichkovs invited me to stay at their estate and I spent two summers with them, as well as visiting them regularly in winter. We became very close friends. To my horror Igor told me that he was reading Kant; Vera had made a vow to meditate daily for three

or four hours. Often she performed her meditation while I was playing the piano. She walked endlessly around a table, her heels tapping
at every small step, inevitably out of time. Now and again a cracking
sound could be heard when she bit off a piece of sugar with her
pretty white teeth. She was perfectly right, of course: sugar stimulates mental activity.

However, although the Anichkovs' elder children behaved like
prodigies, this certainly could not be said about Tanya—at any rate
not while the two of us were together. Disregarding the disapproval
of the peasants, trousers were made for us and we spent days on end
running about the estate (1,250 acres in all), climbing onto the
roofs of granaries and stealing peas and carrots from the gardener.
We were present at the birth of a calf and implored that this wet,
newly-born being should not be condemned to be slaughtered. We
ran in the evenings about the wood, with eyes half-shut, in the hope
of getting lost. We looked for unoccupied horses to ride saddled or
bare-backed. Once we stayed awake all night (Oh, this was hard
indeed but it had to be done) and went out to the main road before
dawn, close to a gypsy camp that had been pitched nearby. We
dreamed of being stolen by the gypsies; they would dye us dark to
make us unrecognizable (I would become a brunette at last), teach
us tight-rope walking and how to jump through a hoop on a galloping horse. Alas! The gypsies not only never stole us but did not
even touch the Anichkovs' horses out of gratitude for being allowed
to camp on their land.

The Anichkov family, and particularly the children, were mon-
archists and very anxious to belong to Court circles, but the political
views of their father and his arrest were a handicap.

The Meyerholds

The summer when I was sent for ten days to visit the Meyerholds brought great happiness into my life, for I became extremely
fond of Marusya, their elder daughter. The Meyerholds lived at
Kuokkala in Finland that summer. Meyerhold himself only appeared
at odd moments. The family consisted of his wife, Olga Mikhai-

lovna, and their three daughters, Marusya, Tanya and Irisha. Irisha was only four or five but had already made up her mind to be a ballet dancer since she yearned to have fame and oceans of flowers at her feet. When I first arrived I was sent at once to see the children in a tiny little garden that had a big heap of sand in the middle. I felt deeply hurt. Marusya was nine, two years younger than me and here I was supposed to play with this mite and in the company of two babies! To bake mud-pies and make mud-balls! Within a quarter of an hour this was exactly what I was doing—oblivious to all the world.

I adored Marusya and regarded her as a saint, as an ideal in every way. She was kind, generous, always in high spirits, and she had a passion for dancing. Whenever dancing was arranged for the children or a children's ball took place, she pleaded so ardently to be allowed to go that no one had the heart to refuse. Yet, the next day, without fail, she was struck down by an attack of pneumonia. A couple of years later we met doctors who insisted on her being sent to Moscow, so she went as a boarder to the Arsenyeva School (very strict and pedantic). The Petersburg air was poison to those suffering from lung troubles, whereas Moscow's climate, dry, cold and sunny, was regarded as salubrious. Marusya came to Petersburg on her holidays but after I left the town we never met again and I heard that she died from tuberculosis while quite young.

Vera entered the College for Women's Higher Education, in the faculty of classical philology; Rostovtsev and Zelinsky were her professors. The Rostovtsevs kept "At Home" days and Vyacheslav and Vera often went to visit them, finding them interesting and entertaining. Vera told me with glee how Rostovtsev once dressed up as a cat with a long fur tail, and walked on all fours on the carpet. A man appeared at that time in Petersburg who maintained that he had discovered a method for extracting all necessary nourishment from grass; there would be no more starvation according to him. At their next party, the Rostovtsevs asked their friends to partake of hay, but when I inquired of Vera what it tasted like she disappointed me by saying that no hay had been served.

I remember Meyerhold talking at the table about his production

of *Tristan* at the Marijnski Theater. He complained about the trivial
gestures of the singers and parodied them amusingly. He told us
with pride of an idea he had had: he commissioned sets which were
most complicated, inconvenient to move about and so unsteady as
to collapse at the slightest movement. Thus the wretched singers
had to stand as motionless as posts for fear of breaking a limb. The
cast was very cross but the director (Meyerhold) rubbed his hands—
he had achieved the result he wanted. Meyerhold took all of us, old
and young, to the dress rehearsal.

Two friends of mine, Cassandra's nieces,[8] had lived in Paris for
a long time and spoke perfect French. Vera had the idea of staging
theatricals for children in French; she left the acting to us and was
concerned only about the production. We performed Racine's *Esther*
and, as a short piece, the farce of *Maître Patelin.* Vera did not have
the text of the farce; she remembered only the general plot from her
literature lessons in Geneva. She narrated it to me and suggested
that I should write it down in my own words, divide it into acts
and sketch in the outline of dialogues. We did not learn any text by
heart but it served as a general plan. When the evening of the
performance came we felt so unselfconscious that we made use of
much improvisation on the spot.

Meyerhold was present. He treated our dramatic play with utter
contempt but was enthusiastic about *Maître Patelin,* said it was a
manifestation of the *Commedia dell'arte* and that the production had
given him valuable ideas.

This performance served as a test to Vera, a preparation for the
realization of her dream: to stage theatrical productions by creating
the Tower Theatre. Long discussions followed about the choice of a
play. In the end Calderón's *Adoration of the Cross* was settled upon.
Planning went on for months and the number of talented people who
became interested and were drawn in grew ever larger. The materials
from Mother's basket eventually fell into the hands of Sudeykin, who
turned them into sets and costumes. Meyerhold came to the dress
rehearsal and started directing everybody. Vera was acting the part
of Eusebio, the chief hero (she had chosen a man's part as always);
she put her whole heart into it. Even I was given a minor comic

part, that of Menga. It was all immensely enjoyable. There seemed to be far more spectators present than the small room could possibly hold, all the more so as part of it was taken up by the stage. This too must have been some trick of Meyerhold's. The Tower Theater was mentioned in the press, and there is Father's poem about it.[9]

I met Meyerhold again years later, in Rome in 1925. It was a great and unexpected joy. He arrived on a well-paid mission to Italy with his young wife, Zinaida Raikh, an actress in his theatre. They were deeply in love with each other. To her he was her husband, her *maître,* her teacher—the man who had created her as an actress. To him she was his last joy; but although the sun was still bright and shone in its glory, the sunset was approaching.

A number of amusing anecdotes arose in connection with this intense mutual infatuation. Once the concierge came to us with a complaint: "Who are those two persons who have come to visit you? Ours is a decent house, we cannot allow kissing on the stairs." "But they are husband and wife." "Well, that is hardly likely; they are too much in love with each other."

Meyerhold was as jealous as Othello of his Zinaida. One evening we went with some friends to eat ice cream at the Villa Borghese. We were in high spirits and Zinaida, with her brand-new Venetian shawl—her husband's latest present—thrown over her shoulders, walked with dancing steps, purring a song. Naturally, the group of Italian sailors who saw this frivolous young beauty began to call out compliments to her. Nobody paid attention to them; but Meyerhold fell silent, his face became deathly pale. We asked "What has happened to him?" Zinaida's answer was "Don't worry. Vsevolod has cut his throat."

Yet complications lay in store for us. Meyerhold had invited us to the smartest night café in Rome. It was full of well-known personalities, fascist hierarchs, generals, and the cream of Roman society. We squeezed through the crowd, sat down at two or three tables, and gave our orders to the pompous waiter for masterpieces of the confectionary art. All of a sudden Meyerhold jumped up with a jerk, moved away among the tables into the illuminated square, went towards the depths of the park and disappeared. Time passed but he did not return. The waiters carried two trays high above the heads of the clients and placed them in front of us. None of us had any money! Zinaida grew anxious: "Vsevolod has cut his throat; we had better go back to the hotel." We had to leave the trays untouched, get up and pass through a battery of scornful looks.

Meyerhold was very amusing when he demonstrated how a bill should be paid in a restaurant if you did not speak Italian. The proprietor brought the bill. Meyerhold examined it for a long time, frowning; then he stared at the proprietor. The proprietor began feeling nervous, took back the bill, made some corrections and brought it back. The procedure was repeated: the scrutiny of the bill, the staring at the proprietor, his confusion, another correction and another return. After one more such pantomime, Meyerhold paid the bill and felt he could now go to bed with an easy mind.

Mussolini had come to power two years earlier. The Roman cafés were packed with youths proudly wearing their black shirts and their black fezzes. Meyerhold was terrified of them and refused to go into any café they might be in. "Vyacheslav!" he would whisper, hurrying away, "Vyacheslav! The fascists!" He had the feeling that if they caught just one glimpse of him they would know that he was a dangerous Bolshevik.

The Auto-incinerated Beard

Once Vyacheslav took a sleigh to the Women's College of Higher Education where he lectured on Greek literature. He wanted to light a cigarette, so he lit a match and, to prevent it from being blown out by the wind, pushed it into the partly open match-box. He never noticed that the tips of the remaining matches were turned toward him; the box burst into flames and half of his beard was burnt off. The students waited in vain that day—their professor was at the barber's. He never wore a beard again and many jokes were made about the "auto-incinerated" beard.

I recall another funny incident. Kostya came home dazzled and jubilant. The Grand Duke Konstantin Konstantinovich had been at the First Cadet Corps that morning. He was a poet; some of his poems enjoyed wide popularity and were set to music and sung everywhere, as for instance, *Nakinuv plashch*.

"I had a personal conversation with him," declared Kostya. All the cadets had been lined up in the courtyard. While inspecting them the Grand Duke stopped at Kostya:

". . . the poet Vyacheslav Ivanov is your step-father?"

"Just so, Your Imperial Highness."

"Have you read his works?"

"Just so, Your Imperial Highness."

"And have you understood them?"

"Just so, Your Imperial Highness."

"Well, in that case, you are more intelligent than I. I have not understood a thing."

A house was rented in Sillomagi, Estonia, for the summer of 1911. It stood amidst a lovely grove not far from the sea. When I arrived from the Anichkovs' estate, I saw a terrace typical of a summer house. Vyacheslav was sitting at the samovar talking to someone unknown to me. This was Gershenzon who spent that summer close by and often came to see Vyacheslav. I think this was when their close friendship began. It was a cozy family life that summer. Matryosha was there, too, with her Flokin. A whole group of professors from Moscow had come to the village nearby for their summer holidays. I remember the names of the historian Petrushevsky and the lawyer Ordynsky. They all gathered in the square after dinner and played games of *gorodki* (a kind of skittles) in which Vyacheslav also took part. It was fun and the game would go on until dark.

Vyacheslav's "Audiences"

There was a special expression in our family: "to ask for an audience." "Vyacheslav, So-and-so asks for an audience." So-and-so came, retired with Vyacheslav into a room and the two had a long talk.

At the "Tower" I was no longer as afraid of Vyacheslav as I used to be in Geneva, yet our relationship was not really free and easy; I felt rather shy in his presence. Once, however, a problem arose that greatly puzzled me and for which I was incapable of finding a solution on my own. At school a girl took my friend and me aside and asked, "Listen, God is almighty, isn't He?" "Yes." "But could He create a stone that He himself would be unable to lift?" We did not know the answer. When I came home this question continued to worry me even more. In the end, I summoned up the courage and, at a suitable moment, asked Vyacheslav: "Could I ask for an audience with you?" Vyacheslav treated my request with affectionate respect and extreme courtesy; he fixed the time. He always behaved toward children, even quite small ones, with polite consideration.

I felt extremely nervous as I entered Vyacheslav's room in the "Tower." He met me affably and offered me the most important (Renaissance) black armchair. Then he asked what was the matter. He listened to me with attention and gave an immediate answer that seemed to me worthy of King Solomon: "God not only could, He has created such a stone. It is man, with his free will." Then Vyacheslav went on explaining to me in detail what was meant by free will. I left him feeling happy and light-hearted.

Having gained confidence, I asked him for another audience after a time, and was received once again with affection and consideration. That time it was a purely intellectual question. At our table I had heard the expression *La propriété c'est le vol,* and I wanted to know what it meant. Vyacheslav gave me a full historical explanation. We parted friends. However, this conversation left no particular impact—the statement was of no deep significance for me nor, possibly, for him.

Vyacheslav worked hard and regularly. Having seen off his friends, he went to bed and worked there until sunrise. It is no wonder that his day sometimes began at 2 p.m. He was a true chain-smoker and smoked up to eighty cigarettes a day, though it must be admitted that his visitors helped him too; the room he was in was always full of thick smoke.

Leaving for France

Spring was approaching. I would be sixteen before long. All

of a sudden Vyacheslav turned to me and asked me to his room in the "Tower" for a talk. We went through the small room on the left. Vera sat there looking at us timidly as we passed. I sat down again in the important black armchair and heard amazing news: Vyacheslav and Vera loved each other and had decided to join their lives forever. This was no betrayal of Mother. Vera was for Vyacheslav a continuation of Mother; a gift from her, as it were. A child was expected. A child always creates new life, new light. Could I accept what Vyacheslav was telling me? If so, I would remain with them. If I found it unacceptable, an independent life of my own would be organized—with Marusya, should I so wish.

The words I heard shattered the whole inward world in which I lived. Vera was a continuation of Mother for Vyacheslav? There they were, both shy and full of anxiety, as if waiting for a verdict from me, a girl in her teens. I was to be their judge? Accept what they were saying? But what if this meant the abandonment of Mother? What if I betrayed her by it? It was a very hard decision to make, a most painful moment. Yet my heart filled with love and I made up my mind: "I am with you." Vyacheslav said: "Whatever happens in our life in the future, I shall never forget this moment." We went to the room next door where Vera was waiting, "She is with us," said Vyacheslav.

A few days later we three left for France and settled down at Neuvecelle near Evion on Lake Leman.

Translated from the Russian by Irina Prehn

Notes

1. Felix Ostroga, son of a Polish émigré, piano professor at the Geneva Conservatory.

2. In Zagorye, Ivanov wrote the cycle of poems *Povecherie* in *Cor Ardens* (*SS*, II, 277–82).

3. Mother used to take with her several young girls, treating them as members of the family. She found them in Russia where she succeeded in saving them from all kinds of hardships and even tragedy. I remember Dunya,

from a fishing village; Anjuta; Olga, the daughter of a sign-painter who drank a lot; she later became the wife of my music teacher, Felix Ostroga. The names of Vasyunia and Kristina also come to my mind.

4. The building is still there, but it now has the number 35. For further information about the "Tower," see SS, II, 692 and 821.

5. Dmitri, son of Vera and Vyacheslav Ivanov.

6. Reproduced in SS, III, 65.

7. For more about Anichkov, see SS, II, 826.

8. "Cassandra's" real name was Aleksandra Nikolaevna Tchebotarevskaya (1869–1925). Sister-in-law of the writer Fyodor Sologub, she was an old friend of Ivanov. See SS, II, 724.

9. SS, III, 54 and 703.

CHRONOLOGY

Chronology of the Life and Works of Vyacheslav I. Ivanov
Valery N. Blinov

1866, 16/28 February

"I was born in my parents' own little house, almost on the outskirts of what then was Moscow, in Gruziny, on the corner of Volkov and Georgiev Lanes, across from the Zoological Garden fence." (*Avtobiograficheskoe pis'mo* [Autobiographical Letter]).

His father, Ivan Tikhonovich Ivanov, was "first a land surveyor, then an employee of the Control Board, an unsociable, opinionated man, a Russian *intelligent* of the 1860s." (O. Deschartes)

"A loner—and an unbeliever." (*Mladenchestvo* [Infancy])

His mother, Aleksandra Dmitrievna (née Preobrazhenskaya) "was the granddaughter of a village priest, the daughter of a Senate civil servant." (O. Deschartes)

"She was ardently religious . . . during portentous times she had prophetic dreams, and she even had visions while awake." (*Autobiographical Letter*)

"She came to love the Bible, Goethe and Beethoven, and in her soul she cherished an ideal of intellectual diligence and high education which she wanted to see embodied in her son without fail." (Ibid.)

"She hated nihilism and flirted with Slavophilism of a liberal tinge; her devotion to the idea of Slavdom was reflected in the choice of my first name." (Ibid.)

"I inherited traits of my mother's spiritual makeup." (Ibid.)

1871, February

Father dies of consumption.
"It was a gray day; I played at home
And I, unwillingly leaving my game,
Was wordlessly brought to the deathbed.
Death's weariness consumed the sufferer;
His sweat ran in a stream.
He made a cross with his hand." (*Infancy*)

1872

"My mother nourished the poet in me. . . . While my father was still alive I came to know the magic of Lermontov's poems . . . the less comprehensible they were, the more magical they seemed." (*Autobiographical Letter*)

"Mother meets the New Year—
Predicts, opening the psalter:
'In my father's family, I, a young shepherd,
Was the youngest. My fingers
Created the stringed psalterion . . .'
'The prophetic pages predict to you
The gift of songs . . .' Their legacy
Since then is inseparable from my soul." (*Infancy*)

1873

"At the age of seven I was deeply shaken and captivated by Uhland's 'Des Sängers Fluch', a verse translation of which I discovered in an old illustrated journal." (*Autobiographical Letter*)

"From the age of seven I began to be taught foreign languages and Russian literature. My teacher was a pretty young lady, the daughter of our landlord . . . and I was agonizingly jealous of her fiancé, a naval officer. This was already the second time I had fallen in love." (Ibid.)

"I was seven years old when my mother told me to read the acathismata in the morning; every day we would read a chapter of the Gospel together." (Ibid.)

"The esthetic was interwoven with the religious even in our little vowed pilgrimages on foot to Iverskaya or the Kremlin on summer evenings." (Ibid.)

"From that time I came to love Christ for life." (Ibid.)

1875

"Until I was nine I attended a private school established . . . by the family of our well-known economist M. I. Tugan-Baranovsky; the Tugan brothers, their cousin, and I made up the upper class, and we competed in the writing of novels." (Ibid.)

First poem, "The Taking of Jericho" (Vzjatie Ierikhona): "I became acquainted with the pride of literary success and the sting of critical insinuations simultaneously: the stupid teacher declared that she had seen something like it somewhere." (Ibid.)

"At nine Vyacheslav was sent to a *gymnasium* housed in a beautiful old building. His entry into school coincided with the visit there of Alexander II, who was idolized by Aleksandra Dmitrievna." (O. Deschartes)

1876

"At ten I was captivated by Schiller's *Die Räuber.*" (*Autobiographical Letter*)

1877

"During my second year of school the Russo-Turkish War was going on; my mother and I were seized with enthusiasm for Slavdom. . . . I sent letters to my brothers in the trenches, full of martial, patriotic poems, which I recognized as childish prattle a year later." (Ibid.)

"Another experience from that time remained unforgettable. Vyacheslav was taken to the unveiling of the Pushkin monument, and to the ceremonial convocation at the University." (O. Deschartes)

1878

"At around age 12 Vyacheslav's piety reached its apogee."
(O. Deschartes)

"At night I would spend long hours standing in front of an icon,
and I would fall asleep on my knees out of fatigue." (*Autobiographical
Letter*)

"I passionately studied Greek a year before the teaching of it began."
(Ibid.)

1879

"Vyacheslav's teaching activity began when he was 13: no matter
how much Aleksandra Dmitrievna economized, by this time nothing
had been saved of the small sum of money that remained after the
prolonged illness and death of Ivan Tikhonovich. . . . He [Vyache-
slav] gave so many paid lessons that he could read and think only
at night." (O. Deschartes)

1880

"Suddenly and painlessly, I realized that I was an extreme atheist
and revolutionary." (*Autobiographical Letter*)

1881, 1 March

Assassination of Alexander II.
"My student compositions, sometimes on themes that were dangerous for me, aroused the amazement of friends who were initiated
into the secret of my worldview, because of the diplomatic adroitness
with which I managed at one and the same time neither to give
myself away nor to play false to myself." (Ibid.)

"My teachers . . . forgave me the errors in my Latin and Greek
assignments because of their generally excellent style and feeling for
language, and they acknowledged my Russian 'compositions' . . .
to be exemplary." (Ibid.)

1883

"The main question tormenting me was that of justifying terrorism as a means of social revolution; my answer matured only toward the end of *gymnasium* and was definitely negative." (Ibid.)

"My free-thinking did not come cheap to me: its consequences were a pessimistic despondency that weighed on me for several years, a passionate longing for death that I celebrated in my poems of that time, and when I was 17 a childish attempt to poison myself with toxic paints I had received from my father." (Ibid.)

"It is noteworthy that at the time of my atheism my love of Christ and dreams about him did not die out, but actually grew more intense." (Ibid.)

First *poema,* "Jesus," about the temptation in the wilderness, with the image of Christ in the spirit of Feuerbach: "May man be proud and free!"

Intimacy with fellow poet Kalabin, "who with pure clairvoyance divined in me the poet concealed from the world." (Ibid.)

"In the 1880s this *gymnasium* student [Ivanov] wrote 'Clarity' (*Jasnost'*), a poem so mature that 22 years later the poet, so demanding of himself, decided to include this early attempt in his second book of poems." (S. Averintsev)

"In his last years in the *gymnasium* Vyacheslav became intimate with his classmate Aleksey Dmitrievsky, with whom he translated a passage from *Oedipus Rex* into Russian trimeter." (O. Deschartes)

"When Vyacheslav graduated from the *gymnasium,* the director offered to arrange for him, the best pupil, to become a fellowship student at the Leipzig Philological Seminar. But this classical seminar . . . seemed to the Russian intelligentsia of the day to be a pernicious institution. . . . For Vyacheslav, to become a fellowship student would mean to be guilty of a traitorous concession to reaction, and he categorically refused." (O. Deschartes)

1884–85

Ivanov studies in the Department of History and Philology at Moscow University.

"The two years of my student life in Moscow were a time of an upsurge of spiritual powers that was bold to the point of excessive presumption. . . . I was an historian . . . through history I dreamed of independently mastering the problems of society and finding a path to social action. Klyuchevsky enchanted me; P. G. Vinogradov gave me . . . German books from his library." (*Autobiographical Letter*)

"The professors immediately noticed and valued Vyacheslav, and in the very first year they awarded him a prize for his work in ancient languages." (O. Deschartes)

The poem "A Legend" (about the conversion to Christianity of a Jewish boy in medieval Spain) is accepted for publication by *Russkij vestnik* (The Russian Herald), but publication is stopped by the author because of the journal's reactionary character.

Close friendship with Aleksey Dmitrievsky's sister, Darya Mikhaylovna.

"Vyacheslav and Darya strolled along the paths of a neglected garden and declared their love for Beethoven, Pushkin, Schubert, and each other. The Hermes of their affair was Aleksey." (O. Deschartes)

"I fell passionately in love with her, and a year later we decided to marry and go off to study in Germany." (*Autobiographical Letter*)

"I could not bear to stay in my homeland: it was suffocating and sinister. Further political inaction, in the event that I remained in Russia, seemed to me to be a moral impossibility. I would have had to throw myself into revolutionary activity, but I no longer believed in it." (Ibid.)

1886, May

Marries Darya Mikhaylovna Dmitrievskaya.

"I was married for the first time in Moscow when I was twenty years and three months old, to Dmitrievskaya. At the time I was mad about her brother. And perhaps if I had not loved the brother so much, I would not have married his sister." (From conversations with M. S. Altman)

"I spent my last summer in Russia on the estate of the Golovin brothers outside Moscow, where I prepared the younger brother Pavel for the sixth year of the lycée . . . and studied a little Greek with the other brother . . . , Fyodor Aleksandrovich (later the Chairman of the Second State Duma)." (*Autobiographical Letter*)

"The Golovins filched my manuscripts, and I was exposed not only as a poet, but as a Symbolist poet, although none of us knew the word 'symbolism' in the sense of a literary movement." (Ibid.)

autumn

Leaves for Germany. Participates in Theodor Mommsen's famous seminar on Roman history at the University of Berlin.

1887

"The first semester (beginning in autumn of 1886) was devoted to mastering the language. At the end of the second semester I presented Mommsen with a trifling bit of research on the tax system of Roman Egypt and was affectionately encouraged by him." (Ibid.)

"On this happy day sarcastic Mommsen
Praised me with a smile"
        (From verse diary of 1887)

"My wanderings in the realm of historical problems began, taking me away from where my inclinations lay—the study of the Hellenic soul." (*Autobiographical Letter*)

Study of the Ravenna exarchate and Byzantine institutions in southern Italy, as well as philosophy, paleography, political economy. Study and personal contact with Hirschfeld, Cumont, Curtius, Zeller, Wattenbach, Schmoller, etc.

1888, spring

"O. Hirschfeld acknowledged the first draft of my future dissertation to be 'solid work.'" (*Autobiographical Letter*)

Contact with visiting Russian scholars: P. G. Vinogradov, Prince S. N. Trubetskoy, A. I. Guchkov, etc.

"As soon as I found myself abroad, mystic searchings began to ferment within me, and the need to recognize Russia in its idea awakened. I began to study Vladimir Solovyov and Khomyakov." (*Autobiographical Letter*)

"On the occasion of Bismarck's resignation, which marked a 'new course,' I wrote a sonnet in which I compared the young Emperor to Phaeton, whose presumptuous daring was sure to entail a world conflagration and the ruin of its perpetrator. Several poems from my student days in Berlin were included in revised form in my first collection." (Ibid.)

Birth of daughter Aleksandra.

1889

"Parting forever with his youthful atheism" (S. Averintsev), he writes a verse epistle to A. Dmitrievsky, "Ars mystica,"
     "May there resound in the ears both familiar and new
     The saving word of the Universal Community."
                                             (*Autobiographical Letter*)

1890

"Nietzsche became ever more fully and powerfully the master of my thoughts." (Ibid.)

"The author of *The Birth of Tragedy* revealed Dionysus to him as an extra-temporal principle of the spirit, as the element of music and holy madness, as the power that delivers from the bonds of individuation." (O. Deschartes)

1891

"Having spent nine semesters in Berlin, and admonished by Hirschfeld to think over my dissertation carefully and draft it in Latin, and also to make a thorough study of the Louvre, I set out for Paris." (*Autobiographical Letter*)

"Over the course of almost a year I did exercises in French stylistics every day. It was also then that I went to England for the first time, on a short visit." (Ibid.)

Meeting with I. M. Grevs in the Bibliothèque Nationale in Paris: "After a meeting on the ground of our common study of Roman history there followed a sincere friendship as well. He imperiously ordered me to go to Rome." (Ibid.)

1892, spring

Tour of Italy and arrival in Rome.

"Here he assiduously frequented the German Archeological Institute, participated together with its pupils . . . in making the rounds of the antiquities, finished his Latin dissertation for Mommsen, and thought of nothing but history and philology." (O. Deschartes)

Contact with Professors Krasheninikov, Speransky, Rostovtzeff, the artist Nesterov, and others.

1893, July

Meeting with Lydia Dmitrievna Zinovieva-Annibal in Rome.

"Through each other, each of us found himself and more than just himself: I would say we found God. My meeting with her was like a powerful, Dionysiac spring thunderstorm, after which everything

in me was renewed, blooming, and green. And not only in me did
the poet reveal himself and recognize himself, freely and confidently,
but in her as well. Our entire life together, full of deep inner events,
could without exaggeration be called a time of almost uninterrupted
inspiration and intense spiritual enthusiasm for both of us." (*Autobiographical Letter*)

"We are two tree trunks set on fire by a thunderstorm,
Two flames in the midnight pine forest;
We are two meteors flying in the night,
The double-pointed arrow of a single fate!
We are two arms of a single cross"
        (*Kormchie zvezdy* [Pilot Stars])

August

Lydia Dmitrievna returns to Russia. The Ivanovs move to Florence.

1894, August

Lydia Dmitrievna's second trip to Italy. She, her children from her
first marriage, and the Ivanov family stay in Florence.

1895, January

Ivanov's "flight" to Rome "for archeological work"; his family and
Lydia Dmitrievna's family remain in Florence.

12–15 March

Lydia Dmitrievna visits Rome and meets Ivanov again.

Summer

Ivanov returns to Florence. Settles on divorce.

"Nietzscheanism helped me—cruelly and responsibly, but in all conscience, correctly—to resolve the choice that faced me in 1895,
between the deep and tender attachment that my feeling of love for

my wife had become, and the new love that had entirely captivated me and that was destined only to grow and spiritually deepen from that time throughout my whole life, but which in those first days seemed both to me and to her whom I loved to be only a criminal, dark, demonic passion. I told my wife frankly about everything, and we decided on a divorce." (*Autobiographical Letter*)

"Dmitrievskaya and I got a divorce, and it was very grim and cruel, but you see, I was a Nietzschean then. . . . Now I perceive it as a murder, because Dmitrievskaya's life was utterly shattered." (From conversations with M. S. Altman)

After his wife departs, Ivanov sets off through Berlin to Moscow, sees his mother, accomplishes the formalities of the divorce and returns to Italy to be reunited with Lydia Dmitrievna Zinovieva-Annibal.

August

Ivanov's dissertation on tax-farming in ancient Rome, *De societatibus vectigalium populi Romani,* is presented to the History Department at the University of Berlin and approved by Hirschfeld and Mommsen.

1896

First meetings with Vladimir Solovyov.

"From that time, over the course of several years, whenever I went to Russia I had meetings with him that were important to me. He was the patron of my muse and the confessor of my heart." (*Autobiographical Letter*)

April

Death of Aleksandra Dmitrievna Ivanova.

16/28 April

Birth of Lydia Vyacheslavovna Ivanova.

Trip to Berlin and visit to Mommsen. His comment: "the dissertation is far above the ordinary level." (*Autobiographical Letter*)

"All I had yet to do was to appear at an examination which, according to Hirschfeld's assurances and a hint from Mommsen himself, was simply a formality; Hirschfeld also assured me that after receiving my doctoral degree I would get a place as a *Privatdozent* in Germany. But I was not destined ever to appear at the examination: the zealous study of specialized papers and thick books . . . did not insure me against the possibility of missing some elementary question, and my self-esteem could not be reconciled to that possibility. And at that time my heart was already full of something else." (Ibid.)

"Not only internal but external reasons deprived Ivanov of the possibility of working peacefully at Berlin or Moscow University. . . . Lydia's husband refused to give her a divorce, and the legal dissolution of a marriage that had in reality long ceased to exist took many years and the most complex proceedings. While waiting for the opportunity of marrying, Vyacheslav and Lydia had to lie low and hide Lydia's children, whom their father was threatening and trying to abduct. A time of wandering began. They traveled around Italy, France, England and Switzerland; they also visited their homeland to meet with relatives, but they came separately and without their children." (O. Deschartes)

1897

Stay in London: "I had not, however, abandoned Rome for Hellenism, and during our almost year-long stay in England I assiduously collected materials in the reading room of the British Museum in London, for a study of the religio-historical roots of the Roman faith in Rome's universal mission." (*Autobiographical Letter*)

1898

First publication of poems, in *Kosmopolis* and *Vestnik Evropy* (The Herald of Europe), on the initiative of Vladimir Solovyov.

1899, winter

Lydia Dmitrievna Zinovieva-Annibal's divorce from her first husband, Konstantin Semyonovich Shvarsalon. Marriage of Vyacheslav Ivanov and Lydia Dmitrievna Zinovieva-Annibal in Greek Orthodox Church in Livorno.

autumn

Vladimir Solovyov's invitation to visit him in his "little hermitage"—"a rare privilege for the philosopher's spiritually closest friends" (O. Deschartes). Ivanov, however, lost his way: "He looked for the hermitage for many hours without success; finally, by nightfall he trudged into some railroad station or other, took the first available train and returned to town. And in vain Solovyov waited for him patiently all day. The appointed meeting never took place." (O. Deschartes)

Publication in a separate brochure of translation of Pindar's First Pythian Ode.

1900

"From 1900 a settled life began, and a house was taken in Geneva. There, far from the time of troubles in the homeland, our parents settled the family. And this also freed them for literary activity. They took an apartment in St. Petersburg which acquired the name the 'Tower,' and only came to see the family for rather short stays." (L. Ivanova)

"Our little villa in Geneva, 'villa Java,' was darling, with two stories and yet a third story on top, where there was a garret and mansards. A very large garden surrounded it." (L. Ivanova)

The children were raised under the supervision of Marija Mikhailovna Zamyatnina, a friend of Lydia Dmitrievna Zinovieva-Annibal's youth, who became a trusted member of the Ivanov family.

summer

"In the middle of the summer of 1900, Vyacheslav Ivanovich and Lydia Dmitrievna visited Vladimir Solovyov in St. Petersburg, and, in fulfillment of his tacit will, they set off directly from his home to Kiev, as pilgrims to the Cave Monastery." (O. Deschartes)

Vladimir Solovyov approves of the title of the first collection, *Kormchie zvezdy* (Pilot Stars), which refers to the collection of ecclesiastical law: "'Nomocanon . . .—they will say that the author is a philologist, but that doesn't matter. Very good, very good.'" (O. Deschartes)

31 July

Death of Vladimir Solovyov.

1902, spring

"From Athens Lydia Dmitrievna Zinovieva-Annibal and I went to Palestine for Easter and visited Alexandria and Cairo along the way. After this trip I fell ill in Athens, with typhus of such a lingering and dangerous strain that the doctors were already almost despairing of my recovery." (*Autobiographical Letter*)

"Thinking of my possible death, which in itself had always been a desired object to me, I was glad that I was leaving *Pilot Stars* behind me: the book had been published in Russia." (Ibid.)

"In Athens, where I spent a year, I was already entirely devoted to the study of the religion of Dionysus. This study was prompted by an insistent inner necessity: this was the only way in which I could overcome Nietzsche in the area of problems of religious consciousness." (*Autobiographical Letter*)

"Ivanov assiduously studied epigraphy in the Museum, participated in Derpfeld's archeological expeditions and collected materials on questions of Greek myths and cults, which lay at the basis of all his scholarly works." (O. Deschartes)

<u>1903</u>

"In spring Ivanov returned to his family in Châtelaine. The Ivanovs lived there until 1905. 'Lived,' however, is not an entirely apt word; more precisely, Vyacheslav and Lydia came there from time to time, as before. They would visit Russia, spend the whole winter in Paris, and were often away in various cities and countries for more or less extensive periods of time." (O. Deschartes)

"In Châtelaine Ivanov studied Sanskrit with De Saussure." (O. Deschartes)

Publication of first book of poems, *Pilot Stars*.

"The debutant emerges . . . as a real master who understands the contemporary tasks of verse and works at them. . . . All times and countries are equally congenial to him; he gathers his honey from all flowers. He handles the sonnet with the refined elegance of the Italian masters, its creators; he is strict and powerful in his terzinas, free and classically lucid in his hexameters and elegiac distichs; he adapts the Alcaic and Sapphic strophes to Russian poetry, lending an amazing lightness to these alien meters and bringing them close to Russian verse; at one moment he approaches the harmoniousness of Pushkin's melodies, at the next he renews the intoxicated sounds of Yazykov, then again he uses the form of our folk songs in a new way." (V. Bryusov)

"In 1903 Ivanov went to Paris to give a course of lectures on the Hellenic religion of Dionysus in the 'University of Social Sciences' that had been established for Russians by M. M. Kovalevsky. The lectures were a huge success: they were attended not only by pupils of the school, but by the professors; they were also attended by representatives of the Russian elite who were visiting Paris." (O. Deschartes)

"There I met Valery Bryusov, who came to my lecture, and who had already reviewed my book of poems. Merezhkovsky wrote and asked me to send my lectures on Dionysus to *Novyi put'* (New Path)." (*Autobiographical Letter*)

"The relationship with Valery Bryusov was a series of the most complex vicissitudes, shifting from genuine intimacy to unpleasant clashes and back again." (O. Deschartes)

"How strange amid the noise of our arguments,
Our ardent blindness,
Is the melody of your victorious choruses
To undying beauty:

And joining our northern lyre
To an Aeolian chime,
You proclaim to me and the world
A native and near horizon!" (V. Bryusov)

1904, spring

Arrival in Moscow.

"Ivanov! Ivanov! Ivanov! Ivanov!" (A. Bely)

"But I was captivated, conquered, touched, when I visited the Ivanovs, who were staying in a house that stood on the place where now a monument to K. A. Timeryazev has been erected." (A. Bely)

"Vyacheslav Ivanov, who hasn't been living in Russia, has just been here, among us; he flashed with brilliance, perplexed, enchanted, many didn't like him; and he left; we didn't know him." (A. Bely)

"The next year my wife and I met the Moscow poets. Bryusov, Balmont, Baltrušaitis solemnly recognized me as 'the real thing,' and we just as solemnly became good friends." (*Autobiographical Letter*)

Trip to St. Petersburg: "And following that we also became acquainted with the Petersburg circle 'New Path.'" (Ibid.)

"Ivanov's relations with Balmont were established immediately and for his whole life: they were sincerely friendly and featured neither outbursts nor ruptures." (O. Deschartes)

"Ivanov's friendship with Baltrušaitis was deep, tender, and true." (O. Deschartes)

"A brilliant, doomed monologist, inexhaustible in 'tête-à-tête conversations'—Vasily Rozanov—became intimate." (O. Deschartes)

"The friendship with Merezhkovsky, which endured stormy arguments and long periods of separation, remained unfailingly strong up to the death of the two writers." (O. Deschartes)

Return to Switzerland. Work on *Tantal* (Tantalus).

Publication of second book of poems, *Prozrachnost'* (Transparency), published by Skorpion.

"There is a sort of person who is destined to steep all the convolutions of his life in the blood of thought, who is accustomed to take the whole many-storied edifice of human history into account. Such people will derive true enjoyment from Vyacheslav Ivanov's book. . . . It is valuable as a lesson in an at times steely verse, as a combination of verbal and logical forms that is fascinating sometimes in the boldness of its conception. In this respect it resembles a chiseled miniature in which movement is depicted so precisely, with such perfection on the part of the artist-caster, that it may at times be taken for a living figure." (A. Blok)

Publication of poems and articles in *Severnye tsvety* (Northern Flowers) and *Vesy* (The Scales).

"During Russia's difficult years my parents did not want to abandon their homeland. They seldom came to see us, and were entirely absorbed in the literary activity of St. Petersburg." (L. Ivanova)

"During the time of Ivanov's stay in Russia in 1904 he began to doubt whether it was admissible, spiritually permissible for him to continue his quiet life far from his homeland." (O. Deschartes)

"Ivanov's Paris course of lectures was published, in the form of a series of articles, in the monthly *New Path* of 1904 and in the monthly *Voprosy zhizni* (Questions of Life; which replaced *New Path*) of 1905." (O. Deschartes)

1905

The events of the first Russian revolution.
Poetic cycle, *Godina gneva* (The Year of Wrath).
Publication of the tragedy *Tantalus* in *Northern Flowers*.

"Vyacheslav Ivanov has imprinted a tragedy of a bright moment with magic force in the dazzling *Tantalus,* his drama, which grips our soul." (Andrey Bely)

Publication of articles in *The Scales* and *Questions of Life.*

autumn

"In early autumn 1905 they left the Villa Java for good." (O. Deschartes)

Beginning of "Tower" period.

"The house at 25 Tavricheskaya was at the corner of Tverskaya Street. The form of the house was peculiar: its corner was built in the shape of a tower. Half of this tower had external walls with large windows, and the other half was part of the inner section of the apartments. A cupola rose over the tower roof, and one could cautiously climb up there to enjoy the marvelous view of the city, the Neva, and its environs. I would often betake myself there, and now and then even Vyacheslav and his guests would too. In the apartments below us the tower formed a large round hall (on the first floor was the Znamensky Dancing School, on the second a public reading room). In our apartment the tower hall was divided into three small rooms with a tiny dark foyer. The shape of the rooms was whimsical, since they were sections of a circle. In each room there was a very big window with a view of the sea of treetops in the Tavrichesky Garden. Father's room was the central one in the tower. Our apartment on the fifth floor was a modest one. All the rooms except the tower had small mansard windows." (L. Ivanova)

"Vyacheslav Ivanov had just then moved in and was getting acquainted with the Petersburgians. . . . He would very politely envelop his interlocutor in his amazing understanding of everything, his unusual erudition, which he knew how to spread softly under his interlocutor's feet; it often seemed as if he was weaving a web of ideas, connecting unconnectable people and enchanting all of them." (A. Bely)

"The first foundation of the people making up the era of 'brilliant Wednesdays' was laid; they were D. Merezhkovsky and his wife, Berdyaev and his wife, Blok, and Rozanov." (A. Bely)

"Soon the Wednesday *jours fixes* turned into 'Ivanov Wednesdays,' about which entire legends arose. People of quite various gifts, positions and tendencies met there. Mystical anarchists and Orthodox, decadents and professors, poets and scholars, artists and thinkers, actors and public figures—all came peacefully together at the Ivanov 'Tower' and peacefully conversed about literary, artistic, philosophical, and occult topics, about the literary news of the day and about the final, ultimate problems of existence." (N. Berdyaev)

"V. Ivanov is the best Russian Hellenist. He is a universal man: poet, learned philologist, specialist in Greek religion, thinker, theologian and theosophist, a publicist who dabbles in politics. He could converse with anyone on the topic of that person's expertise. He was the most remarkable, the most skillful *causeur* I ever met in my life, and a real *charmeur.* He was one of those people who have an esthetic need to be in harmony and correspondence with their milieu and the people around them." (N. Berdyaev)

"It was a talent for imperceptibly introducing each person into the atmosphere of his own interests, his own themes, his own poetic and mystical experiences by way of the path each person was taking toward life." (N. Berdyaev)

"Those two—Vyacheslav Ivanov and Lydia Zinovieva-Annibal—were happy in their own inner fullness, in a way that Russian people are not, in a way they were not then, with the stifled days of December behind them. They seemed to be not of the first decade of the twentieth century, but newcomers from the great, the heroic century, contemporaries of Beethoven." (E. Gertsyk)

"In 1905 I myself promoted the meeting between Ivanov and Blok, seeing in it the beginning of the selection of people for a collective. . . . Ivanov captivated the Bloks." (A. Bely)

"A little stooped, not old, not young,
All an emanation of secret forces,
Oh, how many souls' desert coldness
Have you pierced with your own coldness!

And many charms, and many songs,
And the beauties of ancient visages . . .
Your world, miraculous indeed!
Yes, you are an autocratic tsar." (A. Blok)

Participation in Religio-Philosophical meetings.

1906 January

Participation in the almanac *Fakely* (Torches). Article, "On Non-Acceptance of the World." Beginning of polemics about "mystical anarchism."

"Harsh attacks on 'mystical anarchism' in general and Ivanov in particular began in *The Scales* immediately and continued until 1908." (O. Deschartes)

summer

"An unexpected letter from Sologub, again full of a sort of bifurcating love-hate, with beautiful verses on the name 'Vyacheslav.' A kind of new attempt at sorcery." (*Diary*, 1906)

Society of Hafizites at the "Tower."

"I turn to you, oh Hafizites. My heart and mouth, eyes and ears have turned to you. And here I stand alone among you. Thus my solitude is one with me among you." (*Diary*, 1906)

June–August

Lydia Dmitrievna Zinovieva-Annibal visits Switzerland.

"In the summer of 1906 we rented a chalet with our friends the Wulfs, high in the mountains, in Comballaz over the city of Aigle. Mamma came there to see us for a very short time. It was her last trip to Switzerland, and she made it without Vyacheslav." (L. Ivanova)

August–September

Platonic "affair" with Sergey Gorodetsky, "from the cradle of the autumn moon to the second waning." (O. Deschartes)

"A young man who wrote poems began to visit the "Tower" assiduously. He was tall and well-built. A supple, mobile, 'adolescent' body. A large aquiline nose, large receding forehead, and a small chin that also receded lent a birdlike air to his face; a luxuriant head of hair standing on end, and a somewhat bobbing, flighty step also confirmed the impression of a long-legged bird. The young man was 22 years old." (O. Deschartes)

"Pages of experiences made of fire and blood poisoned with the subtlest venoms. A chronicle of unheard-of suffering and happiness of an unheard-of completeness." (*Diary,* 1906)

"A shapely aspect at the threshold . . .
Sweetness and anxiety in the heart . . .
No breath . . . No light . . .

Half-adolescent, half-bird . . .
The summer lightning of storm-clouds under his brows
Rocks the dim reflection."
        (*Eros*)

November

Meeting with Margarita Sabashnikova, the wife of Maksimilian Voloshin.

"At the summons a woman appeared." (O. Deschartes)

"Lydia and Vyacheslav decided very quickly that Margarita, intelligent, spiritually troubled, was quite capable of being *a third*." (O. Deschartes)

"A mysterious hand shines
In your maidenly and prophetic dreams,
Where birds of the sun, on amber vines,
Drink the juice of the grape clusters, having hastened here from afar,

And the shades of white cavalry—clouds—
Torment the azure in unresolved thunderstorms,
And the bees of midday swarm on the roses
Of the wreath you haven't finished plaiting."
        ("Zolotye zavesy" ["Golden Curtains"])

"Finally the two competitors in applying to life the theory of the merging of three began to doubt the correctness of the very way the question was posed." (O. Deschartes)

winter

Lydia Dmitrievna Zinovieva-Annibal falls ill. Anna Mintslova appears at the "Tower."

"Theosophist, mystic, shaken from within by a chaos of spiritual forces: she appeared from who knows where, there where a tragedy was ripening, and catastrophe was threatening." (E. Gertsyk)

Preparation of the collection *Cor Ardens* for publication. Appearance of book of poems, *Eros*. Work with the publishing house "Ory." The article "*Ty esi*" ("Thou Art")—first draft of the future "Anima."

1907 February

Margarita and Maksimilian Voloshin move into the "Tower."

"The year 1907 was the apogee of Andrey Bely's audacious speeches against 'mystical anarchism,' 'the overcoming of individualism,' 'ecumenicity.'" (O. Deschartes)

spring

"During the spring of 1907, my parents decided to break up the Geneva home and finally move to St. Petersburg." (L. Ivanova)

"It seemed as if they had grown sick of the decadent, orgiastic whirlwinds swirling at their Wednesdays. . . . They were drawn toward work. They undertook to begin publishing a journal in the fall, an artistic-philosophical organ of the Symbolists who dissociated themselves from the estheticizing *Scales*." (E. Gertsyk)

summer

"Vyacheslav Ivanovich and Lydia Dmitrievna spent the summer of 1907 in the sticks, at Zagorye, a distant estate in the province of Mogilyov. They wanted quiet and solitude." (O. Deschartes)

"When Mamma caught sight of Zagorye and entered her new home, the beauty of the place agitated her: she became excited and suddenly started to cry." (L. Ivanova)

17 October

Lydia Dmitrievna Zinovieva-Annibal's unexpected death from scarlet fever.

"Just before the end Lydia became lucid and, fully conscious, said distinctly, 'A wave of bright light; Christ is born.' With that she passed on." (O. Deschartes)

"He to whom my lyrics are not dead hieroglyphics will know what that meant for me; he knows why I live and what I live by." (*Autobiographical Letter*)

"Death answered me: 'Look: my light scorches.
I am love's flame-bearer. Your Psyche,
Desiring the holy font,
Flew ahead into my fire. It will slake
The desire of souls whom the Spirit orders
To light the Earth, shining and flaming.

The dearest shade went off to what was dear to her. Later
Your fused monolith will melt." (*Cor Ardens*)

November

"At the end of November 1907 he appeared in Moscow. . . . One
was struck by his now gaunt, suffering, somewhat nacreous profile."
(A. Bely)

"Mamma's death abruptly breaks off the whole course of our life.
One period ends and another begins. A varied, rich life goes on all
around us, but we all seem to be living and acting in a sort of
straitened and half-real atmosphere, as if a dark stormcloud were
hanging over us. . . . It took years for it to disappear." (L. Ivanova)

"Life flowed on as before at the 'Tower': literary, bohemian-academic
gatherings at night, abundant supplies of wine in simple jugs, mint
cakes, flickering candles stuck in whatever came to hand—cande-
labra, candlesticks, bottles—symposia with friends until morning.
Ivanov was constantly surrounded with admirers and adversaries:
poets, artists, and scholars came from the towns of the homeland
and from foreign lands and stayed for long periods in the strange
and hospitable house on Tavricheskaya." (O. Deschartes)

1908

"I am working in the new tower, already long orphaned . . . on the
ordering of Her works." (*Diary,* 1908)

winter

Anna Rudolfovna Mintslova moves into the "Tower" "almost of her
own accord." (O. Deschartes)

"I perceived Mintslova's influence to be completely negative and even
demonic." (N. Berdyaev)

"She came to Ivanov unbidden, clasped his hand with her soft, always very hot hand, and whispered, 'She is here, she is close by, no need for despair, she can hear, you will hear. . . .' She came to the Tower and never went away again. She settled in." (E. Gertsyk)

spring

Johannes von Günther arrives at the "Tower" from Germany. Translation of *Tantalus* into German in the meter of the original, by Henry von Heiseler (publ. 1940).

summer

"Vyacheslav Ivanov spent the summer with us in Sudak. . . . We put him in a room with a balcony—the attic of our old home. Again an astrologer in a tower, to which a spiral staircase wound its way." (E. Gertsyk)

Abatement in the polemic about "mystical anarchism."

A. Bely "began to depart from the intimacy with the 'faction' of authoritarian Symbolism, an intimacy that was against his nature, and again became close to Ivanov; moreover, the very struggle between the two different tendencies of Symbolism lost its intensity." (O. Deschartes)

winter

The "heard" Latin poem, "Breve aevum separatum."

1909

"Vyacheslav worked a great deal and regularly. After sending away all his guests, he would lie in bed and work until sunrise. Naturally, his morning sometimes started at two in the afternoon. He chain-smoked, in the true sense of the word." (L. Ivanova)

"I never again had occasion to meet a more discussion-oriented person than the Vyacheslav Ivanov of the prewar period. . . . In his love of conversation there was not so much partiality for the battle of opinions as love for the feastlike play of the spirit. Even when attacking an opponent, Ivanov never ceased to attract him with his enchanting amiability. . . . All his public and semi-public speeches were distinguished by a singular combination of profundity and brilliance, erudition and improvisation, weightiness and inspiration." (F. Stepun)

"I want to measure hearts truly,
Weigh them correctly—and in a viscous gaze
I craftily submerge my gaze,
Spreading the conversation like a net."

(Cor Ardens)

Visit to the "Tower" by V. Khlebnikov, "who was drawn to him and feared him, and whose poetic talent Ivanov immediately valued." (O. Deschartes) Appearance of O. Mandelshtam at the "Tower."

"Once a grandmother brought her grandson to be appraised by Ivanov, and we were very amused both by this poet's grandmother and by the boy himself, Mandelshtam, who read precise porcelain poems." (E. Gertsyk)

"He not only recognized Mandelshtam as a genuine poet, but felt a great, almost fatherly tenderness for the frail and ardent young man." (O. Deschartes)

"Vyacheslav Ivanov is more of the people and more accessible (in the future) than all the other Russian Symbolists." (O. Mandelshtam)

June

"I am translating Novalis's *Geistliche Lieder.*" (*Diary,* 1909)

Break with Margarita Sabashnikova.

"After Lydia's passing all the significance of former relationships disappeared for Ivanov, but Margarita began to live on the hope of a new sort of intimacy between them. This was natural on the woman's part, but completely intolerable for Ivanov." (O. Deschartes)

"Friday is the beginning of the final break (M.'s arrival from Finland). Tuesday, Wednesday, Thursday—without her. I hope that tomorrow is the last meeting. . . . And at the same time I do not want to let her go with the impression of external discord, with offense at a harsh word." (*Diary*, 1909)

July

"It is difficult and terrible to describe the merciless battle of recent days, the pitiless, cruel felling of an accursed forest, verdant and tender but poisonous and inhabited by malicious demons. It seems as if I am killing off something agonizingly vital, which gazes touchingly and tries with its final malice to sting me fatally." (*Diary*, 1909)

August

Move to the "Tower" of Mikhail Kuzmin, "whom he loved ardently for his impeccable artistic taste and genuine poetic gift, and with whom he constantly and just as ardently clashed and argued over his impermissible escapades." (O. Deschartes)

"But if, exciting the heart,
I see a dear phantom glitter for a moment,
You will divine me."

(*Nezhnaja tajna* [Tender Mystery])

"I awakened late. Lydia [Dmitrievna] had long been with me in my dreams. I had a joyful and amazed conviction that her return had actually been realized." (*Diary*, 1909)

September

"I was awakened by a sharp pain and a cry from the soul *de profundis*, summoning Lydia. I remember that I had to call her with all my will, with all the pain of separation, to contain all its anguish and terror in that thrice-repeated summons. And when I called her, her answering call faintly resounded. And for an instant before I awoke,

I was able to feel all the happiness and all the hope that blazed up in me at that reply." (*Diary,* 1909)

"In the latter half of that month Innokenty Fyodorovich Annensky (1857–1909) and Ivanov met almost every day, helping S. K. Makovsky put together *Apollon,* the first issue of which appeared in October." (O. Deschartes)

"That year the *Apollon* literary group was born. While thinking highly of several of the young poets, future Acmeists, Vyacheslav Ivanov fiercely attacked the estheticizing spirit of the circle." (E. Gertsyk)

"The discussion of the end of Symbolism began in jest." (A. Bely)

"No matter how Ivanov responded to Acmeism in the period of its beginnings, all his life he ingenuously and unfailingly loved the three main representatives of that literary movement." (O. Deschartes)

"Among the conversations at table were a sort that enthralled my father and me alike. These were Gumilyov's stories about Africa, which he alternated with readings of his poems." (L. Ivanova)

"Andrey Bely was one of the Muscovites who would come to visit us literally with suitcase in hand. . . . At that time he was writing his novel *Petersburg,* and would read new parts to Vyacheslav as they were composed." (L. Ivanova)

"He was fusing Blok's themes, mine, and his own, as if preparing for the union of Symbolists, which he realized through patient effort, making peace with Blok; the union was realized in 1910 and flowered into Musagete; he really knew: we are made akin by the feeling of crisis." (A. Bely)

Active participation in the Religio-Philosophical Society. Publication of first book of articles, *Po zvezdam* (By the Stars).

1910, spring

Disappearance of Anna Mintslova.

"When she understood, in the spring of 1910, that the relationship between Vyacheslav and Vera was taking a turn that was dangerous for her, she bluntly announced to Ivanov that he was destined to play a beneficial role in the fate of his country, but that in order to do so he must live in the world like a monk, taking a secret vow, and remain celibate so as not to dissipate the powers that would be granted him. Ivanov answered with a decisive refusal. . . . She went away. Forever. No one who had known her in Russia ever saw her anywhere again. . . . Strange surmises and rumors began to be spread around the city." (O. Deschartes)

"With every glance at your surroundings, every time you feel the touch of things, you must recognize that you are in contact with God, that God appears before you and reveals Himself to you, surrounding you with Himself; you will contemplate His mystery and read His thoughts. Every movement of your feelings must become benediction and reverence, directed outside yourself and your body, which flows in God. Incessantly glorifying God in this way, in external objective reality, your soul will merge with everything, for its praise will be an affirmation of divine reality in you yourself." (*Diary*, 1910)

April

Production by V. E. Meyerhold of Calderón's mystery play *La Devoción de la Cruz* at the "Tower."

"The plan for the production was months in the making, and the enterprise attracted the interest of an ever greater number of the talented people in our circle." (L. Ivanova)

"Thus the advent of Bacchus,
Without loss to art,

In nineteen hundred and ten
Performed Calderón's play."
    (*Tender Mystery*)

<u>summer</u>

Collection of materials in Italy for a book on Dionysus. Vera arrives
from Greece.

"As it had been with her mother, everything was decided in Rome."
(O. Deschartes)

"Between the columns, where Persephone shines,
In the folds of a damp chiton I see
Your bowed neck.

Tender pilgrim to the shrine,
Childish copy of the daughter-goddess
Who stepped across the forbidden threshold." (*Tender Mystery*)

"A vivid but insane life shook the foundations of the times."
(A. Bely)

"Even Ivanov's 'Wednesdays' were already Thursdays." (A. Bely)

"There was no limit to the hospitality, the cordiality, the affection
shown to his guests by Vyacheslav the Magnificent; Shestov called
him that." (A. Bely)

"Soon, having shaved off his beard and even his mustache, somehow
drawing himself up straight, even seeming younger in his frank old
age, clearly gleaming with the silver of the gray hair that was advancing on him, he became a lecturer at the University and a collaborator with Zelinsky, having turned away from mystical
anarchism and turning to Greece, to rhythmics, to 'mere poetry';
he was already philosophizing about our own contemporary life, not
Cretan; he appeared with a face grown younger, like a cross between
Tyutchev and Mommsen." (A. Bely)

"With his head wrapped up, he would be buried in proofs on the low sofa-bed, working without getting dressed, sipping black tea brought right to the bed. . . . By 7:30 in the evening he would appear as if it were morning—pink, fresh as a rose, washed, dressed—to have supper." (A. Bely)

Movement of the "younger," religious or realistic Symbolism—Vyacheslav Ivanov, Blok, Bely—centered around the publishing house Musagete.

"Realistic Symbolism admits as a symbol any reality, taken in conjunction with the higher reality, that is, that which is more real in the series of the real. For realistic Symbolism the higher reality is found through a single act of intuition either outside the lower reality which reflects it, or immanent to the lower reality which envelops it. Realistic Symbolism seeks in things the sign of their ontological value and connection." ("Simbolismo")

Publication of Latin dissertation on Roman tax farming. Beginning of teaching in Raev's Women's Classes. Participation in "Society for the Development of the Artistic Word."

1911

"One day in 1911 the poet Gumilyov brought his young wife, who wrote poetry, to the 'Tower'. . . . She ventured to read. . . . Everyone waited to see what Ivanov would say. . . . He silently rose, walked up to the young woman, kissed her hand: 'I greet you and congratulate you. Your poems are an event in Russian literature. You will be a famous poetess.'" (O. Deschartes)

"Once Anna Akhmatova demonstrated her suppleness on the carpet in the center of a circle formed by the guests: bending backward, still standing, she had to seize in her teeth a match that had been stuck vertically into a box lying on the floor." (L. Ivanova)

"Having recognized Akhmatova immediately for who she was, he subsequently rejoiced at her spiritual growth and poetic fulfillment." (O. Deschartes)

Publication of third book of poems, *Cor Ardens,* in two volumes.

"I seem to hear the words 'with fear and trembling' when I try to speak about the best, most significant, and perhaps at the same time the most intimate book by one of our major teachers and leaders in poetry. . . . Vyacheslav Ivanov's poetry is the sound of trumpets and flutes, the rustling of wings, the running of white horses who moan with a tender neighing only in the hour of sacrificial quiet. . . ." (M. Kuzmin)

summer

"In the summer of 1911 a dacha was taken in Sillamiagi (Estonia). The dacha stood in the middle of a marvelous grove, not far from the sea." (L. Ivanova)

"Gershenzon . . . was also living in a dacha not far from us, and he would often stop in to see Vyacheslav. I think this was the beginning of their fast friendship." (L. Ivanova)

1912, spring

"Spring of 1912 was setting in. Soon I would be 16 years old. And suddenly Vyacheslav turns to me and invites me to come to his room in the 'Tower' so that he can have a little talk with me. We pass through a little side room on the left. Vera is sitting in it and watches timidly as we pass. I am again seated in the solemn black armchair and hear improbable things." (L. Ivanova)

"In the spring of 1912, Ivanov set off for Switzerland with Vera, who was expecting a child, and his daughter.

June

In June they moved to France, to Savoie, and settled in a small villa near the hamlet of Neuvecelle." (O. Deschartes)

The 'Tower' period ended. A completely new time of life began. I had the sensation that the stormcloud, the gloom, which had hung over us in St. Petersburg even at joyful moments, had dispersed. It was as though morning had come." (L. Ivanova)

12 July

Birth of Dmitri Vyacheslavovich Ivanov.

Work on a book of poetry, *Tender Mystery.*

autumn

"We moved to Rome and made our home in a pension on the Piazza del Popolo that belonged to a certain Englishwoman. . . . The situation, on the corner of the Via del Babuino, was delightful. Several windows looked directly out onto the square, and several overlooked the park of Monte Pincio. Vyacheslav was happy and gay in his beloved Rome." (L. Ivanova)

"There were meetings of friends passing through; but the most valuable thing was that in Rome his friendship with Vladimir Frantzevich Ern was strengthened. The friendship was only broken with Ern's death." (L. Ivanova)

"Vyacheslav Ivanov would visit the learned monk Padre Palmieri, a zealous advocate of the reunification of the churches." (E. Gertsyk)

Beginning of work on translations of Aeschylus.

"But if there is anyone before whom he would not be ashamed to bow down, it is the poet-priest of ancient tragedy; and if there is a service by means of which he might surpass those services he has heretofore rendered, it is the recreation of Aeschylus in Russian poetry." (F. Zelinsky)

Beginning of work on the long poem *Infancy* and the book *Dionis i pradionisijstvo* (Dionysus and Predionysianism). Participation in the journal *Trudy i dni* (Works and Days), which advances the platform of "younger Symbolism."

1913, summer

Marriage to Vera Konstantinovna Shvarsalon.

"Vyacheslav and Vera remained for the summer in Italy, where they were married in the Greek Orthodox Church in Livorno and where Dima was christened, in Florence." (L. Ivanova)

autumn

"The final move to Moscow, to 25 Zubovsky Boulevard, took place in the autumn. . . . The view from all three windows was magnificent, since the apartment was located on the upper floors and there were no high buildings in front; a wide and open panorama of the whole city was spread out before us." (L. Ivanova)

"Life was more normal in Moscow than in St. Petersburg, although there were no fewer friends. Perhaps the existence of a small child itself created a certain rhythm." (L. Ivanova)

Active participation in Religio-Philosophical Society and close contact with N. Berdyaev and P. Florensky.

Meeting with A. N. Skryabin. "My friendship with him in the last two years of his life was a deeply significant and bright event on the paths of my spirit." (*Autobiographical Letter*)

"And my family clavier remembers
The magical touch of his fingers . . ."
   (*Vechernij svet* [Evening Light])

Publication of fourth book of poems, *Tender Mystery*.

"His verse has acquired the power of confidence and impetuosity, his images have acquired precision and color, his composition—clarity and a beautiful simplicity. On every page you feel that you are faced with a great poet who has reached the utter peak of his powers." (N. Gumilyov)

1914

Publication of book of translations of poems and fragments by Alcaeus and Sappho.

1914, 30 January

"Vyacheslav Ivanov takes part in a public debate about the theater. In a long speech with sketches Vyacheslav Ivanov demonstrated that the scenic art consists of three elements: the social, mimesis, and heroics." (*Russkie Vedomosti* [Russian Record])

March

Participates in the collection *Sirin*.

October

Vyacheslav Ivanov joins the lecture committee "War and Culture," for the organization of public readings in the capital and the provinces, on behalf of the Townspeople's Union. S. I. Bulgakov, S. A. Kotlyarevsky, P. B. Struve, and others also join.

1915, 16 January

Vyacheslav Ivanov gives lecture, "Čiurlionis and Problems of the Synthesis of the Arts."

21 January

Vyacheslav Ivanov participates in a public debate on contemporary literature, held by the Symbolists in the Kalashnikov Exchange Building.

1 March

The newspaper *Utro Rossii* (Russian Morning) publishes an address "To the Russian People," demanding equality of rights for the Jewish nation. Among the signers are Vyacheslav Ivanov, Leonid Andreyev, Nikolay Berdyaev, and Fyodor Sologub.

Work on the melopoeia *Chelovek* (Man) and the essays "Icon and Masks of Russia," and "*Legion i sobornost'*" ("Legion and Ecumenicity"), devoted to themes connected with the melopoeia. Completion of the tragedy *Prometej* (Prometheus).

September

Vyacheslav Ivanov participates in the collection *Shchit* (The Shield), which has as its aim the struggle against anti-Semitism.

1916, April

Publication of second book of articles, *Borozdy i mezhi* (Furrows and Boundaries).

summer

"In the summer of 1916 we rented a dacha, along with the Erns, in Krasnaya Polyana, several dozen versts from Gagra. It was a Greek settlement of several dachas, built by a group of professors from various universities." (L. Ivanova)

autumn

"After Krasnaya Polyana and after taking a two-week mud cure in Matsesta (near Gagra), Vyacheslav settled along with Vera and Dima in the 'Svetlana' pension in Sochi, and did not return to Moscow for the winter but stayed the whole year in his beloved South." (L. Ivanova)

"He had received a commission from the Sabashnikov publishing house for a translation of Aeschylus, and during his long stay on the shores of the Black Sea, among the 'swarthy cypresses,' in the shade of the plane trees, he translated almost all the tragedies of his favorite writer, in the original meters." (O. Deschartes)

October

Emergence of first plans for *Povest' o tsareviche Svetomire* (Tale of Prince Svetomir).

"He dreamed of the image of the novice-prince; he is trampling the grapes for the communion wine; a monastery, a pointed mountain, the sea; the Virgin in a bark. . . . The prince is singing. Ivanov wrote down his song. He learned his name—Svetomir." (O. Deschartes)

Essays on war, Russia, and the spiritual essence of the Slavic people, to be included in *Rodnoe i vselenskoe* (Matters Native and Universal).

1917, winter

"Autobiographical Letter to S. A. Vengerov" for the book *Twentieth-Century Russian Literature*, edited by Vengerov.

"At present I am occupied primarily with translating the tragedies of Aeschylus and Dante's *Vita Nuova*." (*Autobiographical Letter*)

February

Revolution in Russia. Overthrow of the autocracy.

"It was decided to compose a new hymn to Russia. Vyacheslav and Balmont wrote it." (L. Ivanova)

Publication of third book of essays, *Matters Native and Universal*.

autumn

"Everyone returned to Moscow relatively early." (L. Ivanova)

October coup in St. Petersburg. Fighting in Moscow.

"The October Revolution burst upon us like thunder over our heads. Our house was on the front line. The fighting in Moscow lasted six days. Cannons thundered, and people told us they were shooting from the Sparrow Hills into the center of town—in other words, the

shells were flying over us. But there was also constant shooting of
rifles and machine guns in the streets." (L. Ivanova)

Attempt by a group of Red Army soldiers to arrest Ivanov: "But
something in his calm, his voice, perhaps a sort of spiritual power,
affected them, and they suddenly seemed to sink, they were almost
embarrassed . . . and they left." (L. Ivanova)

Completion of printing of *Ellinskaja religija stradajushchego boga* (The
Hellenic Religion of the Suffering God).

"V. Ivanov's great significance as one of the forerunners of this
[Slavic] Renaissance derives from the fact that he is both a poet and
a student of antiquity. He began his career as a philologist, and he
has remained a philologist to this day. His philological paper, in
Latin, on publicans, his book about the suffering god (Dionysus),
and his introduction to Homer show him to be a conscientious and
patient student of antiquity, that maternal soil of his ideas."
(F. Zelinsky)

"Directly opposite our windows, which gave onto such a broad horizon, a huge conflagration was blazing. By night the hellish glow
enveloped half the sky. These were buildings that were burning, in
one of which the Sabashnikov publishing house was located. In the
printing shop there, all the copies of Vyacheslav's just-printed book
The Hellenic Religion of the Suffering God were reduced to ashes."
(L. Ivanova)

"The building burned to the ground, and in it the entire edition of
the book along with the manuscript perished on the eve of its publication. One of the proof copies . . . was in the author's possession,
and it is still intact; another or others remained in Moscow. Their
fate is unknown." (O. Deschartes)

1918

"We began to try to get a transfer to another apartment, since the
water pipes in ours were beginning to burst from the frost. Vyacheslav was allotted half an apartment on the former Afanasievsky

Lane, to which we moved. The apartment was furnished and had been abandoned by someone; they gave us three rooms in it and a kitchen shared with the neighbors." (L. Ivanova)

"In the first years of the October Revolution, open public debates were often arranged. . . . Ivanov often appeared at them in defense of religion. At one of these debates he happened to speak immediately after People's Commissar for Education A. V. Lunacharsky. Lunacharsky was a good orator. He eloquently declared for pure atheism. Thunderous applause resounded after his speech. Ivanov came out onto the platform. In a quiet voice (this quiet voice could be heard everywhere), as if imparting a cherished mystery, he spoke of Christ and the Antichrist, of the suffering God, of God's chosen people. . . . He read poems, recounted legends. The crowd listened spellbound. When he finished and fell silent the silence held. It could be felt as a presence. . . . Suddenly it disappeared in a burst of applause." (O. Deschartes)

"In 1918, when the persecution of the Church intensified, Sergey Bulgakov entered the priesthood. Ivanov was present at his ordination. Their friendship deepened." (O. Deschartes)

"The more people were tormented and mired in their everyday life, the keener and more vital became their longing for a genuine existence: circles were formed, and receptive youths, thirsting for knowledge, would gather. Listeners and scholars would come poorly dressed, frozen, but enthusiastic and ardent in spirit. Ivanov loved to converse with them about religion, poetry, Hellas; he taught them versification . . . , he demanded that they guard the purity of the language." (O. Deschartes)

"When the Theatrical Department of the People's Commissariat for Education was formed in 1918, Ivanov began working there. Here he encountered many old friends from the literary theatrical world." (O. Deschartes)

Participation, along with Blok and Bely, in the journal *Zapiski mechtatelej* (Dreamers' Notes), organized by S. Alyansky, published by "Alkonost." Publication of the poem "Infancy."

1919

"Hunger was approaching gradually but implacably." (L. Ivanova)

Death of M. M. Zamyatnina.

"Vyacheslav endured all deprivations stoically, never complained, calmly bore all the inevitable, morbid nervous outbursts at home, and continued his thinking and his work." (L. Ivanova)

March

Work on the epilogue to the melopoeia *Man*.

"I don't recall any large gatherings of friends in those years. There were only intimate meetings." (L. Ivanova)

Publication of the tragedy *Prometheus*.

"The present lyrico-dramatic work is a tragedy—in the first place, of action as such; in the second place, of the active personality's exhaustion of himself in action; in the third place, of the continuity of action. In general, it is a tragedy of a titanic origin, like the primal sin of human freedom." (From the author's preface *O dejstvii i dejstve* [On Action and the Drama])

autumn

Vera and Dmitri, both ill, stay in a sanatorium in the small town Serebryany Bor.

December

Ivanov visits his wife and son in the sanatorium.

"His *Zimnie sonety* (Winter Sonnets) deal with that Christmas of 1919. From them and from the photographs of that time, in which he wears a beret, one can guess the hell that was in his soul then. Outwardly he was still just as calm and open to everyone." (L. Ivanova)

"And I see, as if in a crystal ball,
My family in a nearby sanctuary,
In the mellifluous light of holiday candles.

And my heart, wearied by the secret closeness,
Awaits a little spark in the midst of the pine forest. But the sleigh's
Straight flight rushes past, past"
    (*Winter Sonnets*)

"To endure . . . is not enough—but what he was able to do in 1919, when we all were silent, to turn his feelings into art, that is what has some meaning." (A. Akhmatova)

<u>1920</u>

"In the beginning of 1920, thanks to Lunacharsky's patronage, Balmont and Vyacheslav were granted permission for trips abroad. Our case was particularly exceptional, since trips with one's family were usually not permitted. Everything was already arranged and even the day of departure, some time in May, had been fixed. Vera, and all of us as well, dreamed of the departure for Davos. We believed that there she would be able to recover from her pulmonary tuberculosis. . . . When Lunacharsky wangled the trips for Balmont and Vyacheslav, he asked them to personally give their word of honor that when they got out of the country they would not speak out against the Soviet government, at least for the first few years. He took responsibility for them. Both of them gave their word. But as soon as Balmont, who left first, had gotten to Revel, he sharply criticized Soviet Russia. As a result of Balmont's speech, Vyacheslav's trip was cancelled. I can remember the tragic look on Vera's face . . . when she heard this news." (L. Ivanova)

<u>spring</u>

Last meeting with A. A. Blok.

"Outwardly there was no great closeness between Ivanov and Tsvetaeva, but at times their inner bond would unexpectedly be revealed to me." (O. Deschartes)

"You write on the sand with your finger,
And I have approached and am reading.
Already gray hair on the temple.
My head is golden.

And the twilight steals up like a thief,
Like a black and fatal army . . .
You know, in order better to read,
Oh Rabbi!—I close my eyes . . .

You write on the sand with your finger . . ." (M. Tsvetaeva)

June–July

Composition of *Perepiska iz dvukh uglov* (A Correspondence from Two
Corners) by Ivanov and M. O. Gershenzon.

"They had both received permission to spend six weeks in a sanatorium for writers outside Moscow, and they were allotted a common
room." (L. Ivanova)

Ivanov's definition of culture as the "cult of memory," as the "ladder
of Eros and the hierarchy of reverence."

"There will be an epoch of great, joyful, all-embracing return. Then
springs will begin to gush out from between the old flagstones, and
rose bushes will sprout forth from gray tombs." (*A Correspondence
from Two Corners*)

8 August

Death of Vera Konstantinovna Shvarsalon.

"A slow finger completes its appointed circle,
And a hammer suddenly strikes the heart"
    (*Evening Light*)

"After Vera's death Vyacheslav was seized by a horror of spending
another winter in Moscow. He asked at work for permission to take
a trip, to Italy if possible, but if not, then somewhere in the South,

where he would not have to see snow, where everything would be different. Meanwhile, in order to give him a chance to rest, he was sent with his family . . . to a sanatorium in Kislovodsk for six weeks." (L. Ivanova)

autumn

"Life flowed by peacefully in Kislovodsk, until a certain day when suddenly the sounds of cannonade could be heard from early in the morning." (L. Ivanova)

October

"Soon after this it was announced to us that the Kislovodsk Sanatorium was to be closed down. All the patients were asked to write down where they would like to move. The choice was between Moscow, two towns in central Russia, and Baku." (L. Ivanova)

"Vyacheslav was firm in his choice of Baku. It's in the south, and the border is close by. Who knows, maybe one could manage to cross it, and then get to Italy by a roundabout way?" (L. Ivanova)

"On the ninth day Train no. 14 reached Baku. All the passengers alighted except us: we had nowhere to go. Vyacheslav went to have a look at the town and suddenly ran into Gorodetsky. It turned out that he and his family were living in Baku . . . It was impossible to find living quarters in the town, but for the first few days he lodged us in a dark passageway in an apartment stuffed with numerous families." (L. Ivanova)

"It transpired that a University had been founded in Baku not long before our arrival. Its initial nucleus was a group of professors from the University of Tiflis, since all Russian professors had been expelled at the time of the short-lived national government in Georgia. Professors from various cities gradually began to converge on Baku University . . . The People's Commissariat for Education immediately sent Vyacheslav to the University, where he was greeted with open arms." (L. Ivanova)

"His new colleagues sacrificed their smoking room in order to install us in it." (L. Ivanova)

"Our room was located on a corridor in the University, and so people were constantly dropping in. Students with whom Vyacheslav had an especially close relationship would come by. Among them, Moisey Altman would drop in at least once every day." (L. Ivanova)

November

Ivanov is selected as Professor Ordinarius of Classical Philology and Poetics.

"At that time the University was quite young, and one could sense that the professors and students regarded it lovingly. As yet it had little contact with the central government, and it adhered to the old traditional structure. Vyacheslav worked there with enthusiasm." (L. Ivanova)

"Everyone loved to hear Ivanov. He lectured in the first auditorium, which held 600–1000 people, and students from all departments would gather, and be standing in the aisles." (S. Makovelsky)

"Ivanov took an active part not only in the scholarly, administrative and economic life of the University, but in the cultural life of the entire town. He participated in the selection of scholarly personnel, in the organization of the library, in the purchase of equipment, in the housing commission, and played a large role in the organization of the theater and the cinema." (O. Deschartes)

"But Ivanov's chief concern and delight was his contact with talented students. Several of them became real scholars, significant representatives of scholarship. Ivanov's inner, spiritual influence on his students was of particular importance. Former Baku students later testified that in difficult moments of their lives they would remember their teacher's words, and these words would lend them faith in their own powers and would help them overcome the difficulties. Their inner contact with their teacher ceased neither with parting nor with Ivanov's death." (O. Deschartes)

1921

"Vyacheslav Ivanov was a gentle man, but it was a catlike, tigerlike gentleness, gentle and strong-willed. For all his gentleness, his interlocutor always felt himself taken firmly in hand. At the same time, never simplifying and sometimes speaking of things that were incomprehensible to us at our age and stage of development, Ivanov never humiliated his interlocutor with the sense of that infinite distance between himself and us. . . . Ivanov was wisdom itself. But he displayed such loving personal interest that one could speak with him as with a father, as with a person who is wiser than you but who talks to you like an equal, although you know that equality is out of the question." (V. Manuilov)

"The other day I was given an examination by Vyacheslav Ivanov. Our conversation lasted about an hour. In the course of it we examined a plan of Athens and photographs of the ruins, and he told me about them. He read me entire lectures on Dionysus and pre-Dionysus. And just at random he would ask me sly questions." (E. Millior)

"At that time Khlebnikov suddenly appeared in Baku. One beautiful morning he turned up completely unexpectedly. . . . Vyacheslav was terribly happy, since he loved him very much." (L. Ivanova)

"Aleksey Kruchonykh, still an unknown, beginning poet, was also living in Baku. He would come to see Vyacheslav and they would eagerly converse. Kruchonykh was preaching his trans-sense language." (L. Ivanova)

Nominated for the post of Dean of the University, but declines.

Publication of *A Correspondence from Two Corners.* "The most important thing to be said about humanism since Nietzsche." (E. R. Curtius)

1912

"A poetic circle called 'The Chalice' was formed. Its members were not only Vyacheslav's closest students." (L. Ivanova)

In the summer of 1922 we rented rooms with some friends on a very deserted and beautiful peninsula, Zykh, near Baku." (L. Ivanova)

"On Zykh there is neither a vine
Of clustered grapes nor a fig tree:
The heat has burned everything up, the thirsty heat has drunk
  everything up,
And I drowsed in the cool hut
Till mid-September"
    (*Evening Light*)

"And the smile, the humor, the seriousness of Vyacheslav Ivanov. He is really here, I see him every day, several times a day." (E. Millior)

1923

"During the third year of our time in Baku, Kabanov, the University bursar, died and his apartment was divided between us and his widow and her niece." (L. Ivanova)

Ivanov participates actively in the scholarly life of the university, but refuses to be nominated for administrative positions.

"Since we are on the topic of Vyacheslav Ivanov's participation in the election of the Rector and deans, we must point out the groundlessness of the reports . . . that Ivanov was the Rector of the Azerbaidzhan State University, and even a People's Commissar for Education in the Azerbaidzhan Republic. In point of fact, Ivanov was only nominated at the meetings of the appropriate bodies for the post of Dean in 1921 and Rector in 1923, but both times he withdrew his candidacy, and indeed the number of votes nominating him was not great." (N. Kotrelyov)

Publication of *Dionysus and Pre-dionysianism*.

"The first book about Dionysus, *The Hellenic Reform of the Suffering God,* described the nature of Dionysian ecstasy and was concerned with the problem of the Dionysian psychology and the mysticism of Dionysian sacrifice; in the new book Ivanov examines Dionysianism as a system of conceptions, perceptions, and initiations, and tries to recognize the god in all his metamorphoses and migrations, in all the tales about him: he looks far and wide for the Dionysian roots of the Dionysian religion." (O. Deschartes)

Appearance of first German edition of A *Correspondence from Two Corners*.

1924

Composition of libretto for the operetta *Ljubov'—mirazh?* (Is Love a Mirage?)

"At the end of May 1924, Ivanov was summoned to Moscow to deliver a speech at a jubilee conference celebrating the 125th anniversary of Pushkin's birth." (O. Deschartes)

"He went by himself, and Dima and I continued our peaceful everyday life. Suddenly we received a telegram from Vyacheslav in Moscow informing us that we were going to Venice and instructing us to collect all our things and get to Moscow. . . . Vyacheslav's speech in the Bolshoi Theater was a success. He took advantage of the auspicious moment and renewed his request to be allowed to go abroad with his family. There was always an alternation of periods in the government: for a while everything is easy and simple, everything is permitted; then everyone is pulled up short, everything is refused. Vyacheslav's petition came at a happy moment. He was authorized to spend six weeks in Venice for the opening of the Soviet Pavilion at the Biennale. And, most difficult, his family was allowed to accompany him." (L. Ivanova)

"And now after a rather complicated journey we ended up in Moscow. We were given a room next to Vyacheslav's in Tsekubu, an establishment on Kropotkin Street (formerly Prechistenka), and there ensued a long period of endless bureaucratic fuss about the departure for abroad." (L. Ivanova)

Meetings and beginning of friendship with Olga Aleksandrovna Shor (Olga Deschartes).

"She became a beloved member of our family." (L. Ivanova)

"Among the many voices of her contemporaries—almost always alien to her—the young seeker, who ponders Memory and Existence, distinguishes sounds that are intimate and kindred to her. Vyacheslav Ivanov constantly sings of memory—Mnemosyne in his poems." (D. Ivanov)

"To you, my guardian genius,
Doctor of spiritual wounds and flesh,
Guide of my visions in the twilight,
Interpreter of my earthly fate,

To you, who beyond the boundary of phenomena
Remember the world of heavenly villages
And hear the flight of angels,
Presiding over everyday custom

Humbly-wisely, anonymously."
    (*Evening Light*)

"She knew how much evil and how much good there was in the world, and she struggled inwardly, and made a constant prayer, just as, most likely, the saints do." (D. Ivanov)

"Vyacheslav delightedly met old and new friends. From morning till night the premises of Tsekubu were full of people who wanted to see him." (L. Ivanova)

"While still at a distance I caught sight of a long, winding line; it began at the door leading into Ivanov's room, extended across the corridor, descended a small staircase and trailed off somewhere in the garden. . . . When I approached, I saw Pasternak in the crowd. Bending slightly, he was sketching something with pencil in a notebook. . . . I regret to this day that I did not stay there for their last meeting." (O. Deschartes)

Last meeting with V. Ya. Bryusov.

"Their conversation was very significant and crucial. . . . Ivanov walked up to Bryusov sternly, greeted him and said roughly the following: 'Well, Valery, look at what you have done with your life, and most importantly, with your creative gift.' And Ivanov began severely and angrily to express his opinion of Bryusov's latest poems of the revolutionary period." (V. Manuilov)

"'I am going to Rome to die,' he told his friends." (O. Deschartes)

August 28

Departure abroad with daughter and son.

"Then there was the border: passports, the long customs procedure. Again we all boarded the car. The train started off, and at first we went very, very slowly. A Red Army soldier who was sitting with a sheaf of some sort of documents in his hands got up, went to the door of the car and jumped off. The train started to pick up speed. A long ditch appeared through the window, and a large sign affixed to two posts and directed to the foreign side: 'Proletariat of all nations, unite!'" (L. Ivanova)

Again, true pilgrim of your vaulted past,
I greet you, as my own ancestral home,
With evening "Ave Roma" at the last,
You, wanderers' retreat, eternal Rome.
    (*Rimskie sonety* [Roman Sonnets])

Meeting and friendship with Ettore Lo Gatto, historian of Russian literature.

December

"I have received your beautiful poems, accept my most sincere gratitude, Master." (M. Gorky)

"The feeling of salvation, the joy of freedom has not lost its freshness to this day. To be in Rome—so recently it seemed like an unrealizable dream!" (*Diary*, 1924)

"The whole time I have been abroad I say over and over: Hannibal ad portas! I mean communism. Everyone has said in one voice: falsehood. . . . Communism is the social expression of atheism if only because it alone can be a surrogate for faith, and it answers the question about the meaning of life in almost cosmic terms." (*Diary*, 1924)

"I went walking without an overcoat—and come what may, I walked myself up a store of Roman happiness." (*Diary*, 1924)

"He had taken along whatever he had managed to grab: old notebooks, journal offprints, newspaper clippings of poems." (O. Deschartes)

1925

"In spite of his happiness in Rome he was depressed because of his concern for our future." (L. Ivanova)

"From Russia there come suggestions that we return. In Moscow, L. S. Kogan hopes that Vyacheslav will want to become a member of the Academy of Arts and Sciences." (L. Ivanova)

Frequent meetings with Pavel Muratov and the circle of his Italian and Russian friends, and with O. I. Reznevich-Signorelli, to whose salon comes all literary and artistic Rome.

Ivanov meets Vsevolod Meyerhold and Zinaida Raikh during their visit to Rome. At Meyerhold's request Ivanov writes an article about "The Inspector General."

1926

Publication of *A Correspondence from Two Corners* by M. Buber in the journal *Die Kreatur.*

January

Lectures at the University of Pavia on the Russian spirit and culture.

March 4

"On the day that was St. Vyacheslav's Day in Russia . . . Ivanov read the formula for joining the Catholic Church before the altar of St. Vyacheslav in Rome's Cathedral of St. Peter . . . and then, after standing through a Church Slavic mass in the chapel over the grave of the Apostle, he took communion in two kinds, in the Orthodox manner." (O. Deschartes)

For the first time I felt myself to be Orthodox in the full sense of the word, the owner of a sacred treasure that had been mine from the day of my baptism, but the ownership of which had to that time been clouded, over many years, by a feeling of a sort of dissatisfaction that became more and more agonizing with the consciousness that I was deprived of the other half of that treasure of holiness and paradise, that I was breathing like a consumptive, with only one lung." (*Letter to Charles Du Bos*)

autumn

Father Leopoldo Riboldi, Rector of the Collegio Borromeo in Pavia, invites Ivanov to become a permanent professor and lecturer for students of French, German, and English literature.

"There, in semi-monastic seclusion, Ivanov reexamined, tested, reevaluated the spiritual legacy and cultural achievements of humanity." (O. Deschartes)

"Ivanov's monastic seclusion in the sumptuous Renaissance palazzo was often disturbed by visits from French, Italian, and German poets, writers, and philosophers of from French, Italian, and German poets, writers, and philosophers of various schools. . . . Once Benedetto Croce suddenly appeared, accompanied by several of his followers." (O. Deschartes)

1927

O. A. Shor (Deschartes) arrives in Rome.

"Only O. Deschartes can write about the real me, and she knows my life and all my writings as no one else does." (Ivanov, quoted by S. Makovsky)

"And has your Hymettian honey really sated me?
Who stole your idol from the myrtle grove?
Or did I smash it myself in prophetic horror?
Have I really stopped loving you, Hellas?

And I ran away, and in the foothills of the Thebais I eat
The wild honey and tough locusts of silence"
                    (*Evening Light*)

"In 1927 Ivanov wrote 'Palinodia,' so that after a short renunciation of humanism he could find it in the spirit of Christianity, as a *docta pietas*." (O. Deschartes)

March

Martin Buber visits Ivanov in Pavia. Their close friendship begins.

1928, September

Beginning of work on *The Tale of Prince Svetomir.*

"On the morning of September 28 Ivanov cheerfully and embarrassedly told me, 'I have begun writing.' And after a brief silence he added, 'It's prose.' " (O. Deschartes)

"If the tale did not come into being earlier, it is only because it took Ivanov a long time to find a form of expression. He tried both in rhymed and blank verse. . . . It all seemed not quite right. Only abroad did he find the desired form: a prose *skaz* in the spirit, perhaps, of a chronicle account, with a division into strophes of uneven length which are connected into chapters." (S. Makovsky)

"The entire summation of his spiritual experience was to be reflected . . . in this work; it was conceived by the poet as his *Faust,* Part II." (S. Makovsky)

Travel to Switzerland. Lectures in Zürich and Lucerne.

1929, summer

Another trip to Switzerland. In Davos, Ivanov meets his old friend E. K. Metner. Detailed discussions about C. G. Jung (Metner was his close friend and collaborator).

1930

Publication in the journal *Vigile* of French translation of *A Correspondence from Two Corners,* by Charles Du Bos.

October

Letter to Charles Du Bos.

"Sympathetically, with a tender and loyal hand, you gathered up the pale leaves that, set whirling in the vortex of the Revolution, were carried off and flew to your garden; and immediately, without wavering, you made up your mind to appeal to me for the confessions you needed to interpret the news of the wind that blows wherever it pleases. . . ." (*Letter to Charles Du Bos*)

1932

Italian edition of *A Correspondence from Two Corners.* Publication of *Dostoevsky* in German in Tübingen (the Russian original is lost).

1933

Publication of Spanish translation of *A Correspondence from Two Corners* by Ortega y Gasset in *Revista de Occidente.*

July

Death of Ivanov's first wife, Darya Mikhaylovna Dmitrievskaya.

December

Appearance of special issue of the journal *Il Convegno,* devoted to Ivanov, with articles about him by E. R. Curtius, F. Zelinsky, F. Stepun, G. Marcel, and A. Pellegrini.

1934, February

Letter to Pellegrini about *docta pietas*.

"Universal anamnesis in Christ—this, then, is the goal of human-istic Christian culture: because this is the historical prerequisite for the realization of worldwide ecumenicity." (Letter to A. Pellegrini about *docta pietas*)

"Ivanov spent eight years in Pavia. For vacations he would go some-where by the sea, or to Switzerland, or most often to Rome." (O. Deschartes)

Invited to University of Florence as Professor Ordinarius of Slavistics.

"Ivanov spent the early autumn of 1934 in Rome. The vacation had ended and courses had begun at the universities when news of an unexpected rejection came from Florence: the minister of education had rescinded the Department's decision because Ivanov was not a member of the Fascist Party, and such membership was then obli-gatory for a newly selected professor." (O. Deschartes)

Publication of the article "Anima" in the journal *Corona*.

1935

At his daughter's request, Ivanov writes a drama in verse, *Nal and Damayanti* (unfinished). Work on the German edition of *Dionysus and Predionysianism*.

1936

"In February of this year Vyacheslav Ivanov turned 70. We, his friends, the witnesses of the rapid flowering of his distinctive talent . . . have every reason to remember him as the most versatile, but at the same time the most integral figure of the Russian Symbolist school. For the disclosure of the supreme idea of Russia, which according to Dostoevsky consists of the reconciliation of all ideas, Vyacheslav Ivanov was given exceptional talents and powers. Nature generously endowed him with the gifts of a poet, philosopher and scholar. . . . The result: a unique combination and reconciliation of Slavophilism and Westernism, paganism and Christianity, philosophy and poetry, philology and music, archaism and publicistics." (F. Stepun)

February

Lecture on Pushkin during ceremonies on the anniversary of his death.

March

Ivanov moves to a house on the via Monte Tarpeo.

"Ivanov was noticeably beginning to weary of wandering among strange rooms and little pensions. He decided to rent an apartment and finally begin to live *en famille,* in his own home. As if by magic, a dwelling was found on the Capitoline itself, with a view that in its beauty and grandeur was quite exceptional even for Rome." (O. Deschartes)

"And there is the magical staircase of the Capitoline. . . . Skirting Marcus Aurelius, we walk along a narrow side street, between old buildings. We are already on the famous cliff. . . . There is not a single step from the steep side street into the house where Ivanov lives. But the old houses on the Tarpean Rock have their surprises. If you pass through the anteroom and the tiny dining room, and through the glass door of their little balcony, there is a ravine, and a very long staircase along the outer wall: it is rickety, elbow-shaped, with miserable steps, and resembles a fire escape. It leads to a dark, dense little garden." (Z. Gippius)

"A murmuring little garden, and behind it
Your naked relics, Rome!
There is laurel in it, fig trees, and roses,
And vines in heavy clusters"
        (*Evening Light*)

"True, he no longer has golden curls; but gray-haired, he has come to resemble more a Greek sage (or an old German philosopher). He has the same gentle, extremely gentle, amiable manners, the same attentively lively eyes. And a detailed response to everything." (Z. Gippius)

Among the visitors to the Tarpean Rock, besides the Merezhkovskys, are F. Zelinsky, I. Bunin, B. Zaitsev, G. Papini.

spring

At the invitation of the Rector, Father Phillippe de Régis, Ivanov begins to teach Slavic languages and read lectures on Russian literature in the Russian Catholic Seminary ("Russicum"). He receives an offer to give a course on Slavic languages in the Eastern Institute of the Vatican ("Orientale").

summer

"In the summer of 1936 an offer came from the Swiss publishing house Benno Schwabe to publish Ivanov's works on Dionysus in German. Of course Ivanov gladly agreed, but under the condition that he would check the translation himself and add new notes to the old text. . . . The publisher was in a hurry. The author took his time. Time passed. The war broke out. . . . During the first two years of it the publisher stubbornly insisted that Ivanov send *Dionysus*. Then he died. So the book did not appear." (O. Deschartes)

1938, spring

Private audience with Pope Pius XI.

"At the end of a long conversation the Pope said that the peoples of the West and of Russia would soon be subjected to difficult trials, but that then better times would come, the unnatural discord among the churches would cease and the longed-for union would be realized." (O. Deschartes)

1939

Publication of long poem *Man.*

"Once Pavel Florensky . . . suddenly said, 'It's a beautiful work, but hardly anyone will understand it. Would you like for me to write notes to it?' Of course, Ivanov was delighted with such an offer. . . . Florensky began to write the notes, but slowly.—War, revolution; the publication was delayed and never came about." (O. Deschartes)

"And, Good Spirit, save our souls.
Source of blessings, Choir-leader of life,
Show us God's City in the earthly homeland"
      (*Man*)

Beginning of World War II.

1940, January

Move to apartment at Via Leon Battista Alberti 25 on the Aventine.

"Let the space be built up at sunset
By a ring of neighbors' dwellings,
All the same, from behind roofs and laundry
I am favored to see the Dome"
      (*Evening Light*)

1941 June

Germany invades Russia.

Beginning of work on introductions and notes to *Acts of the Apostles* and the *Revelation of St. John.*

1943, September

Rome is occupied by German troops.

1944

Roman Diary, 1944 is written.

"And suddenly, in that difficult, fatal time, unexpectedly for Ivanov

himself, 'the sealed spring began to play' within him, and that
source gushed through all of 1944. The poems were immediate lyric
responses to the events of the day, as well as quiet meditations."
(O. Deschartes)

June

Liberation of Rome by the Allies.

"Soon after the liberation of Rome, before the end of the war, an
American officer from the front unexpectedly appeared at Ivanov's
home—the well-known writer Thornton Wilder, with whom Ivanov
had previously been personally acquainted. An incredible closeness
was immediately formed, a penetrating, heartfelt understanding of
each other, of a sort that seldom occurs even among old friends."
(O. Deschartes)

December

"Goodbye, my lyric year!
You accompanied
The sublunary round-dance of the Horae
With the private play of strings
And, obedient to the step of the planets,
You led thought to clarity and feelings to harmony"
          (*Evening Light*)

1945

Intense work on *The Tale of Prince Svetomir.*

Among the visitors to the house on the Via Leon Battista Alberti
are J. Maritain and G. Marcel.

1946

Letter from Professor S. A. Konovalov at Oxford, offering to print
Ivanov's new poetic works.

"That was when it was essentially decided to set about publishing a collection of poems." (O. Deschartes)

Work on the preparation of fifth book of poems, *Evening Light*.

"The magnificence and inner energy of the word have made Vyacheslav Ivanov the prophet-philosopher of twentieth-century Russian poetry and a unique druid of European poetry of the Modern era." (A. Rannit)

Publication of Italian translation by Rinaldo Küfferle of the long poem *Man*.

Publication of *Acts of the Apostles* and the *Revelation of St. John* with forewords and notes by Ivanov.

1947

Publication of English translation of *A Correspondence from Two Corners* in the journal *Mesa*.

autumn

Isaiah Berlin and Maurice Bowra come from Oxford for the manuscript of *Evening Light*.

"And so, to the poet's delight, three Oxford professors became patrons of his muse. . . . Thinking of his imminent death, Ivanov was glad that Oxford intended to make public his last songs." (O. Deschartes)

Essays, "Forma formans and forma formata," and "M. Lermontov."

1948

English publication of *A Correspondence from Two Corners* in the American journal *Partisan Review*.

"In 1948 the 82-year-old man received a "spiritually profitable" commission from the Vatican: to write an introduction and compile notes to the Psalter. He finished this task several days before his death." (O. Deschartes)

1949

"On parting I asked the poet his opinion of the future of European thought. He answered, smiling, that he knew nothing about the fate of European culture, but that he knew one thing for a certainty: if he were not permitted to read, speak, and write Greek in the next world, he would be deeply unhappy." (A. Rannit)

"The poet violated the Muse's interdiction against writing poetry three times. The last of these three poems was a sonnet. Ivanov began writing it in February 1949; he reworked it many times; he introduced final changes on July 14. . . . The sonnet ends with the words the poet wrote two days before departing this life: 'Death cleaved with a merciless pole-axe.' " (O. Deschartes)

July 16

"Two hours before his death he said to me: 'Save my Svetomir'. . . . 'Finish it. You know it all. I will help.' He sighed. He was silent for a bit. 'Save my Svetomir.' And he said no more." (O. Deschartes)

Death at 3:00 in the afternoon.

Vyacheslav Ivanovich Ivanov was buried in Rome in the Catholic cemetery of Verano.

> —Translated by Susanne Fusso; passages from *Infancy* translated by Carol Ueland; passage from *Roman Sonnets* translated by Lowry Nelson, Jr.